Dressing in Feathers

Dressing *in* Feathers

The Construction of the Indian in American Popular Culture

edited by
S. Elizabeth Bird

WestviewPress
A Division of HarperCollinsPublishers

Copyright © 1996 by Westview Press, Inc., A Division of HarperCollins Publishers, Inc.

Published in 1996 in the United States of America by Westview Press, Inc., 5500 Central Avenue,
Boulder, Colorado 80301-2877, and in the United Kingdom by Westview Press, 12 Hid's Copse Road,
Cumnor Hill, Oxford OX2 9JJ

Library of Congress Cataloging-in-Publication Data
Dressing in feathers : the construction of the Indian in American
   popular culture / edited by S. Elizabeth Bird.
      p.   cm.
   Includes bibliographical references and index.
   ISBN 0-8133-2666-4 (hc.). — ISBN 0-8133-2667-2 (pb.)
   1. Indians in popular culture—United States.   I. Bird, S.
Elizabeth
E98.P99D72   1996
305.897—dc20   96-4555
                                                                                CIP

The paper used in this publication meets the requirements of the American National Standard for
Permanence of Paper for Printed Library Materials Z39.48-1984.

10   9   8   7   6   5   4   3   2   1

For my sons, Thomas and Daniel Tobin

Contents

List of Figures   ix
Acknowledgments   xii

1   Introduction: Constructing the Indian, 1830s–1990s,
     S. Elizabeth Bird   1

2   The First but Not the Last of the "Vanishing Indians":
     Edwin Forrest and Mythic Re-creations of the Native
     Population, *Sally L. Jones*   13

3   The Narratives of Sitting Bull's Surrender: Bailey, Dix & Mead's
     Photographic Western, *Frank Goodyear*   29

4   Reduced to Images: American Indians in Nineteenth-Century
     Advertising, *Jeffrey Steele*   45

5   "Hudson's Bay Company Indians": Images of Native People
     and the Red River Pageant, 1920, *Peter Geller*   65

6   Science and Spectacle: Native American Representation in
     Early Cinema, *Alison Griffiths*   79

7   "There Is Madness in the Air": The 1926 Haskell Homecoming
     and Popular Representations of Sports in Federal Indian
     Boarding Schools, *John Bloom*   97

8   Indigenous Versus Colonial Discourse: Alcohol and American
     Indian Identity, *Bonnie Duran*   111

9   "My Grandmother Was a Cherokee Princess": Representations
     of Indians in Southern History, *Joel W. Martin*   129

10   Florida Seminoles and the Marketing of the Last Frontier,
     Jay Mechling   149

11   Segregated Stories: The Colonial Contours of the Little Bighorn
     Battlefield National Monument, *C. Richard King*   167

12   A War of Words: How News Frames Define Legitimacy in a
     Native Conflict, *Cynthia-Lou Coleman*   181

13   Going Indian: Discovery, Adoption, and Renaming Toward a
     "True American," from *Deerslayer* to *Dances with Wolves*,
     Robert Baird   195

14   "Her Beautiful Savage": The Current Sexual Image of the
     Native American Male, *Peter van Lent*   211

15   Cultural Heritage in *Northern Exposure*, *Annette M. Taylor*   229

16   Not My Fantasy: The Persistence of Indian Imagery in
     Dr. Quinn, Medicine Woman, *S. Elizabeth Bird*   245

17   *Moo Mesa*: Some Thoughts on Stereotypes and Image
     Appropriation, *Theodore S. Jojola*   263

18   What Does One Look Like? *Debra L. Merskin*   281

Bibliography   285
About the Book   303
About the Contributors   305
Index   309

Figures

CH.1 - 11   CH.13 - 13
CH.2 - 12   CH.14 - 12
CH.3 - 11   CH.15 - 14
CH.4 - 15   CH16 - 14
CH.5 - 11   CH.17 - 16
CH.6 - 13   CH.18 - 4
CH.7 - 13
CH.8 - 15
CH.9 - 17
OH.10 - 15
CH.11 - 12
CH.12 - 11

1.1   Photocopied announcement posted on a bar wall in
      Wisconsin, early 1990s   5
1.2   Sketch by Frederick Opper in *Bill Nye's History of the
      United States*   6

2.1   Edwin Forrest in the title role of John Augustus Stone's *Metamora*   23

3.1   Sitting Bull, 1882   34
3.2   One Bull, nephew of Sitting Bull, 1882   35
3.3   Sitting Bull and family, 1882   39
3.4   Sitting Bull and Buffalo Bill Cody, 1891   40

4.1   Trade card, Duryeas Improved Corn Starch   49
4.2   Trade card, Abe Loebenberg's Arcade Clothing House   49
4.3   Trade card, "Tippecanoe" Spring Preparation   50
4.4   Advertising booklet, "The Golden Secret of the 'Oswego,'"
      Austen's Oswego Bitters, 1882   52
4.5   Trade card, Indian Queen Perfume   53
4.6   Trade card, Bradley's Super-Phosphate of Lime   54
4.7   Trade card, "A Corned Indian," Diamond Lawnmowers   55
4.8   Trade card, Enterprise Bone, Shell, and Corn Mill   57
4.9   Trade card, Arbuckle Brothers Coffee   58
4.10 Trade card, Arbuckle Brothers Coffee   60
4.11 Trade card, Arbuckle Brothers Coffee   61
4.12 Trade card, Keystone Line of Agricultural Implements   62

5.1   Red River Pageant, 1920. Chief Kinnewakan has filled the
      pipe of peace and passes it to Sir Robert Kindersley   69
5.2   Red River Pageant, 1920. Group of Wood Cree Indians,
      Athabasca District   71
5.3   Hudson's Bay Company's 250th Anniversary celebration, 1920   72

6.1   Crow Indians acting as Custer Scouts in a reenactment of the
      Battle of the Little Bighorn   85

6.2   President Wilson's speech being played on a phonograph to
       the Umatilla tribe in Pendleton, 1913   87

7.1   Photograph of Haskell's Homecoming Parade float   103
7.2   Cover of official Haskell Homecoming Game program   106

8.1   Sketch by Frederick Opper in *Bill Nye's History of the
       United States*   118
8.2   Tenskwatawa, "the Shawnee prophet"   121

9.1   Mary Musgrove and her husband "invading" Savannah, Georgia   131
9.2   Osceola   136
9.3   Detail from large mural of the Battle of Horseshoe Bend,
       featured in the Museum of the Horseshoe Bend National
       Military Park   144

10.1   Postcard (1949)   154
10.2   Postcard (c. 1940s–1950s)   155
10.3   Postcard depicting alligator wrestling   156
10.4   Postcard (c. 1940s–1950s)   157

11.1   Monument to Seventh Cavalry soldiers killed in the Battle
       of the Little Bighorn   172
11.2   "The Doomed Battalion" museum display case   175
11.3   "Indian Medicine" museum display case   177

13.1   Lt. John Dunbar (Kevin Costner), Kicking Bird (Graham
       Greene), and other Sioux scout out a herd of buffalo in the
       film *Dances with Wolves*   200

14.1   Rodney Grant as Wind-in-His-Hair, from *Dances with Wolves*   213
14.2   *The Model,* painting by Ozz Franca, reproduced by
       Leanin' Tree, Inc.   215
14.3   Cover of recent Indian romance novel   216
14.4   *Where Eagles Soar,* painting by Marilyn Bendell, reproduced
       by Leanin' Tree, Inc.   220
14.5   *Sleeping Indian,* painting by David Bradley, reproduced
       by Garfinkel Publications   223

15.1   The cast of *Northern Exposure*   234

16.1   Joe Lando as Byron Sully and Jane Seymour as Dr. Quinn   247

17.1 The C.O.W.-Boys of Moo Mesa   265
17.2 Geronimoo, packaged as an action-figure toy   266
17.3 Early draft of Phil Thomas character, showing Plains
      Indian characteristics   269
17.4 Phil Thomas in his antelope incarnation   273
17.5 First version of J.R. as a Pueblo character   274
17.6 Second draft of J.R.   275
17.7 Third draft of J.R.   276
17.8 J.R. with his Amish look   277
17.9 Final version of J.R.   278

18.1 What does one look like?   282

Acknowledgments

Any edited collection is dependent on the quality and commitment of its contributors. I wish to thank all sixteen writers who contributed to this volume, not only for their fine scholarship but also for their prompt attention to suggestions and deadlines and for many helpful comments about the book as a whole.

I also appreciate the day-to-day friendship and support of my colleagues in anthropology and humanities at the University of Minnesota, Duluth, especially Eve Browning Cole, David Smith, Tom Bacig, and Fred Schroeder. Terrie Gimpel, office assistant in the Department of Interdisciplinary Programs, has been an invaluable help in typing sections of the manuscript and organizing the bibliography. Graduate assistant David Woodward also helped assemble the bibliography and undertook many other tasks, such as checking references and setting up the interview schedule for my field study.

Gordon Massman at Westview Press has been friendly, helpful, and encouraging throughout the writing and editing process. I am especially grateful to Michele Wynn for her meticulous and sensitive copyediting of the manuscript.

I would like to thank the students at the University of Minnesota, Duluth, who participated in my focus group research, as well as the College of Liberal Arts for partial funding of the focus group project. In particular, I thank the American Indian participants, not only for their contribution to my own chapter, but also for helping me formulate and think through many of the issues raised by the entire project. Thank you, Jerry Ojibway, Kim King, Mike Munnell, Ty Juoni, Bill Howes, Bev Clark, Tom Drumbeater, Ardene White, and Paul Ojanen.

Finally, I thank my husband, Graham Tobin, for his love, support, and patience throughout the creation of this book.

S. Elizabeth Bird

1

Introduction:
Constructing the Indian, 1830s–1990s

S. Elizabeth Bird

When Walt Disney's animated film *Pocahontas* opened in June 1995, it was greeted by a barrage of contradictory reactions. Although most movie critics agreed that the animation was superb and some liked the story, too, the main focus of academic discussion was on the way the movie portrayed American Indians[1] in general and the historical Pocahontas, in particular.

Although American Indian activist Russell Means lauded the film as "the single finest work ever done on American Indians by Hollywood,"[2] others disagreed, sometimes vehemently. Ted Jojola dismissed Means as "himself . . . an American Indian movement stereotype."[3] Over one hundred members of the electronic mailing list NatChat, many of them American Indian, signed a protest calling on parents to boycott the movie, citing its historical inaccuracies and saying, "Disney has let us down in a cruel, irresponsible manner."[4] In particular, many people were appalled by a centerpiece song, "Savages," that reiterated many of the traditional stereotypes of Indians as bloodthirsty heathens. Within the context of the movie, it was clear that the audience was supposed to condemn the derogatory view of Indians that the English settlers expressed in song. However, many were concerned that the song, already selling millions of copies on the sound track compact disk, was likely to be taken out of context and serve only to perpetuate hatred. That possibility is very real, since clearly audiences frequently hear what they want to hear—one need only recall, for example, the way the bitter Bruce Springsteen song "Born in the U.S.A." became an anthem for Reaganite youth in the mid-1980s.[5]

No one could deny that *Pocahontas* bears little relationship to history. The voluptuous, dark-skinned beauty and her blond, square-jawed suitor, both appearing to be in their twenties, are a far cry from the (probably) twelve-year-old Pocahontas and (probably) forty-two-year-old Captain John Smith. It seems fairly certain that whatever happened between them did not include falling in love. Possible relationships between Smith and Pocahontas range from slight acquaintance, with Pocahontas perhaps rescuing Smith, to the scenario that the NatChat members and others suggest, in which the middle-aged Smith raped the preteen Pocahontas.

In all the debate about what "really" happened between Pocahontas and Smith, what seems to be forgotten is that we will likely never know the truth. The entire narrative is built around one or two brief episodes in Smith's writings, and none of those events may have happened at all. The revisionist interpretation of Smith as a rapist may or may not be true—it is essentially just another piece of (counter) mythmaking.

The Mythical Indian

Mythmaking is what the story of Pocahontas is all about. The Disney version comes after two centuries or more of narrative construction, during which Pocahontas became a multifaceted symbol for the White United States. As Robert Tilton demonstrates, the story "had become by mid-[nineteenth] century so pervasive in American culture that no appeal to the historical record could have had any serious effect."[6] In 1825, a relief of the Smith rescue by sculptor Antonio Capellano was mounted over the west door of the rotunda in the Washington, D.C., Capitol: "Its inclusion in the Capitol at this early date makes clear that the rescue of Smith by Pocahontas had long been perceived as a crucial generative moment in the history of the United States."[7]

The point here is that the Pocahontas story, like other national myths about Indians who helped Whites, such as Squanto and Massasoit, are *White*, mainstream myths.

> What tied the stories of these virtuous Indians together was that for such figures to be seen in this light they generally had to act against the best interests of their own people . . . This elevation saw the actual histories of these figures replaced by mythic narratives depicting the crucial moments when aid was given to the whites, such as the first Thanksgiving dinner in New England and the saving of John Smith.[8]

Thus, these stories, at a mythic level, explain to Whites their right to be here and help deal with lingering guilt about the displacement of the Native inhabitants—after all, the "good" Indians helped us out and recognized the inevitability of White conquest.

And that is the essential "cruelty" that the NatChat members saw in *Pocahontas*. As Tilton points out, it would be, to say the least, "extremely problematic" to present the Pocahontas story from an Indian point of view. Pocahontas and the other (white) mythic Indians of the past are people who sided with the invaders and are not heroic figures to their own people. In many ways, it seems ridiculous to raise the question of historical inaccuracy in an animated film—all Disney cartoons are fantasy, and people would find it ludicrous to question the reality of whether lions can speak or teapots can dance. But one question still arises: Since all other Disney cartoons have been based on fairy-tale, imaginary worlds, why did the Disney company choose the Pocahontas legend as its first homage to American Indians? Perhaps it is because from the viewpoint of the Anglo-American tradition, the issue of historical accuracy is indeed beside the point. *Pocahontas,* for Whites, is as comforting a fairy tale as *Cinderella.* Disney strove to make the film's portrayal of American Indians "authentic," and the company has come a long way from the offensive portrayals in earlier films like *Peter Pan.* But ultimately, the Indians of *Pocahontas* are, yet again, the objects of White concerns and White fantasies. As Pauline Turner Strong observes, "Disney has created a marketable New Age Pocahontas to embody our millennial dreams for wholeness and harmony, while banishing our nightmares of savagery without and emptiness within."[9] It is clear whose dreams and nightmares Strong is referring to in this construction.

Pocahontas, then, is the latest incarnation of what Robert Berkhofer, Jr., calls "the White Man's Indian." In his now classic analysis, Berkhofer points out that "the essence of the White image of the Indian has been the definition of Native Americans in fact and fancy as a separate and single other. Whether evaluated as noble or ignoble, whether seen as exotic or downgraded, the Indian as an image was always alien to the White."[10]

This book is about the fabrication of the Indian by White culture, and the essays included here are presented in the hope that by understanding this myth-making process more clearly, we can think of ways to counter and transform it. We will see that although changes have occurred and some of the more grossly distorted imagery has been superseded, there are many elements in the fabrication of the Indian that have remained consistent. As Strong points out, for example, "the animated Pocahontas is necessarily located within the entire colonial tradition of noble savagism: the natural virtues, cultural critique, and self-sacrifice she embodies are those found in Montaigne and Rousseau and Cooper and Kirkpatrick Sale."[11]

Thus the "noble savage" has been with us for generations, along with his alter ego, the "ignoble savage." With the ebb and flow of cultural images of who *we* are, so the image of the Indian changes— now becoming everything we fear, in the person of the marauding, hellish savage, then becoming everything we envy, in the person of the peaceful, mystical, spiritual guardian of the land who is in vogue in the 1990s. These images have not been mutually exclusive, of course. For another important dimension of the White image is that Indians are akin to primitive children—in a rude state of nature they are nobly innocent, but when crossed they will turn wild and uncontrollable. Thus Thomas McKenney, chief U.S. administrator of Indian affairs from 1816–1830, wrote in his memoirs, "The Earth was their mother, and upon its lap they reposed. Rude wigwams sheltered them. Hunger and thirst satisfied, sleep followed—and within this circle was contained the happiness of the aboriginal man."[12] At the same time, and without any sense of contradiction, McKenney wrote that the Indian was a "man who would scalp an infant in his cradle."[13]

However they are pictured, Indians are the quintessential Other, whose role is to be the object of the White, colonialist gaze. Once Indians were no longer a threat, they became colorful and quaint. A writer in *Harper's*, describing a trip to Arizona in 1883, sums up the White attitude of the time. Getting off the train at Yuma, he hopes to see Apaches, but after an initial disappointment, finds the local Indians acceptable: "They were not Apaches, it is true, but a subsequent acquaintance with the general field proved them to be even more picturesque. They were of that satisfactory type of savages who wear little clothing, and none of the European."[14]

Nineteenth-century tourists wanted to see traditional clothing and quiet nobility, and that has not really changed. Now that few "real" (i.e., frozen in history) Indians remain to be viewed, mass culture has replaced them with movies, television, and romances, which are almost invariably set in the past. Opportunities to see contemporary Indians playing mainstream roles are few and far between.

And when Indians refuse to be quaint, White culture's imagery condemns them. In the nineteenth century, those who resisted domination were painted as bloodthirsty savages, whereas those who did not fit the mold of the picturesque Indian were portrayed as dissolute, pathetic drunks and misfits. In the 1990s, although it is clear that the Noble Savage has gained ascendancy in mass culture, we must be careful not to assume that the negative imagery has disappeared. It becomes clear that as long as Indians are powerless (or safely dead), it is easy to portray them as noble. But at least in some parts of the country, Indians are very much alive and are asserting their own rights to identity. In Minnesota and Wisconsin, for example, Ojibwa people[15] have in recent years begun to reclaim their treaty rights to spearfish on lakes. Some White anglers became incensed, and the conflict unleashed a flood of virulent racism against Indians, or "timber niggers," as protest signs often dubbed them. Crudely copied signs, like the one pictured, appeared on the walls of Wisconsin bars in the early 1990s (Figure 1.1). Many people in the area also stereotype Indians as government-funded deadbeats, who are dirty, drunken, and refuse to work. Jokes that reflect that view are widespread:

Q. How do you starve an Indian?
A. Hide his food stamps under his work boots.

White culture seems to feel angry at Indians who do not fit the romantic mold. In the 1890s, satirical writer Bill Nye wrote disgustedly about the "true Indian princesses," who were filthy and ugly, unlike their fictional counterparts (Figure 1.2). The same image lives on in a 1995 joke:

1ST ANNUAL
INDIAN SHOOT

TIME: EARLY SPRING, BEGINNING OF WALLEYE RUN.

PLACE: NORTHERN & CENTRAL WISCONSIN LAKES

RULES: OPEN SHOOT, OFF HAND POSITION ONLY
            NO SCOPES, NO SLINGS, NO TRIPODS

            OPEN TO ALL WISCONSIN RESIDENTS PAYING TAXES
RESIDENTS ON WELFARE, ADC, FOOD STAMPS OR ANY OTHER GIVEAWAY NOT
ELIGIBLE. (NOTE: DO NOT COMPLAIN ABOUT DISCRIMINATION, YOUR SHOOT WILL
BE ANNOUNCED LATER.)

SCORING: WISCONSIN RULES APPLY. POINT SYSTEM WILL BE USED

PLAIN INDIAN   5 POINTS

INDIAN WITH WALLEYES   10 POINTS

INDIAN WITH BOAT NEWER THAN YOURS   20 POINTS

INDIAN USING PITCHFORK   30 POINTS

INDIAN TRIBAL LAWYER   100 POINTS
  does not have to be spearing)

JUDGES: GOV. TOMMY THOMPSON   REV. JESSE JACKSON

PRIZES: BAGS OF PEANUTS AND SIX PACKS OF TREATY BEER

SPONSOR: SOCIETY HELPING INDIVIDUAL TAXPAYERS OWN NOTHING
                                              (known as SHIT ON)

ENTRY BLANK
        I _____ WILL ATTEND SHOOT

        I WILL_____ WILL NOT _____ BE TAKING SCALPES

Figure 1.1   *Photocopied announcement posted on a bar wall in Wisconsin, early 1990s.*

Q: How do you compliment an Indian woman?
A.   Nice tooth.

Now that Indians have gained some real economic power, through their operation
of gaming casinos, negative imagery continues to grow. Even as casinos have come
to rely almost exclusively on White customers, those same customers are often re-
sentful of the fact that their habit is enriching Indians. In Minnesota, which has
several highly successful Indian gaming establishments, it is common to hear comments that Indians "do not deserve" their riches and that they "can't manage" their
money. This amounts to an ironic reversal of power—in the past, Whites sold alcohol to Indians, exploiting a potential weakness, whereas today, Indians sell slot
machines to Whites, exploiting their weakness for gambling. It remains to be seen
how this new situation will ultimately affect White imagery of Indians.

THE INDIAN GIRL OF STORY.   THE INDIAN GIRL OF FACT.

Figure 1.2   *Sketch by Frederick Opper in* Bill Nye's History of the United States *(London 1894), a satiric "history."*

Gambling revenue, among other things, has offered American Indians the chance to begin taking back ownership of the imagery that has defined them for the White world. The ability to define imagery is a consequence of power, an important point that several authors in this collection raise. And as American Indians gain both cultural and economic power, they can wield that power to fight back. At the informal, interpersonal level, Indians have been doing that for years, creating a rich humor that plays on and subverts dominant stereotypes, mocking White attitudes, federal agencies, and so on.[16] And Indian authors and filmmakers are producing their own art that speaks about who they are.[17]

Changing the Stereotype

Nevertheless, American Indians have had relatively little impact on mass cultural images. How, then, can Indians work to counter the stereotypical imagery of mass popular culture? Clearly, this is not a simple question, and American Indians are

far from unified on the solution. This in itself should not be surprising—to expect one single "Indian view" is to slip into the familiar stereotype of viewing "Indians" as some monolithic, undifferentiated class. *Pocahontas* was viewed positively by some American Indians, who saw it as a genuine step on the way toward
reappropriating the imagery. When a reporter for a newspaper in Duluth, Minnesota, asked local Ojibwa teenagers about the film, they were generally enthusiastic, praising its treatment of the Indians' relationship with nature.[18] Although
some American Indians thought *Dances with Wolves* was wonderful, others were
offended because, yet again, it told the story from the White point of view.

　　Thus, the question arises: If prevailing popular cultural depictions of American
Indians are wrong, what would be right? What would be perceived as a positive
depiction? This question has no straightforward answer. Some American Indians,
for example, have turned the familiar stereotypes to their own advantage. Thus,
Cherokee Henry Lambert has "dressed in feathers" for tourists in the Smoky
Mountains National Park for over forty years, having his photo taken for money:
"I've put my six children through school doing this and movies and a little construction. My son Patrick went to law school down at Chapel Hill," he comments.[19] Indian-run gaming casinos, museums, and cultural centers may use inauthentic artifacts and popular symbols for their own purposes. Some American
Indians fume over such "selling out" or lack of "authenticity," whereas others perceive it as taking back power.

　　Disagreements also focus on how American Indians should be portrayed in
movies and on television. Some argue that progress comes when Indian actors are
cast in generic roles, without any reference to their ethnicity. Others say that
doing this erases the real cultural identity of Indians—certainly they are individuals who are not *solely* defined by their ethnicity, but at the same time, their cultural identity is a crucial element of who they are.

　　This book does not attempt to provide solutions. Rather, the authors offer careful case studies that describe the dominant cultural fabrication of the Indian. To
understand current imagery, it is essential to understand the history of its making, and the seventeen essays mesh to create a powerful, interconnected tapestry
of image creation over the last one hundred and fifty years.

　　The authors of the first six chapters choose particular historical moments and
use these to analyze the representations of American Indians at those times,
showing how these representations perpetuate older images and foreshadow
those to come. Berkhofer has suggested that it was popular culture rather than
elite culture that became the defining medium for the image of the Indian by
around the 1840s. One reason for this was a reaction among the literary elite to
the proliferation in the 1830s of popular plays that defined the archetypical Noble
Savage, now that the Indian in the East was safely vanquished. These plays became
so ubiquitous that they were eventually mercilessly burlesqued and parodied, and
for a time the Indian was seen as no longer an appropriate subject for serious art.
It is fitting, then, that this collection should begin with Sally Jones's analysis in

Chapter 2 of a defining theatrical production of that period, in which the actor Edwin Forrest interpreted *Metamora,* or *The Last of the Wampanoags.* As Jones points out, *Metamora* was important in codifying many of the characteristics that were already becoming standard fare—the monosyllabic grunts, the noble, defeated warrior who recognizes the inevitability of doom, and so on.

In Chapter 3, Frank Goodyear offers a close reading of a series of photographs taken of Sioux leader Sitting Bull and his family after their surrender. Goodyear argues that these photos can be seen as providing the structure for the western narrative, again marking the nobility of the silent, defeated Indian against a background of inevitable White progress. Jeffrey Steele then takes up the story in Chapter 4 to show how images of the Indian proliferated in nineteenth-century advertising, again codifying some of the features that were becoming standard— the Indian princess, the affinity of the Indian with nature, the doomed Indian, and also the savage marauder, for the Indian wars were not yet over. Steele makes the important point that other ethnic groups, although also stereotyped, were usually seen as integrated into the contemporary scene. Indians were already perceived as a kind of anachronism, only conceivable in White culture as traditional and rooted in the past. That notion of the only "real" Indians being historical ones is still pervasive today.

In Chapter 5, Peter Geller, moving a little ahead in time, takes up the same theme in his reading of a special event—the 1920 Hudson's Bay Company anniversary celebration in Canada. Once again, Indians had a defined place in the event—as "traditionals." Geller describes how Indians were, in effect, costumed and inscribed as remnants of the past, for the entertainment of White culture. For, as Daniel Francis has eloquently argued, Canadian mainstream culture appropriated "Indianness" just as fully as U.S. culture did.

In Chapter 6, Alison Griffiths discusses the role of early ethnographic film in the development of popular notions of the Indian. She points out the importance of the developing anthropological discourse in defining the Indian for the general public as the Other—as exotic, with strange customs that were dying out but that should be recorded for posterity.

During that same time period in the early twentieth century, an important theme was the "improvement" of the Indian. Although Indian exoticism was viewed as well and good for history and museums, if actual Indians were to survive, it was thought they must be molded into imitation Whites, hence, the creation of the Indian boarding schools. The effect of the boarding schools in alienating Indians from their culture has been extensively discussed. In Chapter 7, John Bloom takes a look at a specific moment at the Haskell Institute, showing how the Haskell Homecoming celebration brought into sharp focus the prevailing discourses on "improving" the Indian. At the same time, the echoes of both the noble and the savage Indian resound in the narratives about the school.

The next three essays offer thematic overviews that demonstrate the overall pattern—that the same images persist over time. In Chapter 8, Bonnie Duran selects one aspect of the "ignoble savage" stereotype, that of the Drunken Indian. Duran explores the way the stereotype evolved from earlier images of the "wild man" and the way it became a very useful part of the view that Indians were doomed and disappearing. After all, Indians were voluntarily killing themselves with alcohol and thus deserved to disappear. Duran shows how American Indians can counter this negative imagery, discussing the way several Native movements have worked to overcome the alcohol issue, from the nineteenth century through the present.

In Chapter 9, Joel Martin takes on the way the Indian was used by the White South to help define its cultural identity. Arguing that the South is too often seen in biracial (Black-White) terms, Martin shows that southern identity has been tied to Indianness since early settlement. At a national level, White Americans have exploited Indian connections to prove their ties and rights to the land, but no more so than in the South. Within the southern context, Martin delineates the ambivalence that White culture exhibits toward the Indian—wanting connections, yet also needing to define Indians as everything "we" are not.

Jay Mechling's essay on the Seminoles in Chapter 10 also concerns the South and touches on many similar issues. Mechling raises complex questions about control over the narrative construction of Indianness. He points out that it is not always a simple matter to say which are "White" and which are "Indian" narratives. The Seminoles are, in many senses, a "constructed" people, but constructed by whom? White popular culture certainly found in them a perfect picture of the wild, undefeated, yet nonthreatening Indian, who lived a romantic, idyllic, and natural life. The Seminoles were very important in the development of the Boy Scout or woodland camp kind of approach to Indianness. Yet the Seminoles participated in this construction, adding to it and developing it, and they continue to use it for their own purposes today.

Mechling's essay raises important issues of authenticity that perhaps suggest that authenticity is less a matter of historic accuracy and more a matter of power. That is, authentic imagery comes about when American Indians have the power to define and use that imagery, even if some aspects of it originated with White culture. Richard King's essay in Chapter 11 moves us squarely into the present and takes up anew the issue of authenticity and power. Analyzing the Little Bighorn Battlefield National Monument, he shows that in spite of numerous attempts to revamp the museum to suit modern sensibilities, the spectacle presented is still largely a White vision. The ethnographic "otherness" described by Griffiths surfaces again here, with American Indian culture being portrayed as locked in history, impersonal, and generic, whereas the culture of Custer's forces is shown as dynamic, understood through personal identification, and very specific. Moreover, it is not that the artifacts and displays are historically "inauthentic," but rather that one authentic narrative voice is subordinated to the other.

The theme of power continues in Chapter 12, in Cynthia-Lou Coleman's analysis of popular newspaper coverage of a dispute over natural resource exploitation in Wisconsin. Once again, Native voices were marginalized through the power of language, as news stories cumulatively portrayed Native protesters as opposed to progress, somewhat backward, and irrational. In the 1990s, words like "savage" have disappeared and the message is more subtle, but it is still there.

Dances with Wolves was undoubtedly a defining moment in the surge of infatuation with historical Indians during the 1980s and 1990s. In Chapter 13, Robert Baird presents an insightful argument that meshes with the theme of many of the other essays in this collection. The film, he says, is not about Indians at all but is firmly about White concerns. In particular, it is the latest incarnation of an American obsession with "going native," as reflected in arts and literature for the last two hundred years. As Americans yearn for something better, Indian culture has filled a Utopian role, representing a lost Eden. Baird adds an interesting postscript explaining the way elements that contradicted that Edenic picture were excised from the original theatrical release, although they were reinstated in a later TV version, perhaps in response to criticisms of the film's romanticism.

Noble and beautiful "savages" abounded in *Dances with Wolves.* Peter van Lent takes up that theme in Chapter 14, investigating the way the image of the Indian male has become an important cultural icon in the 1990s. Perhaps in response to cultural uncertainties about "correct" male roles, the Indian man, invariably and safely placed in a "dead" historical context, can become all things to all women. He is breathtakingly handsome and virile, with the potential for decisive action when pressed, yet he is tender, loving, and vulnerable. Van Lent's essay underlines an important point about the development of the Indian image—over the last century or so, that image has become increasingly defined as male. Although the importance of the Indian grandmother myth still persists,[20] developed Indian female characters have become increasingly rare. It remains to be seen if the revival of the *Pocahontas* myth will change that.

The next two essays analyze contemporary television representation. In Chapter 15, Annette Taylor points out that the now-canceled program *Northern Exposure* broke new ground in its portrayal of Native Alaskans. The program is set in contemporary times, which is in itself unusual, and the Native characters are unique, not just because they are Native (in many contexts, identifying a character as Indian is presumed to say it all, without further character development) but also because they have individual character quirks, just like everyone else on the show. Nevertheless, Taylor points out that the producers still tended to present the characters Marilyn and Ed as generic "Indians" rather than as members of unique cultural groups. However, in my essay on *Dr. Quinn, Medicine Woman* in Chapter 16, I argue that although the producers of that show strive for "authenticity" and fairness, the series is locked in established White mythologies of the Indian.

Part of my research involved discussions with both White and American Indian people about *Dr. Quinn* and their ideas about Indian representation generally. A clear message from these discussions was that, indeed, popular culture does reflect White concerns, while trivializing and marginalizing those of Indians. Furthermore, White people probably do not even realize this, believing that Indians would approve of the very imagery they may actually find offensive. Thus it falls to Indian people to counter the stereotypes. Ted Jojola's essay in Chapter 17 deals with his involvement in an attempt to do just that, when he was brought in as a consultant in the development of a children's cartoon series. His discussion brings into vivid focus the gap between White and Native perceptions, as he describes the gradual transformation of the proposed character from the ferocious Geronimoo, through the New Age cowboy Phil Thomas, to J.R., whom Jojola modeled on his grandfather. There were obviously frustrations involved, but because of Jojola's efforts, yet another gruesome stereotype was avoided.

Finally, on a very personal note in Chapter 18, Debra Merskin relates the way she confronts White stereotypes of Indians by her very appearance, as a mixed-blood Indian who has to deal with the fact that she "does not look like one." Her essay has wide implications for all Native Americans, whether mixed or full-blooded, who have to confront the expectations of White society that "real Indians" should wear buckskins or do war dances.

Conclusion

The images produced by popular culture play a real role in shaping people's perceptions. When my son was six, he once announced to me that "there aren't any real Indians left, are there"—even though the largest ethnic minority in our region is the Ojibwa. He had never seen a costumed, and therefore "real," Indian. Local Ojibwa writer Jim Northrup recently wrote wryly about his experiences visiting New York City, where he was regularly spotted as Indian and treated as a minor celebrity: "One cab driver took a $10 bill out of his wallet for us to autograph. I signed as Kevin Costner, and I believe my wife used the name Pocahontas."[21]

The current wave of Indian images might seem benign—who would not want to be presented as perfect, beautiful, and all-knowing? But this benign image is deeply impersonal and distanced, once again ignoring Indian people as individuals and allowing real Indian people no subjectivity. In a recent essay, Ted Jojola describes a "little tin Indian" he was given by a friend and goes on to mention *The Indian in the Cupboard*, a popular children's book recently made into a film. "In fact," he comments, "we Native people were never behind that cupboard in the first place. No, because tin Indians like that were fabricated totally in the minds of ancient Europeans and their New World evangelists. It was a mind that was subconsciously molding tin into something that was their image gold."[22] Real Indian people are neither tin nor gold, but flesh and blood, and it is time for popular imagery to recognize their living, breathing presence among all other Americans.

Notes

1. Many people, of course, prefer to use the term "Native Americans" to refer to this country's original inhabitants. In my state, Minnesota, like everywhere else, there is no agreement on the preferred terminology. However, in general, "American Indian" is commonly

used by both native and non-native people, so I have decided to use that term throughout my own work. Some of the authors of essays in this volume prefer to use "Native American"; where this is the case, their terminology stands.

2. Pauline Turner Strong, review of *Pocahontas,* distributed electronically through H-Net (H-Net@uicvm.uic.edu), June 30, 1995.

3. Ted Jojola, "Some Preliminary Notes on *Pocahontas,*" *American Indian Libraries Newsletter* 18 (1) (Fall 1995), p. 1.

4. "Pocahontas Protest: Final Letter," distributed by members of NatChat, an electronic community of native and non-native people interested in issues pertaining to the world's aboriginal peoples, July 1995.

5. See S. Elizabeth Bird, "Is That Me, Baby: Image, Authenticity, and the Career of Bruce Springsteen," *American Studies* 35 (2):39–58.

6. Robert S. Tilton, *Pocahontas: The Evolution of an American Narrative* (Cambridge: Cambridge University Press, 1994), p. 174.

7. Ibid., p. 95.

8. Ibid., pp. 52–53.

9. Strong, review of *Pocahontas.*

10. Robert Berkhofer, Jr., *The White Man's Indian: Images of the American Indian from Columbus to the Present* (New York: Vintage Books, 1979), p. xv.

11. Strong, review of *Pocahontas.*

12. Michael Paul Rogin, *Ronald Reagan: The Movie, and Other Episodes in Political Demonology* (Berkeley: University of California Press, 1987), p. 141.

13. Ibid., p. 144.

14. "Across Arizona," in *The West: A Collection from Harper's Magazine* (New York: Gallery Books, 1990), p. 4.

15. Known officially as Chippewa, though their original name is Anishinabe.

16. See the chapter on Indian humor in Vine DeLoria, Jr., *Custer Died for Your Sins: An Indian Manifesto* (Norman: University of Oklahoma Press, 1988).

17. See, for example, Elizabeth Weatherford, "Starting Fire with Gunpowder," *Film Comment* 28 (1992):64–67, for a discussion of the work of independent Indian filmmakers.

18. Beth Krodel, "Teens Praise Cultural Focus," Duluth *News-Tribune,* pp. 1A, 9A.

19. Geoffrey Norman, "The Cherokee: Two Nations, One People," *National Geographic* 187 (5):83.

20. See DeLoria, Jr., *Custer Died for Your Sins;* Rayna Green, "The Tribe Called Wannabee: Playing Indian in America and Europe," *Folklore* 99 (1) (1988):30–55.

21. Jim Northrup, Indian Issues column, Duluth *News-Tribune,* July 26, 1995, p. 7A.

22: Jojola, "Some Preliminary Notes," p. 3.

2

The First but Not the Last of the "Vanishing Indians": Edwin Forrest and Mythic Re-creations of the Native Population

Sally L. Jones

When Edwin Forrest (1806–1872), the first American-born actor to achieve recognition as a tragedian, announced the first playwriting competition for American dramatists in 1828, his stipulation was that the "hero, or principal character" of the five-act tragedy "shall be an aboriginal of this country."[1] The prizewinner, *Metamora; or the Last of the Wampanoags,* by John Augustus Stone, was first performed in New York City on December 15, 1829. For over forty years after that, Forrest accumulated his fortune by performing the part that had become synonymous with his title as "the American tragedian."

Embodying the traits of the noble-yet-savage characters in James Fenimore Cooper's novels and Washington Irving's story "Philip of Pokanoket," Metamora became the "model Indian" on the stage and in public life. Taverns, sailing vessels, and steamboats were named after him, and signboards and wayside resorts sported his likeness. Lines from the play became instantly recognizable catchphrases. A wave of stage Indians followed, with producers attempting to cash in on the popularity of the noble sachem, which prompted one commentator in 1846 to complain that Indian dramas had become "a perfect nuisance."[2]

The character Metamora represents the historical figure Metacom,[3] a sachem, or hereditary chief, of the Wampanoag tribe that inhabited the coastal regions of southern New England. (Newspaper speculation was that Stone changed the name because of his ear for "euphony.")[4] Metacom's father was the famed Massasoit who had greeted the Pilgrims upon their arrival on his shores and had formulated a

13

peace treaty with their leaders in 1621. Peace was generally maintained between the white settlers and the Wampanoags until Massasoit's death in 1661. When Metacom succeeded, his name was recorded as "Philip of Pokanoket," but he was nicknamed "Prince" Philip by the colonists for his regal bearing and their perception of his role among his people. The sachem became derisively known as "King" Philip when war erupted between colonists and the native population in 1675. That armed conflict, which nearly leveled the Massachusetts Bay Colony, has been known both popularly and historically as King Philip's War.[5]

Although information on the origin and circumstances of the war is scarce, its outcome is undeniable: Over half of the native population of New England was eradicated. When Philip, the nominal figurehead of the war, was betrayed by a defector and killed in an ambush at his hideaway in August 1676, his severed head was taken to Plymouth and displayed on a spike in that town "for decades."[6] Narratives often overlook the fact that even without the presence of the Wampanoags' supposed "chief in command," peace was not achieved until 1678.[7] After the war, hysteria and already rampant prejudice gripped the white population, which allowed no clemency for any still-existing native peoples.

Differing interpretations of events have served Americans in the successive stages of their political development. Not surprisingly, during colonial times, Philip was painted as a diabolical savage, or devil incarnate, while the Puritans were presented as defending their God-given existence. This interpretation was revived during the Revolutionary War to bolster the image of the independent first settlers on American soil. Accordingly, the settlers were viewed as heroically wresting the land from uncivilized brutes while distanced from their mother country, which rewarded their efforts by further exploiting them. However, with the dawn of the nineteenth century and the final military confrontation with the English in the War of 1812, the romantic imagination combined with the urge to create a mythic past separate from England's, and the Indian came to stand as a symbol for the past virginity of the continent.[8] This developing phenomenon is vividly manifested in the diary of the captain who ambushed Metacom, Benjamin Church of Little Compton, Rhode Island. The first edition in 1716 of the *Diary of King Philip's War* was 120 pages long, without notes or illustration. Four years before the landmark date of 1776, a longer edition included an account of Church's life and an engraving of Philip by Paul Revere. The engraving, titled "Philip. *King of Mount Hope*," shows a grim and squat man, pygmy-like and shrivelled, with one hand on his hip, the other on his gun, and a tomahawk at his feet. A little over fifty years later, in 1825, antiquarian and editor Samuel Drake published a 304-page edition of Church's notes. His book, although still focusing on America's heroic forefathers triumphing over savages, introduced a new image for Paul Revere's Philip. This engraving, called simply "King Philip," shows a tall, muscular man with elongated legs and expanded chest. His knife is tucked in his belt, and the tip of his rifle rests in the hand of a regally extended arm. His other hand covers his heart, and four tall feathers comprise his crown. Public response was so favorable to this edition that Drake published an even larger one in 1827 of 360 pages.[9] When Forrest called for his play in 1828 to have an "aboriginal" as its hero, the public was ready.

Although the influence of Jean-Jacques Rousseau on romantic thought rescued the Indian from the depths of infamy, the new philosophy only placed the Indian on a correspondingly high and heroic pedestal. Washington Irving embraced the concept of the noble savage, and two of his *Sketch Book* essays directly address the "North American savage." In the first, "Traits of Indian Character," one finds a romantic eulogium on the first inhabitants of the New World, a rebuttal of their defamation, and an attack on the first colonists. Irving draws a parallel between the Indian's habits and character and the American "scenery" in which he lived—"its vast lakes, boundless forests, majestic rivers, and trackless plains"—glorifying the country that bore these beings. Their defiance of white colonists he likens to that of the stoic Roman senators when the Gauls "laid waste the city of Rome."[10] The sense of a lost golden age permeates Irving's essay and continues more specifically in "Philip of Pokanoket," in which he selects the story of Metacom to "furnish us with nearer glimpses of human nature, and show what man is in a comparatively primitive state." In his attempt to correct the history of the "unfortunate King Philip," he rehabilitates him in nationalistic terms as "a patriot attached to his native soil."[11] He translates the Wampanoag's actions into the adjuncts of the white romantic ideal and creates an Indian chief-cum-soldier-cum-patriot of the nineteenth-century world.

As Irving was publishing his sketches, the figure of the Indian was being enlisted onstage to promote patriotic feeling against the English in Mordecai M. Noah's *She Would Be a Soldier; or The Plains of Chippewa* (1819). This play was first performed on June 21, 1819, at the Anthony Street Theatre, New York City. It was performed until 1868, with half the performances taking place on July 4, on Evacuation Day, or on Washington's birthday.[12] It was in this drama concerning the War of 1812 that Forrest enacted his first Indian character. The play was normally produced on Evacuation Day (November 24), the day set aside to celebrate the departure of British troops from New York City in 1783, marking the end of the Revolutionary War. Noah's nameless Indian, a chief, is not a very large role; the character acts as a guide to an imperious and imbecilic British captain in a comic subplot. The contrast between the steadfast, sensible Indian and the buffoonish Brit serves more than comic ends, however. The few but lengthy speeches of the Indian display his loyalty and patriotism, as well as an inherent nobility and independence of spirit. When the chief is captured by the Americans, he displays stoic courage and offers a passionate argument for his hatred and defiance of the American invaders:

Indian.   You came with the silver smile of peace, and we received you into our cabins; we
     hunted for you, toiled for you; but when your numbers increased, you rose like wolves
     upon us, fired our dwellings, drove off our cattle, sent us in tribes to the wilderness, to
     seek for shelter; and now you ask me, while naked and a prisoner, to be your friend! . . .
     Think you I would be your enemy unless urged by powerful wrongs? No, white man,
     no! (3.1 140)[13]

The response to the Indian's charges fully exonerates the American side and makes an ally of the Indian: "We have not done this, deluded man; your pretended advocates, over the great waters, have told you this tale" (3.1 140). The Indian and American, who live "in one territory," are thus united in the play against "jealous foreigners" who would tear their land asunder.

Indian.   Brother . . . forgive my rage, . . . protect our warriors and wives; guard their wig-wams from destruction; soften their prejudices and remove their jealousies. Do this, and the red man is your friend. (3.1 140)

The reconciliation of the Indian and the American casts the American as a custodian of the land and its peoples. In this way, the symbol of the Indian is taken from British hands in the play and is identified as an American entity. The Indian is now American property and has become an ally in creating a national identity.

Although the noble savage had become an archetype in romantic European and North American thought, American attitudes differed from those of Europeans because in America, these original people still lived among them. The people's hero, Andrew Jackson, elected president in 1828, had won his fame by killing eight hundred people of the Creek nation in 1814. On May 28, 1830, Congress made the provision for forced population removal, which it euphemistically described as "voluntary emigration." The movement to construct a national identity and heritage for the young country, coupled with the political imperative to expand national boundaries, created an almost schizophrenic view of native peoples in the new nation, as the loss of such savage majesty was bewailed, on the one hand, and the removal of the existing descendants of that legacy was condoned, on the other. Jackson's secretary of war, Lewis Cass, identified a "principle of progressive improvement . . . in human nature," which he stated could not be found "in the constitution of our savages."[14] Rousseau's pre-Darwinian theory of the stages of society was thus used to leave the savage in the dust of advancing civilization—and in the dirt of the present one. Written at a crucial point during the enactment of Jackson's Indian Removal Policy, *Metamora; or the Last of the Wampanoags* addressed the heritage of the American continent by imbuing America and its native inhabitants with a mythological grandeur, envisioning the supplanting of the Indian by virtuous, freedom-loving Americans. Stone's Metamora is ultimately defeated by the ineluctable "march of civilization" and his own intractable nature, but before his demise, he manages to kill an evil English lord, foil an exiled regicide's devious plans, and befriend the honest, plainspoken Walter and the warm-hearted Oceana, who signify the "new world order." In this way, President Jackson's course was supported, and an unforgettable hero and emblem of America's past was created.

The character of Metamora was thus constructed to instill a sense of the exotic and of "otherness," while at the same time retaining attributes with which the audience would identify. Furthermore, as an emblem, Metamora had to be noble and reflect the greatness of the virgin continent he represented. In the play itself, Walter enumerates Metamora's "native virtues":

Oceana.   Teach him, Walter; make him like us.

Walter.   'Twould cost him half his native virtues. Is justice goodly? Metamora's just. Is bravery virtue? Metamora's brave. If love of country, child and wife and home, be to deserve them all—he merits them.

Oceana.   Yet he is a heathen.

Walter.   True, Oceana, but his worship though untaught and rude flows from his heart, and Heaven alone must judge of it. (1.1.208)

Bravery, justness, and patriotism are his attributes, coupled with devotion to domestic life. His great devotion to his god, Manitou, is all that differentiates him from the ideal male Jacksonian, but even so his spirituality is translated into God-fearingness. His virtues spring from nature, "rude and untaught"; he is a Jacksonian child of nature on a grand scale.

Sympathy lies with Metamora, as Stone presents a surprisingly strong defense of the Indian's position. Walter explains to Oceana why the white people "love him not": "He stands between them and extended sway" (1.1.207). When Oceana calls the warrior a fiend and murderer during an attack on the white settlement, Metamora replies, "The white man has made me such. Prepare." His Indian virtues prevail, however, for when Oceana herself brandishes the eagle plume with which he had pledged that no harm would befall her, Metamora relents: "The Wampanoag cannot lie" (3.4.217).

Although some viewers may have squirmed in response to the condemnation of white society's motives and treatment of the Indian, most probably did not. There is only one anecdote extant that indicates how an audience could interpret *Metamora* as an indictment of current policies. Actor James Murdoch reported that he was playing an engagement in Augusta, Georgia, when Forrest performed the role there in 1831. According to Murdoch, Forrest's exit in the council scene was followed by loud yells and hisses, the play ended to "unqualified disapprobation," and Forrest was accused of insulting the people of Augusta. For the only time on theatrical record, *Metamora* played to an empty house when it was repeated the following night.[15]

Whether *Metamora* was true or fictitious, it was within the play's power to expose a nerve among the white population. How was Stone able to adhere to the Jacksonian party line when the destruction of such a magnificent hero seems to stand as a protest to removal policies? Textually, on a facile level, the two groups of characters in the play are categorized as the Indians and the English. Stone did not overtly identify Metamora's enemies as American. The Indian was facing British enemies who could well be characterized as unscrupulous, intolerant of different religions, and exploitive in American eyes. Although Metamora's thunderous cry, "Red man, arouse! Freedom! Revenge or death!" (3.1.215), might have struck fear in the midst of a frontier settlement, on stage its reverberations recalled the ideals ascribed to the founding of the American nation. The line, with the substitution of "slaves" or "bondmen" for the call to the "red man," echoes in all of Forrest's famous American plays.[16]

As a patriotic piece, *Metamora's* nationality and vengeful attitude took on a different significance in 1861. Two weeks before the outbreak of the Civil War, with rumors flying of Virginia's secession, *Metamora* was played to a highly enthusiastic New York audience. The reviewer of the *New-York Dispatch* commented that if the principal dancer of the Wampanoag War Dance had been named in the playbill he would have been "undoubtedly called out at the end of the act." Apparently the "Effect of the War Excitement" upon the audience found a vehicle for its release in Forrest's *Metamora:* "It [the audience] encored 'Yankee Doodle'—it demanded 'Hail Columbia'—when Forrest or 'Metamora,' 'The Last of the Wampanoags,' advised the white men to 'Tremble in the East, in the West, in the North and in the South.'"[17]

Forrest's official biographer, William Alger, states that "it was the *genuine* Indian who was brought upon the stage" when Forrest enacted Metamora, "merely idealized a little in some of his moral features."[18] But, as discussed, this was the white man's Indian,[19] perceived through and created for the Jacksonian sensibility; whatever realism Forrest brought to the part of Metamora stemmed from his association in New Orleans with Chief Push-ma-ta-ha of the Choctaws. He reportedly spent a month in the summer of 1825 living with the chief.[20] Such "fact-finding" missions were not new to the romantic school of actors: Forrest went to an asylum to study a man driven insane by sorrow, making observations that he used as the foundation of Lear's madness, as had the English actor David Garrick before him.[21] Details of pantomimic behavior were used to particularize the idealized picturesqueness of actors' presentations. Forrest's experiences and observations merely overlaid the conventions of an art form that strove for an emotional and moral ideal defined by prevailing cultural and social beliefs. The effect could be compared to the tragedian's laying on of the copper-colored makeup over his translucent, white skin, at times in conjunction with the application of a well-groomed mustache and imperial.[22]

Forrest's metamorphosis centered on those physical characteristics with which he chose to represent the Indian. Elements people remarked upon at the time include the carriage of his body, vocal inflections, facial expressions and arm gestures, even down to "the manner his head [was] posed upon his shoulders."[23] Forrest changed his posture by lifting and throwing out his chest "from the small ribs up to the collar bone," and even imitated "the very manner of their breathing."[24] He altered his stance by turning his feet inward, and walked with his feet held parallel in a straight line, or pointing slightly inward,[25] dispensing with the more conventional stances of tragic practice. "New and strange"[26] vocal inflections were supplemented by the Indian's "deep and vigorous gutturals flung out from the muscular base of the abdomen,"[27] alien to the upper-chest breathing of the Victorian era. Some fourteen such "hahs" and grunted "humphs" were interjected by Forrest into the acting script.[28] The actor seems to have made an attempt to convey an "Indianness" within the heightened speech as well. One paper noted that he "tames the Indian's talkativeness" and "keeps him quieter than he had very evidently been intended [by the author] to be."[29] The language flowed "lazily from [his] lips."[30] One perceives here the origin of the stereotypical, taciturn, grunting savage. Daniel Francis identifies the prototype for the "stern, emotionless, stoical" Indian as the famous cigar-store advertisement. Made of wood, they say little but feel deeply; on the surface they appear dull witted, but inside, they are perceived to "contain all the world's wisdom."[31] In the tradition of the tragic stage, however, Metamora is more than eloquent when he describes the white men, and Forrest's "declamation seemed to make the whole tragedy of the story of the American Indians breathe and swell and tremble."[32]

Obviously, the "realism" lay with the perceived typicality of the actions and their effect on the audience, not on the actions themselves. Forrest's performance impressed people as realistic—because it matched their own preconceptions. The source of these conceptions is difficult to pinpoint, but during the 1830s, Black Hawk, Red Jacket, and other native Americans were paraded before the American people, so some of the urban populace had had the experience of "seeing first-hand" what Indians were like. Although Rosemarie K. Banks feels "natives" negotiated their own identities through these public displays, they could as well have played to public expectations: The room for self-expression would seem limited by the objectification of being displayed like clothes on a runway.[33] In 1833, the *New-York Mirror* declared that Forrest's performance was "in strict accordance" with their "*notions* of the Indian character," claiming "he is the complete embodiment of our *idea* of King Philip."[34] Apocryphal stories abounded to certify the accuracy of Forrest's impersonation. Delegations of Indian tribes were reported to have seen him in Boston, New York City, Washington [D.C.], Baltimore, Cincinnati, and New Orleans and to have expressed their approval. One such incident allegedly took place in Boston's Tremont Theater, where some "western Indians" were "so excited by the performance, that in the closing scene they rose and chanted a dirge in honor of the death of the great chief [Metamora]."[35] Forrest supposedly averred that the greatest compliment to his acting came one evening in Charleston when he gave a war whoop for the benefit of a tribe in the audience, and they all responded to the genuineness of his cry in kind, startling the more timid members of the audience.[36]

His emotional expression as Metamora was thought to be quite distinctly Indian as well. A quality of repressed emotion characterized the role, accomplished by the actor with "sudden muscular movements"[37] and "explosive bursts of voice."[38] His voice was the primary vehicle for expressing the pathos of his character—because "the Indian warrior never weeps"; the actor conveyed the character's emotion "without tears or gesture." When Metamora discovers his son is dead, Forrest used "a soft voice quivering with the tears not suffered to mount to the eyes."[39] A fervent admirer and Democrat, Gabriel Harrison, claimed that "Forrest's pathos in Metamora was a pathos that could belong to none except the red man." This pathos was of a stoic nature, "not wet with tears . . . as distinct as is the color of [the brave Indian's] complexion."[40] Moreover, the stolid bearing of the chief, with his "abrupt, dignified, and unconventional" action, imbued Metamora with a grandeur identified with the noble savage.[41]

Forrest used his grand physique to enhance the nobility of Metamora. In the opening scene, a glen was represented on stage with ledges of rocks "rising to a considerable height at the back of the stage," while trees, shrubs, twisting vines, and wild flowers hung "in festoons."[42] Oceana tells Walter about the Indian who had saved her from a panther the previous day: "High on a craggy rock an Indian stood, with sinewy arm and eye that pierced the glen. . . . Firmly he stood upon the jutting height, as if a sculptor's hand had carved him there. With awe I gazed as on the cliff he turned—*the grandest model of a mighty man*" (1.1.207, emphasis added). As Walter replied that this must have been Metamora, two "Indian" gutturals came from offstage: "Hah! Hah!" Looking toward the sound, Oceana gave the cue for Metamora's entrance: "Behold his dread encounter with a wolf" (1.1.207). With another two gutturals, Forrest, entering on the highest part of the "projecting rock" in the background, recreated Oceana's description of the mighty man. Alger fills in the details with his description of

> the leading character seen, in his picturesque, aboriginal costume, standing on the highest rock in an attitude that charmed the eye. Leaning forward on his firmly-planted right foot, the left foot thrown easily back on its tip, he had a bow in his hands, with arrow strung to its head. As the arrow sped from the twanging string he raised his eyes with eager gaze after it, gave a deep interjection, "Hah!" bounded upon a rock below, and vanished.[43]

Poised for action against the craggy rocks, Metamora became part of the majestic landscape. The actor graphically demonstrated the association that was growing in American minds about the character of the nation, its glorious past and future, and its natural geography, in much the same way the Hudson River School of painting strove to invest their landscapes with mythological resonance.

The facets central to Metamora's character are his love of nature, his hatred of the intruding race, and those honorable traits enumerated by Walter. His kingly and noble attributes are established in the first half of the play, whereas the last acts contain more fury and fustian, as well as violent action, for example, the burning of houses. In the first scene of act 2, one can find all the aspects of Metamora's character clearly delineated and exhibited at various tempos. The scene begins with a description of Metamora's foreboding dream and contains the ultimatum by the colonists that he come to their meeting. To describe the Indian's vision of war with the white man, Forrest formed a tableau, placing his wife and child by his side, "a group that was a fit study for pictorial illustration."[44] The actor utilized a "sub-sonorous voice, full of superstitious suggestion,"[45] growing in intensity as he uttered the words: "Nahmeokee, the power of dreams has been on me, and the shadows of things to be have passed before me. My heart is big with thoughts. When I sleep, I think the knife is red in my hand and the scalp of the white man is streaming" (2.1.210).[46] Harrison commented that the "deep and tremulous quality" of Forrest's voice was "like the subdued bass of the great organ," and that the stage reverberated as a sounding board with his tones, lending "an additional awe to the words."[47] After uttering these words, Forrest accentuated the reflective mood with a pose that distilled the nobility and sympathetic quality of the man: "Here he gave an additional height to his figure, a slight downward inclination to his head and eyes, dropped his left arm listlessly, and while the two halves of his whole form were seen finely distinguished along the median line, with his right hand, extended to its fullest distance straight from the shoulder, grasped his bow, which stood perfectly erect from the ground."[48] With one half of his body firmly extended and the other half drooped in tiredness and despair, Forrest underlined the inevitable, undeserved fate awaiting Metamora.

Although Metamora is sympathetically drawn, Stone also incorporated the bloodthirsty traits of the "red menace" into the chief's stalwart defiance, playing on the sense of the Indian as a threat to society. Metamora is charged with conspiracy in the council scene (2.3.) and stabs the Indian informant dead on the spot, although historically, the Wampanoag who collaborated with the colonists was found dead some days after. Within the grandiose sweep of his final speech in this act are contained the vengeful and dreaded qualities attributed to his race:

> My knife has drunk the blood of the false one, yet it is not satisfied! White man, beware! The mighty spirits of the Wampanoag race are hovering o'er your heads; they stretch out their shadowy arms to me, and ask for vengeance; they shall have it. The wrath of the wronged Indian shall fall upon you like a cataract. The war whoop shall start you from your dreams at night, and the red hatchet gleam in the blaze of your burning dwellings! From the east to the west, in the north and in the south shall cry of vengeance burst, till the lands you have stolen groan under your feet! (2.3 214)

An actor, a contemporary of Forrest, described the vocal prowess of the tragedian during this speech as Metamora "tower[ed] alone in solitary and solid grandeur":[49] "His voice surged and roared like the angry sea lashed into fury by a storm . . . the serpent hiss of hate was heard, at intervals, amidst its louder, deeper hoarser tones . . . it was a whirl-wind, a tornado, a cataract of illimitable rage!"[50] As the soldiers were ordered to fire upon him, Metamora/Forrest threw a man in front of him, who fell wounded—"Thus whiteman do I smite your nation"—and hurled his hatchet into the floor, center stage, exiting up center. A tableau was formed, in contrast to the preceding frenetic action, framing the still-moving hatchet handle; then a "*Quick curtain*" fell amidst "*general confusion*" (2.3.214).[51] The violence and action of the scene is unmistakable, and it was quite thrilling for the audience. Imbued with Forrest's electrifying power, the image of the tomahawk quivering in the floor, with its associations of scalping and bloodshed, became a signal symbol of Metamora's defiance, creating an unforgettable visual climax to act 2. The threat of the bloodthirsty savage was thus ingrained in the spectator's mind.

Such a menace must of course be eliminated. Stone's title itself effectively removes Metamora from contemporary and future societies. *The Last of the Wampanoags* is but one of many works (*The Last of the Mohicans, The Last of the Serpent*

Tribe, The Last of the Norridgewocks, The Last of the Shkikellemus, and so on)[52] that constructed the wish-fulfilling myth of a vanishing breed. This myth was very important to the ideology that expanded the new country and established white hegemony. Its pervasiveness has served interests from the nineteenth through the twentieth century, besides filling the coffers of Edwin Forrest.[53] In 1976 the Wampanoags of Mashpee, who had not participated in the war, instituted a suit to reclaim Wampanoag land incorporated into the town of Mashpee in 1869. The property in question, undergoing development, was worth $30 million in 1977. The move was defeated in court on the grounds that the Wampanoag tribe had been exterminated in King Philip's War three hundred years earlier. Even though anthropologists, ethnohistorians, and others testified to the contrary, the Mashpee Wampanoags were told that they did not exist.

In summary, attitudes toward Forrest's characterization changed both with time and with the native population's ever-diminishing fortunes in the country. If, in 1831, it was felt Forrest's Metamora was "a remarkable and highly finished picture of the American Indian,"[54] in 1855, his "feathers, beads, moccasins, and red-ocher" were seen as the only "Indian characteristics" of the role.[55] This change was not due to any greater understanding of native peoples, but rather to the increasing movement toward the west by the American population. In fact, in 1838, Louisa Medina's adaptation of *Nick of the Woods* brought a hero to the stage whose sole obsession was the extermination of the evil "redskins" of her play.[56] The perception of the Indian as a beast that must be eliminated grew in intensity as Americans began their appropriation of lands beyond the Mississippi. By 1844, the native population east of the Mississippi had been reduced from 120,000 (in 1820), to fewer than 30,000. By 1870, when only 12,534 aboriginals existed from coast to coast, Metamora became known as an "Eastern Indian."[57] (Ironically, this is the only accurate comment ever made about the character, as "Wampanoag" literally means "dawn people" or "people of the East"). The American-cum-noble-Indian-chief had been replaced with a rival in the public's consciousness—the western Indian. Thus, in reference to Forrest's Metamora, the Washington *Intelligencer* wrote in the 1860s that not only "Indian dramas" but native peoples themselves had become a "nuisance": "True it is that experience has destroyed the romance of Indian character—the Indian has become a nuisance; but nevertheless, as long as the virginity of this continent is remembered, as long as our bloody and priceless frontier traditions shall live, so long will the American Indian exist *as a portion of the poetry of Nature* wherein he is cradled."[58]

By embodying such a mythic and poetic past for a politically young nation, Metamora/Forrest served the burgeoning nationalistic interests of Jacksonian America. His performance and characterization of Metamora's "rude and savage, yet noble nature,"[59] as refracted through the Jacksonian sensibility, combined both the "pesky injuns" and "noble savages," advancing the ideology of a necessarily vanishing race. Through an ephemeral art form, Forrest gave his audience moments to preserve in their collective memory. In this way some of the unpublished

Figure 2.1 *Edwin Forrest in the title role of John Augustus Stone's* Metamora, *painting by Frederich Styles Agate, c. 1830. National Portrait Gallery, Smithsonian Institution.*

lines became "constant quotations." Contemporaries report that young boys mimicked Metamora's weighty, "Metamora cannot lie!"; "older persons" would use Metamora's reply in the council scene that "the good man's heart should be a stranger to fear and his tongue ever ready to speak the words of truth." These moral assertions were just as popular as the defiant air that the actor used when

Metamora entered the council chambers, facing soldiers who had reached for their weapons but who were struck dumb with astonishment: "You have sent for me and I have come. If you have nothing to say, I'll go back." Forrest's "bold and fearless manner" so impressed his audience that "their tongues were ever ready to quote the pertinent words."[60]

In effect, these pithy statements became "household words," in Harrison's experience "as familiar upon the public's tongue as the name of Washington."[61] Their reiteration reinforced the artist's fame and contributed to the verbal mythology that is vital to the process of nation building. Associated as these sayings were with the "American" Edwin Forrest, they soon became accepted emblems of national identity, usurping a native identity. In the National Portrait Gallery in Washington, D.C., hangs a painting of Forrest in the role, entitled "The Last of the Wampanoags" (Figure 2.1). Wampanoags may still exist, but their image pales against the performance of an actor of whom it was claimed: "And Metamora and Mr. Forrest have passed away together."[62]

Notes

1. *The Critic: A Weekly Review of Literature, Fine Arts, and the Drama,* 1, November 22, 1828.

2. See Cornelius Matthews, *Sun* (New York), July 5, 1881; Gabriel B. Harrison, *Edwin Forrest: The Actor and the Man* (Brooklyn, N.Y.: Brooklyn Eagle Book Printing Dept., 1889), pp. 39–40; See Laurence Hutton, *Curiosities of the American Stage* (New York: Harper and Brothers, 1891), pp. 13, 17–18.

3. His name appears variously as Metacom or Metacomet in English language histories. In the twentieth century, the editors of Colonel Benjamin Church's *Diary of King Philip's War, 1675–1676* use the name "Metacomet" (Alan and Mary Simpson, eds. [Tiverton, R.I.: Lockwood Publications, 1975]), whereas historian Russell Bourne uses "Metacom" (*The Red King's Rebellion: Racial Politics in New England, 1675–1678* [Oxford: Oxford University Press, 1990]). In the nineteenth century, author Washington Irving refers to the Wampanoag as "Metacomet" (see "Philip of Pokanoket," in *The Works of Washington Irving,* 10 vols. [London: Henry G. Boker, 1854], vol. 2, pp. 216–229).

4. *New-York Mirror,* 7 (23) (December 12, 1829).

5. Bourne, *Red King's Rebellion,* pp. 1–2, 10–11, 85–86, 95–96; Simpson, *Diary,* pp. 7, 16, 26–28; A. Bingham, *Mashpee: Land of the Wampanoags* (Falmouth, Mass.: Kendall Printing Co., 1970), p. 32; Nanepashemet interview by the author, Plymouth Plantation, Plymouth, Mass., August 10, 1991: Thomas Hutchinson, *The History of the Colony and Province of Massachusetts-Bay,* vol. 1, ed. L. Mayo 1764; reprint, Cambridge: Harvard University Press, 1936), p. 236.

6. Bourne, *Red King's Rebellion,* pp. 3, 199–201; Hutchinson, *History of Massachusetts-Bay,* pp. 251–260; Simpson, *Diary,* pp. 142–156; Ibid., pp. 32–35.

7. Even Kevin Costner's recent "500 Nations" (Part 2) television retelling of the story followed traditional narratives and ended with Philip's head on a spike.

8. See Bourne, *Red King's Rebellion,* pp. 2–6; Simpson, *Diary,* pp. 56–57, and in the same work, "The Mythical History of King Philip," pp. 179–180; see also Jeffrey Mason's

recent article on Metamora, pp. 95–96 ("The Politics of *Metamora*," in *The Performance of Power,* Sue-Ellen Case and Janelle Reinelt, eds. [Iowa City: University of Iowa Press, 1991], pp. 92–110).

9. A description and history of these editions are given by Alan and Mary Simpson, *Diary,* pp. 43–54. A reproduction of Revere's engraving appears on p. 51 of their work, and Drake's appears on p. 56. Revere's is also reproduced in Bourne, *Red King's Rebellion,* p. 147.

10. Irving, "Traits," in *Works of Irving,* pp. 207, 215.

11. Irving, "Philip," in *Works of Irving,* p. 229.

12. Mordecai M. Noah, "She Would Be a Soldier," in Richard Moody, ed., *Dramas from the American Theatre, 1762–1909* (Boston: Houghton Mifflin, 1969), pp. 120, 123–142. All quotations in this essay are from this text.

13. As in Howard Zinn, *A People's History of the United States* (New York: Harper and Row, 1980), p. 130.

14. John Augustus Stone, "Metamora, or the Last of the Wampanoags," in *Dramas from the American Theatre, 1762–1909,* ed. Moody, pp. 205–227. All quotations in this essay are from this text unless otherwise noted.

15. James E. Murdoch, *The Stage* (Philadelphia: J. M. Stoddart and Co., 1880), pp. 298–300. Alger reports that Forrest was in Georgia in 1831 but mentions his visit in an entirely different context (William Rounseville Alger, *Life of Edwin Forrest, the American Tragedian* [Philadelphia, 1877; reprint, New York: Benjamin Blom, 1972], p. 170). See also B. Donald Gross's article, "Edwin Forrest, *Metamora,* and the Indian Removal Act of 1830" (*Theatre Journal* [May 1985], pp. 181–191), in which he examines this incident and the play's relevance to prevailing attitudes and policies of the time.

16. See *The Gladiator,* 2.3., "Ho, slaves, arise! it is your hour to kill! . . . Freedom and revenge!"; *Jack Cade,* 4.2., "England from all her hills, cries out for vengeance! . . . For liberty and vengeance!" For a more complete discussion of the old world/new world, English/American dichotomies in the play, see Sally L. Jones, "The Original Character of Edwin Forrest and His American Style," (Ph.D. diss., University of Toronto, 1992), pp. 136–140.

17. *New-York Dispatch,* March 30, 1861, in Forrest Scrapbook (University of Pennsylvania, Special Collections).

18. Alger, *Life of Edwin Forrest,* p. 240.

19. Robert Berkhofer, Jr., uses the term "white man's Indian" as his title in *The White Man's Indian: Images of the American Indian from Columbus to the Present* (New York: Vintage Books, 1979).

20. Alger, *Life of Edwin Forrest,* pp. 137–138. All the biographies of Forrest repeat Alger's account of this; Harrison's does so the most colorfully, perhaps.

21. Alger, *Life of Edwin Forrest,* p. 354; "The Madness of Lear," n.d., Harvard Theatre Collection Clipping File, Harvard University.

22. In 1855, the *Boston Daily Journal* complained of his imperial in Hamlet, which, the paper noted, he "wears, even when playing Metamora" (November 24, 1855), but the *Boston Daily Courier* of 1861 commended Forrest for "dispensing with his moustache and imperial in Metamora (November 13, 1861). Forrest had photographer Matthew Brady record his character without imperial or moustache (reproduced in Alger, *Life of Edwin Forrest,* p. 230).

23. Harrison, *Edwin Forrest,* p. 35; see also Alger, *Life of Edwin Forrest,* pp. 239–240. Alger's descriptions coincide largely with those of Gabriel Harrison, many times verbatim.

Harrison, who published his work twelve years after Alger, denied in that work any plagiarism on his part, explaining that he had sent Alger his notes on Forrest's performances to help him with the biography (p. 157). Harrison included a letter he received from Alger that stated, "I shall avail myself of all you have written freely" (p. 158).

24. Harrison, *Edwin Forrest*, p. 38; see also Catherine Winslow, "The Actor, the Man and His Influence," n.d., Harvard Theatre Collection.

25. Harrison, *Edwin Forrest*, p. 35; Alger, *Life of Edwin Forrest*, p. 240.

26. Harrison, *Edwin Forrest*, p. 35.

27. Ibid., p. 35; Alger, *Life of Edwin Forrest*, p. 240.

28. Acting Side, "Metamora," handwritten manuscript in the Furness Collection, Van Pett Library (University of Pennsylvania).

29. *New-York Dispatch,* March 30, 1861, in Forrest Scrapbook.

30. The *Times* (London), March 27, 1845.

31. Daniel Francis, *The Imaginary Indian: The Image of the Indian in Canadian Culture* (Vancouver, British Columbia: Arsenal Pulp Press, 1992), pp. 85–86.

32. Alger, *Life of Edwin Forrest*, p. 243.

33. See Rosemarie K. Banks, "Staging the 'Native': Making History in American Theatre Culture, 1828–1838," *Theatre Journal* 45 (4) (December 1993), pp. 461–486.

34. The *New-York Mirror,* 14 December 1833, emphasis added.

35. Alger, *Life of Edwin Forrest*, p. 240; see also H. P. Phelps, *Players of a Century: A Record of the Albany Stage* (Albany, N.Y., 1880; reprint, New York: Benjamin Blom, 1972), p. 149.

36. The source of this information is an article titled "His Greatest Compliment [from the *Washington Post*]," a clipping of which the author found in Forrest's home. The elderly man who recalled the story and related it to the press claimed that the famous Indian chief Osceola was in the audience on the occasion.

37. Alger, *Life of Edwin Forrest*, p. 240.

38. Winslow, "The Actor, the Man and His Influence."

39. Alger, *Life of Edwin Forrest*, pp. 246, 247.

40. Harrison, *Edwin Forrest*, p. 44; see Alger, *Life of Edwin Forrest*, p. 246. An actor himself, Harrison was a member of the left-wing faction of the Brooklyn Democratic Party, an acquaintance and admirer of Edwin Forrest, and an associate of Walt Whitman. The fact that the most graphic and favorable descriptions of Forrest as Metamora emanate from such a source reinforce the extent to which his portrayal appealed to nationalistic tastes.

41. *New-York Dispatch,* Forrest Scrapbook, March 30, 1861.

42. Harrison, *Edwin Forrest*, p. 40.

43. Alger, *Life of Edwin Forrest*, p. 141; see Harrison, *Edwin Forrest*, pp. 40–41.

44. Harrison, *Edwin Forrest*, p. 42.

45. Ibid., p. 41.

46. Both Alger (*Life of Edwin Forrest*, p. 244) and Harrison (*Edwin Forrest*, p. 42) quote this speech.

47. Harrison, *Edwin Forrest*, p. 42.

48. Alger, *Life of Edwin Forrest*, p. 244; see also Harrison, *Edwin Forrest*, p. 42.

49. Alger, *Life of Edwin Forrest*, p. 245.

50. George Vandenhoff, *An Actor's Note-Book; or, the Green-Room and Stage* (London: John Camden Hotten, 1865), p. 201.

51. The *Times* (London) mentions "a dozen shots [that] followed Metamora as he left the council-room" (March 27, 1845).

52. Eugene Jones, *Native Americans as Shown on the Stage, 1753–1916* (Metuchen, N.J.: Scarecrow Press, 1988), p. 63. In the list of plays Jones provides at the end of his work, one also finds *Sharratah; or The Last of the Yemassees* (1842) and *The Last Night of a Nation* (1884). See Jones's chapter, "The 'Last Indian' Syndrome," pp. 63–81.

53. Seven more land claim suits were brought against the Massachusetts House in 1983, over land worth $1 billion; the cases failed. Although the Gay Head peoples are now recognized by the federal government as an official tribe, the Mashpee are categorized as "ethnic Indians," belonging to no tribe. James D. St. Clair, attorney for Richard Nixon during the Watergate trials, represented the town of Mashpee.

54. *New England Galaxy,* November 12, 1831.

55. *Boston Daily Journal,* November 28, 1855. The reviewer is echoing William Stuart's comments in the New York *Tribune* of that October.

56. See Jones, *Native Americans on the Stage,* pp. 75–77.

57. Census table, Appendix 2. In *Harvard Encyclopedia of American Ethnic Groups* (Cambridge: Harvard University Press, 1980), p. 1045.

58. *Intelligencer* (Washington), clipping in Special Collections, University of Pennsylvania.

59. *Brooklyn Daily Times,* February 20, 1862, Forrest Scrapbook.

60. Harrison, *Edwin Forrest,* pp. 39–40; Alger, *Life of Edwin Forrest,* p. 245.

61. Harrison, *Edwin Forrest,* p. 39.

62. Hutton, *Curiosities of the American Stage,* p. 14.

3

The Narratives of Sitting Bull's Surrender: Bailey, Dix & Mead's Photographic Western

Frank Goodyear

General Sherman has called the twenty years of constant Indian warfare following the War of the Rebellion, "The Battle of Civilization." That battle, on this continent, of course made that period an epoch by itself. . . . The field of "The Battle of Civilization" was the vast trans-Missouri region, and civilization did not, during that period, satisfy itself with a gradual advance of its line, as formerly, but became aggressive, pierced the Indian country with three trans-continental railways and so ultimately abolished the frontier. A very large portion of the army . . . was at one time or another occupied with the task and many heroic deeds were done, but the conspicuously successful leaders were few.

—G. W. Baird

In his 1891 *Century Magazine* article "General Miles's Indian Campaigns," Major G. W. Baird, a retired army officer, recounted the glory days in the West fighting under General Nelson A. Miles's command.[1] Illustrated with engravings by Frederic Remington, the article celebrated Miles's Indian-fighting career from its beginnings at Fort Dodge, Kansas, in 1874 to its conclusion at Wounded Knee, South Dakota, in 1890. Baird described the string of successes that Miles achieved in his fight against such famous Indian leaders as Geronimo, Chief Joseph, Lame Deer, Crazy Horse, and Sitting Bull. With the belief that "there are but two goals for the Indians—civilization or annihilation," Baird concluded his essay on a sympathetic note by calling on "the American people, those who really wish and hope to save the Indians from extinction and degradation . . . to use great patience and summon all their wisdom" in an effort to rescue "the savage of today."[2] By making such an appeal, he suggested that this long period of warfare with the Plains Indians was finally a closed chapter in American history books and that a new period of constructive reform was to follow.

The "Battle of Civilization" that Baird describes has been and continues to be the topic of many popular narratives, from the nineteenth-century dime novels of Erastus Beadle and John Adams to the twentieth-century Western movies of John Ford. Indeed, each generation recreates this historic conflict. Whether based on the activities of fictional heroes or on the supposed exploits of real men like Buffalo Bill Cody and Wild Bill Hickock, these tales all purport to relate the true "spirit" of this conflict, reflecting the dominant culture's desire for stories that not only dramatize but also confirm its history.

Since the earliest days of colonial settlement, the American Indian has been a source of fascination. Over the years, a large number of often contradictory myths have emerged from the dominant culture concerning the Indians and their society. In the American public's imagination, the Indian has represented such positive virtues as simplicity, beauty, and freedom. At the same time, this "noble savage" has also been portrayed as the epitome of barbarianism, poverty, and dependence. Forever being constructed, destroyed, and then resurrected, the popular image of the Indian fluctuates to meet the needs of the dominant culture and to justify its treatment of the native.[3] During the late nineteenth-century Great Plains conflicts, the images that were used to bring home the news of this struggle reflected society's belief in the righteousness of the conflict.

Sitting Bull's surrender to federal authorities at Fort Buford in the Dakota Territory on July 19, 1881, marked an important occasion in the "Battle of Civilization." Having been pursued by the U.S. cavalry for more than five years following the famous massacre at the Little Bighorn, Sitting Bull represented, in the eyes of the dominant culture, the most potent symbol of Indian aggression and resistance. For that reason, his capture was particularly noteworthy not only to military officials involved in the struggle on the plains but also to the American public, which hungered for information and evidence of his seizure.

In addition to the large number of newspaper reporters and tourists who flocked to see Sitting Bull during his two-year incarceration at Fort Randall, photographers also took this opportunity to capture the famous Sioux chief on film. One such individual was William R. Cross, a local Nebraskan photographer who was commissioned to assemble a series of twenty-four photographs that dramatized this historic event. In this essay I use that series of photographs, twenty-one of which were stereographs, to suggest the ways in which the dominant culture constructed a popular image of the Indian during these transitional years in Indian-Anglo affairs. Commissioned and marketed by Joshua Bradford Bailey, Dr. George P. Dix, and John L. Mead, three local men who saw the opportunity to make money, these images not only represent an early form of photojournalism in their narration of Sitting Bull's capture, but when viewed as a series, they also form a type of photographic Western.[4]

Although the formula Western did not emerge until the early part of the twentieth century, this set of photographs anticipates this theatrical and cinematic genre. Not only are the setting and costumes authentic, but the central Western conflict in which civilization and savagery meet on the frontier is also present. In addition, the characters involved prefigure the stereotypical Western characters who were later to popularize the American West in the twentieth century on stage and screen. There are the outlaw Sioux Indians led by their famous chief Sitting Bull. There are the agents of civilization represented by the white settlers who appear in a number of the photographs. Finally, there are the military heroes who appear in the photographs as four companies of the Twenty-fifth Infantry led by Captain Charles Bentzoni. Most important, though, the photographs presage the later Westerns in enacting a morality play in which the lawless Indian is forced to surrender to the progress of white civilization.

In this way, the photographs not only celebrate but also legitimize the tremendous transition occurring in the West. Forced to abandon their life as nomadic tribes, the Plains Indians were being coerced to accept a new life on the reservation. The image of the Indian in the eyes of the dominant culture mirrors this transformation. No longer portrayed as "noble savages," the Indians that William Cross photographed for Bailey, Dix & Mead were a defeated and dependent band whose future revolved around the reservation. Only later, when the transition to reservation life was complete, did the earlier romantic image of the Indian return in the paintings of such popular artists as Frederic Remington and Charles Russell and in the photographs of Edward Curtis. In 1882, however, nostalgia played little role in the documentation of Sitting Bull's surrender and imprisonment at Fort Randall. This set of photographs acted not only to satisfy the eastern public's thirst for visual documentation of this momentous event but also to educate them about the transition that was the result of America's long-fought "Battle of Civilization."

Sitting Bull's surrender at Fort Buford on July 19, 1881, attracted the attention of the entire nation. At the time, it shared front-page headlines in national newspapers with the assassination of President James Garfield, who had been shot less than three weeks earlier and lingered in critical condition for three months before dying. Special dispatches from the *St. Paul Pioneer Press* reached large city papers on both coasts the next day. For the next two weeks, the *New York Times* ran several further stories about the event in addition to a lengthy one and one-half column interview with Sitting Bull himself. In that interview, published August 7, Sitting Bull responded to an assortment of questions about topics as diverse as his treatment by the government and the number of wives he had. He was even asked to comment on his feelings concerning the president's assassination and the "coward" who shot him. Indeed, Sitting Bull became a national celebrity.

Only five years earlier, his place in American history had been assured because of his participation at the Battle of the Little Bighorn. Since that time, he and four thousand Sioux Indians had taken flight from the U.S. army, which had redoubled its efforts to subdue the "Indian menace" on the Upper Missouri frontier. Fleeing from the forces under General Alfred Terry, Sitting Bull's band of refugees sought sanctuary across the Canadian border. Not wanting to set off an international conflict, officials in Washington rejected several plans to go after Sitting Bull in

Canada. With the belief that "Sitting Bull and his outfit . . . have had enough of Indian hostilities," General Philip H. Sheridan proclaimed in 1878 that in time the Sioux would "sneak back to their agencies."[5]

True to his prediction, hunger and the realization of their hopeless predicament caused the large band to come apart slowly. Finally, on July 19, 1881, at Fort Buford, Sitting Bull and 187 followers became the last of the Sioux to "surrender." In his interview in the *New York Times*, Sitting Bull declared stubbornly,

> I came in to claim my rights and the rights of my people. I was driven in force from my land and I now come back to claim it for my people. I never made war on the United States Government. I never stood in the white man's country. I never committed any depredations in the white man's country. I never made the white man's heart bleed. The white man came onto my land and followed me. The white man made me fight for my hunting grounds. The white man made me kill him or he would kill my friends, my women, and my children. . . . I expected to stay but a few days at Buford. When I came in, I did not surrender. I want the Government to let me occupy the Little Missouri country. There is plenty of game there. I have damages against the Government for holding my land and game. I want the Great Father to pay me for it.[6]

Ten days later, under the protection of twenty soldiers from the Seventh Infantry, Sitting Bull was transported on the steamer *Sherman* to Fort Yates and the Standing Rock Agency, where his fellow Sioux were now located.[7] Out of fear that his presence would cause unrest on the Sioux reservation, the army transferred Sitting Bull and 172 of his followers to Fort Randall two months later. As the *New York Times* reported on September 2, "It is the intention to treat Sitting Bull as one who will bear watching, and not give him further opportunity by cunning counsel to stir up strife among the Sioux."[8] Despite swearing "that he would never go to Randall alive," Sitting Bull was relocated as a "prisoner, not a pensioner of the Interior Department."[9] He would spend the next two years imprisoned at Fort Randall.

The excitement caused by Sitting Bull's capture can be measured by the frenzied scramble to obtain both images and artifacts of the fallen Sioux leader. In nearly every newspaper article concerning the incident, there were reports of Sitting Bull selling his autograph and personal trinkets. In the *Chicago Tribune* of August 1, 1881, it was reported that he "sold a pipe for $100 and goggles for $5."[10] Orlando Scott Goff, a frontier photographer working in Bismarck, North Dakota, became the first individual to take Sitting Bull's picture. On August 1, while on his passage from Fort Buford to the Standing Rock Agency, Sitting Bull was offered fifty dollars to sit for his portrait by Goff. Having never been photographed before, he first refused, then later allowed Goff to make one negative.[11]

It was under these excited circumstances that George Dix and his partners Bailey and Mead commissioned William Cross to assemble his unique set of photographs.[12] Despite the absence of documents concerning this transaction, evidence from local newspapers and letters suggests that these three local civilians were present around Fort Randall at the time of Sitting Bull's incarceration. Although they were not photographers themselves, they saw the opportunity to make a quick profit, creating attractive images that could be sold to local inhabitants, potential settlers from the East, or visitors who passed through on the newly completed railroad line.[13] After this project, Bailey, Dix & Mead never published another photograph.

Given the entrepreneurial spirit behind this undertaking, it is significant that all but three of the photographs in the Bailey, Dix & Mead series are stereographs. By the 1880s, the stereoscope, the handheld viewer that produced the three-dimensional illusion of the image on the stereograph card, had become a common item in the middle-class Victorian home. It is estimated that there were over six thousand stereographers at work in the United States and Canada during the latter half of the nineteenth century.[14] By the time mass production of stereographs was made possible in the 1870s, large stereograph firms could manufacture over three thousand views each day to meet the demands of this expanding market.[15] By choosing to use stereographs to relate their narrative, Bailey, Dix & Mead were targeting a wide audience. Having compiled a trade list of more than two thousand stereographs during his forty years as a photographer in Nebraska and South Dakota, Cross had made a career creating images that would satisfy the American public's appetite for vicarious adventure in the world of the Indian on the Great Plains. Given the national demand for a visual record of the events surrounding Sitting Bull's surrender and the nature of the stereograph to provide this type of narrative, the opportunity was ripe for the creation of Bailey, Dix & Mead's photographic series.

A close examination of the twenty-four photographs that comprise this photographic Western reveals a record of the relationship between the white and Native American cultures during this transitional period. Not only are the captions helpful, but the numbered sequence of the stereographs also provides clues to understanding the dominant culture's attitude toward the Indian's subjugation and removal to reservations.[16] Indeed, much care has been taken to order the images in such a way as to construct a clear narrative. Through the dramatic story of one Indian's defeat, the series presents a familiar tale, one that had been heard before and would continue to be played out in the years ahead.

The narrative begins with an autographed cabinet-card portrait of Sitting Bull before a plain cloth backdrop (Figure 3.1). This is altogether fitting, as it introduces the viewer to the title character in the story that is about to unfold. In order to confirm the authenticity of the image for an audience that had never seen him before, a fixed caption reads, "The above is a true Photo and Autograph of 'Sitting Bull,' the Sioux Chief at the Custer Massacre." On the mount's reverse, a paragraph presents a number of statistics about him, including his height, weight, and the number of wives he has. The reverse also announces the fact that Sitting Bull, who is "too shrewd to acknowledge to having killed any whites," and his band of "Uncapapa Souix [sic] Indians" are now "prisoners of war at Fort Randall." In the

TATONKAIYOTONK. *Sitting Bull*
The above is a true Photo and Autograph of "Sitting Bull," the Sioux Chief
at the Custer Massacre.

Copyrighted, 1882, by Bailey, Dix & Mead.

Figure 3.1   *Sitting Bull, 1882. Courtesy Nebraska State Historical Society.*

first image of the set, the viewer directly confronts the notorious villain. While celebrating his long-awaited surrender, the photograph also presents the central conflict of the larger narrative through the placement of two symbolic items on his lap—a peace pipe and a small club. Is Sitting Bull ready to accept "civilization," or, unwilling to live on a reservation, will he continue to oppose the white man's advance?

The two other cabinet-card portraits in the series introduce the viewer to Indian characters who represent these two opposing views. The kneeling portrait of Steps, a "Nes Perce [sic] Indian" who has "lost his feet above the ankles" and "his right hand" in a "severe snow storm," suggests that the Indians were finally in a position of helplessness and had no other alternative except to give way to white society.

Copyrighted, 1882, by Bailey, Dix & Mead.

Figure 3.2   *One Bull, nephew of Sitting Bull, 1882. Courtesy Nebraska State Historical Society.*

In contrast, the portrait of One Bull (Figure 3.2) gives quite a different impression. Brandishing a club in his right hand, One Bull, a nephew of Sitting Bull, appears as the quintessential picture of Indian courage and might. In the caption on the mount's reverse, he is identified as having "had to be knocked down and carried aboard the boat to be brought as a prisoner to the fort." This incident had been recognized earlier in newspaper reports recounting the prisoners' transfer from the Standing Rock Agency to Fort Randall. The *New York Times* of September 12, 1881, reported a "slight disturbance" in which "a nephew of Sitting Bull made some resistance and was knocked down with the butt end of a musket. . . . It is thought that the preparations at Fort Randall are such as to prevent trouble there."[17] These two portraits remind the viewer of the conflict that is at the heart of this narrative.

Having acquainted the viewer with this conflict, Bailey, Dix & Mead next provide their audience with glimpses of the stage on which this play will be enacted. The next image, simply entitled "Winter Quarters," is the first of four stereographs that present an iconographic representation of the Native American tepee in the woods. In addition to describing the surrounding scene in which the camp is set, the caption on the mount's reverse also claims that "we have endeavored to give to them a much richer and attractive appearance than is shown in the bleak and dreary character of such views in general." A close examination does suggest that the foreground has been swept clean of any debris. Not only do these camp scenes give the viewer an idea of what an "actual" Indian camp looked like, but they also propagate the myth of the simple life for which the Indian was popularly known. In an age in which American society was undergoing dramatic technological and industrial changes, this camp scene "situated in a beautiful grove of box elders" further romanticized Indian culture. Indeed, Bailey, Dix & Mead's narrative is played out before this sanitized romantic set.

A number of the images make a point of depicting traditional Indian objects and customs in order to give the scene an "authentic" look. This practice of including colorful aspects of Native American culture in the image was employed for the same reason by many nineteenth-century artists who traveled into the West. Cross's recurring habit of depicting Indian objects in the foreground of his stereographs followed in the tradition of such popular Eastern painters as Albert Bierstadt and Worthington Whittridge. Although Cross worked in a different medium, all these artists were as concerned about heightening the mystique of a "disappearing" Plains Indian culture as they were about bringing back accurate ethnographic records. In his stereograph titled "Medicine Teepe [sic]," for example, Cross structures his image around the animal skins and barrel staves in the picture's foreground and the tepee and totem pole in the background. The caption on the mount's reverse dramatizes the scene:

> Here the Indians congregate evenings, to sing and dance, until the medicine man, who sits by the side of a drum, "made of a tin boiler," beating it with a stick, calls out that he has made his medicine, "in thoughts," when they all retire to their Teepes' [sic] to awake the morning dawn, when they again congregate in front of the medicine teepe [sic] to learn the medicine man's dream or vision.

By constructing a "realistic" scene of traditional Indian life, Bailey, Dix & Mead were appealing to their white audience's interest in Indian folkways.

Although the retention of some aspects of native culture was significant, it was also important that the Indian be presented as assimilable. If Indians were to make a successful transition from "savagery" to "civilization," they would have to give up many of their traditional customs and adopt not only the farming practices but also the social structure on which the dominant society was built. One of the prevailing criticisms of Indian culture by white society was the apparent laziness of Indian men. One stereograph entitled "Women's Rights" shows, according to its caption, "two squaws sitting beside their teepe [sic], resting after carrying the wood seen beside them on their backs, as seen in view No. 19, for half a mile, while their liege lords and masters, (the noble red men,) are smoking." The notion of the "noble red man" that dominated white society's thinking during the first half of the nineteenth century had become displaced over time with a revised idea about the stature of the Indian male. The satirical characterization of the "Goshoot Indians" in Mark Twain's 1871 novel, *Roughing It,* also suggests this change. Calling them the "wretchedest type of mankind I have ever seen, up to this writing," Twain compared his Goshoot Indians to the "Bushmen of South Africa."[18]

> Such of the Goshoots as we saw, along the road and hanging about the stations, were small, lean, "scrawny" creatures; in complexion a dull black like the ordinary American negro;. . . a silent, sneaking, treacherous-looking race; taking note of everything, covertly, like all the other "Noble Red Men" that we (do not) read about;. . . savages who, when asked if they have the common Indian belief in a Great Spirit, show a something which almost amounts to emotion, thinking whiskey is referred to.[19]

Thinking that he had been "overestimating the Red Man while viewing him through the mellow moonshine of romance," Twain created a sketch that illustrated the radical change in white society's perception of the Indian male.[20] Cross's stereograph affirms that the Indian male would have to overcome this perceived laziness and lack of responsibility in order to make a smooth transition into white society.

The civilizing force in this photographic Western appears in the form of the Twenty-fifth Infantry, a unit of black soldiers who were at the time led by Captain Charles Bentzoni. Cross's stereograph entitled "Battalion Drill" shows the unit in parade formation at Fort Randall. Originally established during the Civil War and made up of former slaves led by white officers, the Twenty-fifth Infantry was one of two black infantry units at the time. This unit was originally stationed after the War at Fort Davis on the western frontier in Texas but was transferred in the summer of 1880 to Fort Randall in order to supplement the military force guarding both the new settlers pouring onto the Plains and the construction of the Northern Pacific Railroad from Indian attacks. The order and discipline exhibited in the stereograph by this military unit stands in stark contrast to the posture of the Indian men, who are sitting around lackadaisically throughout the set of images. Indeed, the very next image in the series, titled "Issuing Rations," is telling. The caption reads, "An Indian with a pipe in his hand in the foreground watching the artist, some officers and their families with Indians standing and squating [sic] around them." Forced to accept handouts from the agency (the specific details of these rations are printed on the mount's reverse), the reservation Indian was a far cry from the noble red man of yesteryear.

However, just as the example of the Twenty-fifth Infantry shows how "civiliza-tion" is able to transform an "other" into a strong, fighting American, so too are the agents of "civilization" shown to be compassionate in their treatment of the fallen Indians. The next image, entitled "Issuing Supplies," shows the "issuing of annuity goods to the prisoners of war . . . by the Post Quartermaster." The list that follows describes the articles issued to each "Buck," "Squaw," and "Family." Given the number of Indians that were at Fort Randall (one caption lists the total as 161 men, women, and children), the amount of goods issued appears from the de-scription on the mount's reverse to be quite generous. For example, "each squaw" received the following items: "1 Shawl, 1 Blanket, 6 yards Calico, 5 yards heavy Flannel, 3 yards Flannel, red for Leggings, 3 yards Bleached Muslin, 2 Undershirts, 2 pair Stockings, 1 pair Scissors, 1 doz. spools Thread, 1 paper Needles assorted, 1 Thimble, 1 fine Comb, 1 coarse Comb, 1 Scarf, 1 Handkerchief." Additional cooking supplies were also included for each family. Both the photographs and the details on the reverse of each mount give the impression that Sitting Bull and his band of Sioux followers were well treated during their incarceration. This charitable attitude toward the Indian was part of the effort to construct a heroic portrait of the men who were responsible for ridding the Plains of the "Indian menace."

The progression of this photographic narrative leads the viewer to a most pre-dictable conclusion. In the final images of this set, the effects of the advance of white society are captured. Whereas no white settlers are shown in the first ten images, they play a conspicuous role after the introduction of the military. In the portrait of Sitting Bull accompanied by part of his large family (Figure 3.3), a fe-male settler in a pleated skirt sits beside Sitting Bull, while Captain Bentzoni watches over the scene on his white horse. No mention is made of the woman in the caption, but she and others appear regularly throughout the rest of the narra-tive. In fact, one stereograph near the end of the series represents exactly the same view as an earlier image. The only difference between the two is that the later image introduces this same white woman, her child, and Captain Bentzoni into the picture. Loaded with signs of white domination and power, Bailey, Dix & Mead's narrative recounts this "inevitable march of progress" across the Plains.

However, this photographic Western does not end simply with the introduction of settlers onto the former lands of the Indian but instead leaves the viewer with the impression that the Indians under the defeated Sitting Bull are ready to accept the future under the white man's rule. In three of the final five images in the set, an Indian and "his squaw" are pictured sitting peacefully in front of their tepee. Hori-zontally arranged in front of their tepee, the "renowned chief [Sitting Bull] with his interesting family" is shown now in a posture of submission. No longer the fiery insurgent of Figure 3.1, Sitting Bull appears at the end of this photographic sequence as one who is willing to comply with white society and its ways. The final two images, both entitled "Summer Views," suggest that peace and order have fi-nally been instilled on this formerly hostile land. As in later twentieth-century

Figure 3.3 *Sitting Bull and family, 1882. Courtesy Nebraska State Historical Society.*

Figure 3.4 *Sitting Bull and Buffalo Bill Cody, [1885] 1891. Courtesy Nebraska State Historical Society.*

Westerns, the heroes from the dominant culture win out in their battle against the forces of "savagery" that stand in the way of "civilization's" westward advance.

Sitting Bull remained under watch at Fort Randall for almost two years before he was released in May 1883 and allowed to return to the Standing Rock Agency where most of his people were located. In the years after his time at Fort Randall, Sitting Bull continued to be the focus of national notoriety. Acquitted of the charge that he was the person who killed General George Custer, the famed leader quickly became the representative Indian spokesperson at public ceremonies. In September 1883, he traveled to Bismarck to participate in the ceremony that marked the official completion of the Northern Pacific Railroad. Because of his tremendous drawing power, he was even recruited by Buffalo Bill Cody to appear in his famous Wild West Show during the summer of 1885. Traveling throughout the United States and Canada, the Wild West Show drew tremendous crowds that came to see the famous "Killer of Custer" in real life.[21]

Having been familiarized to the villainy of Sitting Bull and his band of Sioux Indians in the many stories and pictures that were produced after Custer's Massacre, the national public longed to see a living part of this infamous event. William Cross's photo of Buffalo Bill and Sitting Bull in full regalia before a painted backdrop is just one of the many souvenir images of the famous two men that was produced at this time (Figure 3.4).[22] Although Cody invited him to join the show on its tour of Europe in 1887, Sitting Bull declined in order to lead the fight against white encroachments on designated Sioux lands. Sitting Bull continued in this struggle up until his tragic assassination on December 15, 1890, at his new home on the Standing Rock Agency.

The death of Sitting Bull, the "bloodthirsty savage," though, had taken place nearly a decade before, when the photographer played an integral role in transforming the public's image of the Indian from a "wild savage" to a mild reservation dweller. Indeed, it was not so much the cavalry or infantry that ultimately brought Sitting Bull to his knees as it was the camera, with its power both to record and make history. Through the medium of Bailey, Dix & Mead's photographic Western, the subjugation of Sitting Bull entered the public's imagination. In 1882, after decades of fighting the Indians on the Great Plains, it was important to recognize the final surrender of one of the leading agitators in that "Battle of Civilization." Once tamed, the Indian could again be romanticized by the dominant culture. In the illusory world of photography, the "truth" about a mysterious, alien people was shaped and molded in order to convey the dominant culture's own record of history. This act of history making was central to the photographs of Bailey, Dix & Mead.

Notes

1. G. W. Baird, "General Miles's Indian Campaigns," *Century Magazine,* July 1891, p. 351.

2. Ibid., p. 370.

3. See Brian Dippie's *The Vanishing American: White Attitudes and U.S. Indian Policy* (Middletown, Conn.: Wesleyan University Press, 1982) and Robert Berkhofer, Jr., *The White Man's Indian: Images of the American Indian from Columbus to the Present* (Lawrence: University Press of Kansas, 1982), for a further discussion of this idea.

4. There are several facts that suggest that this series of twenty-four photographs, twenty-one of which are stereographs and three of which are 4-inch × 6-inch cabinet cards of individual Indians, were intended to be seen and read as a complete set. The uniformity of the mounts and the written texts on the mounts' reverse both reflect this idea. Included on the back of each photographic mount is the title of the photograph, a checklist of the other images in the set, and an extended caption that both describes the photograph itself and provides additional statistics and information on the Hunkpapa Sioux, the Indian band that is the subject of this work. In several cases, the caption on one mount refers specifically to other images in the series.

5. Quoted in Robert Wooster, *The Military and United States Indian Policy, 1865–1903* (New Haven: Yale University Press, 1988), p. 182.

6. "A Talk with Sitting Bull," *New York Times,* August 7, 1881, p. 2.

7. Alfred Terry, *Report of the Secretary of War* (Washington, D.C.: Government Printing Office, 1881), p. 98.

8. "The Band To Be Transferred as Prisoners to Fort Randall," *New York Times,* September 2, 1881, p. 5.

9. "Sitting Bull Protests Against His Removal," *New York Times,* September 11, 1881, p. 1.

10. "At Last," *Chicago Tribune,* August 1, 1881, p. 2.

11. Elmo Scott Watson, "Orlando Scott Goff, Pioneer Dakota Photographer," *North Dakota History* (January–April 1962), p. 212. An enlarged print of this famous negative was later exhibited at the Chicago World's Exposition of 1893.

12. The attribution of these photographs to William R. Cross, a local photographer who ran a studio in Niobrara, Nebraska, can be made since a number of the Bailey, Dix & Mead images can also be found on Cross's own studio mounts at this same time. It was not uncommon for frontier photographers not only to accept commissions but also to exchange and sell negatives to other frontier studios. Indeed, two Dakota photographers, Stanley J. Morrow of Yankton and William H. DeGraff of Bismarck, both sold images from the Bailey, Dix & Mead series under their own name several years later.

13. By trade, Dix was a traveling dentist whose March 4, 1881, advertisement in the *Niobrara* [Nebraska] *Pioneer* stated that he made "regular monthly professional visits" to Niobrara and several other small towns in the region. Fort Randall was only a short distance from Niobrara. A 1942 letter from George Dix's daughter to Martha Turner, the woman in charge of the photographic collections at the Nebraska State Historical Society, confirms her father's involvement in the project. Although the identity of Bailey and Mead has never been confirmed, it would not be unreasonable to speculate that Bailey is Joshua Bailey, who in 1883 received an appointment as the post trader at the Yankton Agency located next to Fort Randall on the opposite bank of the Missouri River. The idea that Mead is John L. Mead of Herman, Nebraska, is even more speculative. The only clue that suggests a possible relationship between him and Bailey and Dix is the fact that Mead is buried next to Bailey in the Herman town cemetery.

14. William Darrah, *The World of Stereographs* (Gettysburg, Pa.: W. C. Darrah, Publisher, 1977), p. 6.

15. Ibid., p. 45.

16. It is unclear who the author of these captions was and where the information for them was obtained. However, given the specific nature of many of the statistics, it is reasonable to assume that the author was closely connected, if not living at, Fort Randall at this time.

17. The *New York Times*, "Removal Has Been Safely Accomplished," September 12, 1881, p. 5.

18. Mark Twain, *Roughing It* (New York: Viking Penguin, 1987), p. 131.

19. Ibid., pp. 131–132.

20. Ibid., p. 132.

21. Following Sitting Bull's death, Buffalo Bill recalled the effect of his presence on the Show's white audience: "The first time I ever saw him to know him was when he joined my show at Buffalo, coming with eight or nine of his chosen people from Grand River. He appeared there before 10,000 people, and was hissed so it was some time before I could talk to the crowd and secure their patience. The same thing occurred at almost every place. He never did more than to appear on horseback at any appearance and always refused to talk English, even if he could." Quoted in W. Fletcher Johnson, *Life of Sitting Bull and the History of the Indian War of 1890–91* (New York: Edgewood Publishing Company, 1891), pp. 192–193.

22. Although Cross sold this image on his own studio mount, the original photographer was a Canadian, William Notman of Montreal, who took this picture during the Wild West Show's 1885 tour.

4

Reduced to Images: American Indians in Nineteenth-Century Advertising

Jeffrey Steele

Stereotypes sell. To this day, consumers recognize the stylized Indian chief on cans of Calumet baking powder and the kneeling Indian maiden on packages of Land O'Lakes butter. The athletic fortunes of the Braves, Indians, Chiefs, Redskins, and Black Hawks are followed by professional sports fans across the country. In the past, images of Indian warriors, chiefs, and maidens helped to market products as diverse as Bow-Spring dental rubber, Hiawatha canned corn, Cherokee coal, Red Warrior axes, and Savage rifles.[1] From the late nineteenth century to the present, numerous manufacturers, promoters, and advertisers have chosen the image of an American Indian to symbolize their products. Although some of these symbols and trademarks were designed as recently as the 1950s, the majority date from the period 1870–1910—the era of warfare and legislation that effectively contained American Indian cultures on the margins of U.S. society.

This containment of cultures is evident in the forms of racialized entertainment that arose in the closing decades of the century. Emerging at roughly the same time, the minstrel show and the Wild West show both reinforced racial stereotypes during an era when the roles of African-Americans and American Indians were rapidly changing. After the departure of federal troops from the South during the 1870s, the civil and voting rights of American blacks became the source of violent contention. With their images of happy slaves and benign songs and dances, minstrel shows helped to perpetuate the myth that the old days of plantation slavery represented the high point in black-white relations. In answer to the more disturbing racial anxieties of the time (such as those expressed in the growing epidemic of lynchings), the images of happy, banjo-playing plantation laborers reassured viewers that "blacks were under control."[2]

In many respects, Wild West shows, with their mock combats showing the defeat of Indian warriors, enacted a similar containment. Maintaining the illusion that American Indians dwelled in regions far removed from eastern urban centers, extravaganzas like "The Wild West: Buffalo Bill's and Doc Carver's Mountain and Prairie Exhibition" constructed "the image of the Plains Sioux as the quintessential American Indian."[3] From the safety of their seats in the grandstand, viewers were exposed to "Indians as savages from a wild land . . . inimical to civilization"; in one scene, for example, "Buffalo Bill and his cowboys would ride to the rescue of [stagecoach] passengers before Indians could commit their final treachery."[4] It is ironic that such racial myths came into conflict with the official policy of the Bureau of Indian Affairs, which attempted "to break up the reservations and accelerate the transformation of Indians into property owners and U.S. citizens" after the passage of the Dawes Act in 1887.[5] But not surprisingly, the image of assimilated Indians with 160-acre farms was much less appealing to the popular imagination than Buffalo Bill's horse-riding, stagecoach-attacking warriors.

Rather than acknowledging a continuity between their world and that of American Indians, such shows fixed the image of the Indian in time "as if the only true Indian were a past one."[6] In this format, the heroism of Indian braves could be appreciated as a remnant of vanquished and "vanishing" cultures that posed little threat to the hegemony of white civilization.[7] Forcibly removed from any contexts that would threaten the imaginative security of consumers, American Indians (like African-Americans) were being turned into fetishized images that satisfied the hunger for entertainment and disposable commodities.

Contemporaneously with the rise of the Wild West show, images appropriated from native cultures began to appear on advertisements for products found in numerous American households. As "the volume of American advertising increased by more than tenfold" from 1870 to 1900, advertising trade cards became the most important form of mass-market advertising.[8] Produced in the thousands, these postcard-size, lithographed images were widely distributed in stores and as premiums packaged with some products. The "narrative richness" of these cards, limited by little more than the imaginative energies of printers, artists, and manufacturers, is of great interest to the modern historian.[9] A form of what is now known as "printed ephemera," trade cards were given away by merchants, who quickly restocked new cards to feed the growing hunger for images and the commodities they represented.

In a few cases, manufacturers hit upon stable images that solidified into recognizable trademarks; but most often, designs proliferated, as one eye-catching image after another was used to lure potential customers. As chromolithography became the most effective technology for mass-producing images, there emerged a "swelling trade in images" that contributed to what Jackson Lears has characterized as the "rich and complex carnivalesque tradition" operating "in nineteenth-century American advertising."[10] Many products (especially patent medicines) seemed "to conjure up the magic of self-transformation through purchase"—a magical "aura" that was captured by the fantastic "floating signifiers" found on trade cards.[11]

This riot of images, churned out by numerous printers, facilitated the release of racial fantasies that might have been contained in more stable circumstances. Since "advertisers using trade cards were able to avoid the editorial constraints imposed by periodicals and even more public forms of advertising," nothing prevented their producers from digging deep into the mine of racial fantasy.[12] Focusing upon the characteristics of various racial and ethnic minorities, many advertisements created a sense of white, middle-class consumer solidarity at the expense of subordinate groups. Although they were not totally without buying power, Irish servants, African Americans, Chinese Americans, and American Indians were often depicted in demeaning postures and caricatures that reveal the assumption that such individuals stood outside the mainstream of American consumerism. As a result, nineteenth-century trade cards remain to this day the most graphic examples of racial and ethnic stereotypes being used as marketing tools.

On some cards, eye-catching humor (often cartoons at the expense of blacks and the Irish) captured the attention of white consumers. On others, specific product characteristics were highlighted through association with racialized attributes of marginalized groups. Manufacturers of both thread and stove polish, for example, promoted the blackness of their products through images that exploited stereotypes of African-Americans. On one card, an African-American boy riding a spool of "fast black" thread points to a worried-looking sun and proclaims that "We never fade!!" In similar fashion, an image promoting Dixon's black stove polish shows an African-American mammy washing a young white girl who has gotten into the stove polish—a whitening operation that the mammy cannot perform on herself.

Both images depend upon the exclusion of a racial other whose marginalized presence buttresses the identity of white consumers. The dynamics of this process are perhaps most apparent on a remarkable card produced to market Muzzy's cornstarch: A Chinese laundry worker holds up before a white, middle-class family a freshly starched and ironed shirt, which is so shiny the woman can see her own reflection. In this image, we find depicted a mythologized image of identity construction in which whiteness (we notice that the laundry worker holds up a *white* shirt) depends upon the presence of a subordinate, racialized other. Recently, Toni Morrison has argued that the white imagination depends upon the presence of a racial other in the form of an "Africanist presence"; in her eyes, the most fundamental white American ideals—"freedom . . . autonomy . . . authority"—were "made possible by, shaped by, activated by . . . Africanism, deployed as rawness and savagery."[13] Images of American Indian "savagery" served a similar function, validating the smug self-certainty of nineteenth-century proponents of what is now called "scientific racism": the belief that the different races of human beings exist on an evolutionary continuum ranging from "savagery" through "barbarism" to "civilization."[14]

To explore the role that racial ideologies played in the early stages of product identification and marketing psychology, it is useful to compare images of African-Americans and American Indians on trade cards. Not surprisingly, African-Americans are depicted in a wide variety of occupations, including sports, domestic roles, and public performances; American Indians, by contrast, are found in a narrower range of occupations and activities—imagery that suggests a more alien status in the white imagination. African-Americans, wearing familiar clothing, are often depicted indoors in domestic or vocational scenes, whereas American Indians are almost always shown outdoors in traditional, native attire (for example, moccasins, leggings, and headdresses). It is extremely rare to find black cards that refer to specific historical events; Indian cards, on the other hand, often refer to specific treaties and scenes of warfare, as if the image of the Indian were fixed at a specific time.

According to Robert Jay, in the late nineteenth century, "the Indian was little more than a romanticized abstraction for most white Americans, and was seen firsthand only in medicine and wild west shows, if at all"—a situation that gave Indians an "exotic appeal" that made them "a natural vehicle for advertising."[15] More accurately, those American Indians still remaining east of the Mississippi, many of whom had adopted western dress and manners, had become largely invisible. The Indian maidens and warriors depicted on trade cards belonged to worlds that stood outside those of white, eastern consumers. Either they were located in historical scenes from the past or they were shown in picturesque locales far removed from the domain of middle-class, urban homes. As in the case of picture postcards mass-produced a generation later, such representations created a fictitious sense of "reality" in which contemporary American Indians found little reflection of their daily lives.[16]

For example, an advertisement for Duryeas Improved Corn Starch depicts a scene far removed from eastern cities (Figure 4.1). In the foreground, an Indian man attempts to quiet a bucking horse, which he holds by the bridle. In the background, Indian women near tepees cultivate corn, prepare food, and care for children. Other cards produced during this era illustrate plains Indians hunting buffalo on horseback or fighting with government troops. The clothing on many cards enforces a similar sense of distance. For example, the young man and woman on a card advertising Abe Loebenberg's Arcade Clothing House (Figure 4.2) wear traditional outfits that cut them off from the cosmopolitan world of Washington, D.C., portrayed in the background. On a card advertising Tippecanoe Spring Preparation (Figure 4.3), eight Indians in various types of tribal attire carefully conduct their birch bark canoe through rapids. Their canoe does not tip and presumably, these hardy warriors do not suffer from motion sickness and thus are immune from "dyspepsia," "stomach disorders," "feeble appetite," or any of the other disorders of civilization that the Tippecanoe nostrum allegedly cures.

Figure 4.1 *Trade card, Duryeas Improved Corn Starch. Bren-Dor Americana; photo, Jeffrey Steele.*

Figure 4.2 *Trade card, Abe Loebenberg's Arcade Clothing House, 10 West Washington Street, Indianapolis. Bren-Dor Americana; photo, Jeffrey Steele.*

Figure 4.3 Trade card, "Tippecanoe" Spring Preparation. Bren-Dor Americana; photo, Jeffrey Steele.

In this instance, the advertiser exploits the perceived distance between Indian and white cultures (signified through setting and dress) by the suggestion that "the red man, in his unique communion with nature, possessed knowledge of its curative powers unrevealed to civilized man."[17]

The Kickapoo Indian Remedy was one of numerous patent medicines to exploit the myth that American Indians were more closely attuned to the rhythms of nature. One of the more elaborate variations of this theme is found in a sixteen-page advertising booklet produced to market Austen's Oswego Bitters in 1882 (Figure 4.4), which contains a short story entitled "The Witch-Woman's Revenge; or, the Golden Secret of the Oswego." In a familiar fairy-tale plot, Winona, a beautiful Indian girl, is forbidden by her mother (the "witch-woman") to marry the son of the man who killed her father. Illustrating the way that images of American Indians were fixed in the past, this tale is set in the distant era before the "foot of a white man had trod" the country now covered by the city of Oswego, New York. In order to enforce the separation between Winona and her beloved Wanketo, the witch-woman has cast a curse that is rapidly killing all the members of his tribe. Miraculously, a lightning bolt kills the wicked mother, freeing Winona to use her family's herbal lore to save Wanketo's village. Gathering "simple herbs which none has ever thought to use as medicines," she administers the "health-giving" and "life-giving" remedy.

Through some miracle of transmission, the booklet concludes, this remedy has come into the possession of "the well-known firm, W. J. Austen & Co., Oswego, N.Y.": "Gradually its benefits were extended to the whites, and as the Indians faded away before the onward march of civilization the secret passed from their hands into those of the conquering race." "Almost as soon as they had taken the Indians' land," Jackson Lears comments, "white settlers began to claim access to their medical lore."[18] In striking support of such cultural imperialism, this booklet provides a compendium of nineteenth-century racial myths: The Indian characters, existing lower on the scale of civilization, live closer to nature and its secrets; as a 'vanishing' race, Indians yield effortlessly to the "onward march of civilization"; Winona is a "wonderfully beautiful" Indian maiden; her betrothed, "a perfect specimen of forest manhood," exhibits the characteristics of the "noble savage."

Superimposed on this racialized framework is a seductive narrative that exploits nineteenth-century stereotypes of age and gender. The attractive and healthy young couple prosper in their "free and simple lives," while the "withered crone" (Winona's interfering mother) dies. Youth (and, by implication, the sexual energies of youth) conquer in this simple tale that culminates with the marriage of Winona and Wanketo, who become the progenitors of "many generations." Similar associations are found in the trade cards produced to market Indian Queen Perfume. On one card (not pictured here), an attractive Indian woman, standing in the midst of luxuriant foliage, cradles a bow in her left arm as she gathers nectar dropping from a flower into a shell held in her right hand.[19] In an image that "represents the colonized world as the feminine," the exploitable bounties of nature are associated with the eroticized image of a native woman from a dominated race.[20]

Figure 4.4   *Advertising booklet, "The Golden Secret of the 'Oswego,'" Austen's Oswego Bitters, 1882. Bren-Dor Americana; photo, Jeffrey Steele.*

Another card advertising Indian Queen Perfume makes even more explicit the conjunction of racialized myths of beauty, nature, and female fecundity (Figure 4.5). A demure-looking Indian woman, with limpid eyes and bowed head, cradles an infant in her left arm, while she holds a magical-looking feathered wand in her right hand. Wearing a cowrie-shell necklace, feathered headdress, and surrounded by luxuriant foliage, she seems the mythical embodiment of nature's maternal, soothing power. In the terms of Jackson Lears, she is a mythical representation of the female source of abundance—a symbol commonly found in nineteenth-century advertising.[21] To complete the picture, a butterfly (a sign of grace or immortality) hovers above her child's head in an apparent blessing.

In somewhat different fashion, male figures are used to symbolize nature's abundance. In an advertisement for a fertilizer called Bradley's Super-Phosphate of Lime (Figure 4.6), an Indian man in traditional dress stands in a field of corn; he holds a (phallic-looking) lance and stares into the distance. Behind him are two corn plants: a short plant with the legend "without phosphate" and a tall plant labeled "with phosphate." This figure's kingly potency (associated with the generative qualities of Bradley's *fertilizer*) is reinforced by a verse from Ecclesiastes: "The

Figure 4.5 *Trade card, Indian Queen Perfume, Bean and Brother, Philadelphia. Bren-Dor Americana; photo, Jeffrey Steele.*

profit of the earth is for all; the king himself is served by the field." Significantly, the image on this card is framed by a border that appropriates this regal and generative power for the white-controlled arena of scientific agricultural management (an act that narrows the definition of the earth's "profit" to an idea of commercial gain). "Bradley's Phosphate furnishes the elements of plant-food in proper proportions," this border reads. "By using Bradley's Phosphate you return to the soil the plant-food constituents your crops are constantly taking from it."

Nature's masculine abundance is even more apparent on an 1886 card used to advertise Diamond lawnmowers (Figure 4.7). An example of the popular and widely used "vegetable people" series, this advertisement depicts a "corned Indian" whose body is an ear of corn; hands and feet, corn husk. Melded with this agricultural motif is the figure of an Indian whose posture, clothing, and staff resemble to a close degree those found on the previous card. An even more primordial representation of natural bounty and potency, this image suggests the extent to which racial myth (based upon the deep-seated association of American Indians with their staple, corn) could be blended with fantasy and desire in the service of commerce. Merging deeply rooted images of oral gratification, masculine sexuality,

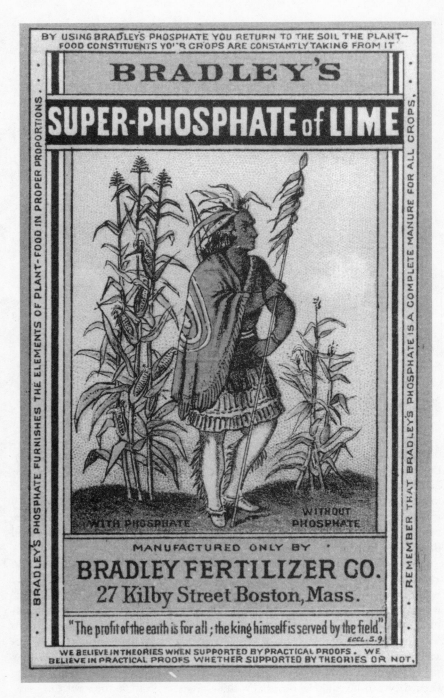

Figure 4.6 *Trade card, Bradley's Super-Phosphate of Lime, Bradley Fertilizer Co., Boston. Bren-Dor Americana; photo, Jeffrey Steele.*

Figure 4.7 *Trade card, "A Corned Indian," Diamond Lawnmowers, C. W. Hackett Hardware Co., St. Paul, Minn.; printed 1886 by L. P. Griffith & Co., Baltimore. Bren-Dor Americana; photo, Jeffrey Steele.*

and racialized iconography, this card represents the American Indian as a consumable product—as food. In the face of white imperialism, this card suggests, Indian cultures (like the products appropriated from them) could be absorbed at will.

Such disposition is even more apparent on trade cards that used images derived from history. William Penn's 1682 treaty with Delaware tribal leaders might seem like an odd choice for a nineteenth-century advertisement. But the use of this event on two different trade cards suggests some of the ways in which historical references served commercial ambitions. Although Penn's treaty was famous for "acknowledging Indian title to land, and establishing strict and fair procedures for its purchase," white settlers "managed to evade regulations . . . through leases of Indian lands," "outright encroachment," and "official fraud."[22] Two hundred years later, in the 1880s, it was easy to use this historical event as a self-congratulatory symbol substantiating whites' "enlightened" policy toward Indians (at least in the East). Why go to the trouble of conquering Indian territories, these cards suggest, when they can be easily appropriated through seemingly fair treaties? On both cards, the "treaties" represented are actually advertisements: for Ayer's Cherry Pectoral and for Enterprise Bone, Shell, and Corn Mills, respectively.

The Enterprise card (Figure 4.8) is especially interesting—both for its graphic design and because of a verse embedded in the center of the card. The text reads:

> In sixteen eighty two, you surely have heard
> How William Penn an honest treaty made.
> All good Indians mourn him still
> And remember his proclamation of good will
> To use the Enterprise Bone, Shell, and Corn Mill.

In this context, Penn's "honest treaty" commits unwitting Indians to the consumption of the product he is peddling—in an unequal relationship that cements the image of white paternalism. According to this card, "good Indians" know their place and their proper role—to be unquestioning consumers. But in reality this card advertises a form of agricultural technology of little use to the American Indians depicted, who seem to have stepped out of a cartoon world. Their function, it would seem, is to signify an act of consumption that they cannot fill, for more than anything, they seem to be playing with the Enterprise mill.

The visual categories pioneered by Erving Goffman can be applied to this card to reveal a number of familiar signs of dominance and subordination. This power differential is reinforced by the placement and posture of the figures: a smug-looking William Penn stands in the background overlooking three Indian figures who seem totally absorbed with (if not amazed by) their new mill. The position of the figures provides an obvious "function ranking": Penn stands in a paternal position of control, "a little outside the physical circle," surveying the entire scene and holding pen and paper (the tools of literacy), while the Indian figures have their attention more narrowly focused on the mill.[23] The playful, even childish, expressions on the faces of the Indian figures express an emotionality and lack of restraint that diminishes their status in contrast to the more staid figure of Penn and suggests their distance from his mastery.[24]

In addition to the portrayal of human figures, this card conveys its message through the conjunction of "multiple planes of meaning" (to use Lears's phrase) that are conjoined but do not meet.[25] The Enterprise mill (a modern machine) belongs to a world distinct from that of William Penn and his seventeenth-century treaty with the Delawares. The effect of this disjunction is to underscore the distance between the world of native culture and the nineteenth-century realm of technological and mechanical power. In another way, the gap between white and Indian cultures is signified by the presence, at the bottom of the card, of an imposing edifice designated the "Electrical Building." As an aspect of the card's design, this building seems out of place. But as a signifier demonstrating the evident 'superiority' of white civilization, it bespeaks a kind of economic manifest destiny. The three Indian figures depicted above the Electrical Building are provided with no valid place in a world where such structures exist.

In contrast to treaties, scenes of Indian warfare and violence were an even more popular subject on trade cards. As is to be expected, depictions of Custer's Last

Figure 4.8 *Trade card, Enterprise Bone, Shell, and Corn Mill, Enterprise Mfg. Co., Philadelphia; printed 1893 by Donaldson Brothers, N.Y. Bren-Dor Americana; photo, Jeffrey Steele.*

Stand made their way onto these advertisements. One unusual card, for example, depicts the "Death of Custer" as part of "Forepaugh's Equestrian Spectacular Tragedy"—evidently a Wild West show staging scenes from recent history.[26] Other cards, which had the merit of not raising unsettling questions about recent U.S. Indian policy, portrayed military scenes from the past. The 1811 Battle of Tippecanoe (fought in Indiana) was featured on an 1883 advertisement for Tippecanoe tonic—a graphic card that depicts a number of Indian warriors in the act of being slaughtered. A sensational scene from the Black Hawk War, identified on the back as "Defeat of Black Hawk and his Indians, 1832," was one of three vignettes of Wisconsin history depicted on an 1892 card for Arbuckle Brothers Coffee (Figure 4.9). Part of a series of fifty cards "giving a pictorial history of the United States and territories," the Arbuckle card is worth closer examination. Both the pictorial elements on the front of the card and the text on the back (a synopsis of Wisconsin history) contribute to a complicated act of racial mythmaking.

The battle scene, occupying the center of the card, is given visual emphasis by the diagonal lines at the left (the French explorers "Marquette and Joliet crossing the portage from the Fox to the Wisconsin River"), a visual element echoed in the position of muskets and arms in the center panel. The right-hand scene, which provides a sense of closure to the design, portrays a party of white tourists in contemporary dress on top of "Stand Rock in the 'Dells.'" Both the left- and right-hand panels place human figures in recognizable natural landscapes, while presenting a visual narrative that stresses the progression from exploration to

Figure 4.9   *Trade card, Arbuckle Brothers Coffee, Arbuckle Bros., N.Y.; printed 1892 by Donaldson Brothers, N.Y. Bren-Dor Americana; photo, Jeffrey Steele.*

present-day tourism. In contrast, the center panel stands out from the card as an intrusion; it contains no natural features and seems to have been unscrolled, rolling across and disrupting the narrative of exploration, implied settlement, and tourism. The text on the back of the card reinforces this narrative of "manifest destiny" by asserting that "the Black Hawk War (1832) was an important factor in the opening of the region to public view."

Appealing to consumers' prurient interest, the central panel shows a scene of close combat in which a bare-breasted Indian woman, kneeling over a dead man, raises her arm in a futile effort to stop the killing. Significantly, this image depicts an Indian woman in a state of seminudity that no white woman could occupy.[27] In the visual economy of this advertisement, the American Indian is implicitly identified with this figure, whose state of vulnerable undress seems a sign of "savagery," at the same time that her resistance seems particularly pathetic and ineffectual. The viewer's sympathy is stirred but quickly overwhelmed by the implied message: Here is a powerful emblem of the "vanishing Indian," powerless to resist the white military pressure that was successful in "opening the region [like this female figure] to public view." Just as this eroticized image of an American Indian woman was made available for white-male erotic fantasy, Indians (in general) were reduced to images that could be made to play allotted roles in nineteenth-century fantasies of cultural imperialism.

In different ways, a number of trade cards (some of them illustrating historical subjects) contributed to the argument for "manifest destiny" by illustrating scenes of savagery and violence. As a group, these cards provide graphic images of "the Indian as . . . alien to the White."[28] A Kickapoo Indian Medicines booklet, for example, depicts a sleeping Indian who dreams of hunting, Custer's Last Stand, and a massacre.[29] In the massacre scene (placed directly beneath the word "Indian"), a number of warriors slaughter and scalp white men, women, and children. The motif of scalping was picked up in even more graphic fashion on a card advertising Taylor's Sure Cure.[30] A sleeping Indian, his gun leaning against him, dreams two scenes: embracing a large, life-size bottle labeled "Fire Water"; and killing a horrified missionary, his tracts scattered at his feet and eyes wide open, who prays for his life. Superimposed on this amazing image is the following verse:

> The Indian dreams of days gone by,
> When he raised hair, his knife for a lever;
> His country is gone, but then he has left
> Taylor's Sure Cure for chills and fever.

In this vision of commercial expansion, the lost lands and violent past of the Indian figure are compensated for by his new "role" as consumer. But in reality, the sleeping Indian is not being presented as a potential customer but rather as a source of entertainment for a white populace whose sense of identity is bolstered by its perceived distance from such "savagery."

Images on two Arbuckle Brothers coffee cards reinforce this stereotype of savagery. The first, part of the series illustrating scenes from state history, depicts as one of three historical tableaux a scene identified on the reverse as "Massacre by the Sioux" in Iowa (Figure 4.10). The explanatory text relates that "in 1830 the Sioux annihilated a large party of the Sacs and Foxes (including ten chiefs) on the Mississippi River, near Dubuque." The only problem with this explanation is that the inflammatory image on the front portrays a white family being killed and scalped. Perhaps it was unthinkable for the anonymous artist who drew this scene to imagine anyone other than white settlers as the victims of American Indian violence! The lapse is revealing and eloquently illustrates the ways in which stereotyped images of American Indians took on a life of their own.

The second Arbuckle card (dated 1893), titled "American Indians," is particularly interesting because it is part of an ethnocentric series of fifty cards "giving a pictorial history of the Sports and Pastimes of all Nations" (Figure 4.11). In addition to hunting, spearfishing, and riding, one of these "pastimes" was the war dance. In this illustration, a ceremony related to the cultural survival of American Indian nations (who were subject to constant encroachment and attack from white troops and settlers) is turned into an amusement, as if it were no more serious than the waltz or polka. The text on the reverse continues this vein of cultural chauvinism: "The war-dance, principal of their terpsichorean exercises was more horrible than graceful, and suggested the sanguinary atrocities of bloodshed." The Latinate euphemisms ("terpsichorean," "sanguinary") make a show of disguising

Figure 4.10 *Trade card, Arbuckle Brothers Coffee, Arbuckle Bros., N.Y.; printed 1892 by Donaldson Brothers, N.Y. Bren-Dor Americana; photo, Jeffrey Steele.*

American Indians.

Figure 4.11 *Trade card, Arbuckle Brothers Coffee, Arbuckle Bros., N.Y.; printed 1893 by Kaufmann & Strauss. Bren-Dor Americana; photo, Jeffrey Steele.*

the bloody "reality" behind the war dance, as if more direct language would offend the reader's "civilized" sensibilities. But in actuality, these terms (as well as the text as a whole) reveal a colonizing mind-set that uses ornate language as a sign of cultural superiority and presumed distance from "sanguinary atrocities" (as if only American Indians were responsible for savage acts of violence).

Equally revealing is the writer's use of the past tense throughout the explanatory text (which provides a graphic example of the image of the "noble savage"): "No hardier or more rugged race than the Indians of North America *ever existed*. Their endurance and tenacity *were* more than human, their stoicism *was* remarkable, their courage *shrank* from nothing, and their skill and agility *were* the development of generations of outdoor life." In the scale of cultural evolution, this suggests, the American Indian represented an earlier, more primitive race that had long since been superseded by the "civilized" races of the world, who fit more clearly into the scale of humanity (not being "more than human").

Very few nineteenth-century trade cards escaped from the cultural imperialism of the cards described above. This should not be surprising, considering that most of these cards were produced in the late 1880s and early 1890s, at the end of two decades of active warfare between government troops and Indian nations in the West. After the completion of the transcontinental railroad in 1869, western settlement had rapidly accelerated. Armed conflicts became inevitable as struggles broke out over valuable lands. Between 1866 and 1886, wars were fought with the Teton Sioux, Cheyennes, and Arapahos in Wyoming and Montana; with the Paiutes

62   *Jeffrey Steele*

in Oregon and Idaho; with the Cheyennes, Arapahos, Sioux, Comanches, and Kiowas in the Central Plains; with the Modocs in California; with the Lakota Sioux, Cheyennes, and Arapahos in Montana and Wyoming; with the Nez Percé in the Northwest; with the Bannocks, Paiutes, and Cayuses in Idaho and Oregon; with the Utes in Colorado; and with the Apaches in the Southwest.[31] By 1890, after the conclusion of these armed conflicts, millions of acres of ceded land were being opened up for white settlement throughout the West.

As these wars ended and especially after the passage of the Dawes Act in 1887, the roles of American Indians were rapidly changing. In the eyes of many whites, Indian cultures—vanquished by the U.S. military—had disappeared. Other more enlightened individuals realized that surviving members of tribes would need a new economic foundation for their cultures, since traditional patterns of hunting and food gathering had been destroyed by the numerous wars and the consequent relocation of Indians to reservations. The Dawes Act, with its system of land allotments, represented an attempt to transform American Indians into citizens and farmers. The Salishan author Mourning Dove captured the turmoil of this situation in her posthumously published autobiography:

> My birth happened in the year 1888. In that year the Indians of my tribe, the Colvile, were well into the cycle of history involving their readjustment in living conditions. They were in a pathetic state of turmoil caused by trying to learn to till the soil for a living, which was being done on a very small and crude scale. It was no easy matter for members of this aboriginal stock, accustomed to making a different livelihood

Figure 4.12 *Trade card, Keystone Line of Agricultural Implements, Keystone Manufacturing Co., Sterling, Ill.; printed c. 1890 by G. H. Dunston, Buffalo, N.Y. Bren-Dor Americana; photo, Jeffrey Steele.*

(by the bow and arrow), to handle the plow and sow seed for food. Yet I was born long enough ago to have known people who lived in the ancient way before everything started to change.[32]

Not surprisingly, very few trade cards illustrated these changing circumstances. One card that did, however, was produced to advertise Keystone Agricultural Implements around 1890 (Figure 4.12). Uncle Sam stands in front of an illustration of a new disc harrow, which he points out to sixteen male viewers. All of the members of his audience represent recognizable ethnic types, among them Scottish, Irish, German, Scandinavian, Turkish, Chinese, Arabian, and African. Significantly, this family of nations includes an American Indian, who looks on as attentively as the others. In this unusual advertisement, the American Indian is granted space, along with the others, to join in the cultivation of the nation. Although such space rarely appears in nineteenth-century trade cards, its presence in this instance suggests how varied and rich a medium they represent. Advertisers used whatever would help sell their products; and as the nation began to change at the turn of the century, even American Indians (long used as emblems of racial otherness) gained a foothold in the nation's commercial culture. No longer positioned solely as entertaining icons used to symbolize products, they began to gain a role as accepted consumers in their own right.

Notes

1. Hal Morgan, *Symbols of America* (New York: Viking Press, 1986), pp. 57–59, 61–62.

2. Eric Sundquist, *To Wake the Nations: Race in the Making of American Literature* (Cambridge: Harvard University Press, 1993), p. 473.

3. L. G. Moses, "Wild West Shows, Reformers, and the Image of the American Indian, 1887–1914," *South Dakota History* 14 (fall 1984):195.

4. Ibid., pp. 194, 197.

5. Ronald Takaki, *A Different Mirror: A History of Multicultural America* (Boston, Toronto, London: Little, Brown, 1993), p. 234. Moses (cited earlier) notes that "by the end of the 1880s, considerable sentiment against the use of Indians in shows rose among leaders in Indian policy reform" (p. 199).

6. Robert F. Berkhofer, Jr., *The White Man's Indian: Images of the American Indian from Columbus to the Present* (New York: Vintage Books, 1979), p. 67.

7. In a modern example of this viewpoint, Morgan in *Symbols of America* observes that "after the last Indian resistance in the West had been crushed," it "became safe to look back fondly on a great and noble culture that had been largely destroyed" (p. 57).

8. Robert Jay, *The Trade Card in Nineteenth-Century America* (Columbia: University of Missouri Press, 1987), pp. 34, 39.

9. Ibid., p. 60.

10. J. Lears, *Fables of Abundance: A Cultural History of Advertising in America* (New York: Basic Books, 1994), pp. 41, 54.

11. Ibid., pp. 42, 20, 55.

12. Jay, *The Trade Card,* p. 60.

13. Toni Morrison, *Playing in the Dark: Whiteness and the Literary Imagination* (New York: Vintage Books, 1993), pp. 38, 44.

14. For a discussion of these matters, see Berkhofer's *White Man's Indian,* chapter 2, under the section "'Scientific' Racism and Human Diversity in Nineteenth-Century Social Sciences."

15. Jay, *The Trade Card,* pp. 70–71.

16. Patricia C. Albers and William R. James, "Utah's Indians and Popular Photography in the American West: A View from the Picture Post Card," *Utah Historical Quarterly* 52 (winter 1984):91.

17. Jay, *The Trade Card,* p. 71.

18. Lears, *Fables,* p. 64.

19. Kit Barry, *Reflections: Ephemera from Trades, Products, and Events,* vol. 1 (Brattleboro, Vt.: Iris Publishing, 1993), p. 52.

20. David Spurr, *The Rhetoric of Empire: Colonial Discourse in Journalism, Travel Writing, and Imperial Administration* (Durham, N.C. and London: Duke University Press, 1993), p. 170.

21. Lears, *Fables,* pp. 107, 109.

22. Carl Waldman, *Atlas of the North American Indian* (New York and London: Facts on File, 1985), p. 171.

23. Erving Goffman, *Gender Advertisements* (New York: Harper and Row, 1979), pp. 32, 39.

24. Goffman discusses a similar dynamic in the advertisements he studies, in which "the female is likely to be exhibiting a more expansive expression than is the male" (p. 69).

25. Lears, *Fables,* p. 153.

26. Barry, *Reflections: Ephemera from Trades, Products, and Events,* vol. 2 (Brattleboro, Vt.: Iris Publishing, 1994), p. 27.

27. One famous example of contemporary standards of erotic display involved a Merrick Thread card depicting a mother playing with two children at the ocean. In its original state, the woman, shown seated on a rock, was depicted with bare breasts, but because of public outcry, the printer was forced to alter the card by covering the offending flesh with extra hair.

28. Berkhofer, *White Man's Indian,* p. xv.

29. Barry, *Reflections,* vol. 1, p. 123.

30. Barry, *Reflections,* vol. 2, p. 173.

31. Waldman, *Atlas,* p. 129.

32. Mourning Dove, *A Salishan Autobiography,* ed. Jay Miller (Lincoln and London: University of Nebraska Press, 1990), p. 3.

5

"Hudson's Bay Company Indians": Images of Native People and the Red River Pageant, 1920

Peter Geller

The spring and summer of 1920 brought an unprecedented public display by one of the major corporations doing business in Canada when the Hudson's Bay Company (HBC) initiated a variety of activities to celebrate the 250th anniversary of its incorporation (May 2, 1670). Competitions, service medals, improved pensions, and an extra month's pay were provided for employees, and an essay contest on HBC history was held for school children. The *Anniversary Brochure,* a brief history of the HBC and its current activities, was distributed, free of charge, to libraries, schools, and other public repositories. *The Romance of the Far Fur Country,* portraying the "romantic and picturesque side of the Company's work" on film, was screened in theaters across the country.[1] And at the numerous HBC fur trading posts, local celebrations featured feasts, games, dances, and medal ceremonies honoring the company's Native trappers and customers.[2]

The most elaborate and spectacular of these public anniversary celebrations were the historical pageants, coinciding with HBC Governor Robert Molesworth Kindersley's visits to the major cities where the company operated its department stores. In Victoria, Vancouver, Edmonton, Calgary, and Winnipeg, employees enacted events from the company's glorious past and paraded through the cities' streets in period costumes. According to the glowing report in the first issue of the company's staff journal, the *Beaver:*

> Never in the history of Edmonton, it is said, had such crowds been witnessed. . . . Besides the spectacular review of happenings during the past 250 years, depicted on

floats, there were large bands of mounted Indians, ox carts, and prairie schooners, which the Hudson's Bay Company furnished. The city of Edmonton took a prominent part also. No less than sixty floats representing various organizations in the city lined up at the rear of the parade, making a magnificent spectacle. The procession was estimated to be three miles long.[3]

Although all the pageants featured the representation of the relationship between Aboriginal people and the HBC, it was Winnipeg's Red River Pageant that focused entirely on this theme. In addition, the Red River Pageant accorded a central role to Native people themselves. On May 3, 1920, spectators gathered along the banks of the Red River to watch the costumed participants, brought to Winnipeg from First Nations communities throughout western and northern Canada, reenact a canoe and York boat fur brigade excursion. Then, at Lower Fort Garry (a former HBC fur trading post just outside the city), the assembled crowd viewed the Indian Reception, featuring the ceremony of the smoking of the peace pipe between the governor and the Indians. An examination of this carefully constructed event and the documentation produced to commemorate it exposes the presentation of an intriguing and persuasive image of the Indian, as well as the ways in which this image was conveyed and manipulated by the officials of the Hudson's Bay Company.

An appropriate introduction to this Indian imagery, HBC-style, is found in the Red River Pageant album.[4] Opening this weighty volume, the viewer is presented with a likeness of "'Kinnewakan'/Chief of Sioux Tribe or Plains Cree." Seated on a wicker chair, the chief, attired in a feather headdress and an ornately beaded and decorated buckskin jacket, stares gravely into the distance. Kinnewakan strikes a similar pose in the photograph on the following page. P. H. Godsell, HBC post manager, is then introduced; he stands, hands on hips, beside "'Ben Charles' Chief of Wood Cree Indians, Athabasca District." Following this introduction, a series of formal portraits highlight the participating "tribes" and individual Natives. The empty grounds of Lower Fort Garry, located some thirty-two kilometers north of the company's Canadian head office in Winnipeg, function as a pictorial backdrop for the Native men in their ceremonial dress. After a further two pages of group portraits and one page of miscellaneous views of the fort, the viewer is one third of the way into this commemorative volume. The images then shift to the portrayal of the events of the pageant itself: The York boat and canoe brigades, manned by the colorfully dressed Indians, proceed down the Red River; disembarking at Lower Fort Garry, they are joined by Red River carts and pack ponies. The ceremony begins: Godsell, on behalf of the assembled tribes, addresses the governor of the Hudson's Bay Company and the party of officials and friends. Governor Kindersley then accepts the "pipe of peace" from Kinnewakan. He distributes medals to the Indians, speeches are exchanged and translated, and Indian dances presented. Following the formal portion of the ceremony, the Indians partake in a feast prepared for them, all the while observed by the throngs of spectators gathered to witness this staged event.

The Red River Pageant album provides, on one level, a simple record of this company-sponsored celebration. Yet it is also the most imposing and impressive surviving artifact of the commemorative material created by the HBC on the occasion of its 250th anniversary.[5] Prepared for the Canadian head office in Winnipeg to be sent to company headquarters in London, this photographic chronicle of the pageant suggests the importance attached to the public presentation of Native peoples and the HBC-Indian relationship. In addition, the recording of these events in 1920 reveals the desire to control and extend this image through the medium of photography, a circumstance that calls for a particularly close reading of the pageant album by the researcher. In the individual images and in its general organization, the album presents a way of viewing the pageant that blends the viewpoints and choices of the individual photographers with the emphases of the organizers and officials who constructed the event and directed its documentation.

The photographs of the pageant, then, provide visual clues that may be used to unravel the meanings of this public ceremony—conceived and presented as a spectacle. "See the Red River Pageant," urged a poster advertising the event. It featured a map of the procession of the Red River Brigade to guide viewers and information on special streetcars to Lower Fort Garry was also provided to encourage spectators to attend.[6] In fact, part of the pageant's attraction to HBC officials was related to its visual appeal and its capacity to be captured by the camera's eye. The initial proposal by Land and Fur Trade Commissioner James Thomson to hold a central gathering of Indians in Winnipeg, which played up the publicity value of such an event, proved attractive to celebration organizers. As Thomson foresaw: "What an opportunity for films! As an object lesson, and an attraction for the public, it would be a superb show."[7] The presence of photographers was, in fact, an essential element in the proceedings and not an intrusive component. Photographers and their equipment were given a central space in the pageant, seemingly encircling the seated Native participants.

F. C. Ingrams, the HBC's secretary in London, similarly stressed the importance of "a complete and careful film record" being made under the company's auspices.[8] Ingrams, however, added a note of urgency concerning both the enactment and the documentation of the presentation, as "in a few short years the opportunities for such a reconstruction of the costumes, manners and customs of former days will have passed away."[9] Yet the pageant was not about capturing the material culture of the "vanishing Indian" but was instead a reaffirmation of the continued existence of the image of the "Hudson's Bay Company Indian," as visualized by the organizers and documenters of this anniversary celebration.

Pageant participants were identified and categorized not only according to tribal groupings ("Wood Cree Indians," "Siwash," "Sioux or Plains Cree," "Swampy Cree Indians")[10] but also by the district categories used by the HBC for the administration of its Fur Trade Department. The captions accompanying the photographs in the Red River Pageant album highlighted this assumed identification of the Indians with the HBC, as both groups and individuals were described according to district affiliation. As an organizing principle, the association with the Fur Trade District was further enhanced by the district buttons the participants wore. And in the organization of the pageant itself, the Natives were seated separately by district, each group having an appointed headman acting as spokesperson.[11]

Such categorizations point to the ongoing project of perceiving the Native in terms classifiable and manageable by the administrative structures of the HBC. Defined according to the imperatives of non-Natives, these roles implied a dependence and reliance on white institutions. In William Schooling's company-sponsored *Anniversary Brochure,* the chapter called "Indians" elaborates on this perception of Native peoples. After initially identifying the many different Indian "stocks" and the differences of character and disposition among individual Natives, Schooling then plunges headlong into generalizations about Indian lifeways and the "native mind," paying little attention to the complexities and diversity of Aboriginal societies, both past and present. Individuals are neither named nor are their activities described. Although Schooling briefly recognizes that the interaction between Indians and the HBC influenced both parties, he focuses on Aboriginal people as the dependent recipients of the advantages of the white man's "civilization" and on their gaining comfort and affluence as a result of this contact. Schooling then notes the proud claim of many Natives to the title of "Hudson's Bay Company Indian." The perception of the "dependence" of Native people on the HBC and the company's duty to "manage" the inferior Indian tribes finds expression in this rhetorical description.[12]

In the performance of the Red River Pageant, this perceived relationship was dramatized in the celebration of the "two hundred and fifty year old friendship" between the Hudson's Bay Company and Aboriginal peoples, as HBC publicity termed it.[13] Given the concept of a pageant, with its implications of spectacle and effect, artifice and historical allegory, how was this "friendship" depicted? A number of panoramic views of the Indian Reception capture the sweep of the ceremony and its orderly nature.[14] The governor and his party are raised above the ground on a wooden stage, the HBC flag hanging behind them. The Native delegates, seated on the ground in a semicircle in front of the stage, are separated from the HBC party by a large empty space. This spatial separation reproduces the social distance between the two groups, while the levels on which they sit indicate the differences in status as envisioned by the organizers of the pageant. The Indians are only seen briefly entering this central space, when making speeches to the governor and presenting him with the pipe of peace. The spectators, meanwhile, remain on the periphery, cordoned off from the scene of action by a rope barrier, while Royal Canadian Mounted Police, spaced at intervals on the edge of the crowd, enforce the orderly division between the public and the pageant participants.

The plans for the Indian Reception demonstrate how Aboriginal rituals and symbols were appropriated by pageant organizers as evidence of Native compliance with this scenario of the ideal HBC-Indian relationship. After describing the ceremony of the smoking of the peace pipe, the program outline notes: "A special pipe of excellent workmanship has been prepared for the occasion, the stem having been symbolically carved and painted to depict the friendship that has existed and shall continue to exist between the Company and the different tribes present, each tribe being registered on the stem with an animal representing the totem of the head man of each band."[15] The pipe was then to be presented to the governor as a souvenir of the occasion, leaving little doubt as to who, in the minds of HBC officials, controlled this representation of Indian imagery.

Visually, this theme of HBC-Indian friendship achieved its most salient expression in a photograph of Chief Kinnewakan presenting the pipe of peace to Governor Kindersley; both men, pictured in full profile, are frozen in the solemnity of the moment[16] (Figure 5.1). Although not singled out in the Pageant album, this photograph was widely reproduced in the press. And as the cover of the "Two Hundred Fifty-Second Anniversary Number" of the company's staff magazine, the *Beaver,* it stood not only for the Red River Pageant but for the whole of the anniversary celebrations.[17]

The governor dominates the scene, towering over Kinnewakan and HBC interpreter W. C. McKay; Kindersley's chair is elevated on a podium above the wooden stage, while his top hat adds further height to his imposing frame. He leans

Figure 5.1 *Red River Pageant, 1920. Chief Kinnewakan has filled the pipe of peace and passes it to Sir Robert Kindersley. Courtesy Hudson's Bay Company Archives, Provincial Archives of Manitoba.*

slightly forward to accept the pipe from Kinnewakan, who holds the offering up to Kindersley. In addition to the height difference, the two men are separated by a table; Kinnewakan can come only so close before encountering this physical barrier. Their dress also accentuates their differences, Kindersley's sharply defined black formal attire contrasting with the loose-flowing, brightly colored outfit worn by Kinnewakan. This photograph, then, highlights the distance between the HBC and its "Indian friends," reinforcing the separation of the key participants at the same time that it celebrates their joining together in a common ritual.

Throughout the events of the Indian Reception, two figures occupy the space between Kindersley and the Natives, befitting their roles as intermediaries. McKay, an HBC employee, is depicted interpreting the governor's address to the various tribes. Godsell, the local organizer of the pageant and the officer in charge of the Native delegates, appears as director, surveying the events and occupying the central space between the Indians and the governor.[18]

Godsell's impression of "Indian behavior," and of the importance of his own role in monitoring and directing such behavior, is evident in his description of the pageant, published fourteen years later: "One by one I introduced the Indians [to Kindersley], each chief being permitted to make a little speech. I had warned McKay beforehand that if any of them talked foolishly, as they are sometimes apt to do, he was to substitute words of his own more suited to the occasion."[19] Godsell was not alone in viewing the Natives as passive participants, both in the anniversary celebrations and in the history of their dealings with the HBC, as a reading of the Red River Pageant album and Schooling's official history reveals. Yet a variety of motivations figured into what appears to be a willingness by Aboriginal people to join in the celebrations.

In the first place, the Native delegates were provided with transportation, food, shelter, clothing, and a tour of Winnipeg in exchange for taking part in the anniversary events. And given the actual reliance of many Native people on the HBC for employment, credit, and supplies at this time, a show of loyalty by answering the call to come to Winnipeg made good economic sense. Secondly, a desire to meet with other First Nations people at HBC expense, coupled with a willingness to share their sense of cultural identity with outsiders are other probable contributing factors.[20]

Although Native people participated in the pageant for their own reasons, pageant organizers attempted to define and limit their appearance and actions as "Indians." Elaborate dress, in particular, tended to affirm, and conform to, these perceived roles (for both Natives and whites). Yet there remained a tension between assumed and "authentic" appearances. A comparison of the image of "Wood Cree Indians, Athabasca District" with the individual portraits of these men in the Pageant album suggests that appearances may be just that.[21] Several of the men in the former picture are dressed in plain suits and hats. Without their "tribal" attire, they call attention to the dressing up and artifice of the pageant (Figure 5.2). This relationship between dress and identity is further highlighted

Figure 5.2   *Red River Pageant, 1920. Group of Wood Cree Indians, Athabasca District. Courtesy Hudson's Bay Company Archives, Provincial Archives of Manitoba.*

by the photograph of "Louis E. Wilson/Director of pageant/(in Sioux costume)." Wilson, an Englishman brought to Canada to supervise the anniversary celebrations, appears in the photograph to be as "Indian" as the portraits that surround him. Only the accompanying caption removes the ambiguity and establishes Wilson as a non-Native employed by the Hudson's Bay Company.[22]

Yet to what extent were the Native participants also in "costume," dressing up for the occasion? The instances of ill-fitting buckskin shirts and feather headdresses raise a question about the extent to which the Native people themselves were involved in the preparation of the pageant. Godsell, in addition to having responsibility for the Natives during their stay at Lower Fort Garry, assisted in the development of the program, duties that included supervising "the assembling of the necessary material and equipment," such as tepees, canoes, and costumes.[23]

An article in the *Winnipeg Bulletin* acknowledged that the Indians dressed for comfort rather than style, wearing "ordinary 'hand-me-down' suits" when the press paid a visit to their encampment at Lower Fort Garry several days before the pageant.[24] They were undoubtedly clothed like the men who gathered at the various HBC posts for the local 250th anniversary celebrations.[25] Yet the photographs accompanying the *Bulletin* article portrayed Indians in ceremonial attire, striking noble poses. Almost all of the visual images that survive of the Red River Pageant, in fact, reproduce this idealized view of the "real Indian" in "traditional" dress.

The ceremonial regalia of the pageant "Indian" carried over into other public displays and performances, extending a unified concept of Indianness beyond the immediate environment of the historical enactment at Lower Fort Garry. The participants wore their costumes not only when paddling the canoes and York boats down the Red River and at the ceremony at the fort but also during an automobile tour to various sites in Winnipeg the following day, which included a stop at the Allen Theater (Figure 5.3). The dimension of role-playing and dressing up was carried beyond the historical reconstruction of the pageant into more public and less formal settings, where the confusion between representations of an idealized past and present became more pronounced than in the ceremony itself. Furthermore, the impressions and reactions of the "Hudson's Bay Company Indian" were then described and interpreted according to the role he was supposed to play. Thus a photograph of a man in headdress, seated in the cockpit of a stationary airplane, is entitled "Indians' amazement at White Man's Giant Bird," despite the absence of any sign of amazement on the face of this man or in the expressions of the Natives and non-Natives who watch him.[26]

This aspect of Native people "playing Indian," of conforming to the expectations and role models of Europeans and North Americans, can be considered as part of a larger complex of North American popular culture. These cultural expressions, as delineated by Rayna Green, include orally transmitted and formal literary texts, artifacts, dramatic performances, and, indeed, the Red River Pageant ritual reenactments were such cultural expressions. Rooted in the forced display of "savageness" by early Indian and Inuit visitors to Europe, playing In-

Figure 5.3   *Hudson's Bay Company's 250th Anniversary celebration, 1920. Natives in front of the Allen Theater. Photo, L. B. Foote. Courtesy Hudson's Bay Company Archives, Provincial Archives of Manitoba.*

dian underwent a variety of transformations and refinements, incorporating non-Natives into the role of Indian and at the same time developing a unique vocabulary and costume: "The performers speak in a measured speech . . . of 'The Great Spirit,' 'the big water,' the 'happy hunting ground' and so on, complete with the raised arm gestures, and often accoutrements of Plains Indians costume and behavior."[27]

The Red River Pageant allowed for (and encouraged) a portrayal of several types of Indian, but the central Native role was reserved for the Sioux warrior Kinnewakan, who incorporated those elements described by Green as the "definitively male and be-feathered 'Lord of the Plains.' "[28] In fact, despite the important role of Native women in the fur trade and the prevalence of available "Indian princess" imagery, the Red River Pageant offered up an exclusively male picture of the Indian.[29] Created by the male management of the HBC to be enacted by Aboriginal men, the Indian Reception presented a masculinized version of the HBC-Indian relationship. In addition to agreeing with a view of history that exalted the heroic exploits of men and ignored the place of women, the pageant's highlighting of the exchange between male leaders effectively submerged any hints of sexual desire and union between white and Native.

The pageant's portrayal of the Indian leader was elaborated upon by contemporary newspaper and magazine reports, as in the following account from the *Winnipeg Tribune*: "The old chief, with the classic, furrowed features, body and head arranged in a brilliancy of colours, the pens, beads, furs and leathers making a graceful and striking combination, approached the stately Governor, pipe of peace in hand, and looking heavenwards, called upon the Great Spirit to witness the compact of confidence about to be sealed afresh between their White Father and the Indians of all the Canadian Tribes."[30] In this piece the *Tribune* reporter played up the spiritual associations of the "Indian chief," at the same time elevating Kinnewakan to the status of leader of all the "Canadian Tribes." As noted in a recent biography of an Ojibwa healer and religious leader, however, the very category of "chief" is problematic, tending toward the mystification of complex individuals into stereotypic Others.[31] Not surprisingly, in both the spectacle of the pageant and in its documentation, these very categories were those most readily seized upon by HBC officials and the press.

The image of the "Hudson's Bay Company Indian" conformed to popular stereotypes of "Indianness" prevalent in the first decades of this century, but it also represented a particular manifestation of this imagery—one that could come into conflict with other perceptions. Thus, the Canadian government's Department of Indian Affairs at first refused to sanction Native participation in the pageant.[32] Although both HBC officials and government bureaucrats shared similar paternalistic assumptions about Aboriginal peoples, federal policies tended toward a different image of the ideal Indian. One of the major objectives of federal Indian policy at this period, under the direction of Deputy Superintendent General Duncan Campbell Scott, was to transform "the native population into civilized and productive members of the 'industrial and mercantile community.'" This effort translated into the discouragement and suppression of Aboriginal customs, including the prohibition of potlatching among the Pacific Coast tribes and the banning of dancing by the prairie provinces' First Nations.[33]

This government policy to control behavior among Native peoples also manifested itself in attempts to curb public displays of "Indianness." In the first decades of the twentieth century, country fairs and exhibitions, in addition to their function of promoting agricultural methods and competitions, provided amusement for the rural residents of the Canadian prairies.[34] Echoing the popular entertainments of the Wild West shows of the 1880s and 1890s, Indian encampments and parades became a feature of the festivities. In one sense the show of exotically costumed and befeathered, yet tame, "Indians" reflected the perceptions of many non-Natives. In this view, Aboriginal people, although maintaining a distinct identity, were no longer seen as a threat to settlement and society. In another sense, the exhibitions provided an outlet for Native people to publicly display, in the face of repressive measures, the vitality of their culture. In response to this threat to the official assimilationist view, in 1914 federal bureaucrats drafted an amendment to the Indian Act (subsequently approved by Parliament) forbidding Indians in the provinces of Manitoba, Saskatchewan, Alberta, British Columbia, and in the territories from participating in "Indian dances" outside their own reserves and from appearing in shows or exhibitions in "Aboriginal costume."[35]

In keeping with this avowed aim of protecting Native people from "being exploited as a savage or semi-savage race, when the whole administrative force of the Department is endeavoring to civilize them," government officials sought to limit the ways in which Aboriginal peoples were presented in public.[36] Yet, when influential parties (such as the Hudson's Bay Company) were involved, government cooperation was usually forthcoming. After a personal visit to Ottawa, HBC pageant organizers obtained the necessary permissions to stage their event, but only after they agreed to the Indian Department's demands. As Deputy Superintendent Scott stated: "The reproduction of barbaric costumes or custom will form no part in the entertainment. . . . The HBC will bear all expenses, proper arrangements will be made for the care of the Indians, their remuneration and so forth."[37] With the necessary approval in hand, the HBC proceeded to orchestrate its own version of the public display of "Indianness" in its elaborate historical pageant.

Playing up the "historical significance of the occasion" of the company's 250th anniversary sprang from quite pragmatic concerns, because HBC officials recognized that directing the celebrations along the lines of a commercial advertising project would discourage press and public support.[38] By building on the portrayal of the company as a progressive influence on Native people and in the development of Canada as a whole, the celebrations capitalized on the Anglo-Canadian enthusiasm for the colonization of the West and the extension of empire. The "peaceful" nature of the conquering of the Canadian wilderness—and of its inhabitants—constituted a major aspect of this view. Thus the cooperation of the

Indians and their continued friendship with the Hudson's Bay Company occupied a central place in this popular recounting of the past.

Exploiting its long history of economic and social exchanges with Aboriginal people, the HBC contributed its own version of the image of the "Indian" to the Canadian public—that of the ideal "Hudson's Bay Company Indian." Although introduced to the benefits of civilization (pageant participants were driven around in automobiles and taken to the movies), the "Hudson's Bay Company Indian" never traded in his colorful costume for the white man's attire. He smoked the pipe of peace with his more civilized brothers and then dutifully returned to the wilds to engage in the "traditional" pursuit of trapping, thereby guaranteeing a steady supply of furs for the company and customers for its trade goods. The performance of the Red River Pageant and the related 250th anniversary celebrations marked 1920 as a unique year in the history of the HBC's public representations. However, the company continued to construct images of Native people in the following decades. In the pages of the company's magazine, the *Beaver*, in its museum collections and displays in the Winnipeg department store, and in the organization of a company archives and publication program in London, the HBC institutionalized the presentation of its history and the HBC-Indian relationship, generating a rich legacy of "Indian" images in the process.[39]

Notes

Acknowledgments are due to Jennifer S. H. Brown for helpful comments and editorial advice on an earlier version of this essay; to the Social Science and Humanities Research Council of Canada, the University of Manitoba, Rupert's Land Research Centre (University of Winnipeg), and the Faculty of Graduate Studies and Research (Carleton University) for financial support; and to the staff of the Hudson's Bay Company Archives, Provincial Archives of Manitoba for facilitating this research.

1. In the course of the year, 1,159 copies of the anniversary brochure by Sir William Schooling, entitled *The Hudson's Bay Company, 1670–1920* (London: Hudson's Bay House, 1920), were distributed. The anniversary film was produced by the American Educational Film Corporation. See Hudson's Bay Company Archives, Provincial Archives of Manitoba (hereafter HBCA), A.102/53, Anniversary Brochures; and RG2/1/2, Canadian Advisory Committee, September 15, 1919.

2. See HBCA, RG2/3/227, Governor's Itinerary and The *Beaver* (October 1920), pp. 2–5, 7–9. The cost of the celebrations to the Canadian office of the HBC was $333,545.00 (HBCA, RG2/74/1, Hughes to Harman, February 11, 1921).

3. "Echoes of May Celebrations," The *Beaver*, (October 1920), p. 2.

4. HBCA, Album No. 35, *The Red River Pageant May 3rd, 1920, Commemorating the Hudson's Bay Company's 250th Anniversary*.

5. The photographs were produced by several prominent Winnipeg firms, mounted on thick cardboard, and then bound by a professional printer into a large album that was over three inches thick.

6. HBCA, A.102/47; *See the Red River Pageant*.

7. Ibid., RG2/2/127, Thomson to FitzGerald, October 3, 1919.

8. Ibid., RG2/3/1, Ingrams to Secretary, Canadian Advisory Committee, December 2, 1919. The Educational Film Corporation of New York, under the auspices of the HBC, filmed the Red River Pageant and other anniversary celebrations, and distributed the films through Pathe Weekly in the United States and Canada.

9. HBCA, RG2/3/1, Ingrams to Secretary, December 2, 1919.

10. See HBCA, Album 35, photo nos. 8–11 (references are to individual photographs in the album, as numbered by the archivist).

11. HBCA., RG2/3/2, P. H. Godsell, Programme of Red River Brigade and Indian Reception, April 1920.

12. Schooling, *Hudson's Bay Company*, pp. 35, 37, 45. For a later expression see Robert Watson, "A Company Indian," The *Beaver* (June 1931), pp. 220–222.

13. The undated brochure *The Fort Garry Historical Pageant*, subtitled "Celebrating a Friendship 250 Years Old!" (HBCA, RG2/74/3), and "Renewing Pledges of Friendship," *Winnipeg Tribune*, May 4, 1920, both emphasized this theme of Indian-HBC "friendship."

14. HBCA, Album 35, photo nos. 145–150, 177; these photographs are folded over in the album to accommodate their large size.

15. HBCA, RG2/3/2, P. H. Godsell, Programme.

16. HBCA, Album 35, photo no. 136.

17. The *Beaver*, May 1922, cover. This photograph appeared locally (*Winnipeg Tribune*, May 4, 1920) and abroad ("An Outpost of Empire: The 250th Anniversary of the Hudson's Bay Company," The *Graphic* [London], June 5, 1920, pp. 904–905, for example). In a recent incarnation, this image illustrates A. J. Ray's "The Hudson's Bay Company and Native People," in Wilcomb E. Washburn, ed, *Handbook of North American Indians: History of Indian-White Relations*, vol. 4 (Washington, D.C.: Smithsonian Institution Press, 1988), p. 349.

18. In the album captions, Godsell was described as leading the "Vanguard of the Red River Fur Brigade" from his passenger seat, while the Native men at bow and stern provided the labor. Godsell served as an apprentice clerk, post manager, and district inspector before being dismissed from the HBC in 1929. He subsequently pursued a career as a writer, focusing on "true stories" of the fur trade and Aboriginal people in periodicals and books, including *Arctic Trader: The Account of Twenty Years with the Hudson's Bay Company* (New York: G. P. Putnam's Sons, 1934).

19. Inevitably, in Godsell's telling, one of the Indian speakers confirms his stereotype, and McKay substitutes a more appropriate, "flowery address." Godsell, *Arctic Trader*, p. 171.

20. See Lacey Sanders, "'Real Indians' at Red River: The Hudson's Bay Company's 250th Anniversary Pageant" (Winnipeg: 1991), pp. 24–29.

21. HBCA, Album 35, photo no. 8.

22. HBCA, Album 35, photo no. 76.

23. HBCA, RG2/3/1, Thomson to FitzGerald, January 29, 1920.

24. "Smoke of Tepees Once More Arises at Historic Fort," *Winnipeg Bulletin*, May 1, 1920.

25. See HBCA, 1987/363/A-15/2 for snapshots of the people and activities at Lac Seul, Ontario; and "Celebrations at Fur Trade Posts in Many Districts," The *Beaver* (October 1920), pp. 7–9.

26. HBCA, 1987/363/A-15/120, Native pageant participants with crowd at the Allen Theatre; Album 35, photo nos. 217, 220.

27. Rayna Green, "The Tribe Called Wannabee: Playing Indian in America and Europe," *Folklore* 99 (1) (1988), pp. 30–39.

28. Green, "Playing Indian," p. 41.

29. See Sylvia Van Kirk, *Many Tender Ties: Women in Fur Trade Society, 1670–1870* (Winnipeg, Manitoba: Watson and Dwyer, 1980) on the role of Native women in the fur trade in the nineteenth century. A recent exhibit, *Fluffs and Feathers* (Woodland Cultural Centre, Brantford, Ontario; Deborah Doxtator, curator) presented numerous female images of the Indian in North American popular culture.

30. "A Day of Days," *Winnipeg Tribune,* May 4, 1920.

31. Jennifer S. H. Brown and Maureen Matthews, "Fair Wind: Medicine and Consolation on the Berens River," *Journal of the Canadian Historical Association* 4 (1993), pp. 71–74.

32. HBCA, RG2/3/6, Report of 250th Anniversary Celebration; RG2/3/2, Duncan Campbell Scott (deputy superintendent general, Department of Indian Affairs) to J. Thomson, April 8, 1920.

33. E. Brian Titley, *A Narrow Vision: Duncan Campbell Scott and the Administration of Indian Affairs in Canada* (Vancouver: University of British Columbia Press, 1986), pp. 162–183. In his assessment of the effectiveness of the attempt to prevent "senseless drumming and dancing," Titley concludes that prairie Native cultures resisted the persuasive and coercive aspects of federal policies and practices.

34. See, for example, Ken Coates and Fred McGuinness, *Pride of the Land: An Affectionate History of Brandon's Agricultural Exhibitions* (Winnipeg, Manitoba: Peguis Publishers, 1985).

35. Titley, *A Narrow Vision,* pp. 171–175; see also Daniel Francis, *The Imaginary Indian: The Image of the Indian in Canadian Culture* (Vancouver, British Columbia: Arsenal Pulp Press, 1992), pp. 96–103 and Deborah Doxtator, *Fluffs and Feathers: An Exhibit on the Symbols of Indianness, a Resource Guide,* rev. ed. (Brantford, Ontario: Woodland Cultural Centre, 1992), pp. 16–20.

36. D. C. Scott to R. B. Bennett, July 17, 1916 (cited in Titley, *A Narrow Vision,* p. 176).

37. HBCA, RG2/3/2, Scott to Thomson, April 8, 1920.

38. HBCA, RG2/3/6, Report of 250th Anniversary Celebration.

39. See Peter Geller "Creating Corporate Images of the Fur Trade: The Hudson's Bay Company and Public Relations in the 1930s," in *The Fur Trade Revisited: Selected Papers of the Sixth North American Fur Trade Conference,* ed. J.S.H. Brown, W. J. Eccles and D. P. Heldman (East Lansing: Michigan State University Press, 1994), pp. 409–426; Diedre Simmons, "Annals of the Fur Trade: The Making of the Hudson's Bay Company Archives" and Robert Coutts and Katherine Pettipas, "'Mere Curiosities Are Not Required': The HBC Museum Collection," in The *Beaver* (June/July 1994), pp. 4–12, 13–19.

6

Science and Spectacle: Native American Representation in Early Cinema
Alison Griffiths

Late nineteenth- and early twentieth-century American popular cultural entertainments catered to an enormous public appetite for images of the culturally exotic, and this taste was met by a diverse range of early moving pictures that featured indigenous dances, historical reenactments, colonial pageants, and fictional
narratives. For some early traveling film exhibitors, audience fascination with the
exotic became part of the lecture-presentation itself, as the showmen adopted national costumes to add a touch of "authentic" culture and visual color to the film-
lecture performance.[1] The touristic gaze by means of which early American cine-
matographers constructed the distant Other also characterized filmic depictions
of racial and ethnic groups closer to home, particularly in the representation of
Native Americans. As would be expected, the construction of Native Americans in
early silent film was infused with nationally and historically specific discourses regarding the relations of Native Americans to White society. Moving pictures were
not unique in this respect; their repertoire of representations borrowed freely
from traditional American culture, the repositories of which included popular
fiction (particularly the dime novel), Wild West shows, commercial photography,
paintings, circus and vaudeville performances, theatrical productions, popular
music, and museums of natural history.

In this chapter, I examine films featuring Native Americans that were made by
three White producers—Thomas Edison, Joseph K. Dixon, and Edward Curtis—between 1901 and 1914. I describe these films as "quasi-ethnographic" in order to distinguish such works by nonanthropologists with varying degrees of ethnographic

insight from more narrowly defined applications of film as a tool of field research by professional anthropologists. These early films depicting Native Americans are considered in the context of early twentieth-century public perceptions of Native Americans, perceptions that were shaped both by popular entertainments and by the fledgling discipline of anthropology.

Both popular and anthropological views of Native Americans at the time were animated by a central tension between the idea of Native Americans as historically co-present (coeval) with White society and the conception of a timeless (allochronic) existence suggested in the familiar White image of the Noble Savage. This tension is evident in a number of early twentieth-century forms of cultural exhibition in which the emerging science of anthropology intersected most visibly with popular culture, for example, in filmmaking, world's fairs and expositions, and museums of natural history. Silent filmmakers thus constructed Native American identity through recourse to a version of anthropology compatible with popular ideology. Their films negotiated the conflicting demands of the scientific and the popular with relative ease by trading on notions of ethnographic legitimacy and filmic realism.

The coexistence of the scientific and the popular within this palimpsest is suggested in anthropologist Clark Wissler's 1917 *The American Indian: An Introduction to Anthropology.* In his introduction, Wissler suggests the enormous interest in popular writing about Native Americans ("it may be doubted if there is anywhere in all the land a normal individual who has not acquired some interest in the Indian's history") as a justification for his own academic study of Native Americans.[2] Given the myriad manifestations of the figure of the Native American in the public imagination at this time, the public exhibition site becomes a crucial determinant in privileging certain kinds of ethnographic meaning. Turn-of-the-century spectators' negotiation of hierarchized and context-determined truth-values were shaped by the distinct cultural connotations of diverse exhibition sites; viewing a moving picture in the Brooklyn Institute of Arts and Sciences or the American Museum of Natural History, one imagines, would have been very different from watching a film (perhaps even the same film) in a New York City nickelodeon. Films representing native peoples were thus part of a discursive practice that cannot be reduced to a single site or meaning. In fact, there is no easy way of knowing precisely what kinds of ethnographic meanings these films engendered for spectators in the past, since there are few remaining traces of their exhibition or reception contexts. Nevertheless, it is possible to consider the competing notions of ethnographic authenticity in circulation at the time, which were brought about by singular patterns of filmic exchange, exhibition, and cultural meaning. And the films themselves—or the traces of them that have survived—are important starting points for investigators.

Narrative, character, and iconographic tropes were borrowed freely across different media of the late nineteenth century. An example of this intertextuality can be seen in two 1894 kinetoscope films of Native Americans by Thomas Edison cameraman W.K.L. Dixon, *Indian War Council* and *Sioux Ghost Dance,* both shot at Edison's Black Maria film studio in New Jersey.[3] The Sioux performers' reconstructions of ritual dances were already popular attractions in Buffalo Bill Cody's Wild West Show, a touring spectacle then appearing in Ambrose Park, Brooklyn. *Sioux Ghost Dance* points to the difficulty of differentiating the "authentic" from the "inauthentic" in commercially produced quasi-ethnographic films of the period and to the unstable status of the "real" in quasi-ethnographic filmmaking shot in the motion picture studio.[4]

However, filmmakers and other showmen-entrepreneurs often sought ratification of the ethnographical claims for their representations by establishing links with prominent anthropologists or institutions. This annexing of scientific legitimacy by popular forms can be seen in a series of films produced by Thomas Edison's company in Native American communities in Walpi Pueblo, Arizona, in 1901. Edison and cameraman J. H. White enlisted the aid of the Bureau of American Ethnology (BAE), established as part of the Smithsonian Institution in 1879 to place anthropological expertise in the service of public policymaking. In his agreement with the BAE to allow filming on the reservation, White promised to make motion pictures "representing the industries, amusements, and ceremonies of the Pueblo and other tribes . . . [and to] obtain absolutely trustworthy records of aboriginal activities for the use of future students."[5]

One product of the BAE-sanctioned project, *Moki Snake Dance by Wolpi Indians,* is a one-minute film of a ritual dance featuring live snakes, captured in a high-angle medium-long shot that includes internal spectators (mostly White) at the right corner of the frame. There is little evidence in this film of the technique that film historian Marshall Deutelbaum calls "structural patterning," that is, the construction of internal coherence, or a sense of beginning, middle, and end through circular patterning; White's camera assumes the point of view of a western observer and records the dance fragment without changing position in the single-take film.[6] The film validates the White ethnographer through its use of internal filmic spectators and its recourse to ethnographic legitimacy via its association with the BAE. It represents an indexical tracing of an event and a larger cultural fascination with the abject—the snakes in this context—and with the indigenous rituals of the Other. The repulsion, fear, and fascination of the exotic suggested by the *Moki Snake Dance* is evocative of both the voyeuristic appeal and the essential distance provided spectators by the moving-picture apparatus.

The dance captured in *Moki Snake Dance* had enjoyed great popularity as a tourist attraction on Native American reservations and in the Wild West show, which accounts for its appeal as a film subject for Edison. At the same time, the deleterious effects of still and moving-picture cameras upon the "authenticity" of this Native American ritual were decried by professional photographer George Wharton James in the premier issue of the photographic monthly *Camera Craft* in 1902. James criticized the misrepresentation of Snake Dance performances by (competing) photographers and journalists, claiming that the performances were not dances of spectacle but prayers for rain and a blessing of the harvest. James went on to decry the presence of too many White spectators with still (and on some instances moving-picture) cameras, resulting in parts of the performance either being cut or altered by performers intimidated by the encroachment of the observers: "It cannot be said that the changes are to the advantage of the photographer. They render his work less *certain* and *effective,* and it will not be long before one can write a learned and accurate paper from the standpoint of scientific ethnology on the change in religious ceremonies owing to the camera."[7]

James's concern with both the impact of White observers on indigenous rituals and the camera's inability to differentiate between an "authentic" performance and a fake or imperfect rendition anticipates a perennial and still-lively debate within ethnographic filmmaking. However, efforts to efface the presence of the White observer through rarefied notions of native authenticity can be seen in construction of the centuries-old figure of the Noble Savage. The Noble Savage, whose image could be summoned in the context of White discussions of any American indigenous people, elevated the qualities of a "native," pristine, Edenic existence above the corrupting influences of modern civilization. According to historian Robert Berkhofer, Jr., the idea of the Noble Savage can be traced back to sixteenth-century European homogenizations of the indigenous peoples of America.[8] The conventionalized image is explicit in the work of American painter George Catlin, whose oil sketches of American Indians from the 1830s and 1840s were sold to the American Museum of Natural History in 1912. As early as 1841, Catlin linked the Indian with the vanishing wildlife of the American West and predicted, with a sense of intense loss, the extinction of both man and beast at the hands of the White man:

> Nature has nowhere presented more beautiful and lovely scenes than those of the vast prairies of the West and of *man* and *beast* no nobler specimen than those who inhabit them—the *Indian* and the *buffalo*—joint and original tenants of the soil, and fugitives together from the approach of civilized man; they have fled to the great plains of the West, and there under an equal doom, they have taken up their last abode, where their race will expire and their bones will bleach together.[9]

The tone of melancholic nostalgia in such lyrical accounts of the plight of the Noble Savage suggests anthropology's utility for broader commentaries upon the emerging urban and industrial society of turn-of-the-century America. For Americans disenchanted with the physical and social transformation of the modern American landscape, the myth of the Noble Savage became a mnemonic for cultural loss. More significantly, this positioning of Native Americans as a doomed race created a set of hegemonic images that reinforced a fundamental paradox in Native American representation. Specifically, these images presented an allochronic existence in the obscure past as synonymous with a more "authentic" vision of Native American life. Further, such images reduced the importance of human agency and the contemporaneous experiences of Native Americans in their contact with White society. This paradox is vividly evoked in the praise anthropologist Clark Wissler heaped upon artist George Catlin's earliest sketches from the 1830s, saying they represented "the customs, ceremonies and habitations of the wild Indian tribes . . . at a time when Indian life was *real,* not transitional as later," in 1912.[10] As Berkhofer argues, "if the Indian changed through the adoption of civilization as defined by Whites, then he was no longer truly Indian . . . because the Indian was judged by what Whites were not."[11] Thus, an authentic Native American representation could not exist in an ethnographic present but was typically relegated to a more "authentic" mid-nineteenth-century historical moment before full White settlement of the western frontier had occurred. Anthropologist Roger Sanjek points to an example of this practice in the 1932 obituary notice of Plains Indian Francis La Fleische in the *American Anthropologist.* The photograph accompanying the obituary of La Fleische, who worked at the Bureau of American Ethnology and published widely in the 1910s and 1920s, was retouched so as to remove his conventional White attire, leaving him dressed in the buffalo robe he had been persuaded to don for a single photograph.[12]

Whereas conventional nineteenth-century representations of Native Americans such as Catlin's frequently evoked the tragic and sentimental trope of a "timeless" people paradoxically condemned by history's progress, Native Americans were occasionally inserted into White history in more explicit and self-serving ways, for example, through the use of ethnographic displays of "primitive peoples" at world's fairs. Native Americans were used as a "baseline against which to measure civilized progress," according to historian Curtis Hinsley.[13] For example, *The World's Work* summed up the educational value of the Native American display in the anthropology exhibit at the 1904 St. Louis World's Fair in evolutionist and self-congratulatory terms: "The significance of this exhibit in the Anthropological Section is its showing that a race which cannot of itself make the necessary strides to civilization may be helped; and moreover, that part of the culture development of a civilized people is the growth of an altruism and a sense of justice that prescribe the giving of such help."[14]

The development of a charitable countenance by "civilized" exhibition-goers was as important a justification for this anthropological living exhibit as the object-lesson of native primitivism. In fact, this dualism had never been far from anthropology's quintessence; in 1852, Smithsonian philologist William W. Turner optimistically offered anthropology as an instrument for both the organized religious conversion of the heathen Indian and the eradication of white ignorance and prejudice toward Native Americans.[15] Despite the appeal of notions of the allochronic Other as anthropological subject, the impact of modern cultures upon primitive cultures (and vice versa) thus became an ongoing preoccupation of anthropologists. Within an ascendant positivist epistemology, such "scientific" knowledge about Native Americans provided a legitimizing tool for anthropology at a time when topical concerns over assimilation, reservation policy, and the closing of the frontier became urgent matters of popular and political debate.[16]

Anthropology's task of generating accurate empirical knowledge about the "real Indian" was part of a wider social discourse concerning Native American assimilation into White society. Entrepreneur Rodman Wanamaker entered this debate in 1908 when he sponsored an expedition to obtain still and moving pictures on the Crow Reservation in Montana. Expedition leader Joseph K. Dixon, together with his son Rollin, who operated the moving picture camera, shot still and moving pictures of Native Americans during two trips to the Crow Reservation in Montana in 1908 and 1909, as well as during a touring expedition to Indian reservations around the United States in 1913. According to Joseph Dixon, the primary goals of the 1908 and 1909 expeditions were to "perpetuate the life story of the first Americans and strengthen in their hearts the feeling of allegiance and friendship for their country."[17] These two aims neatly encapsulate the allochronic-coeval paradox, as Dixon's desire to "perpetuate the life story" was firmly entrenched in a discourse of salvage ethnography (a desire to study and record Native American tribes that anthropologists predicted would soon vanish). Dixon declared that "in all these pictures . . . of Indian life, every effort was exhausted to eliminate any hint of the white man's foot" in order that the "spirit of the native environment" would dominate.[18]

Conversely, Dixon's desire to strengthen feelings of national allegiance in the Native American acknowledged the presence of the Indian within history and promoted the U.S. government's assimilationist policy. A major goal of the 1908 expedition was to produce a moving-picture version of Henry Wadsworth Longfellow's epic poem *Hiawatha*, although Dixon also filmed a reenactment of Custer's battle at the Little Bighorn, which used two groups of U.S. cavalry and Crow Indians in place of Sioux (Figure 6.1). According to anthropologist Susan Applegate Krouse, however, the restaged battle epic degenerated into farce as many of the Native American actors failed to take their performances seriously, spoiling the desired dramatic effect, for example, by refusing to play dead properly.[19]

Although much of the Wanamaker footage has been lost, a twelve-minute compilation of film from the 1909 and 1913 expeditions, titled *Indian Communication: Sign Language of the North American Indian,* survives in the Special Collections Archive of the American Museum of Natural History. *Indian Communication* opens with five Sioux chiefs demonstrating sign language. Following a medium close-up of Chief Iron Tail looking at the camera, the film depicts Chief Iron Tail and Buffalo Bill Cody communicating to one another via sign language. The next shot shows Chief Two Moons using sign language to tell the story of Custer's defeat in battle, followed by demonstrations of smoke and blanket signals and an Indian procession to a tepee with the body of a Sioux. The final intertitle tells us that "they then rose up and departed, each one homeward to his wigwam on a long and distant journey."

Although much of the film is composed so awkwardly that the action is lost in the extreme long-shot, three shots are striking in their composition and their negotiation of the tensions between allochronic and coeval constructions of Native American identity. The first of these depicts Buffalo Bill entering and meeting Chief Iron Tail in long-shot; both sit atop gray horses positioned so that the two riders can communicate in sign language facing one another in profile to the camera.[20] The spectator's attention is captured less by the details of the sign language, which are difficult to discern in the long-shot, than by the unexpected aesthetic quality of the nearly symmetrical composition, suggesting something of the formality of a staged and quasi-official ceremony.

This shot is immediately followed by the second striking shot, the film's only medium-close shot—of Chief Iron Tail staring directly at the camera. The shot evokes the potentially threatening quality of the return gaze of the ethnographic subject, while its pictorialism and conventionalized iconography echo the composition of Dixon's famous photographic portraits of Native Americans taken on the expedition. The feather bonnet of Chief Iron Tail reinforces the performative aspects of this shot, doubly inscribed in the staged quality of the sign-language demonstration.

Indian Communication's use of the conventions of allochronic signification are, however, disturbed by the more direct insertion of Native Americans into history. For example, an intertitle announcing the famous 1876 battle between Chief Two Moons and Custer is followed by the third important shot, that of Chief Two Moons standing next to his horse amid tombstones at the side of a mountain. The composition of this medium-long shot of the Chief signing the story of the battle

Figure 6.1 *Crow Indians acting as Custer Scouts in a reenactment of the Battle of the Little Bighorn during the 1908 expedition to the Crow Reservation in Montana. Photo, Joseph K. Dixon (negative 316936). Courtesy Dept. Library Services, American Museum of Natural History.*

to an off-screen figure is extremely aestheticized; the placid horse and tombstones with an American flag in the foreground seem calculated to invoke a sentimental and patriotic response, although the pathos is as much (if not more) triggered by Native American as by White American loss. Indeed, the goal of the final 1913 Wanamaker expedition, according to Dixon, was to inspire "an ideal of patriotism in the mind of the red man—a spirit of patriotism that would lead to a desire for citizenship—a feeling of friendship and allegiance."[21]

As part of Rodman Wanamaker's Expedition of Citizenship, Dixon also shot an official presentation of the American flag to every reservation in the United States, though these presentation ceremonies are not included in *Indian Communication*. The flag ceremony was accompanied by a phonograph playing the "Address of the President of the United States and Other Messages," which predicted the day when the "Red Men, our neighbors, become truly one people with us, enjoying all the rights and privileges we do, and living in peace and plenty as we do"[22] (Figure 6.2). Despite the ostensible historical copresence of Native American and White in the staging of the president's assimilationist rhetoric, the lure of the allochronic is suggested in the profilmic stage management of the filmed ceremony. The Honorable F. H. Abbott, acting commissioner of Indian Affairs, forwarded a letter to the superintendents of the Indian reservations in which he suggested that "as each tribe has a distinctive costume, and as a record will be preserved of the meeting through photographs of Indians who assemble . . . it is highly desirable *for historical purposes* that Indians who may care to do so should appear dressed in their native regalia."[23]

Written in conjunction with his 1913 film, Dixon's book *The Purpose and Achievements of the Rodman Wanamaker Expedition of Citizenship to the North American Indian* begins with the affirmation that "Historic values have been preserved. . . . These records are systematic, extensive and constructive. . . . They not alone furnish exact data, but they are in addition a record of the environment, homes and types of the tribes so that a hitherto unavailable source of information is afforded by yielding data for comparative study."[24] Dixon's rhetoric suggests the use of film as a tool of surveillance and discipline for the classification of Native Americans; however, whatever empirical knowledge was furnished by moving pictures, this information was hardly transparent and value free. Indeed the "data" gathered by Dixon's moving pictures were consistent with a tradition of fabricated and idealized versions of American Indians' cooperation and assimilation.

The conventional suppression of Native American presence in the same historical time as Whites in favor of mythical and allochronic constructions is vividly illustrated in the work of photographer and filmmaker Edward Curtis. His work includes a 1914 film entitled *In the Land of the Head-Hunters*, set among the Kwakiutl Indians of the U.S. Northwest coast.[25] After a successful career as a photographer of portraits and landscapes, Curtis began photographing Native Americans in 1900 on a trip to the Blackfoot Reservation in Montana; in 1906 he started using moving pictures to record special events and ceremonies.[26] Curtis's

Figure 6.2 *President Wilson's speech being played on a phonograph to the Umatilla tribe in Pendleton, Oregon, 1913. Wanamaker's Expedition of Citizenship spent six months touring Indian reservations and presented flags to a total of 169 tribes. Photo, Joseph K. Dixon (negative 316629). Courtesy American Museum of Natural History.*

approach, like Edison's, depends on institutional and scientific validations of filmic and photographic depictions of Native Americans for truth claims. Acknowledging his lack of ethnographic expertise in a letter to J. Pierpont Morgan (from whom Curtis was seeking sponsorship for his twenty-volume *North American Indian* project), Curtis argued that turning over his completed fieldwork to scientific authorities for editing and scholarly commentary would afford his work "unquestionable authenticity."[27] However, Curtis's repeated truth claims (he saw his own photography as an "art science") in both the introductions to the *North American Indian* photographic series and in correspondence with potential sponsors are problematic when the photographer's actual working practices are carefully examined. Although Curtis condemned conventional studio portraits of Native Americans as inaccurate, he continued to take his studio-tent with him into the field and was at great pains to conceal every trace of the subject's contact with white society. Curtis provided a limited inventory of "Indian" props such as feather bonnets, masks, and costumes, which frequently resurfaced haphazardly in his photographs of members of different tribes. In later photographs he used wigs to disguise the short hair worn by many of his Indian subjects and cropped and retouched prints to remove all signs of White contact, thereby enhancing homogenized and allochronic notions of "Indianness."[28]

Curtis opposed the artifice of commercially produced films featuring Native Americans and favored the salvage ethnography of Joseph Dixon's Wanamaker expedition; he thus set out to make *In the Land of the Head-Hunters,* a film that would "illustrate the period before the white man came."[29] Curtis's film narrates an intertribal feud triggered by a jilted Indian sorcerer and can best be described as an "ethnographic fiction." The story of the kidnapping and return of the heroine is punctuated by Kwakiutl rituals, which include a wedding ceremony and animal-costumed dances. Curtis organized the Continental Film Company and outlined his film project in visionary tones in 1912: "Genuine Indian pictures will be far more valuable than regular dramatic subjects. . . . The questions might be raised as to whether the documentary material would not lack the thrilling interest of the fake picture. It is the opinion of Mr Curtis that the real life of the Indian contains the parallel emotions to furnish all the necessary plots and give the pictures all the heart interest needed."[30]

Judged by Curtis as highly marketable, the filmic depiction of the "real life of the Indian" was defined exclusively in allochronic terms; for Curtis, "real Indians" are American Indians who remain ethnographically pristine and uncontaminated by Whites. Moreover, Curtis's evocation of discourses of science and entertainment as selling points echo Clark Wissler's belief in the widespread appeal of Indian subjects in American popular culture in his 1912 book. Attempting to gain financial backing for his film, Curtis sought both to exploit the popular interest in Native American themes and to distinguish his project from the inauthentic products of commercial filmmakers. In a 1912 letter to Charles D. Walcott, secretary of the Smithsonian Institution, Curtis claimed his aim was to record as carefully as possible the domestic and ceremonial life of Native Americans, so that each picture would be an "unquestioned document" instead of "caught fragments of superficial, indifferent matter."[31]

Notwithstanding his own claims, Curtis's work as a photographer and filmmaker was riddled with paradoxes, and his desire to appeal to a nonspecialist audience encouraged him to suppress visual evidence of the contemporary lived realities of his subjects. In a January 1906 letter to J. Pierpont Morgan, Curtis expressed confidence about the "scientific accuracy" of his proposed twenty-volume survey of Native American life, although he admitted his treatment of the history, ceremony, and mythology of the people would be rendered in broad strokes to be, "if possible, interesting reading."[32] In his 1914 film, Curtis eliminated much of the ethnographic detail of everyday life in favor of more sensational topics such as war, adventure, and ceremony and had few qualms about manipulating reality for his desired effect; for example, Curtis paid many of the male Kwakiutl Indians in *Head-Hunters* to shave their beards and wear wigs in order to comply with mythologized images.[33]

Curtis's key collaborator in *Head-Hunters* was the Anglo–Native American George Hunt, who had also been recruited as a photographer and guide for the Jesup North Pacific Expeditions organized by Franz Boas for the American Museum of Natural History between 1897 and 1902.[34] The intricate lineages that emerge during this period between Franz Boas, George Hunt, Edward Curtis, and Joseph Dixon are worth briefly outlining, especially since Hunt, who assisted both Boas and Curtis, was a pivotal figure in the projects of several of these men. Although Hunt was employed by Curtis in the film production (the male lead in Curtis's *Head-Hunters* was played by George Hunt's youngest son, and many of Hunt's other children and grandchildren performed in the film), he was nevertheless critical of Curtis's overall approach. In Hunt's opinion, Curtis failed to present the most important cultural elements from a Kwakiutl viewpoint and elevated visual effect above cultural contextualization and explanation.[35] On another front, seeing a potential rival in Dixon, Curtis disparaged the Wanamaker expedition films, complained of Dixon's plagiarism (Curtis claimed he was the first to initiate a filmic and photographic project), and called Dixon's photographs from the expedition "fakey illustrations."[36] Franz Boas was also critical of Curtis's "ethnography" among the Kwakiutl, although he, too, felt at liberty to alter the version of "ethnographic reality" he constructed among the same tribe via photographic retouching and other techniques.[37]

Curtis's hope that *Head-Hunters* would "possess the interest needed to make [sic] the tastes of the masses or those who are looking for amusement only" and thereby assure its commercial success was not endorsed in W. Stephen Bush's laudatory review of the film in *Moving Picture World* in 1914.[38] Bush judged that the film was not "a feature for the nickelodeon or the cheap houses, but it ought to be welcomed by the better class of houses that are looking for an occasional departure from the regular attractions and that want to give their patrons a special treat."[39] Bush was acutely aware of the class connotations of such educational films and in his effusive review compared the film to Wagner's *Ring of the Nibelung* and *Parsifal:*

> Mr. Curtis has extracted from his vast materials nothing but the choicest and nothing but that which will please the eyes and stir the thoughts of an intelligent white audience. All the actors are full-blooded Indians. The Indian mind is, I believe, constitutionally incapable of acting; it cannot even grasp the meaning of acting as we understand it. Probably nobody understands this better than Mr. Curtis. The picture speaks volumes of the producer's intimacy with the Indians and his great power over them. They are natural in every move; the grace, the weirdness and the humor of their dances has never been brought home to us like this before.[40]

Beyond flattering his "intellectually superior" readership's ability to distinguish Curtis's use of "real" Native Americans from the practice of commercial filmmakers employing White actors to play Indian roles, Bush's reference to the "naturalness" of Curtis's "full-blooded Indians" also pays tribute to the familiar image of the American Indian as Noble Savage. Likewise, Bush's ease in essentializing the Native American and his praise for Curtis's privileged access to and power over his subjects suggests the heroicized figure of the White showman-explorer.

The aesthetic qualities of Curtis's film were also celebrated in 1915 by poet and film theorist Vachel Lindsay, who described visiting the Chicago Art Institute and New York's Metropolitan Museum of Art looking for "sculpture, painting, and architecture that might be the basis for the photoplays of the future."[41] Based on this research, Lindsay argued that "the photoplay of the American Indian should in most instances be planned as a bronze in action [although] the tribes should not move so rapidly that the panther-like elasticity is lost in the riding, running and scalping."[42] For Lindsay, the "action moving picture" called for the mood of bronze figurative sculpture due to the metal's supposed elasticity and its ability to highlight "tendon, ligament, and bone" rather than muscle. Praising Curtis's film as a "work of a life-time . . . [and] supreme art achievement," Lindsay contended that *In the Land of the Head-Hunters* abounded with such "noble bronzes."[43] Lindsay's references suggest an aesthetic analogy to bronze as the classical medium for the representation of movement; however, Lindsay's racial coding (later in the same chapter he describes [African] aborigines in a comedy about cannibalism as being "like living ebony and silver") seems to speak as much about White cultural assumptions about the exotic and aestheticized Other as about classical art history.[44]

Despite such elevated critical praise for *Head-Hunters* and Curtis's own efforts to distinguish his film from more mainstream motion pictures featuring Native American subjects, many commercial films featuring Native Americans around that time evoked similar ethnographic claims. Ethnographic verisimilitude was frequently offered as a normative criterion by moving picture reviewers who scorned the enormous liberties taken with customs, costumes, and settings of Native American culture. Critics also debated whether or not "real" Native Americans should be cast in films, frequently invoking the same ethnographic verisimilitude as when Bush praised Curtis for using "full-blooded Indians." This interest in "ethnographic realism" is clearly part of a larger shift toward more "realistic motivation" in the emerging film industry as a whole.[45] An editorial entitled "The 'Make-Believe' Indian" in a 1911 issue of *Moving Picture World* drew attention to the hypocrisy of critical demands for film realism at a time when Native Americans continued to be played by White actors. Yoking the representation of the American Indian as Noble Savage to the ideology of salvage ethnography, the reviewer posed a question: "While we still have the real Indians with us . . . cannot thoroughly representative films be produced, making them at once illustrative and historic recorders of this noble race of people, with their splendid physique and physical prowess?"[46]

The following week, *Moving Picture World* reported the visit to Washington, D.C., of a group of Native Americans to complain about their filmic representation. The delegation charged that "moving picture promoters in order to get thrilling pictures of the Indians have used white men costumed as Indians in depicting scenes that are not true pictures of the Indian and are in fact grossly libelous" and urged congressional action to regulate moving pictures.[47] In an implicit defense of the representation of Native Americans in the early film Western, the editor of the same issue of *Moving Picture World* published a letter apparently from a Native American reader in Rochester, New York. Although the reader attacked Westerns for their exaggeration of the fighting prowess of White protagonists (such as five pioneers chasing away twelve Indians), he praised the majority of films for their accurate portrayal of Native American life.[48] Around the same time, critic W. Stephen Bush enumerated a taxonomy of stereotypes of Native Americans used by filmmakers of the Western, noting acerbically that "we have Licensed Indians and Independent Indians—the only kind we lack are real Indians."[49] Similar criticism was voiced from anthropological quarters; protesting to the *New York Times* in 1914, Alanson Skinner, assistant curator of the Department of Anthropology at the American Museum of Natural History, argued that "from the standpoint of a student, most of the picture plays shown are ethnologically grotesque farces. Delawares are dressed as Sioux, and the Indians of Manhattan Island are shown dwelling in skin tipis of the type used only by the tribes beyond the Mississippi."[50]

Defending the practice of the filmic convention of using White actors as Native Americans, Ernest Alfred Dench's 1915 book *Making the Movies* warned of the dangers of casting real Native Americans in moving pictures. Dench objected to recent efforts to employ Native Americans on three grounds: because receiving a salary would merely keep Native American actors furnished with "tobacco and their worshipped 'firewater'"; because "they put their heart and soul into work, especially battles with the Whites, and it is necessary to have armed guards watch over their movements for the least sign of treachery"; and because Whites are "past masters" at playing Native American roles and with clever makeup are indistinguishable from actual Native Americans.[51]

Dench's rationalizations for the simultaneous incorporation of representations of Native Americans and their exclusion as actors in those representations may seem extreme, but this dual process operated across a range of filmmaking practices and critical commentary from the period. The appeal of American Indian narratives in a variety of artistic modes and exhibition sites across diverse class strata of early twentieth-century American culture is suggested by anthropologist Clark Wissler in the introduction to his 1917 textbook, *The American Indian,* in which he claims that the American Indian was "the source . . . [for] the most original artist of our present-day culture and a heritage upon which we may realize more and more."[52] Thus, professional anthropologists attempted to popularize their young academic field by using the enormous appeal of Indian subjects in popular visual culture, just as filmmakers and other showmen borrowed the scientific legitimacy of anthropologists in their mass entertainments. Despite the ubiquity of Native Americans as subjects in films and popular culture of the time, however, the issue of who is speaking in these films was rarely addressed by filmmakers or critics. Edison's films illustrate George Wharton James's fear of cultural rituals being reduced to ethnographic spectacle, whereas Dixon's film uses didactic intertitles to interpellate the (White) spectator into the comfortable position of historical witness. These diverse films of dances, historical reconstructions, and fictional narratives are united by the complex negotiations of the tensions between science and popular entertainment and between the Native American as timeless tragic figure versus historical actor. In these negotiations, anthropology was used as a legitimizing discourse by each of these filmmakers to distinguish commercially motivated "caught fragments" of Native American identity from more "authentic" renditions. In addition to recirculating existing ideology and introducing new problems relating to cinema's potential as an ethnographic record, moving pictures featuring Native Americans provide evidence of the larger historical problem of American identity and self-representation, and they highlight some of the enduring conceptual and ethical problems of ethnographic filmmaking.

Notes

I would like to thank Antonia Lant, Richard Allen, Robert Sklar, Karen Schwartzman, and William Boddy, as well as Joel Sweimler at the American Museum of Natural History, Special Collections, for assistance with this essay.

1. For example, see Charles Musser's discussion of the practices of traveling exhibitor Burton Holmes in *High-Class Moving Pictures: Lyman H. Howe and the Forgotten Era of Traveling Exhibition, 1880–1920* (Princeton: Princeton University Press, 1991), p. 82.

2. Clark Wissler, *The American Indian: An Introduction to the Anthropology of the New World* (New York: Oxford University Press, 1922), p. xvi.

3. According to Charles Musser, these performers were brought to Thomas Edison's studio in the fall of 1894. In addition to *Indian War Council* and *Sioux Ghost Dance,* two other films, *Buffalo Dance* and *Buffalo Bill,* were shot, the latter featuring seventeen Native Americans. All these were filmed on September 24, 1894. See Kinetoscope Company, *Price*

Lists of Films, May–June 1895, p. 3, and Edison Manufacturing Company, *Edison Film,* March 1990, p. 19, cited in Musser, *Before the Nickelodeon* (Berkeley: University of California Press, 1991), p. 50.

4. For background information on the Ghost Dance religion see Alice Beck Kehoe, *The Ghost Dance: Ethnohistory and Revitalization* (New York: Holt, Rinehart and Winston, 1983) and James Mooney, *The Ghost-Dance Religion and the Sioux Outbreak of 1890* (Lincoln: University of Nebraska Press, 1991). These Edison films were also part of a wider practice of filmic reconstruction that included subjects such as the Spanish-American War and boxing films.

5. Pierre-L. Jordan, *Premier contact—premier regard* (Marseilles: Musées de Marseille, 1992), pp. 33–34. According to Jordan, five other films produced as part of the same series include *Panoramic View of Moki Land, Parade of the Snake Dance Before the Dance, The March of the Prayer and the Entrance of the Dancers, Line-Up and Teasing the Snakes,* and *Carrying Out the Snakes,* all shot in Walpi Pueblo, Arizona.

6. Marshall Deutelbaum, "Structural Patterning in the Lumière Films," in John Fell, ed., *Film Before Griffith* (Berkeley: University of California Press, 1983), pp. 299–310.

7. George Wharton James, "The Snake Dance of the Hopis," in *Camera Craft* (1) (November 1902), p. 10. Emphasis added.

8. Robert F. Berkhofer, Jr., *The White Man's Indian: Images of the American Indian from Columbus to the Present* (New York: Vintage Books, 1979), pp. 4–5.

9. George Catlin, *North American Indians, Being Letters and Notes on Their Manners, Customs, Written During Eight Years Travel Amongst the Wildest Tribes of Indians in America* (Edinburgh: John Grant, 1841), vol. 1, p. 293, as quoted in Berkhofer, *White Man's Indian,* p. 88. Emphasis in original.

10. Clark Wissler, "The Catlin Paintings," *American Museum Journal* 12 (3) (March 1912), pp. 89–93. Emphasis added.

11. Berkhofer, *White Man's Indian,* p. 29.

12. Roger Sanjek, "Anthropology's Hidden Colonialism: Assistants and Their Ethnographers," *Anthropology Today* 9 (2) (April 1993), p. 14.

13. Curtis M. Hinsley, "The World as Market-Place: Commodification of the Exotic at the World's Columbian Exposition," in Ivan Karp and Steven B. Lavine, eds., *Exhibiting Cultures: The Poetics and Politics of Museum Display* (Washington, D.C.: Smithsonian Institution Press, 1991), p. 350.

14. W. J. McGee, "Strange Races of Men," in *World's Work* 8 (1) (May 1904), p. 5188.

15. Curtis M. Hinsley, "Anthropology as Science and Politics: The Dilemmas of the Bureau of American Ethnology, 1879 to 1904," in W. R. Goldschmidt, *Uses of Anthropology* (Washington, D.C.: American Anthropological Association, 1979), p. 17.

16. Ibid., p. 19. The BAE was headed by John Wesley Powell, who had previously been special commissioner of Indian affairs and was responsible for investigating the conditions of Native American life and reporting his findings to Congress.

17. Joseph K. Dixon, *The Vanishing Race* (New York: Doubleday Page and Company, 1913), p. xv.

18. Joseph K. Dixon, *Wanamaker Primer on the North American Indian* (Philadelphia: Wanamaker Originator, 1909), p. 44.

19. Susan Applegate Krouse, "Filming the Vanishing Race," in Jay Ruby and Martin Taureg, eds., *Visual Explorations of the World: Selected Papers from the International Conference on Visual Communication* (Aatchen: Editions Heridot, 1987), p. 260. A more detailed

version of Krouse's essay, titled "Photographing the Vanishing Race," was published in a special issue of *Visual Anthropology,* edited by Joanna Cohan Scherer, 1990, 3 (2–3), pp. 213–233. According to Krouse, only fourteen reels of film from the over seventy-five taken by Dixon survive. The National Archives Motion Picture and Sound Recording Branch owns twelve of the remaining reels, and the Human Studies Film Archive in Washington, D.C. owns one of the Dixon reels.

20. Dixon's recruitment of Buffalo Bill Cody, whose historical reenactments of Indian-White conflicts were staples in Cody's Wild West Show, brings the film into the culturally mythic territory of history as pageant and carnivalesque spectacle.

21. Dixon, *Vanishing Race,* p. xv.

22. Joseph K. Dixon, *The Rodman Wanamaker Expedition of Citizenship to the North American Indian: Address of the President of the United States and Other Messages* (summer 1913), p. 3. Department of Library Services, Special Collections, American Museum of Natural History (AMNH).

23. F. H. Abbott letter "To the Superintendents of Indian Reservations," in Dixon, *Rodman Wanamaker Expedition,* p. 16. Emphasis added.

24. Joseph K. Dixon, *The Purpose and Achievements of the Rodman Wanamaker Expedition of Citizenship to the North American Indian* (n.p.: summer and autumn 1913), p. 1. Department of Library Services, Special Collections, AMNH.

25. The title of the film itself is indicative of a voyeuristic relation to the Other and was changed by Holm and Quimby to *In the Land of the War Canoes* because they felt the original title "put undue emphasis on what was actually a minor if visible and spectacular aspect of Kwakiutl life." They argue that although Curtis may have anticipated a box-office advantage by referring to headhunting, the use of the term wrongly implied that the custom was more important than it actually was. For a detailed overview of the restoration project that took place between 1967 and 1974, see B. Holm and G. I. Quimby, *Edward S. Curtis in the Land of the War Canoes: A Pioneer Cinematographer in the Pacific Northwest Coast* (Seattle: University of Washington Press, 1980), p. 65. See also Rosalind C. Morris's discussion of the film in her book *New Worlds from Fragments: Film, Ethnography, and the Representation of Northwest Coast Culture* (Boulder: Westview Press, 1994), pp. 39–41.

26. Christopher Lyman, *The Vanishing Race and Other Illusions: Photography of Indians by Edward Curtis* (Washington, D.C.: Smithsonian Institution Press, 1982), p. 17.

27. Ibid., p. 60.

28. See Lyman, *Vanishing Race and Other Illusions,* pp. 62–112, for a discussion of Curtis's photographic practices. For general information on the manipulation and stereotyping of Native American in late nineteenth- and early twentieth-century photography, see Margaret B. Blackman, "Posing the American Indian," *Natural History* 89 (10) (October 1980), pp. 68–74, and Joanna Cohan Scherer, "You Can't Believe Your Eyes: Inaccuracies in Photographs of North American Indians," *Studies in the Anthropology of Visual Communication* 2 (2) (1975), pp. 67–79, and "The Public Faces of Sarah Winnemucca," *Cultural Anthropology* 3 (2) (May 1988), pp. 78–204.

29. Quoted in Holm and Quimby, *Edward S. Curtis,* p. 32.

30. Ibid., p. 113.

31. Ibid., p. 32.

32. Edward Curtis letter to J. Pierpont Morgan, January 23, 1906, quoted in Lyman, *Vanishing Race and Other Illusions,* p. 60.

33. Holm and Quimby, *Edward S. Curtis,* p. 59.

34. Ira Jacknis, "George Hunt, Kwakiutl Photographer," in Elizabeth Edwards, ed., *Anthropology and Photography* (New Haven: Yale University Press, 1992), p. 144.

35. Ibid., p. 145.

36. Lyman, *Vanishing Race and Other Illusions*, p. 118.

37. For a discussion of Boas's own alterations of his ethnographic material, see Ira Jacknis, "Franz Boas and Photography," *Studies in the Anthropology of Visual Communication* 10 (1) (1984), pp. 2–60.

38. Edward Curtis, "The Continental Film Company," 1912, appendix in Holm and Quimby, *Edward S. Curtis*, p. 113.

39. Stephen W. Bush, "In the Land of the Head-Hunters," *Moving Picture World*, December 19, 1914, p. 1695.

40. Ibid.

41. Vachel Lindsay, *The Art of the Moving Picture* (New York: Liveright, 1913), p. 115.

42. Ibid., p. 114.

43. Ibid., p. 115.

44. Ibid., p. 121.

45. See David Bordwell, Janet Staiger, and Kristin Thompson, *The Classical Hollywood Cinema: Film Style and Mode of Production to 1960* (New York: Columbia University Press, 1985), pp. 19–21, for a discussion of their term "realistic motivation." Thanks to Richard Allen for clarifying this point.

46. *Moving Picture World*, March 4, 1911, p. 473.

47. *Moving Picture World*, March 11, 1911, p. 58.

48. *Moving Picture World*, March 18, 1911, p. 600.

49. Stephen W. Bush, "Moving Picture Absurdities," *Moving Picture World*, September 16, 1911, p. 733.

50. Alanson Skinner, *New York Times*, June 3, 1914, p. 12, as quoted in Kevin Brownlow, *The War, the West, and the Wilderness* (New York: Alfred A. Knopf, 1979), p. 329. Despite Skinner's scorn for ethnographic liberty-taking, he had on previous occasions served as a consultant for commercial filmmakers. For example, in early 1913, filmmaker F. E. Moore wrote to Skinner requesting information about Ojibway and Sioux burial customs for his proposed film version of *Hiawatha*. The Department of Anthropology at the AMNH lent Moore a large number of props and costumes for his film, which was later shown at that museum on April 13, 1914. The event was cohosted by the AMNH and the American Scenic and Historic Preservation Society. Department of Anthropology archives, AMNH, Alanson Skinner file.

51. Alfred Ernest Dench, *Making the Movies* (New York: Macmillan, 1915), pp. 92–94.

52. Wissler, *American Indian*, p. xvii.

7

"There Is Madness in the Air": The 1926 Haskell Homecoming and Popular Representations of Sports in Federal Indian Boarding Schools

John Bloom

At the east end of the Carlisle Plaza Mall, on the wall separating the K-Mart from the decorative water fountain in the shopping center's main corridor, there is a glass-encased mural that chronicles "Carlisle Through History." There, shoppers can gaze at artwork depicting a number of scenes from this small Pennsylvania town's past. In the center of the mural, a U.S. cavalry officer in late nineteenth-century uniform sits at a registration desk for the Carlisle Indian Industrial School. In front of him stands a line of very noble and grateful-looking Native Americans who appear eager to have their names placed on the registration list. Next to this image is one of a helmetless football player galloping with a pigskin tucked under his arm. In case one does not recognize the face, mock newspapers surround him with headlines such as, "Indians Scalp Army, 27–6; Jim Thorpe on Rampage."

In the words of the mural's creator, retired U.S. Army Colonel Charles Tyson, the point of this public art piece is to portray events that "put Carlisle on the map." Yet the mural also highlights something that was important to the lives of Native Americans: the Carlisle Indian Industrial School, the federal government's first off-reservation boarding school for Native Americans, opened in 1879 and closed in 1918. The mural's sequence on the school is a story of *progress*, of Indians transforming themselves from noble savages into national symbols of individual athletic success. In fact, sports were a prominent aspect of life at many Indian boarding schools like Carlisle. In this mural, however, athletics serve a specific function. They are a symbol of assimilation, a marker of civilization.

Other off-reservation boarding schools created during the same time period also thrived, becoming nationally or regionally famous for their football, track, baseball, or boxing teams. School administrators generally found sports to be a good source of publicity. Not only did winning teams spread a school's name but they also provided an easily interpreted set of representations that fit well with the boarding-school agenda. Successful athletics signified that Indians were taking to modern life, were dutifully accepting its rules, and were capable of shedding their old cultures.

In fall 1926, however, the Haskell Institute in Lawrence, Kansas, hosted a major sporting event that frustrated supporters of assimilation. It was a homecoming to dedicate a new stadium for its nationally famous football team. The intention, like that of the Carlisle Plaza Mall mural, was to portray Native American cultures as relics of the past and present sports as a symbol of progress and civilization. In the end, however, the Haskell Homecoming generated a far more ambiguous set of images. It was an illuminating moment, in that it reveals how representations of Indian boarding-school sports during the early part of this century contained and framed larger hegemonic struggles over Native American life.

Federal Indian Boarding Schools

Off-reservation boarding schools were the outgrowth of policy changes by the federal government toward Native Americans during the late nineteenth century. They emerged from a more general set of policies designed to assimilate Native Americans into mainstream, Anglo-Protestant norms by transforming the "system of values" that many government officials believed were characteristic of Native American cultures. The government in Washington isolated two areas in which to concentrate this attempt at forced cultural change: land use, and the education of children. Congress addressed the land issue by adopting severalty laws, such as the Dawes Act of 1887, which allotted tribal members individually parceled plots of land to farm and manage.[1]

Boarding schools were the federal answer to the problem of Indian education.[2] Drawing on a model set forth by missionaries, boarding schools took students away from their homes and often from their tribes and provided a rigidly disciplined education.[3] General Richard Henry Pratt, who founded and served as superintendent of Carlisle between 1879 and 1904, was the most influential white activist leading the boarding school movement. A veteran of Indian wars and fervent believer in assimilation, Pratt initiated an educational program among a group of Cheyenne prisoners of war under his charge at Fort Marion in Saint Augustine, Florida. He eventually sought to bring these prisoners into a formal boarding-school setting and in 1878 did so by transferring several prisoners into the traditionally African-American Hampton Institute in Hampton, Virginia.

After a year Pratt moved north again and established a boarding school exclusively for Native Americans at an abandoned army base in Carlisle, Pennsylvania.[4]

Over the next twenty-one years, the federal government rapidly increased its appropriations toward Indian education, and boarding schools became the cornerstone of national Indian educational policy. By 1900, there were a total of 113 federal boarding schools (25 of which were off-reservation) in addition to 47 mission boarding schools. These institutions enrolled 22,832 students, or over 80 percent of all Indian children in school.[5]

At Carlisle, Pratt imposed rigid discipline to bring his students into "civilization." He modeled Carlisle after a military boarding school, an example followed by all of the off-reservation schools created around the country. Students marched in drills and wore military uniforms. They were prohibited from using their Native languages, from wearing their traditional hair styles or clothing, from practicing their native religions, and from using their former names.[6] Students at Carlisle and at the other federal boarding schools more often resembled prisoners than pupils. Many were forcibly removed from their homes when as young as five or six years old.

While at school, students were under constant surveillance by the staff, and a daily schedule occupied nearly every waking moment of a student's life, leaving almost nothing up to an individual's imagination and allowing almost no room for free expression.[7]

Within this context of discipline and assimilation, sports were employed in two important ways. First, they were generally included as part of a more comprehensive physical education curriculum designed both to reformulate the bodies of students and, just as important, to provide some measure of playful recreation. Second, sports were used as a vehicle for public relations. The deliberateness and complexity of this second purpose should not be underestimated, particularly at Carlisle. As early as 1881, only two years after the institution was founded, Pratt wrote in his annual report to the commissioner of Indian Affairs about the construction of a gymnasium for the boys: "Regular physical instruction is given, and from all that can now be seen we may eventually rival Cornell, Amherst, or Columbia in athletic prowess."[8] His words were particularly prophetic—or perhaps they were a self-fulfilling prophesy.

Interpretations of the Representation of Indian School Athletics

Thus, from the outset, one of the most influential boarding-school advocates in the United States showed a keen interest in the representations that sports created for boarding schools. Few scholars have critically examined the meanings of media images of boarding-school athletes, though the work of those who have takes two main directions. Some have tended to see representations of boarding-school athletes as being unambiguously negative and stereotypical. Others have understood them as metaphorical, representing popular ideas about race, but not necessarily anything unique about Indians.

Ward Churchill, for example, has written about the hurtful stereotypes circulated in popular press accounts of boarding school athletic heroes. He sees sports as confirming racist notions that have framed Indians in the public mind as "overwhelmingly physical creature(s)." Although victories on the athletic field might have seemed empowering to many American Indians at the turn of the century, Churchill sees their meaning as effectively neutralized, and even turned against Indians, by the stereotypes and conventions employed in the mass media.[9]

The Carlisle Plaza Mall mural certainly supports Churchill's assessment, presenting Jim Thorpe to contemporary audiences as a kind of raging bull on a "rampage." Yet Churchill generally understands representations of Indian athletes as having an extremely seamless set of meanings. He allows little room for exploring the nuances of sports coverage or its textured meanings to different audiences. Michael Oriard, in his study of popular football journalism during the late nineteenth century, provides a more intimate analysis of specific ways in which Carlisle's football team was represented. Yet Oriard hardly sees Native American history as at all significant to media representations of boarding-school athletics. He writes, "Indians were not a 'problem' in the 1890s; exterminated or confined to reservations, they posed no danger to white Americans." Oriard concludes that newspaper coverage of Carlisle reveals more about racial ideology than it does about Native Americans. "The unspoken subject of Carlisle football was probably the black Americans and Southern European immigrants, who indeed posed unresolved problems for the shrinking Anglo-Saxon majority at the turn-of-the-century."[10]

Unlike Churchill, Oriard does not see American Indians as the primary targets of racial stereotypes, viewing them mostly as stand-ins for those more relevant to the lives of eastern, white, middle-class newspaper readers. Oriard's source material is derived particularly from the New York daily and weekly presses, and he may provide an accurate understanding of what the coverage he describes might have meant to its audiences. However, Indians did not cease to exist in the 1890s, and the federal policies that created schools like Carlisle in the first place suggest that they were indeed a "problem" to some in white society. Representations of Indian boarding-school sports were, in fact, very much linked to the particulars of Native American history.

Local newspapers and Indian service agencies in the vicinity of boarding schools also covered sports at these institutions. They employed a variety of narratives regarding progress, "savagery," civilization, and sexuality that were relevant in specific ways to Native American history. Although these narrative accounts often portray Indians as physical beings, each also manages to contain a symbolic conflict between Indians and whites embodied in boarding-school sports, something that could have sustained the hopes and pride of indigenous populations through difficult times. In other words, press coverage of Native American sports can be seen as part of a hegemonic struggle to contain resistance on a cultural level relevant to the social circumstances and history of white–Native American relations. This struggle over meaning can best be seen at moments when contradictions over sports have risen to the surface, when no account or set of images could completely contain an undertone of Native American refusal to accept dominant society's terms. One such moment occurred in 1926 with the homecoming celebration and football game at Haskell Institute.[11]

Plans for the Homecoming

Between 1925 and 1926, motivated in part by the success and national fame of the Haskell football team during the 1920s, Native Americans from across the United States took part in a massive fund-raising campaign to construct a new, 10,500-seat stadium on Haskell's Lawrence, Kansas, campus. They raised between $180,000 and $250,000, and by fall 1926, the new venue was ready. That Halloween weekend, representatives of over seventy tribes and nations gathered at Haskell to dedicate the stadium in what promised to be the most spectacular homecoming celebration any Indian boarding school had ever seen. In addition to the game scheduled on Saturday between Haskell and Bucknell College, the three-day festivities were to include a powwow, traditional Native American dances, and gatherings of tribes in their traditional clothing. Yet within the context of boarding-school history and the position of sports within the structure of boarding-school life, these festivities were unsettling, for they implicitly acknowledged the continuing survival of vital and diverse Native American cultures. Indeed, boarding-school administrators often stated in explicit terms that football was supposed to promote gentlemanly virtue, sportsmanship, and respect for white opponents, not a return to tribal cultures and traditions.

One of those who objected to the Haskell celebration was E. D. Mossman, superintendent from the Standing Rock Agency in Fort Yates, North Dakota. After receiving a circular pamphlet announcing the event, Mossman wrote to Commissioner of Indian Affairs Charles H. Burke to express his protest. Among other things, Mossman objected to four pictures on the cover of a circular that "depict the Indian as he was and as many of them would still love to be" (he did not describe the circular beyond this). Mossman went on to argue that it should have pictured more desirable role models such as those of the "farmer, laborer or business man." Echoing the rhetoric of Pratt, he wrote of the average Native American, "Either he must be taken into the body politic as a citizen like other citizens or he must perish. The Indian loves to look backward and in my opinion this celebration is a most decisive backward step."[12]

Using terminology common among white reformers of the time, Mossman went on to write that the celebration would only serve to enhance the position of "reactionary" elements among tribes that resisted the "progressive" guidance of "Christian Indians, missionaries or educators."[13]

The Reverend Henry H. Treat from the Red Stone Mission in Anadarko, Oklahoma, expressed similar dismay and was particularly upset by the dances to be performed at the celebration. Expressing both a race and class bias, he wrote to Burke:

> I am hurt, as were all of us missionaries, that just because of a desire for a great crowd at this home coming to Haskell, it should seem to be necessary to undo the work of thirty five years of attempt to help make these Kiowa, Comanche, and others, Christian citizens. We believe that the Department and the School have put themselves on a level with the cheap John white trash of these parts who make rodeos and picnics and keep the Indians going from one dance to another all the summer long.[14]

Treat sent Burke a copy of a resolution drafted by the Annual Conference of Indian Missionary Workers, which met in Anadarko on October 19 and 20, 1926, in which the missionaries characterized traditional Native American dances as "subversive of the teachings of the Christian religion, and of the best that is being developed in the lives of the Indian people." The conference resolved that such customs "are highly detrimental to their economic, moral and religious advancement."[15]

H. B. Peairs, the general superintendent of Indian Education within the Bureau of Indian Affairs, defended his decision to allow such a celebration of Native American cultures by explaining how it fit into the progressive narratives that guided federal Indian policy. "There is no more effective method of teaching a lesson on any subject than by means of making comparisons and contrasts. The program rendered at Haskell certainly was an opportunity to put on several contests which did very positively show progress of Indians through education."[16]

In other words, the display of war dances and "costume" by visiting tribes could be framed as a kind of picturesque relic of the past. Publicly presented, it could demonstrate the evolutionary ideology that guided federal Indian educational policy. The entire celebration could provide a stage for showing Haskell students as formerly primitive beings, earnestly and successfully struggling to gain a foothold on civilization. Far from preserving traditions, the presentation of Native American culture in the present, as a kind of entertainment show for white football audiences, could actually cement them in the past by rendering them meaningless—little more than decorative display. Peairs hoped popular representations would present Indian cultures as a thing of the past and Indians, for all practical purposes, as a dead people.

Framing the Event

This kind of presentation, or framing, was particularly important at the historical moment of the homecoming. In 1924, only two years before the stadium dedication, Native Americans had been granted federal citizenship. Although this move did grant many tribal members new rights, it also burdened them with many more responsibilities (like military service and taxation) and made it easier for their land legally to be taken from them. Recognizing this, some tribes refused to accept citizenship. Others, however, accepted it and struggled to carve out a place for Native Americans in mainstream American life. The fund-raising and con-struction effort to build the stadium was a prime example of such an effort.

On the one hand, Indian boarding-school administrators like Peairs wanted to demonstrate that the next generation of Native Americans was "ready" for citizen-ship (see Figure 7.1). This not only meant that they would be able to wear starched clothing and speak English but that they would accept the subordinate status for which they were being trained at schools like Haskell. On the other hand, the assertion of traditional cultural expressions at the homecoming also suggests that many American Indians may have understood the terms of their cit-izenship in ways that conflicted with the aims of the federal government. The framing of their traditions quite literally *contained* real historical experiences that continued to define Native American groups as a vital and surviving people.

Two print media sources, the local press and the Indian service (which printed the Haskell weekly newspaper and the stadium program on the day of the game), illustrate the extent to which administrators like Peairs were successful in "fram-ing" this event. Papers like the *Kansas City Times,* the *Kansas City Star,* the *Kansas City Journal,* the *Topeka Daily State Journal,* and the *Muskogee Daily Phoenix* all provided extensive coverage of the weekend festivities, including feature sto-ries and captioned front-page photographs. Each tended to present the familiar

Figure 7.1 *Photograph of Haskell's Homecoming Parade float, published in the school's official weekly publication,* The Indian Leader. *Through such public representations, school administrators hoped to display a narrative of progress associated with federal efforts to educate Native Americans. Courtesy Kansas Collection, University of Kansas Libraries.*

narrative of progress—the linear uplifting of Indians from their noble savagery to civilization. Some, however, also employed sensational descriptions that could have been understood in complex ways. Among the most common portrayals of Indians visiting Lawrence that weekend were those that employed the notion of "noble savage."

Popular representations of Native Americans have long employed the motif of the noble savage, which Robert Berkhofer, Jr., has described as that of the Indian as close to nature, simple, brave, and innocent.[17] Such images had long been used by boarding schools to illustrate their progressive mission.[18] Noble Indians were presented as members of a dying race and as holders of long-dead traditions that were no longer a threat to white people, their ambitions, or their values.

Newspapers presented the noble savage image in their coverage of the Haskell Homecoming repeatedly, sometimes explicitly linking it to progressive narratives. The *Kansas City Journal,* for example, published a series of five photographs on page three of its front section the Friday before the game, under the headline "Lawrence Harks Back to Frontier Days as Indians 'Take' City for the Biggest Pow Wow in History." The photos progress from left to right (numbered one through five) and are framed underneath by the following caption: "Indians have captured Lawrence again. But this time it is a pleased Lawrence that watches the influx of representatives of fifty tribes attending the biggest Pow Wow in history on the campus of the Haskell Indian Institute. Above are typical scenes of the Pow Wow."[19]

The photos themselves show a portrait of Osage Chief Bacon Rind in the first frame, followed by a photo of Blackfoot Indians in traditional clothing doing a war dance. The third photo represents a kind of transition, an ironic juxtaposition of an Indian chief dressed in fringed leather leaning against the hood of a car. The caption highlights the irony of this image: "A chief bows to Father Time and substitutes a modern war horse for his traditional pony." This image and caption not only convey humor, but they do so by presenting modern technology as a natural component of the progress of time. This further positions Native American traditions as relics of the past that, in a practical sense, are incompatible with the present. The fourth photo is of a baby who won the "baby contest," dressed in a white-lace outfit, and the final photo is of "Miss Hazel Dupuis" the beauty queen winner who wears makeup and is dressed in a fur-lined coat and a fashionable hat and dress.

This progressive vision was an implicit part of noble savage representations that characterized other less explicitly narrative press descriptions of this event. Such representations emerged particularly in descriptions of the Blackfoot war dances that took place that weekend. For example, the caption for a photo in the *Muskogee Daily Phoenix* read, "Hoop-la, the Redskins are out for scalps again! But only in athletic contests this time. With thousands of Indians celebrating—one of the chief events being a war dance contest—a $250,000 stadium at Haskell Institute, Lawrence, Kansas, now is duly dedicated and ready for 'warfare.'"[20]

The *Phoenix*'s representation of the war dance is very similar to that of the other paper, in that both make light of it as no longer threatening. Football is established as the modern replacement for war. Unlike war, however, the outcome of a football game has no lasting consequences—no land is ceded, nobody is killed, no treaties need to be signed. These war dances then could be observed safely and even humorously by whites. That they were safe to observe proved that an era of Indian resistance was over; indeed, its passing could be nostalgically lamented.

The Indian service press newspaper at Haskell, the *Indian Leader,* which published both the official game program and an extensive postgame issue, also employed the noble savage motif in this manner. The cover of the program is an artistic rendering of an Indian chief in floor-length feather warbonnet and fringed leather shirt and leggings. He passes the newly built Haskell football stadium in his arms to a young Indian boy, who wears only a loincloth, moccasins, and two feathers in his braided hair. They stand on a bluff overlooking a grassy pasture (Fig. 7.2). The following passage was printed inside the program, expressing a theme repeated in press clippings of the day—that theme being amazement that such a friendly gathering of Indians and whites could take place only fifty years after the Battle of Little Bighorn (which had occurred in summer 1876).

> Haskell Institute is the largest Indian school in the world. Its mission is the fitting of young Indian men and women for the problems of life which white civilization has brought to the Indian race. When one stops to consider that Haskell Institute is dedicating a huge stadium just fifty years after ancestors of its pupils fought at the battle of Little Big Horn, some idea of the huge success of Indian education can be gathered.[21]

After the game, the next issue of the *Indian Leader* declared that the pregame festivities and the game itself "presented a thrilling pictorial scene, mingling the past, the present, and the future." Like the popular press, the Indian press took special note of the Blackfoot dances: "A band of Blackfeet in ceremonial costume, arriving Wednesday, October 27, lent picturesqueness to the Pow-Wow and reminded crowds of the rapid rise of the Indian race in the last few decades from the days of prairie warfare to the dedication of a school stadium, comparable to many of the magnificent college stadiums of the country."[22]

Together, these visual and verbal images not only present Native American culture as a thing of the past but also present Indian resistance as no longer existent. They implicitly or explicitly construct a history. This was one way in which the display of cultures at the homecoming was contained hegemonically—the cultures were acknowledged only as a nonthreatening picturesque relic from the past. In fact, public chronicles of the homecoming festivities interpreted the pow-wow itself as an implicit endorsement of boarding-school education. The display of traditional dancing and clothing confirmed a narrative of progress, in which elders representing their vanishing race came to observe their modern children.

This link between noble savagery and progressive narratives was further reinforced in subtle images of gender drawn from the event. One of the most popular

Figure 7.2 *Cover of official Haskell Homecoming Game program. It provides a vivid example of the noble savage motif being employed in the service of a progressive narrative. Courtesy Kansas Collection, University of Kansas Libraries.*

motifs employed in the coverage of Indian school sports was the portrayal of Native American men as unusually good sports who played rough games like football with a high regard for gentlemanly virtue, fairness, and clean play. Oriard describes such treatments as common for Carlisle's players, and they also permeated the local press coverage of teams from schools like Phoenix and Haskell.

Noting the emphasis on such representations is not to deny that Indian school athletes were unusually good sports on the field. In fact, as Oriard mentions, players were instructed to behave in this manner. Nevertheless, this behavior became meaningful in large part through the ways in which it was popularly represented. Accounts of Indian sportsmanship were a part of both Indian service and popular press coverage of the game between Haskell and Bucknell. The game program, for example, describes Haskell's head football coach, R. E. Hanley, as someone whose leadership "won [Haskell students] the reputation of being hard, clean fighters who often fight their way up from behind to win." The *Indian Leader*'s postgame special issue reprinted the following letter sent to the *Topeka Daily State Journal*.

Although it focuses on the behavior of fans, the letter links this to the gentlemanly virtue of the whole school:

> The Haskell Institute last Saturday set a precedent for a football contest that might well be followed by other institutions of learning throughout the country. On arriving at the Haskell grounds and in the Indian village one noticed scores of football fans wearing little tags upon which were the words, "welcome Bucknell.". . . This courtesy to a visiting football team appeared to be a marked contrast to such phrases as "Twist the Tiger's Tail," "Beat the Jayhawks," "Beat the Teachers," and countless other expressions. Football, like other sports, can be played hard and for all that is in it, but courtesy is the first step for a gentleman and an institution to take.[23]

This kind of praise was a double-edged sword for Haskell athletes and fans. Oriard notes, for example, the way it created standards for Carlisle's football players that were far beyond what one might reasonably expect from white teams. In addition, it also created a particularly comforting image of the Native American male as a racial type. The control of Indian men over their passions within a violent game like football confirmed for many that an era of real battle had passed. Provided Indians had a proper, white, paternal leader like R. E. Hanley, they could knock heads with whites on the football field and walk away with no hard feelings, respecting the boundaries between legitimate competition and illegitimate violence.

Such popular representations of the Haskell Homecoming make Peairs look successful in his effort to frame the powwow and dances within an overall narrative of progress and to portray American Indian cultures as having no real place in the present or the future. However, not all press coverage could be understood in this manner. In fact, some of the most sensational accounts actually presented Indians as very much alive in the present. These press accounts portrayed the visitors to Lawrence that weekend as out of control rather than as noble and subdued. They circulated images of the pregame festivities as exotic, strange, and sexually exhilarating. An article in the *Kansas City Times* best exemplifies this type of portrayal of the event. Under the headline "Like Birds and Beasts," the article describes the Friday night dances at the stadium.

> It seemed tonight as if the slinking animals of field and forest and the birds of mountain crag and wood, possessed of demons, came out into the area of the Haskell stadium to dance to frog noises from the Wkarusa and the sobbing cadence of wind . . . Aye-yah-aye-yah sing the . . . Osages, Pawnees . . . Only the must colored blankets around rounded backs are seen, but the measure excites the heart . . . Feathers become tumultuous. Knees bend grotesquely; moccasined feet descend toe downward; arms rise and fall. Beribboned weapons are twirled and swung menacingly. But the dance is stopped before ecstacy comes. Enough is enough.[24]

This journalist paints a scene of emotions uncontained. His description of the dances is almost explicitly sexual. Unlike the accounts of gentlemanly behavior in the football stadium, this article portrays this event as an unrepressed outpouring of shockingly passionate expression.

The animals and birds, squaws and children, sweep over the shadowy field in an inter-tribal dance, the combined tom-toms thundering, the grandstands echoing. It is Custer's last stand, the Halloween of beasts and birds. There is madness in the air. It would not be weird in the sunlight, but in a strip of dim light on a dark night and the air clouded with fogs of a thousand cigarettes, it was diabolism.[25]

These descriptions make the dances seem dangerous and threatening. Yet it is unlikely that the author was actually afraid of the ceremony provoking some sort of violent insurrection. Instead, it was the demonstration of Indian cultures as alive, as expressing the visions and passions repressed by the boarding schools that evoked fears. The Indian dances of that evening were followed by a display of physical education, hygiene, and gymnastics by female students who attended Haskell. This was to provide a neat narrative of progress for the audience. Yet this popular account of the evening represents this display as somewhat anticlimactic when compared to the dances that had taken place earlier: "Seventy-five Haskell girls in black bloomers and white blouses did the dance of health—gymnastics— for the benefit of the big chiefs. They marched, formed a giant letter H; did sitting up exercises."[26]

K. Tsianina Lomawaima has illustrated the significance of bloomers to boarding-school education, noting their association with control of female sexuality and the body and the ways in which such control was tied to a more general lesson of subservience under regimented authority.[27] However, compared to the lurid descriptions of the "Halloween of beasts and birds", the formation of a giant letter H is almost comically boring. This journalist presents progress as dead and the supposedly bygone rituals of Native American life as exciting and alive. No doubt this was not his intention. But no matter how unwittingly conceived, his descriptions of sexually uncontrolled savages also reveal the intense repression that "civilization" implied. These Indians still needed to be tamed. Their identities as Indians were not presented as a thing of the past but as something that was "menacingly" alive in the present. This is the irony of the progressive representations that guided the coverage of Indian boarding-school sports. The motifs employed often made the "past" more alive than the progressive narrative itself. In addition, the progressive narrative identified Indians not as assimilated beings but as Indians battling, and often winning, against white foes on a symbolic field of battle.

These media representations only let us see what whites thought of these events. But the conflicts they evoke provide clues to the ways Indians might have found sports at boarding schools important. Only five years after this event, Haskell discontinued its major college football schedule. With the administration of John Collier at the Bureau of Indian Affairs during the 1930s, Indian schools placed less emphasis on public, high-profile, interscholastic competition and more on intramural athletics and physical education. Such moves were made with the well-intentioned motive of ending the exploitation of Indian athletes by overzealous coaches and school administrators. However, a consequence of such moves may also have been the severance of an important cultural resource for twentieth-century Native Americans. As Lomawaima has written of Chilocco Indian School, although it was created by and for white people, "It was, however, an institution inhabited by Indian students, who created its everyday life. Every student knew Chilocco was an *Indian* school."[28]

On the Saturday of the dedication, Haskell trounced Bucknell 36–0. But the spectacle that football allowed before the game also made it clear that Haskell was an *Indian* school, and its football victories were victories by and for Native Americans throughout the United States.

Notes

I wish to acknowledge the 1993 National Endowment for the Humanities Summer Seminar on Native American History under the direction of Roger Nichols. In addition, I conducted other research for this article while on a fellowship from the American Council of Learned Societies. I would also like to thank Lonna Malmsheimer for directing me toward important resources and Amy Farrell for her critical comments on early drafts of this chapter.

1. This was intended to promote the ideal of independent farming, the patriarchal nuclear family, and individual land tenure, ending communal land ownership. In terms of racial ideology, small farming was seen as the next step up the evolutionary ladder to civilization, and it also made land grabs easier for western settlers and land speculators. See K. Tsianina Lomawaima, *They Called It Prairie Light: The Story of Chilocco Indian School* (Lincoln: University of Nebraska Press, 1994), pp. 3–4.

2. This connection between federal education and land policy is drawn from the analysis of Margaret Connell Szasz in her book, *Education and the American Indian: The Road to Self-Determination Since 1928* (Albuquerque: University of New Mexico Press, 1977), p. 8.

3. See Wilbert H. Ahern, "'The Returned Indians': Hampton Institute and Its Indian Alumni, 1879–1893," *Journal of Ethnic Studies* 10 (4), pp. 101–124; Michael Coleman, *American Indian Children at School: 1850–1930* (Jackson: University of Mississippi Press, 1993); Sally McBeth, "The Primer and the Hoe," *Natural History* 93 (8) (August 1984), pp. 4–12; Lonna M. Malmsheimer, "Photographic Analysis as Ethnohistory: Interpretive Strategies," *Visual Anthropology* 1 (1987), pp. 21–36; Margaret Connell Szasz, "Listening to the Native Voice," *Montana: The Magazine of Western History* 39 (3) (1989), pp. 42–53.

4. Richard Henry Pratt, *Battlefield and Classroom: Four Decades with the American Indian 1867–1904,* ed. Robert M. Utley (New Haven: Yale University Press, 1964).

5. Wilbert Ahern, "'To Kill the Indian and Save the Man': The Boarding School and American Indian Education," in Larry Remele, ed., *Fort Totten: Military Post and Indian School, 1867–1959* (Bismarck: State Historical Society of North Dakota, 1986), pp. 23–59.

6. For an account of the disciplinary procedures at the Santa Fe Indian School at the turn of the century, see Sally Hyer, *One House, One Voice, One Heart: Native American Education at the Santa Fe Indian School* (Santa Fe: Museum of New Mexico Press, 1990).

7. See K. Tsianina Lomawaima, "Domesticity in the Federal Indian Schools: The Power of Authority over Mind and Body," *American Ethnologist* 20 (1993), pp. 227–228.

8. From *The Annual Report of the Commissioner of Indian Affairs to the Secretary of the Interior for the Year 1881* (Washington, D.C.: Government Printing Office, 1881), p. 189.

9. Ward Churchill, Norbert S. Hill, and Mary Jo Barlow, "An Historical Overview of Twentieth Century Native American Athletics," *Indian Historian* 12 (4) (1979), pp. 22–32.

10. Michael Oriard, *Reading Football: How the Popular Press Created an American Spectacle* (Chapel Hill: University of North Carolina Press, 1993), p. 233.

11. George Lipsitz provides an extended discussion of collective memory among marginalized groups in American life that is relevant to my assessment of Indian boarding school sports in his book *Time Passages: Collective Memory and American Popular Culture* (Minneapolis: University of Minnesota Press, 1990). Lipsitz argues that hegemonic popular cultural forms serve to contain the counterhegemonic power of oppositional cultural expressions. Yet he also sees the popular appeal of such expressions as often lying within their submerged oppositional meanings.

12. Letter from E. D. Mossman to the Commissioner of Indian Affairs, September 14, 1926, National Archives, RG 75, box no. 2380-24-750.

13. Ibid.

14. Letter from Rev. Harry H. Treat to Charles Burke, Commissioner of Indian Affairs, October 23, 1926, National Archives, RG 75, box no. 2380-24-750.

15. Resolution from the Annual Conference of Indian Missionary Workers, Anadarko, Oklahoma, October 19–20, 1926, National Archives, RG 75, box no. 2380-24-750.

16. Letter from H. B. Peairs to Rev. Harry Treat, November 12, 1926, RG 75, box no. 2380-24-750.

17. Robert F. Berkhofer, Jr., *The White Man's Indian: Images of the American Indian from Columbus to the Present* (New York: Vintage Books, 1979), p. 28.

18. Lonna Malmsheimer, "'Imitation White Man': Images of Transformation at the Carlisle Indian School," *Studies in Visual Communication,* 11(4) (fall 1985), p. 69. As Malmsheimer has pointed out, the most famous examples of this were the "before" and "after" photographs that Pratt commissioned at Carlisle, in which students were shown in tribal clothing upon their arrival and in starched uniforms and short or combed hair only a year later. Advocates of boarding school education for American Indians, like the Board of Indian Commissioners, expressed in explicitly racist terms characteristics they saw as inherent to Native Americans and that they found worthy of redemption (such as bravery and the ability to endure pain). See *The Annual Report of the Board of Indian Commissioners to the Secretary of the Interior for 1905* (Washington, D.C.: Government Printing Office, 1906), p. 17.

19. *Kansas City Journal,* October 29, 1926, p. 3.

20. *Muskogee Daily Phoenix,* October 29, 1926.

21. *Indian Leader: Haskell Celebration Official Program,* October 27–30, 1926, p. 21.

22. *Indian Leader,* special issue for month spanning October 29/November 5/November 12/November 19, 1926, p. 7.

23. "Like Birds and Beasts," *Kansas City Times,* October 30, 1926.

24. Ibid., p. 9.

25. *Kansas City Times,* October 30, 1926.

26. Ibid.

27. Lomawaima, *Prairie Light,* pp. 98–99.

28. Ibid., p. 99.

8

Indigenous Versus Colonial Discourse: Alcohol and American Indian Identity

Bonnie Duran

One of the many possible historical stories that can be told about Native American communities and alcohol is about the power to define, produce, and disseminate meaning. This story concerns the nature of otherness; it involves a culturally and historically specific form of (European) reason that constructs identity on the boundaries of what it is not, thereby constructing what it is. The tale is about marginalized groups of people who are objects of an attribution of identity and history and tells of the agency of those groups in resisting and generating counterhegemonic meaning. This story is about a struggle to be subjects rather than objects of history and science, and it concerns the location, mode, and idiom of cultural articulation.

The images and identities of tribal people and the meaning and significance of alcohol in those constructions are the site of half a millennium of struggle between Natives and others. The focus of the struggle is not the indisputable fact of alcohol-related problems or the necessity of intervention, issues in which tribal peoples have more concern and interest than any others. Rather, the struggle is over the sign "Indian" as a signifier of ethnicity, ancestry, cultural tradition, geography, and historical experience, versus a stage in a social evolutionary ladder, the embodiment of a genetic wholism or degeneracy, a psychological archetype or a shadow projection of an entire continent. This overdetermined and overloaded sign was, and is, always more and less than real tribal people could ever hope or dread to be. Within American popular and elite culture, Indianness is more than an ethnic assignment (like being Italian or Irish are). To be a real "Indian," one is compelled to fit one of the binary oppositions or cease to be. It was within this field of meaning that the nineteenth- and twentieth-century white reformers, the "Friends of the Indian," exhorted their members to "Kill the Indian and Save the Man."[1]

The last twenty years have shown significant advances in theoretical and empirical investigations of oppression and domination, specifically by postcolonial and cultural studies scholars,[2] French poststructuralists,[3] and the German critical theorists.[4] The terms "colonialism," "colonized," and "colonial discourse" have been used by these scholars to signify similar processes and effects occurring in different historical times and at different analytical levels. Edward Said, a leading postcolonial scholar, defines colonialism as an effect of imperialism that results in settlements on distant territories. Imperialism means the "practice, the theory, and the attitudes of a dominating metropolitan center."[5] Most Native American populations in the United States have been subjected to all or a combination of these processes.

The association of Native peoples with alcohol occurred within the context of colonial discourse.[6] Homi Bhabha defines colonial discourse as an apparatus of power that strategically creates a space for a subject people through the production of knowledges by colonizer and colonized that are stereotypical but antithetically evaluated.[7] Its mechanism is the scientific, moral, or aesthetic writing and other representation that creates the foundation and rationale for the colonial political and economic agenda. A. JanMohamed characterizes colonialist writing as representation of a "world at the boundaries of 'civilization', a world that has not (yet) been domesticated by European signification or codified in detail by its ideology."[8] In my analysis, colonial discourse about Native people and alcohol is identified by the institutions to which it relates and by the position from which it comes and which it marks out for the speaker. That position does not exist by itself, however, and is best understood as a standpoint taken up by the discourse through its relation to another, ultimately opposing, discourse.[9] The opposing discourse about Native peoples and alcohol, both disguised and marginalized, is found in the eastern and midwestern pan-Indian spiritual-political movements that occurred at the turn of the nineteenth century and again toward the middle of that century. The origin of the image of Native peoples starts before colonization in the imagination and folklore of Europe.

The Wild Man

The image of the Native as the exotic Other already existed in European culture before Columbus's initial journey and can be seen as analogous to our current imaginings about extraterrestrials. Among the numerous mythical characters of medieval European stories and drawings, a certain genre appeared whose symbols functioned as the negative self-definition of European culture.[10] The source for the projected image of the American Indian is found in one of these symbols, the Wild Man.[11]

The significance of the Wild Man was profound in the Middle Ages: The creature symbolized pure European alterity and everything that eluded the normalizing gaze of the church. The image of the Wild Man referred to what was "uncanny, unruly, raw, unpredictable, foreign, uncultured, and uncultivated. . . . Man in his unreconstructed state, faraway nations, and savage creatures at home thus came to share the same essential quality."[12] At least the first twenty pictorial images representing Native Americans are of this Wild Man image. Most were created in the fifty years after Colombus's initial journey and all are ethnographically incorrect, depicting Native men with long flowing beards accompanied by various monstrous forms of life.[13] The earliest images of Native peoples in the European imagination reveal the projection of European binary alterity and ambivalence. The portraits chosen to represent Native peoples revealed more about individuals' and groups' own ideology vis-à-vis the burgeoning ethos of modernity than they did about their knowledge or attitude toward real Native people.[14] The savage Wild Man allowed the comparison with a European civilization seen as the pinnacle of social evolution and provided the ideological foundation for the Christian "civilizing" mission. In contrast, the positive Noble Savage stereotype, a man at one with nature and in touch with his instinctual self, functioned as commentary both on Europe's burgeoning capitalism and the envelopment of traditional forms of life.

The imagery of the stereotypical Drunken Indian—violent, lawless, impetuous—emerges clearly in this analysis as one of the instruments that attuned Western collective consciousness to the notion of a North America awaiting the civilizing and rationalizing mission of European settlement. The most striking thing about the Wild Man archetype in Western culture was that after having been one of the most frequently depicted themes in the fourteenth and fifteenth centuries, it "disappeared from the visual arts and literature by the end of the [sixteenth] century."[15] The image disappeared from European art and literature, but it came to embody America's indigenous peoples.

An Oppositional Identity

The association of certain Native American groups with a destructive use of alcohol, the popular Drunken Indian stereotype, dates to the late seventeenth and eighteenth century, when European settlements were established in North America.[16] The development and spread of this image paralleled the growth of the concept of reason, embodied when the state replaced the church and monarchical dictates as the guiding principle in European social organization during the Enlightenment.[17]

The definition and significance of alcohol centers on the struggle of related terms and their binary opposites: tradition/assimilation and savagery/civilization. Alcohol was used as a metonomy by both sides of a power struggle to define both the meaning and value of "Indian" versus white identity and the moral grounding and guiding principles of the colonization.

Colonial Ideology: Benjamin Rush and Indian Tom

European colonial logic universalizes the Western liberal discourse of "civility" to justify its authority, while simultaneously denying the applicability of "civility" to Native people.[18] This subterfuge of logic is overtly and unself-consciously played upon by Benjamin Rush, a primary American Enlightenment and republican philosopher, member of the Continental Congress, signatory to the Declaration of Independence, powerful educator, major architect of American nationalist ideology, and voluminous writer.

In his biography written in 1793, Dr. Rush shared the insights on civility he acquired while on extended medical apprenticeship in Europe between 1761 and 1766. During his time in Paris, he observed many similarities between French culture, "the most civilized of any nation in the world," and the "savages" of North America. The French and Indian cultures, he noted, share a lack of "delicacy in the intercourse of the sexes with each other" in that both French and Indian women do not conceal their sexual desires or needs from their men. The French are fond of "ornamenting their faces with paint, so are the Indians." Natives and French both eat their primary meal in the evening; in both races the people of means are fond of fishing and hunting; and the Indian and French seldom address each other by proper names. In addition, both cultures hold laborious occupations in contempt and highly regard the military arts. From these observations, Rush deduced that there is a circular course in the progression from savagery to civility and noted that "the highest degrees of civilization border upon the savage life."[19] For Rush, the similarities in culture between the French and Native could no sooner attribute civility to tribal peoples than could his own culture admit thievery and genocide.

Rush, in his role as medical educator—a role that would subsequently earn him the title "father of American psychiatry"—had occasion to deliver a paper in 1774 to colleagues in Philadelphia, titled *An Enquiry into the Natural History of Medicine Among the Indians of North America and a Comparative View of Their Diseases and Remedies, with those of Civilized Nations.*[20] During the course of this talk, he expounded on the vices common to the Indians of North America. In addition to "uncleanness" and "idleness," the third most common vice Rush cited was drunkenness. Rush told his colleagues that drunkenness was part of the Indian character and that the savages glory in their fondness for strong liquor. He told the following tale:

A country man who had dropt from his cart a keg of rum, rode back a few miles in hopes of finding it. On his way he met an Indian who lived in the neighborhood, whom he asked if he had seen his keg of rum on the road? The Indian laughed in his face and addressed him in the following words: "What a fool you are to ask an Indian such a question. Don't you see I am sober? Had I met with your keg, you would have found it empty on one side of the road and Indian Tom drunk and asleep on the other."[21]

Within this small description, the logic of colonial discourse at work is obvious. "Indians," whose lifestyles and cultures are incommensurable with colonial America's, are somehow transparent to Rush's medical gaze. In one short story and the construction of the composite "Indian Tom," he ascribes cultural properties and propensities that typify his image of Natives as thieves and drunks who exist totally outside the boundaries of civilized relations. In his position as physician and republican philosopher, he speaks with the double authority of clinician and colonial administrator. Alcohol, as a polysemic cultural artifact, plays a profound role in the production, colonization, and subjection of Native people, both materially and symbolically.

The Political Economy of Alcohol and Legislative Discourse in Colonial America

Very few North American Native cultures had had experience with alcohol before the first wave of European colonization. The Papago and Zuni used alcohol sparingly for either informal secular gatherings or in religious ceremonies.[22] Within these circumstances, its use and effects were rigidly socially controlled and alcohol did not create social problems. The same is true for Natives of Central and South America, where pre-Columbian use of alcohol was more widespread. Intoxication by alcohol was subject to strict prescriptive cultural traditions and did not interfere with tribal life.[23]

Alcohol was introduced to North American Indian tribal communities by white explorers and traders. Jacques Cartier, a French explorer, and Henry Hudson documented the first instances of alcohol being used as a trading commodity in the late 1500s. Both men wrote that initially Indians were distrustful of the effects of alcohol but soon learned to enjoy their interaction with traders. Although alcohol was commonly used by explorers and traders as a means to establish friendship with Native peoples, no early accounts indicate that Indians acted violently or otherwise inappropriately or that they suffered in any way as a result.[24]

Similar experiences were recorded for the initial contacts on the West Coast. In 1778, for example, Captain Cook reported that "when offered spirituous liquors, they rejected them as something unnatural and disgusting to the palate." However, as Native people found uses for intoxication, liquor became a useful item for the explorers. As on the East Coast, no adverse effects of liquor were recorded during the earliest encounters.

This image changed, however, as white encroachment expanded. The explorers soon had to justify their travels by returning with valuable trading goods, particularly furs. Native traders were satisfied with trinkets and basic household goods initially; however, there was only a limited demand for such items and curiosity and demand for them was soon satisfied. Liquor, as a replenishable commodity, became one of the few trade items for which there was an increasing demand.

Alcoholic beverages, then, became the ideal commodity for the "conspicuous consumption" that the traders needed to increase their business and profits. By the 1800s, liquor was the basic bartering item on the frontier, as the Whites used the most deceitful tactics to make large profits. There are numerous reports of traders plying people with rum or whiskey as a show of friendship, then trading watered liquor of the most vile nature (often poisonous) for the valuable furs that were often given away while Natives were intoxicated.

As the liquor trade expanded, the "drunken Indian" stereotype became established. The Jesuits began to see brandy as their primary obstacle to converting Indians. They reported that Natives turned into beasts when they drank and that debauchery, murder, and interfamily and intertribal feuds resulted. European traders also documented the adverse effects of alcohol on their trading partners. John Long, a trader with the Chippewa between 1768 and 1782, reported a period of ten days when three men were killed and two wounded after a dreadful scene of riot and confusion occasioned by the effects of rum.[25] Other trader accounts are similar; it was reported that Indians were heavy drinkers, consumed large quantities in short periods of time, and often combined their drinking with bouts of violence and promiscuity.[26]

Widespread accounts of these incidents soon led to demands, first by the Jesuits and later by the eastern colonists, that the liquor trade be ended. The popular image was that since alcohol unleashed the basic savage nature of the natives, all Indians were totally incapable of holding their liquor and should not be allowed to drink at all.

Early colonial legislation,[27] however, embodies the contradiction between moralistic attitudes and economic benefit. Between 1643 and 1715, Pennsylvania, New York, New Hampshire, Maryland, Virginia, and Massachusetts all enacted statutes prohibiting the trade or sale of alcohol to Native peoples. Although early white settlements took measures to limit alcohol, legislative measures were continuously passed and repealed depending on the economic interests of the traders. These colonies, as well as the future states of Ohio, Louisiana, Florida, and Maine, all eventually outlawed the liquor trade with Natives. But all waited until after the most lucrative benefits had been attained.[28]

W. R. Jacobs, in *Dispossessing the American Indian,* reports an incident that illustrates frontier ambivalence. In 1756, Edmond Atkins, the English superintendent for the Southern Region of the Frontier, recommended that heavy penalties be levied if a trader allowed an Indian to become drunk and that all liquor should be watered. The commander in chief of the British force agreed and did "everything he could" to suppress the rum trade. However, as Northern Superintendent William Johnson noted, these efforts were ill fated since the rum trade was an "absolute necessity" for the economy of the area.[29]

The first federal legislation concerning Indian drinking was passed in 1802 as part of an act that established control of trade and intercourse with the Indian tribes. It read: "The President of the United States [is] authorized to take such measures, from time to time, as to him may appear expedient to prevent or restrain the vending or distributing of spirituous liquors among the all or any of the . . . Indian tribes."[30] This prohibition, however, proved fruitless on the western frontier. On the West Coast, no attempt to control the liquor trade was made until the 1850s. The Supreme Court itself acknowledged the failure in an 1876 decision:

> It may be that the policy of the government on the subject of Indian affairs has, in some particulars, justly provoked criticism; but it cannot be said, that there has not been proper effort, by legislation and treaty, to secure Indian communities against the debasing influence of spirituous liquors. The evils from this source were felt at an early day, and in order to promote welfare of the Indians, as well as our political interests, laws were passed and treaties framed, restricting the introduction of liquors among them. That these laws and treaties have not always secured the desired result, is owing more to the force or circumstances which the government could not control, than to an unwillingness to execute them. Traffic with Indians is so profitable, that white men are constantly encroaching on Indian Territory to engage in it.[31]

Although the founding fathers enacted significant legislation restricting the availability of alcohol to Native people, the liquor trade was not curtailed; in fact, legislatures were more concerned with protecting the trade as a valuable resource. More important than liquor laws were efforts to control practical concerns like raiding and colonial annoyances. In fact the liquor legislation was really part of a long campaign to impose Anglo-Saxon cultural, religious, and moral codes of behavior. Native drinking, despite all statements to the contrary, was encouraged in order to increase trade profit, induce concessions, and sap the strength of the tribes. Alcohol was thus an important element in the inevitable disappearance of the Indian (Figure 8.1). Benjamin Franklin noted this final, most unspoken purpose: "And, indeed, if it be the design of Providence to extirpate these savages in order to make room for the cultivators of the earth, it seems not improbable that rum may be the appointed means. It has already annihilated all the tribes who formerly inhabited the seacoast."[32]

Indigenous Alcohol Discourse

Although an overview of early American drinking legislation provides insight into the colonial view of alcohol and Natives, it does not provide a Native interpretation of alcohol-related problems during colonial times. Edward Said eloquently notes that the United States was forged out of numerous histories, often in conflict and contradiction with each other.[33] The object peoples of many of these histories are now demanding acknowledgment, most profoundly, so that communities of color, the poor, and other marginalized groups may view themselves differently. So it is with Native Americans.

MOVE ON, MAROON BROTHER, MOVE ON!

Figure 8.1 *Sketch by Frederick Opper in* Bill Nye's History of the United States *(London 1894), a satiric "history" that illustrates clearly the prevailing view that liquor had helped send the Indian to his inevitable doom.*

Temperance has either been the major focal point or a dominant theme in many Native social movements over the last two hundred years. The Handsome Lake Religion, the teachings of the Shawnee Prophet (Tenskwatawa), and the spread of the Native American Church all had temperance as a major tenet. Regardless of whether the movement was an attempt at cultural "revitalization" or had a more political agenda or whether it was tribe-specific or pan-Native, alcohol has been a predominant theme in most Native collective action since its arrival among Natives of North America. The meaning of alcohol to Native people, therefore, appears highly symbolic.

The inscription of alcohol-related problems within the case studies outlined below can be seen as a "displacement"[34] of the colonial discourse on alcohol at the time. A religious or spiritual idiom gave the movement leaders and participants an alternative framework to codify their problems and propose solutions. In this section, I will briefly outline the temperance aspects of the social movements previously mentioned, while searching for a Native voice in the construction of alcohol-related problems.

Handsome Lake

Handsome Lake,[35] the Seneca Prophet, preached abstinence from alcohol as early as 1800. The political climate at the time of Handsome Lake's vision provides clues to the colonial struggle to define alcohol's function and meaning. The colonists contended that they had not only won the Revolutionary War against Britain but had also won a de facto war against all of Britain's allies, who included large segments of the Iroquois confederacy. In the Treaty of Paris of 1783 the United States claimed that it now owned all Native territory south of the Great Lakes and the St. Lawrence River and east of the Mississippi River. Treaties were yet to be signed with the Native tribes, but the only matter for negotiation was what lands they would be allowed to keep. The newly formed government badly needed Iroquois land to pay off the enormous debt incurred to soldiers fighting the war, land that could be sold to pay off other debts incurred during the conflict. In addition, private speculators saw great potential profit in selling Native land to settlers.

The resulting Treaty of Fort Stanwix, in 1784, was a fraud. Native leaders were coerced at gunpoint into signing a document that conceded large tracts of land. Many of the Native delegates left before the treaty was signed. The inability of the delegates to adequately represent the interest of their tribes led to the disintegration of the original Iroquois confederacy. Another association of western tribes was formed, united in their continued loyalties to the British. Although the War of the Northwest Territory waged by this group of the Western Iroquois Confederacy put the tribes in a much better negotiating position with the government, many of the Mohawk members of the confederacy had already fled to Canada during the Treaty of 1784, and other members of the traditional confederacy did not support the western confederacy because of its British alliances.

As the original confederacy fragmented, it lost considerable power as a representative and negotiator for the tribes. Soon its members were assigned to reservations, where it became easier for religious organizations like the Quakers to begin their project of Native assimilation. With the support of tribal leadership, the Quakers taught western agriculture, carpentry, and Christianity to the bands confined to reservations. In response, the bands split along generational lines. Older Seneca, tired of fighting, attempted to see the value of the new agricultural lifestyle. The younger generation, angry at its elders for conceding land, saw little merit in the white man's ways. Handsome Lake, the Seneca Prophet, emerged from this conflict.

Handsome Lake's visions, the ensuing religion, and the effects these had on the political and social life of the Iroquois confederacy are considered a form of cultural revitalization. The precepts he taught can be divided into two chronological phases: the apocalyptic and the social gospels. His first visions contained three interrelated themes: the imminence of world destruction, the definition of sin, and the prescription for salvation. Cosmic catastrophe was imminent unless tribal members took steps to avert it. The overriding sin in his prophecy was failure to believe in his vision, a vision that would remedy such other sins as alcohol abuse, witchcraft, love magic, and abortion. The third principle, salvation, was to be accomplished by refraining from sin and by reinstating certain traditional social and ceremonial practices.

There were also three themes in Handsome Lake's second social gospel, which he preached from 1801 until his death in 1815. The first theme related to the use of alcohol.

> Good food is turned into evil drink. Now some have said that there is no harm in partaking of fermented liquids. Then let this plan be followed; let men gather in two parties, one having a feast of food, apples and corn, and the other have cider and whiskey. Let the parties be equally divided and matched and let them commence their feasting at the same time. When the feast is finished you will see those who drank the fermented juices murder one of their own party but not so with those who ate food only.[36]

Temperance remained a prime concern throughout Handsome Lake's mission. He, as well as other tribal leaders, saw alcohol as the leading cause of social instability and therefore of the Senecas' inability to regroup after the reservation confinement. The enactment of temperance was not left to individual conscience but was instituted in the political structure of several communities of the Great League itself. The liquor trade was outlawed by Corn Planter and other village chiefs, and Handsome Lake was praised as being principally responsible for curing the Seneca of "the misuse of that dreadful manbane, distilled spirits."

The second social principle was peace and social unity, which was institutionalized in 1801 when Handsome Lake became the moral censor and principal leader of the Six Nations. His position toward whites was a cautious nationalism: Peace toward the whites, in a separate but equal framework, and unity among the tribe and confederacy (pan-Nativism).

The third principle was the preservation of the tribe's land base. Handsome Lake was adamantly opposed to any further land concessions but promoted profitable exchanges of land that would geographically consolidate the confederacy's lands, thus contributing to community control of disparate clans. The claim that Handsome Lake expanded the social gospel into a fourth principle, acculturation, is a misunderstanding of his intentions regarding white education. "Now let the Council appoint twelve people to study, two from each nation of the six. So many white people are about you that you must study to know their ways."[37] Handsome Lake saw the value of obtaining a white education not because it advanced assimilation into white culture but because it promised an equal negotiating position that would enable the members of the confederacy to retain their unique cultural lifestyle and economic land base. His mission, understood within the milieu of colonial oppression, was more nationalist than assimilationist.

The symbolic meaning of alcohol to Handsome Lake and other confederacy leaders who were trying to maintain their culture amid white economic, religious, and cultural intrusion can be gleaned from the prominent place accorded temperance among other prescriptions for tribal revitalization. Handsome Lake taught that temperance was as important as traditional ceremony, social organization, and maintenance of a land base to the continuity of tribal life, thus providing a clear cultural response to the stereotype, the Drunken Indian.

Tenskwatawa: The Shawnee Prophet

Tenskwatawa[38] emerged from a personal life of great hardship as a leading visionary of the Shawnee and neighboring tribes during a time of intense cultural change (Figure 8.2). Originally named Lalawethika, the prophet was born fatherless in 1775. His mother, a despondent widow with eight children, abandoned her

Figure 8.2 *Tenskwatawa, "the Shawnee prophet," as pictured in Thomas L. McKenney and James Hall's* The Indian Tribes of North America, *1844.*

Shawnee offspring and returned to her Cree relatives in 1779. Tenskwatawa was raised by his older sister and other Shawnee but is generally thought to have been ignored by any real parental figures.

Influenced by this early life of physical and emotional abandonment, Tenskwatawa grew into an alcohol abuser. After sporadic involvement with the tribe's warfare against the invading colonists, led by his brother Tecumseh, Tenskwatawa finally found his calling while undergoing a type of apprenticeship with the clan's medicine man. After the death of his mentor and his failure to be recognized by the clan as the man's rightful successor, Tenskwatawa experienced a series of visions and a death experience initially thought to have been brought on by alcoholic stupor. During these revelations, the Master of Life did not allow Tenskwatawa to enter heaven, though he was permitted to gaze on a paradise, which he described as follows: "a rich fertile country, abounding in game, fish, pleasant hunting grounds and fine corn fields . . . they could plant, hunt, or play at their usual games, and in all things could remain unchanged."[39] According to Tenskwatawa's vision, not all Shawnee were allowed to enter this heaven. Unvirtuous men, allowed only a glimpse of this paradise, were confined to a lodge within which a large fire burned. The most wicked were turned to ashes and others stayed in this place until their sins were atoned. Unrepentant drunkards were particularly mentioned by the prophet. They were "forced to swallow molten lead until flames shot from their mouths and nostrils."[40] Although this type of purgatory had redemptive qualities for some sinners, the less virtuous tribesmen eventually ascended to heaven but never fully took part in the enjoyments of their more virtuous brothers. It was through this and another series of visions that Lalawethika was personally and socially transformed into the Shawnee Prophet, Tenskwatawa.

During the summer of 1805, the prophet and many Shawnee followers moved from their home at White River to establish a new settlement—Prophet's Town—in western Ohio. Tenskwatawa's teachings were similar to Handsome Lake's. First and foremost, he denounced the drinking of alcohol as poison and accursed. In addition to this proscription, he preached against the rising incidence of internal and external tribal violence, sexual promiscuity, and polygamous marriages.

The Shawnee Prophet, again like Handsome Lake, preached the return of traditional Shawnee ritual and ceremonial practices, although he also condemned certain practices and medicine men as corrupt and misguided. Tenskwatawa exhorted his fellow tribal members to give up their medicine bundles, which he claimed had lost their effectiveness. He substituted medicine sticks as a manifestation of personal power. Like the Seneca Prophet, Tenskwatawa urged tribal members to give up the notion of private property, to return to communal life, and to fight any white acquisition of Native land. He instructed his followers to move away from using white man's food, technology, and manner of dress. While praising the traditional life of the Shawnee, Tenskwatawa warned against any close association with the Americans. He went so far as to state that the Master of Life had informed him that the Americans were not made from him (the Master of Life) but were actually children of the evil spirit.

Tenskwatawa's teachings spread quickly among the tribes of Ohio. At the same time, federal attempts to gain Native land through coerced and unfair treaty negotiations drove other tribal members, including some Chippewa, Mohicans, Wyondot, Kickapoos, Potowatomi, Ottawas, Crees, and Assiniboins into the prophet's camp. There is evidence that his doctrines significantly influenced Native-white relations of the time. In 1807, for example, Captain Dunham, an American military commander on the Michigan frontier, heard complaints from traders that the Natives no longer accepted whiskey for trade and were refusing to discuss any further Native land concessions.

Eventually, Tenskwatawa's fate as a spiritual and cultural leader fell prey to the corrupt political manipulations of the encroaching white government and his own foray into the role of warrior. Unable to logistically accommodate the hordes of followers flocking into Prophet's Town and unable to stop federally delegated "representative" tribal members from signing away Native land, his mission, under his brother Tecumseh's guidance, turned more and more political. In November of 1911, Tenskwatawa and his army of followers were defeated at the Battle of Tippecanoe.

Again, the symbolic meaning of alcohol to Tenskwatawa and his followers can be seen in the prominent place that temperance was given in the prophet's doctrine. Abstinence was the first precept taught, since alcohol consumption was paramount among the evil white ways that Natives would have to abandon in order to return to a state of equilibrium with the Master of Life, with fellow tribal members, and with other tribes. Alcohol was associated with assimilation and, like other white cultural artifacts, such as food and clothing, was condemned as a threat to Native identity.

The Native American Church

Approximately seventy years after Handsome Lake and the Shawnee Prophet provided the leadership necessary for pan-Native collective action, another movement with strong temperance themes emerged. The peyote religion[41] had its roots among the pre-Columbian Natives of Mexico. Transported to Natives north of the border by the Mescalero Apaches in 1870, the religion quickly spread to the Kiowa and Comanche. Unlike the two earlier social movements, whose goal was "revitalization," this movement is categorized as one of "accommodation." It abandoned the messianic hopes of the past and instead developed ideology and ceremonies more in line with the realities of Native life in the early twentieth century. The Native American Church ceremony involves all-night meetings, usually held in a traditional Native structure such as a tepee. In the ceremony, participants sing and ingest peyote in order to cure themselves and become closer to the creator via the helper spirit, peyote. An early promoter of the religion stated, "The white man goes into his church house and talks about Jesus, but the Native goes into his tepee and talks to Jesus." Although the religion is not hostile toward Christianity, peyote groups differ in the amount of Christianity incorporated. Christian beliefs form the core rhetoric of some groups, whereas in others Christian references are absent. The Native American Church's major canon is opposition to alcohol. Anthropologists have gone so far as to say that the religion began as a temperance movement, with an anti-alcohol message similar to the temperance movement of white society. Indeed, both movements originated at about the same time.

The beliefs of two early missionaries of the Native American Church, Quanah Parker (Comanche) and John Wilson (Delaware-Caddo), who both converted in the 1880s, typify the major strains of the religion that exist today. John Wilson attributed his cure from alcoholism to the assistance of the spirit of peyote. Wilson, while under the influence of peyote, had visions and received peyote songs, a body of moral and religious teaching, and details of ceremonial procedures. In these visions Wilson saw Christ and was told that at the time of his death he would be in the presence of both peyote and Christ. In contrast, Parker's brand of peyotism had much less Christian influence. Both men, however, stressed right conduct, abstinence from alcohol, and peyote as a cure for disease.

H. W. Hertzberg has delineated twelve reasons why the Native American Church became the most successful pan-Native movement (today it has members among almost all tribes). One important reason was the ability of the church to "cure" alcoholism, which contributed to the stability and health not only of individuals but also of Native communities.

Other movements, such as the Ghost Dance religion, which started at about the same time as the peyote religion, made fewer references to alcohol abstinence, although Jack Wilson, the movement's prophet, is known to have specifically addressed the topic.[42] The Native Shaker Church was founded during the second wave of Native-white contact among the Natives of the northwest coast and northern California regions in approximately 1889. The founding of the church has been interpreted as a response to acculturation pressure and the introduction of alcohol into the region. It is estimated that 76 percent of the religion's members are recovering alcoholics; the religion acts for them as a "culture-based indigenous treatment response to alcohol misuse."[43]

In all these social and religious movements, alcohol carried a symbolic association as an artifact of assimilation and dominance. Social movements "work" insofar as they succeed in "strengthening tribal identity and distinctions between American Native and European populations."[44] The prominence of the alcohol issue within these movements clarifies a category of meaning for this substance. Alcohol historically is associated with Indian identity within Native communities and among the broader dominant population. At the same time, it is viewed by Natives as destructive of Native life. Thus abstinence becomes a symbol of protest and an affirmation of Native identity.

Conclusion

Present-day alcohol prevention and treatment programs under Native control have consciously or unconsciously overcome the inherent biases of standard social science approaches by employing "indigenous theory."[45] Indigenization refers to the replacement of Eurocentric models with Native idioms.[46] Indigenous theory is an advance in treatment and prevention ideology for Native Americans in two ways. First, it utilizes knowledges and idioms produced by Native people from within Native culture, thus creating Natives as subjects (those who know and act) rather than objects[47] (those who are known and acted upon). Second, this form of self-representation compels reflexivity, insight, and agency (called *conscientização*).[48] This indigenization, as it is applied to alcohol prevention and treatment, can be interpreted as the legacy of the eighteenth-, nineteenth-, and twentieth-century Native social movements that produced alternative understandings of alcohol in Indian country. Indigenous approaches to prevention and treatment benefit by being accompanied by postcolonial histories of alcohol. By "postcolonial" I mean the use of "a social criticism that bears witness to those unequal and uneven processes of representation by which the historical experience of the once-colonized comes to be framed in the West."[49] A postcolonial history of alcohol situates the emergence of alcohol-related problems within the phenomenon of colonial discourse.

Eurocentric conceptualizations of Native alcohol-related problems may contribute to the ongoing reproduction of these same problems by denying Native agency, idiom, and epistemology, both historically and in the present. Certainly, to the extent that dominant cultural approaches have been evaluated, they have been found inadequate as a form of alcoholism treatment for people who identify strongly as "Indian."[50]

Thus we must acknowledge and value the burgeoning of present-day indigenous models of etiology and intervention. These models are the legacy of earlier political, cultural, and spiritual movements that sought to resist and deconstruct the dominant image of the Drunken Indian, who succumbed helplessly to the advancing tide of "civilization."[51] Postpositivist investigations into indigenous approaches are needed to evaluate the effectiveness of these models and to disseminate their belief system, thus moving toward a more self-determined construction of alternative, workable Indian identities at this turn of the millennium.

Notes

1. A. Harmon, "When Is an Indian Not an Indian? The 'Friends of the Indian' and the Problems of Indian Identity." *Journal of Ethnic Studies* 18 (2), pp. 95–123.

2. A partial list includes: H. Bhabha, *The Location of Culture* (London and New York: Routledge, 1994); R. Ferguson, et al., eds., *Out There: Marginalization and Contemporary Cultures* (Cambridge: MIT Press, 1990); P. Freire, *Pedagogy of the Oppressed* (New York: Continuum Press, 1990); H. Gates, ed., *Race, Writing, and Difference* (Chicago: University

of Chicago Press; 1985); R. Guha and G. Spivak, eds., *Selected Subaltern Studies* (New York: Oxford University Press, 1988); A. Ong, *Spirits of Resistance and Capitalist Discipline* (New York: State University of New York Press, 1987); E. Said, *Culture and Imperialism* (New York: Alfred Knopf 1993); M. Taussig, *The Nervous System* (New York: Routledge 1992); G. Vizenor, *Word Arrows: Indians and Whites in the New Fur Trade* (Minneapolis: University of Minnesota Press, 1978); C. West, "The New Cultural Politics of Difference," in Ferguson et al., eds., *Out There*, pp. 19–39.

3. J. Derrida, *Of Grammatology* (Baltimore: Johns Hopkins University Press, 1980); M. Foucault, *Power/Knowledge: Selected Interviews and Other Writings, 1972–1977* (New York: Pantheon Books, 1980); J. Lyotard, *The Postmodern Condition: A Report on Knowledge* (Minneapolis: University of Minnesota Press, 1984).

4. J. Habermas, *The Theory of Communicative Action,* vol. 1 (Boston: Beacon Press, 1984) and *On the Logic of the Social Sciences* (Cambridge: MIT Press, 1988).

5. E. Said, *Culture and Imperialism,* p. 9.

6. My definition of colonial discourse is a compilation of the work of two postcolonial theorists, Homi Bhabha and Abdul JanMohamed and a discourse theorist, Diane MacDonnel.

7. H. Bhabha, "The Other Question: The Stereotype and Colonial Discourse," *Screen* 24 (6) (1983), p. 23.

8. A. JanMohamed, "The Economy of Manichean Allegory: The Function of Racial Difference in Colonialist Literature," in Gates, *Race, Writing and Difference,* p. 83.

9. D. MacDonnel, *Theories of Discourse: An Introduction* (Cambridge, Mass.: Basil Blackwell, 1986), p. 3.

10. P. G. Mason, "Deconstructing America," Ph.D. diss., Rijksuniversiteit Utrecht.

11. R. Berkhofer, Jr., *The White Man's Indian: Images of the American Indian from Columbus to the Present* (New York: Vintage Books, 1979), pp. 13–14.

12. Berkhofer, *White Man's Indian,* p. 11.

13. S. Colin, "The Wild Man and the Indian in Early 16th Century Book Illustration," in C. F. Feest, ed., *Indians and Europe* (Herodot, Netherlands: Rader Verlag, 1987), pp. 5–36.

14. J. Hulme, *The Enlightenment and Its Shadows* (New York: Routledge, 1990).

15. Colin, *Wild Man,* p. 29.

16. C. MacAndrew and R. Edgerton, *Drunken Comportment* (Chicago: Aldine, 1969).

17. For an excellent and readable discussion of the sociocultural context of the emergence of "modernity," see S. Toulmin, *Cosmopolis: The Hidden Agenda of Modernity* (New York: Free Press, 1990).

18. Bhabha, "The Other Question," 1983

19. G. Corner, *The Autobiography of Benjamin Rush: His "Travels Through Life" together with His Commonplace Books for 1789–1813* (Princeton: Princeton University Press, 1948), p. 71.

20. B. Rush, "An Account of the Vices Peculiar to the Indians of North America," in B. Rush, ed., *Medical Inquiries and Observations upon the Diseases of the Mind* (Philadelphia: Kimber and Richardson, 1812), pp. 256–260.

21. Ibid., p. 259.

22. J. E. Levy and S. J. Kunitz, *Indian Drinking: Navajo Practices and Anglo-American Theories* (New York: Wiley, 1974).

23. M. Villanueva, "The Use of Alcohol in Pre-Columbian South American Native Cultures," Pacific Graduate School of Psychology.

24. MacAndrew and Edgerton, *Drunken Comportment,* pp. 111–112.

25. W. R. Jacobs, *Dispossessing the American Indian* (New York: Scribner's, 1972).

26. A. M. Winkler, "Drinking on the American Frontier," *Quarterly Journal of Studies on Alcohol* 29, pp. 413–445.

27. All of the legislative references in this section come from J. Mosher, *Liquor Legislation and Native Americans: History and Perspectives,* Working Paper F 136, Berkeley Social (Alcohol) Research Group, University of California, Berkeley, unless otherwise noted.

28. Mosher, *Liquor Legislation.*

29. Jacobs, *Dispossessing.*

30. Mosher, *Liquor Legislation.*

31. United States v. 43 Gallons of Whiskey, 93 U.S. 188, 192–193 (1876). As quoted in Mosher, *Liquor Legislation.*

32. Quoted in D. H. Lawrence, *Studies in Classic American Literature* (New York: Seltzer, 1923), p. 15.

33. Said, *Culture and Imperialism,* p. xxvi.

34. Guha and Spivak, *Subaltern Studies,* p. 9.

35. All references regarding Handsome Lake and the Iroquois are from A.F.C. Wallace, *The Death and Rebirth of the Seneca* (New York: Vintage Books, 1969), unless otherwise noted.

36. Ibid., p. 278.

37. Ibid., p. 282.

38. All references regarding Tenskwatawa are from D. Edmunds, *The Shawnee Prophet* (Lincoln and London: University of Nebraska Press, 1983), unless otherwise noted.

39. Ibid., p. 33.

40. Ibid., p. 33.

41. All references regarding the Native American Church are from H. W. Hertzberg, *The Search for an American Indian Identity* (New York: Syracuse University Press, 1971), unless otherwise noted.

42. Quoted in O. C. Stewart, "Contemporary Documents on Wovoka, Prophet of the Ghost Dance in 1890," *Ethnohistory* 24 (3) (1977), p. 222.

43. L. Slagle, and J. Weibel-Orlando, "The Indian Shaker Church and Alcoholics Anonymous: Revivalistic Curing Cult," *Human Organization* 45 (4) (1986), pp. 310–319.

44. R. Thornton, *We Shall Live Again: The 1870 and 1890 Ghost Dance Movements as Demographic Revitalization* (Minneapolis: University of Minnesota Press, 1986), p. 49.

45. See, for example, P. Weeks, "Post-Colonial Challenges to Grand Theory," *Human Organization* 49 (3) (1990), p. 239; U.S. Department of Health and Human Services, *Breaking New Ground for American Indian and Alaska Native Youth at Risk: Program Summaries,* OSAP Technical Report No. 3, (ADM)90-1705 (ADAMHA, 1990).

46. Y. Atal, "The Call for Indigenization," *International Social Science Journal* 33, pp. 189–197. For an example, see Slagle and Weibel-Orlando, *Indian Shaker Church.* For an excellent discussion of some South American etiologies and cosmologies of disease, see M. Taussig, "Reification and the Consciousness of the Patient," in Taussig, *The Nervous System.*

47. Freire, *Pedagogy of the Oppressed,* p. 20.

48. "*Conscientização* refers to learning to perceive social, political and economic contradictions, and to take action against the oppressive elements of reality," ibid., p. 19.

49. Homi Bhabha, "Conference Presentation," in *Critical Fictions,* ed. P. Mariani (Seattle: Bay Press, 1991), p. 63.

50. For a dismal account of the outcomes of mainstream approaches to Indian alcohol treatment and prevention see: D. Kivlahan et al., "Detoxification Recidivism Among Urban American Indian Alcoholics," *American Journal of Psychiatry* 142 (12) (1985), pp. 1467–1470; J. Query, "Comparative Admission and Follow-up Study of American Indian and Whites in a Youth Chemical Dependency Unit on the Northern Central Plains," *International Journal of the Addictions* 3 (4) (1985), pp. 489–502; J. Westermeyer and D. Peake, "A Ten Year Follow-up of Alcoholic Native Americans in Minnesota," *American Journal of Psychiatry* 140 (2) (1983), pp. 189–194. Equally alarming are reports that Indian specific treatment programs which lack a comprehensive, codified alternative to the negative stereotype are failing as miserably as the non-Native oriented treatment programs. For example, see C. G. Gurnee, "Substance Abuse Among American Indians in an Urban Treatment Program," *American Indian and Alaska Native Mental Health Research* 3 (3) (1990), pp. 17–26.

51. A few of the notables working within academia include Maria BraveHeart Jordon at University of Denver, Billy Rogers at the University of Oklahoma, and Jean Thin Elk at the University of South Dakota at Vermillion. Many local medicine people use indigenous approaches to treat alcohol problems. Some of the more renowned practitioners include Richard MovesCamp and Rick Two Dogs at Pine Ridge and Dan Freeland in Gallup, New Mexico. Most Indian alcohol (and other drug) prevention projects, especially those funded by the Center for Substance Abuse Prevention under Dr. DeJong, build on tribal cultural approaches to reinstate belief and control systems to local communities.

9

"My Grandmother Was a Cherokee Princess": Representations of Indians in Southern History

Joel W. Martin

It is difficult to overestimate the importance that representations of Indians have held within the cultural and ideological life of southerners, from colonial times to the present. Indians have appeared prominently in a wide variety of genres, in legends, humor sketches of the Old Southwest, romance novels, epic poems, historical narratives, plays, and songs. Plentiful in southern literature, Indians are also omnipresent across the southern landscape. Indian names are used for several southern states and for hundreds of hamlets, towns, and cities. Thousands of historical markers and monuments, streams, rivers, mountains, and natural sites feature Indian names. (I am writing this essay in a house next to Watulla Creek, south of Opelika, Alabama, twenty miles west of the Chattahoochee River.) To understand the South and southerners, we need to understand southern representations of Indians, past and present.

In this essay, I argue that the character and significance of Indian representations have changed over time. My research suggests classification into five major time periods: pre-Removal (1783–1830), antebellum (1831–1861), Civil War–closing of the "western frontier" (1862–1893), Jim Crow era (1894–1945), and civil rights struggle (1945–present). In this essay, I concentrate on the first two periods, then due to space limitations here I briefly describe the third, skip over the fourth, and jump ahead to the contemporary scene. I argue that although southern Indians have been represented in ways familiar in other regions, the standard figures have been painted with distinctly southern accents.[1]

In this essay, I call attention to this regional specificity and offer a tentative, and definitely preliminary, explanation for its existence. My discussion focuses on three key historical factors that all affected how southeastern Indians were represented. First, a region-specific history of conquest and resistance has left its peculiar marks on the southern imagination. Second, the struggles around slavery, secession, and Reconstruction led white southerners to try to define and justify a distinct southern culture. Third, the defining role that race discourses have exercised in southern culture has shaped how white and Black southerners view Indians. Southern Indian images are not timeless archetypes but highly politicized icons. The Indians of Dixie are symbols produced in historical struggles over land, politics, and race.

The Pre-Removal Period, 1783–1830

In 1752, an Indian woman married to a white man helped lead a diplomatic mission from the colony of Carolina to the Indian peoples of the southeastern interior, for which action she became a famous, controversial figure among whites and Indians. In 1799, a U.S. Indian Agent visited an Indian town on the Tallapoosa river and was impressed with the wife of Zachariah McGirt. Because she had the "neatness and economy of a white woman," the agent considered her a model for her people.[2] In 1812, Indian men killed a white woman on the Cumberland Plateau. Heroes to Indians involved in a revolt against the United States, they became the incarnation of evil for white settlers in Tennessee.

I have highlighted these three disparate events and the contrasting representations they elicited—Indian as cultural broker, Indian as cultural convert, Indian as cultural enemy—because they point to three major ideologies that organized southern white perceptions of Indians during the pre-Removal period. One ideological formation respected the autonomy of Indian peoples and recognized their importance in the contact situation. An antithetical formation sought to crush Indian sovereignty and projected Indians as savage obstacles in the path of the white civilization. Somewhere between these two, a third formation, based on the idea that whites and Indians shared a common humanity, tried to assimilate Indians into white culture peacefully. During the pre-Removal era, these three major ideologies shaped how Indians were represented, with the ideology of Indian-hating ultimately prevailing.

Eighteenth-century representations had centered on border-crossing types, individuals who moved freely between Indian and non-Indian cultures. These included Scottish traders, their Indian wives, African American runaways who fled to Indian country where they dreamed of being free, and bicultural Indians, such as Mary Musgrove. Musgrove, who was a Creek Indian married to an English preacher named Thomas Bosomworth, claimed to be descended from an important Creek leader and used her putative status successfully in negotiations with colonial officials. During the mid-eighteenth century, she and Bosomworth were employed by the colony of Carolina on important diplomatic missions to the Indian interior. Their border-crossing activities attracted considerable attention and have sparked the imagination of many southern writers, historians, and myth-makers (Figure 9.1). Other bicultural Indian leaders were highly regarded and courted by white officials.[3] At the same time, not all border-crossers were viewed positively, but rather were seen as ambiguous characters of uncertain loyalties. Anglo-American traders, for instance, were considered by Indians and Anglo-Americans alike to be a coarse and unprincipled group of men.[4]

Figure 9.1   *This picture of Mary Musgrove and her husband "invading" Savannah, Georgia, appeared in Lawton B. Evans's* First Lessons in Georgia History *(New York, 1913). The picture is an imagined scene, graphically illustrating the perceived role of Musgrove as mediator between two cultures.*

Whether regarded positively or negatively, border-crossers were considered by most eighteenth-century southerners to be key players in the economic and social life of the southeastern interior. The same can be said for Indian peoples in general. Regarded alternatively with mistrust and respect, they were never ignored, because the South, during much of this period, was a true "middle ground,"[5] in which native peoples such as the Cherokees, Creeks, and Choctaws participated in multiple exchange networks. During the seventeenth and eighteenth centuries, southeastern Indians, Africans, and Europeans learned to communicate across linguistic and cultural barriers, bringing their cultures into contact and transforming one another as a result. Indians, European settlers, and African slaves traded deerskins, cloth, rum, corn, and horses, but they also intermarried, mixed genes, and produced bicultural peoples. They swapped ideas, songs, poems, stories, and symbols. They exchanged and compared religious perspectives. It was in such a context that stories and images of figures such as Mary Musgrove first became popular. To people living on the middle ground, she seemed an emblematic figure.

As the eighteenth century unfolded, the middle-ground ideology was challenged by a counterideology promoted by Anglo-American settlers and planters. Dependent far less upon access to Indian trade and far more upon access to Indian land, they held that there was no place for Indians in the Southeast. Their ideology started to gain prominence after the departure of the French in 1763,[6] as representations of Indians as savages became more popular in the Southeast.

Southeastern expansionists and planters found their spokesperson in Andrew Jackson, a Tennessee slaveholder (who later became president). No friend of the middle ground, Jackson despised its protocols, ambiguities, and complexities. His representations of Indians were saturated with the rhetoric of savagery, captivity, and miscegenation. He was not fascinated with a figure such as that of Mary Musgrove, but rather with the figures of bestial Indian warriors attacking innocent white women. In May 1812, just before he became nationally famous, Jackson gave voice to his obsession, describing the death of a frontier woman and calling for vengeance. "When we make the case of Mrs. Manly and her family and Mrs. Crawley our own—when we figure to ourselves our beloved wives and little prattling infants, butchered, mangled, murdered, and torn to pieces, by savage bloodhounds, and wallowing in their gore . . . we are ready to pant for vengeance . . . the whole Creek nation shall be covered with blood."[7] In Jackson's world, Indians were savages, irremediably in conflict with civilization. They needed a punishing, violent father. This ideology would become dominant in the early decades of the nineteenth century, climaxing with the Indian Removal Act (signed by President Andrew Jackson in 1830). Around 1800, however, this ideology was still emergent, Jackson was just a lawyer and slaveholder, and a third ideology was temporarily dominant.

Promulgated largely by the federal government and its cultural missionaries, this ideology provided a less violent vision of Indian-white relations and used a different set of images. It was a Eurocentric view that nonetheless acknowledged the potential humanity of natives. It held that Indians could be assimilated to white ways, become Christians, learn to respect law, and practice intensive, commercial agriculture on much less land. This ideology projected Indians as children, in need of paternalistic instruction in the ways of civilization. Intermarriage with Indians was sanctioned, not to forge intimate bonds between interdependent peoples but as a means of diluting Indian blood. Federal proponents launched "experiments" to prove Indians could be civilized, sending Indian agents and Christian missionaries among the Creeks, Choctaws, and Cherokees. There they labored to save Indians by transforming them into white people.[8]

Encountering these three conflicting ideologies and images, Indian peoples reacted in different ways, the sharpest division occurring among the Creeks. A significant faction, numbering about nine thousand individuals, believed that whites were determined to drive them out of the Southeast. These Creeks found the government's assimilationist program objectionable and feared the exterminationist rhetoric of leaders such as Andrew Jackson. They were persuaded when the Shawnee leader Tecumseh, who visited them in 1811, called for massive pan-Indian renewal and resistance. They developed a set of pan-Indian symbols and actions to mark authentic Indianness, valuing the wild over the tame, turkeys and deer over chickens and cows. They tried to abandon European manufactures and to reduce the cultural and political influence of white Indian agents. When push came to shove, they decided to fight. Since these rebel Creeks wielded red battle clubs, they became known as the Redsticks.

The Redsticks had some initial successes, defeating a Mississippi militia in a skirmish at a place called Burnt Corn. They captured the frontier stronghold of Fort Mims, where, after losing many lives themselves, the Redsticks killed many men, women, and children. This provided whites with the pretext for an unprecedented invasion of Creek lands. Three American armies, including one led by Andrew Jackson, marched into their nation. In March 1814, at the Battle (or Massacre) of Horseshoe Bend, Jackson's army killed more Indians than any U.S. army before or since, including "too many women and children."[9]

This bloody slaughter and the entire Creek war would provide some of the Southeast's most important and lasting representations of Indians, to be discussed later in the section on the contemporary scene. For now, the point is that Creeks became associated with "savagery," warfare, and conflict. A different symbolic fate awaited the Cherokees. Because they had fought and lost earlier (defeated by the British in 1760 and by the Whigs in 1776), they also had been vilified as savages deserving extermination.[10] But since they never fought against the United States proper, they would not be memorialized as enemies of the nation-state itself. Whereas Creeks were destined to be remembered as warriors, the Cherokees were cast as the model converts to white culture.

In the years after the Revolution, a Cherokee elite emerged. Heavily missionized and increasingly acculturated, this elite attracted national praise, as Anglo writers heralded their agrarian, mercantile, religious, and social achievements.[11] The Cherokees, it was implied, were exceptional Indians who vindicated the dreams of the assimilationists. It was often overlooked that among the Cherokees, as among other southeastern peoples, many Indians did not belong to the elite class. Indeed, the great majority of Cherokees did not convert to Christianity, attend school, hold elected office, run houses of entertainment, own slaves, or publish newspapers. Their dreams were not necessarily those of the elite or of their white friends.

But because the Cherokees had a unique national reputation, what happened next seemed the cruelest of all tragedies. During the Gold Rush of 1829, whites entered their land by the thousands. Georgia extinguished Cherokee sovereignty on June 1, 1830. Whites stole Cherokee property with impunity and drove Cherokees from their farms. In 1838, the great majority of Cherokees (sixteen thousand people) were forced to remove west in a murderous march that cost thousands of lives.[12] This long march became known as the Trail of Tears. The primary images associated with this march were of Indians as tragic victims, innocent parties crushed by vast, inevitable historical forces. Choctaws, Chickasaws, Creeks, and Seminoles were also forced to leave their homelands and suffered terribly. Yet, because they were not considered to be as "civilized," their suffering was discounted and did not achieve permanent mythic value in southern culture.

The Antebellum Period, 1831–1861

A brave warrior surrendered to a white general. A noble Indian chief made a sad speech as he abandoned the land of his ancestors. Meanwhile, a less noble, intoxicated Indian was cheated out of his land by a white con man. Whites came to believe that no actual Indians remained in the South but used Indian names with abandon to designate landscape features and invoke the memory of their martial spirit with respect. Far from being uncommon, Indian representations were central to southern culture during this period.

Scholars who theorize about southern distinctiveness often point to 1831 as a turning point. The Nat Turner revolt occurred in 1831, after which date, white southerners repressed criticism of slavery and locked themselves on a course that would lead to secession and the Civil War.[13] Yet, if the Nat Turner revolt was a critical event, so too was Indian Removal. The expulsion of tens of thousands of Indians from the South drastically changed the region, not least by bolstering the strength of state's rights and providing new land for the expansion of cotton culture. It was to these lands that many of the children of planters in Carolina, Virginia, Georgia, and Tennessee moved with their African-American captives. They expanded old southern states and created the new states of Louisiana (1812), Mississippi (1817), Alabama (1819), Arkansas (1836), and Florida and Texas (1845). In sum, the antebellum white South, devoted to slavery at all costs, was expanded, empowered, and consolidated by Indian Removal.

In this new South it might seem that representations of Indians would decrease in importance, that the white South would abandon figurative Indians as fully as it had purged real ones. The opposite happened. In what must be one of the least-studied developments in southern culture, representations of Indians proliferated. Indian place-names were adopted by the thousands, particularly in the newly absorbed areas. And Indians infiltrated nearly every genre of writing. Indeed, the literary genres that are considered distinctively southern—humor sketches of the Old Southwest and the romance novel—centered on Indians. Other important literary genres in the South, for example, historical works, reminiscences, and natural histories, likewise gave a prominent place to Indians.[14]

Why was this happening? Perhaps it represents an attempt by whites to come to terms with the violence of the Removal. Having dispossessed the aboriginal inhabitants, white southerners needed to legitimate this invasion and did so by retelling the history of conquest as either inevitable or humorous. Writings that took the former approach tended to portray Indians as proud, nomadic peoples, destined to be overwhelmed by civilization. Such writing implied that victorious whites should be generous enough to recognize that a few individual Indians had fought with bravery; romantic fiction thus celebrated noble, defeated, yet gracious Indian warriors, who recognized that they had been beaten by honorable men.[15]

The most influential literary work that projected this new view was William Gilmore Simms's historical romance *The Yemassee: A Romance of Carolina* (1835), a work often compared to James Fenimore Cooper's *The Last of the Mohicans*. Even authors writing in other genres were shaped by Simms and his representations of Indians. For instance, the poet Albert Meek dedicated his epic *Red Eagle* to Simms. And historian Albert J. Pickett, while working on his *History of Alabama,* corresponded with Simms, seeking advice on research and writing style.[16] Their writings, like Simms's, are colored with rapturous descriptions of natural beauty, spiced with historical references, and punctuated with battle scenes. Like Simms, they produced a text that justified conquest but also voiced a lament. Whites were destined to prevail; the least they could do was write a respectful epitaph for the defeated.[17]

Simm's novel provided the literary model for romantic representations of Indians and Indian wars, but an actual Indian, Osceola, became the real-life incarnation of the noble enemy (Figure 9.2). Osceola was the headman who led the Seminoles in conflict against the United States from 1835 to 1837. After his capture under a flag of truce in 1837, he was imprisoned at Fort Moultrie in Charleston. His fame soared, as Charlestonians avidly sought to catch a glimpse of this real Indian leader. George Catlin closed his New York gallery in order to travel south to paint him. After Osceola's death, the attending doctor decapitated the corpse and kept the head as a treasured artifact, reputedly displaying it at his drugstore. Apparently Osceola stood for something special to antebellum southerners and

Figure 9.2   *Osceola, as pictured in Thomas L. McKenney and James Hall's* The Indian Tribes of North America, *1844.*

other Americans. Theda Perdue suggests that his "capture and death symbolized the end of 'savagery' in the East. . . . In the defeat of Osceola, the quintessential 'savage,' Anglo-Americans confirmed that they were right: Failure to become 'civilized' resulted in death, albeit a heroic and romantic death."[18] Having hated and "removed" most literal Indians, southerners fell in love with figurative ones.

   Although similar trends were unfolding in the Northeast, there was something particularly southern about these noble Indians, in that they were deployed in a manner that reinforced the honor of white men.[19] Consider the climactic scene of Alexander Beaufort Meek's epic poem *The Red Eagle: A Poem of the South* (1855). The Creek Redstick leader William Weatherford surrendered to Andrew Jackson with words that Meek considered to be "the finest specimen of Indian eloquence":

> A soldier I have fought
> Your people long and bravely, as I ought;
> They were my foes,—and all the harm I could
> I did them. With an army still, I would

Fight to the last. But all my braves are gone,
And I am left my nation's woes to mourn. . . .
A brave man knows a brave man's heart!—And I
Upon your generosity rely![20]

As this passage suggests, an emphasis on the dignity of the individual Indian warrior could be used to underscore the magnanimity of his conqueror. And the Indian's recognition that his day has passed helped absolve whites of any guilt. In popular stories told by whites, Indian chiefs heading west on removal marches talked "in eloquent pathos of their bitter grief on leaving their hunting grounds and the graves of their fathers."[21] The message was clear: Literate white southerners with a generous heart could lament the passing of a brave opponent, and after a momentary pause of nostalgia, they could get back to business.

Quite a different approach was represented in southwestern humor, in which genre Simms also wrote, along with Augustus Baldwin Longstreet, Johnson Jones Hooper, William T. Porter, "Davy Crockett," and many others. These works tended to be short sketches that appeared in local newspapers and then were collected and reissued as books. They focused on frontier scoundrels and their scams, characters like the fictional Simon Suggs, whose motto was "It is good to be shifty in a new country." The Indians in these works were gullible, dirty, hard-drinking fools who did not understand American laws regarding land ownership. Because southwestern humor focused on petty incidents involving a few characters in isolated settings, the genre gave the impression that conquest had been a chaotic, even accidental, affair in which all sides lacked morals and manners and Indians usually got duped.

Yet, although southwestern humor did not lament fallen Indians and was often explicitly racist, it did provide space for a critique of conquest, in the form of parody. The best example of this is Hooper's story "Simon Becomes Captain" (1845).[22] The story begins by equating "the nation's Jackson and the country's Suggs." A biography of the latter's rise to power follows that replays Jackson's. The year is 1836 and several persons have been murdered by "'inhuman savages' . . . Consternation seized all! 'Shrieks inhuman' rent the air" (p. 82). To the rescue comes Simon Suggs, a roving, backwoods con man. He exaggerates the danger in language that is very close to that used by Jackson in 1812. "'Gentle*men*,' said he impressively, 'this here is a critercle time; the wild savage of the forest are beginnin' of a bloody, hostile war, which they're not a-goin' to spar nither age nor sek— not even to the women and children!'" (p. 85). In its details and parodic use of the rhetoric of frontier hysteria and campaign biography, the author iconoclastically attacks Jackson. Although the immediate political intent was to rally Whigs against Democrats in the 1840s, the story also carried a truly subversive message. Just as historical romances revealed a subtle, if safe, sympathy for Indians, southwestern humor called attention to the hypocrisy of southerners, their heroes, and their "civilization." Even though humor, like romance, served the needs of the hegemonic class, it nonetheless gave voice to criticisms of conquest. Indeed, the precise ideological work of these genres and one of the keys to their popularity may have been this: to stimulate critical impulses, then to contain them.

Even as middle-class whites were busy reading stories about noble and ignoble Indian characters, they were appropriating Indian names by the thousands to designate settlements, post offices, streams, and other natural features of the newly acquired lands. Whites exiled real Indians, but they brought symbolic "Indianness" close to their hearts. In Alabama, for instance, they gave Indian names to most of that state's streams and to almost all of the state's rivers, some ten thousand miles of waterways.[23] Why this marked preference for Indian names? Why not use English names, easier to pronounce and spell, evocative of locations mentioned in English poetry and song?

Several reasons suggest themselves. Indian names were colorful and romantic. They added flavor to the landscape and heightened a sense of regionalism, serving, for instance, to mark insiders, who could pronounce them, from outsiders, who could not. Perhaps most important, on a symbolic level, Indian names enabled southerners to claim an archaic connection between themselves and the land. Call a town Irwinton and it might as well be in England or Connecticut. Call it Eufaula and it almost had to be in Alabama or Oklahoma, that is, in a place where Muskogee Indians had lived. An Indian name made it seem as if the new town had been there forever, as if it was all right for whites to be living there. Finally the names were like trophies: Much like Indian arrowheads, pots, and artifacts, Indian names were prized possessions, signs that whites used to assert that they had inherited the land and its history. In a deep sense, southern whites were claiming Indian ancestors, even as they repudiated contemporary Indians and denied them their birthright. The actual living Indian had been exiled; the fictive dead Indian was romanticized. The former was the precondition for the latter, if not the cause.

As if translating conquest and invasion into romance and humor was not enough to keep southern writers busy, they were also "burdened" with the job of defending slavery during a period when it was being attacked from both within and without. These pressures affected authors such as Simms, Meek, Pickett, and Hooper. Although they disagreed on the issue of secession (Simms and Meek opposed it, Pickett and Hooper championed it), they wrote self-consciously as "southerners" eager to defend their class, race, and region. Meek arranged for the simultaneous publication of his epic poem in New York and Mobile, Alabama.[24] Pickett, at great expense, had his book published in Charleston, South Carolina, in 1851. "The whole work," he said of his *History*, "will be *Southern*—except the pictures."[25] It should come as no surprise that writers employed Indians on behalf of southern propaganda. Specifically, they constructed Indians in such a way that African captivity was legitimated and white honor bolstered.

The previous text has shown how authors used pre-Removal conflicts with Indian enemies to underscore white heroism—the more honorable the opponent, the greater the victory. But these authors also sanctioned the southern culture of honor and the class hierarchy it legitimated. As countless retellings of the William Weatherford legend emphasized, the Indian leader strode past common soldiers, entered Jackson's tent, made his speech of surrender and gave his bow and arrow to Jackson. The message was clear: Only an honorable knight like Jackson was worthy to receive Weatherford's "sword." To emphasize the point, Meek has Jackson defend the Indian from common soldiers who cry for his execution. Thus, romantic Indians were used to support the southern hegemonic class and its ideology. White patrician slaveholders were men of honor: They should be in charge.

But the romantic, free, warlike Indian had greater utility. He provided a damning contrast to the African captive, who, according to white authors, loved bondage. Later in the nineteenth century, Ben Tillman, rabid advocate of segregation, summed up this contrast: "We all respect the Indians because they were too brave to ever consent to be made slaves while the negroes have submitted to slavery and seemed to thrive on it."[26] Antebellum literature typically portrayed Africans as happy in their captivity, obedient as dogs, eager to play their roles in the great southern play. Romantic and rebellious Indians served to dramatize by contrast the docility of Blacks.

This was the racial system constructed by whites, the one that informed southern literature and politics, the one that whites would fight and die for. Yet the system was continually put into crisis when actual Indians or Blacks refused to conform. Whites viewed with considerable ambivalence the small minority of Creeks, Choctaws, and Cherokees who themselves had African-American slaves, doubting if Indians knew how to "manage" their slaves properly. But if Indian slaveholders posed an interpretive problem, the Seminole wars, the last Indian wars fought in the Southeast, presented an even greater challenge, because of the active participation of Blacks alongside Indians.

Throughout the colonial period, whites had tried to regulate the interaction of Indians and slave populations. Indians had been on the borders, slaves "within the bosom" of the South. The Seminole wars changed this. Now, there were warlike slaves on the borders, united with hostile Indians. Was this an Indian war or a slave insurrection? Whatever it was, southern fiction avoided it. There was no established genre capable of handling the protracted, code-busting Seminole wars. Historical romance had portrayed Blacks as docile; southwestern fiction had been a white-red affair with surprisingly few Blacks present; historical writing focused on the mighty acts of white heroes. The Seminole struggle could not be made to fit; this mismatch may explain why these wars produced relatively little antebellum southern literature.

When the white South seceded from the union, it invoked the symbolism of the American Revolution. During the Revolution, Americans had sometimes dressed as Indians to define themselves against England. As Philip J. Deloria has demonstrated, there was precedence for this type of symbolism well before the Boston Tea Party, and there were many subsequent times when Americans, for various purposes, assumed Indian identities. In contrast, in their moment of crisis, southerners did not do this in any widespread manner.[27] Republican imagery clearly dominated their rhetoric, providing the archetypes for rebellion. For example, the seal of the Confederacy featured a mounted George Washington. Nevertheless, Indian representations were not entirely absent or useless, especially as white southerners contemplated a possible invasion of "their" land. For instance, toward the end of his *History of Alabama,* published in 1851, Albert James Pickett lauded the Creek rebels as positive examples of people willing to spill their life's substance to defend their ancestral homeland.[28] Such strategies helped to legitimate warlike patriotism and rebellious nationalism, the glorification of a lost cause, and the notion that shedding blood in defense of land was honorable, noble, and redemptive.

From the Civil War to the
Closing of the Western "Frontier," 1862–1893

Indians disappeared from the South at the time of Removal—or so the dominant narrative claimed. It was not true, but try telling southerners that. In the period after the Civil War, Indians were represented less frequently, yet southerners continued to draw psychic energy and narrative drama from symbolic Indians. Indeed, new types of representation emerged. On the one hand, all southerners began connecting living Indians with the West. On the other hand, southern whites linked the rhetoric of (Indian) savagery to African-Americans. And finally, southern African-Americans started dressing as Indians in carnival celebrations. Thus, as the literal Indian became associated with the West, in the South the figurative Indian became associated with African-Americans, in negative and positive ways. An already strange history of representations grew stranger.

The Civil War marked a watershed—as in so many things—in the history of southern representations of Indians. After the war, white southerners' ideological needs changed dramatically. Instead of needing to legitimate Removal, they needed to defend their prewar commitment to slavery and justify continuing a race- and class-based hierarchical social order. Indians did not help achieve either of those goals. The two genres that had centered on them had to change. Southwestern humor picked up and moved west, leaving the Old Southwest behind. Romance novels now concentrated more on the plantation, portraying it as a happy place where white ladies helped childlike Blacks unable to face the world on their own and where planters forged intimate bonds with faithful retainers. As white readers grappled with the war and its loss, memorialized their dead, and worked to undermine Reconstruction, they found little use for fiction focused on Indian conflicts.

During the late nineteenth century, Indians became "westernized," even in the South. As newspapers proliferated and filled their pages with stories of Sioux uprisings and Apache skirmishes, and dime-store westerns became popular, southerners started thinking of Indians as other Americans did—as vanishing, horse-mounted, buffalo-hunting nomads roaming the Great Plains.[29] In the twentieth century, the ultimate result of this would be that southerners visiting Cherokee, North Carolina, would not believe they were seeing a "real" Indian unless he was wearing a warbonnet. To this day, Cherokees dressed in such bonnets make money posing with tourists, an activity called "chiefing."[30]

Viewed from a distance, it seems there was a great national division of labor taking place in the production of discourses on race. The West would become the locus for discourses on Indians, as whites were charged with figuring out the "Indian problem." Meanwhile, southern whites had the burden of dealing with the "Negro problem." In the West, this meant an allotment policy designed to pulverize western Indian landholdings and obliterate their cultural identity. In the South, it meant Jim Crow laws (Plessy v. Fergueson, 1896) mandating rigid segregation of Black from white, and political disenfranchisement for African-Americans. Culturally, it meant southerners increasingly thought of the South in biracial terms.[31]

As southern whites and Blacks were polarized, it is not surprising that their respective creation and use of Indian representations served contrary purposes. Whites invoked many of the stereotypes of the savage that had been generated in the Indian wars, but because the South no longer had an "Indian problem," these stereotypes could now be applied to African-Americans. As Joel Williamson has shown, the late nineteenth century was a period in which a new radical racism emerged in the South.[32] Unlike earlier forms, it held that African-Americans were not only incapable of civilization, unacceptable as citizens, and inferior as a race but were regressing to a savage state. Without "the direct training and discipline" provided by the "school" of slavery, whites were sure African-Americans would devolve or return to a state of bestiality.[33] Popular journalism spread this racism, concentrating on the figure of the "black beast rapist." In response to the mere rumor of such an outrage against a white woman, white men formed lynch mobs. They killed hundreds of Black men during the 1890s.[34] This form of state-tolerated terrorism was justified in part through use of old rhetorical forms generated in the Indian wars. "Bad negroes" prone to "criminality" lurked along isolated paths. A "black devil," "a fiend of hell" might be hidden behind the next tree.[35] Although these "fiends" were not called "Indians," the basic form of demonization was familiar. Now, in the 1880s and 1890s, it was as if the savage had reappeared in the South, in a Black body.

Facing this terrorism and virulent forms of racism, southern Blacks fought back, protesting, boycotting, and organizing petitions.[36] And in New Orleans, during the carnival season of Mardi Gras, they assumed a more fantastic identity, that of "wild injuns." Just as white southerners had long associated Indians with savagery, so Black southerners had long associated them with freedom. Wearing elaborate feathered costumes, Black Mardi Gras Indians temporarily stepped out of the biracial South and assumed a third identity characterized by improvisation, proud public display, ceremonial conflict and competition, and undeniable beauty. Although scholars later linked these costumes to Caribbean cultures, participants insisted they were "Indian." Thus, even as both Black and white southerners were inclined to believe that Indians had disappeared, both found the symbolic appeal of "Indianness" too great to resist. Whites found a new use for hysterical rhetorical forms generated in the long colonial war against indigenous peoples. Blacks found a new use for liberative symbols in a land where Indians seemed to be the freest people of color.[37]

It should not surprise us that generations after Removal, even in the context of a landscape imagined in strictly biracial terms, the figure of the Indian remained a vital part of southern cultural expression. Indians were charged symbols in a region shaped by contact, colonialism, and racism. Space does not permit discussion of the manifold ways in which modern southerners continued to connect themselves to Indians: placing historical markers dealing with Indians along highways, establishing state archives and creating museum exhibits focused on Indians, naming sports teams after Indians, collecting Indian artifacts, preserving sites associated with Indian history, creating military parks related to Indian battles, marketing art with Indian motifs, painting murals, performing pageants, organizing scout troops, and so on.

The Present Era

This remains true today: Southerners continue to create and consume images of Indians. The Neville Brothers, for example, recently wrote a song celebrating the Mardi Gras Indians of their hometown:

> Under the yellow moon
> while the sky is black and dark
> All the injuns head uptown
> to meet in Shakespeare Park
> They all gonna be pretty,
> have no kind of fear
> They all sew brand new suits,
> to mask in every year
> Wild injuns down in New Orleans.

Elsewhere in the South, Indian imagery is common. In Florida, for example, images of Osceola abound. In Alabama, Chief Tuscaloosa, who fought Soto, and Menawa, the leader of the Redsticks, are often represented. By invoking these figures, contemporary southerners seem to be claiming a wild past, seeking to affix the romance of the "frontier" to their region's narrative. The images reinforce southern regionalism and pride, even as they unite southern history with the larger national story. Much like the innkeeper who boasts that George Washington slept here, southerners employ images of southeastern Indians to connect their home with American History—with a capital H.

Given this conservatism, it is not surprising that these images have changed little from the time they were first generated. Cherokees continue to be remembered in art, literature, and drama as tragic victims inevitably steamrollered by history.

In their ancestral lands in North Carolina, a historical pageant titled *Unto These Hills,* depicting the Cherokee Removal, draws large crowds every evening during the summer. Its popularity is remarkable, says a great deal about Southerners, and warrants closer scrutiny. For now, it is important to note that no such pageant exists for other southeastern Indians. Southerners associate Removal first and foremost with the Cherokees, thus displaying a selective historical memory. This bias is reflected in another way. Even when history and geography might suggest an Indian ancestor from a different group or none at all, an astonishing number of southerners assert they have a grandmother or great-grandmother who was some kind of Cherokee, often a "princess."[38]

Meanwhile, Creeks are still represented as savages. Newspaper feature articles, history books, museum exhibits, novels, and works of art continue to recall the Fort Mims "massacre", describe the canoe fight[39] (with white frontiersmen as invincible), and contemplate William Weatherford's surrender to Jackson.[40] Indeed, the defeat of the Creek "enemies" was the foundational event in Alabama history.

Even contemporary museums perpetuate this stereotyping. On March 24, 1995, the newly overhauled Museum of the Horseshoe Bend National Military Park in Dadeville, Alabama, opened, purporting to tell the true story of the Battle of Horseshoe Bend. Unfortunately, the museum gives new life to the worst forms of anti-Creek propaganda. Located dead center in the exhibit and mounted on a large panel, a sepia-shaded sketch depicts maniacal savages (wearing Mohawk haircuts!). They wrestle white women and lift their tomahawks over white soldiers (Figure 9.3). A small text panel provides a body count of the people killed in the fort, but no Redstick casualties are mentioned, even though the Indians suffered severe, faith-testing losses. The rest of the exhibit downplays the active participation (on all sides) of African-Americans, with none depicted in illustrations or in dioramas. The war appears to have been solely a red-white confrontation, which it was not.

The conflict at Fort Mims was won by Indians, whereas the clash at Horseshoe Bend was won by whites. In descriptive captions, the former is termed a "massacre," whereas the latter is termed a "battle," suggesting that the outcome of the war was laudable and morally legitimate. There is little, if any, suggestion that whites fought in order to gain land for the expansion of slavery and cotton culture. Similarly, the nine thousand Creeks who fought with the United States receive little attention. And contemporary Creeks, two thousand of whom are organized as a federally recognized tribe in Alabama (the Poarch Band of Creek Indians), are simply elided. The major message of the exhibit seems to be that Indians went crazy and had to be subjugated through military force.

Hardly mentioned in the Horseshoe Bend museum, contemporary Creeks are also ignored in the Indian exhibit at the Alabama Department of Archives and History in Montgomery. That exhibit, which represents state-of-the-art scholarship and does a good job with early history, begins ten thousand years ago and stops with Indian Removal. When I asked a museum official about this, he said that the standard narrative of Alabama history deals with Indians first, then turns

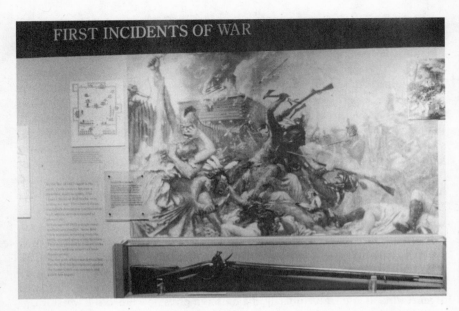

Figure 9.3   *Detail from large mural of the Battle of Horseshoe Bend, featured in the Museum of the Horseshoe Bend National Military Park in Dadeville, Alabama. Photo by Joel Martin.*

to consider statehood, leaving Indians behind. This implied that Indians only belong at the beginning, not in the middle or at the end of historical narratives. When pressed, he said that if the Creeks want to be represented, they have enough money to create their own exhibits. Thus, in defending images of Creeks as dead or gone, or both, he invoked newer and still-forming images of the Poarch Creeks as people who enjoy unnatural, even scandalous, special treatment from the federal government, including the right to operate bingo establishments and grow rich. I have heard other white southerners say the same, in much more bitter tones, about Florida's Miccosukee and Seminole Indians, and Mississippi's Choctaws. As Poarch Creeks attempt to gain approval for Alabama's first casino, we can expect their status and identity will be questioned by southerners who prefer images of pre-Removal Indians to real Indians today.

The non-native preference for fantasy over reality was demonstrated recently in a controversy over the name of the Atlanta Braves, a major league baseball franchise. Like a verbal magnet trolled through the cesspool of American racial discourse, this word invites images of Indians as ignorant fools and "blood-thirsty, tomahawk-waving savages."[41] (At Braves games, thousands of fans chop the air with plastic "tomahawks" to express their excitement.) Protests by Indians against these stereotypes have been dismissed by fans. Long accustomed to representing Indians as they see fit, contemporary southerners are the heirs of a long history of appropriation of Indian lands, images, and Indianness itself.

It will do little good to criticize Braves fans, although such criticism is certainly justified. It might do more good to study how Indian representations became important to southerners and why these representations have continued to possess symbolic and ideological value. Such study will show that representations have always been important to southerners, that they have changed in different periods, and that they have served diverse ideological ends. These representations were formed in the context of a long-term, ongoing historical process of violent expropriation that has affected nearly every southerner.

In a sense, most southerners are like Braves fans—too ready to trade in stereotypes, to pretend that they are Indians, to ignore real Indians, or to discount their subjugated knowledges. Like insecure aliens living in someone else's home, we southerners know the land belongs to other peoples—to Cherokees, Creeks, Chickasaws, Choctaws, Seminoles, Catawbas, and other southeastern Indians—in a way it can never belong to us. Unwilling to do what it will take to make the situation right—for Indians, for ourselves, for our progeny—we perpetuate settler ideologies of Indians as natural beings, savages at worst, anachronisms at best. We try to keep real Indians distant. Until the complicated consequences of colonialism in the South are fully addressed, we can expect that southerners will continue to generate and depend upon fantastic representations of Indians, and we can predict that scholars will continue to analyze these representations.

Notes

1. See Rayna Green, "The Tribe Called Wannabee: Playing Indian in America and Europe," *Folklore* 99 (1) (1988), pp. 30–55.

2. Benjamin Hawkins, "A Sketch of the Creek Country in the Years 1798 and 1799," in *Letters, Journals, and Writings of Benjamin Hawkins,* vol. 1, ed. C. L. Grant (Savannah, Ga.: Beehive Press, 1980), p. 292.

3. William McDowell, Jr., ed., *Documents Relating to Indian Affairs, May 21, 1750–August 7, 1754* (Columbia: South Carolina Archives Department 1958), p. 288; Rodney M. Baine, "Notes and Documents: Myths of Mary Musgrove," *Georgia Historical Quarterly* 76 (2) (1992), pp. 428–435.

4. Joel W. Martin, *Sacred Revolt: The Muskogees' Struggle for a New World* (Boston: Beacon Press, 1991), p. 76.

5. For the metaphor of "middle ground," see Richard White, *The Middle Ground: Indians, Empires, and Republics in the Great Lakes Region, 1650–1815* (New York: Cambridge University Press, 1991), p. 33.

6. The French departure left southeastern Indians without any available counterweight to check the influence of the British, who came to believe that most of the North American continent should belong to them and invaded western territories on a massive scale. This provoked Indian resistance movements, which in turn fueled more intense forms of Indian hating among whites.

7. Quoted in Michael Paul Rogin, *Fathers and Children: Andrew Jackson and the Subjugation of the American Indian* (New York: Alfred A. Knopf, 1975), p. 147.

8. William G. McLoughlin, *Cherokees and Missionaries, 1789–1839* (New Haven: Yale University Press, 1984); Martin, *Sacred Revolt,* pp. 87–113.

9. This phrase appears on a map of the battle by Colonel William Carroll, inspector general, Tennessee Militia; notes and map are contained in General Joseph Graham's Letter Book, P.C. 60-1, Folder 8 (1814), North Carolina State Archives, Raleigh, North Carolina. On the Redstick revolt, see Martin, *Sacred Revolt.*

10. See David Cockran, *The Cherokee Frontier, 1540–1783* (Norman: University of Oklahoma Press, 1962); Marvin Thomas Hatley, "The Dividing Paths: The Encounters of the Cherokees and the South Carolinians in the Southern Mountains, 1670–1785," Ph.D. diss., Duke University, 1989.

11. E.g., Isaac McCoy, *The Practicability of Indian Reform, Embracing Their Colonization* (Boston: Lincoln and Edmands, 1827), pp. 27–28, describes the way Cherokees took to education and commercial agriculture.

12. Harold David Williams, "The North Georgia Gold Rush," Ph.D. diss., Auburn University, 1988; Mary Young, "Racism in Red and Black: Indians and Other Free People of Color in Georgia Law, Politics, and Removal Policy," *Georgia Historical Quarterly* 73 (fall 1988), pp. 492–518; Russell Thornton, "The Demography of the Trail of Tears Period: A New Estimate of Cherokee Population Losses," in *Cherokee Removal: Before and After,* ed. William L. Anderson (Athens: University of Georgia Press, 1991).

13. Charles Reagan Wilson, "History and Manners," in *Encyclopedia of Southern Culture,* ed. Charles Reagan Wilson and William Ferris (Chapel Hill: University of North Carolina Press, 1989), pp. 583–595.

14. Edward Watts, "The Changing Critical Placement of Humor of the Old Southwest," *Mississippi Quarterly* 44 (winter 1990/1991), pp. 95–103; Terry Roberts, "The Reconstruction of a Poet," *Mississippi Quarterly* 44 (spring 1991), pp. 203–207; Michael Kreyling, "Southern Literature: Consensus and Dissensus," *American Literature* 60 (1) (March 1988), pp. 83–95.

15. Green, "Tribe Called Wannabee," p. 34.

16. William Gilmore Simms to A. J. Pickett, December 4, 1847; March 18, n.d. (c. 1848), Albert J. Pickett Papers, Alabama Department of Archives and History, Montgomery, Ala.

17. Richard Drinnon, *Facing West: The Metaphysics of Indian Hating and Empire Building* (Minneapolis: University of Minnesota Press, 1980), p. 143.

18. Theda Perdue, "Osceola: The White Man's Indian," *Florida Historical Quarterly* 70 (1991), p. 484. See also Patricia R. Wickman, *Osceola's Legacy* (Tuscaloosa: University of Alabama Press, 1991).

19. Perdue, "Osceola," p. 484.

20. Alexander Beaufort Meek, *The Red Eagle: A Poem of the South* (Written in 1845, first published in 1855; reprint, Montgomery, Al.: Paragon Press, 1914. pp. 114, 105–107; Benjamin Buford Williams, *A Literary History of Alabama: The Nineteenth Century* (Rutherford, N.J.: Fairleigh Dickinson University Press, 1979), pp. 39–57.

21. Thomas Clinton, "Emigration of the Creek Indians, 1836–37," *Arrow Points* 3 (6) (1921), p. 3.

22. Johnson Jones Hooper, *Adventures of Captain Simon Suggs, Late of the Tallapoosa Volunteers; Together with "Taking the Census" and Other Alabama Sketches* (Tuscaloosa: University of Alabama Press, 1993), pp. 82–95.

23. Peter A. Brannon, "Alabama Postoffice and Stream Names, 1922," *Arrow Points* 6 (1) (1922), pp. 3–7; "Macon County: Present Day Place Names Suggesting Aboriginal Influence," *Arrow Points* 5 (1) (1921a), pp. 5–9; "Tallapoosa County: Present Day Place Names Suggesting Aboriginal Influence," *Arrow Points* 5 (6) (1921b), pp. 104–108.

24. Williams, *Literary History of Alabama,* p. 45.

25. Pickett to Absolom Jackson, March 7, 1851, Albert J. Pickett Papers, Alabama Department of Archives and History, Montgomery, Alabama.

26. Quoted in Joel Williamson, *The Crucible of Race: Black-White Relations in the American South Since Emancipation* (New York: Oxford University Press, 1984), p. 381.

27. Philip J. Deloria, "Playing Indian: Otherness and Authenticity in the Assumption of American Indian Identity." Ph.D. diss., Yale University, 1994.

28. Albert James Pickett, *History of Alabama, and Incidentally of Georgia and Mississippi, from the Earliest Period* (Birmingham, Ala.: Birmingham Book and Magazine Company, 1962).

29. Brian W. Dippie, *The Vanishing American* (Lawrence: University Press of Kansas, 1982); Roy Pearce, *Savagism and Civilization* (Baltimore: Johns Hopkins Press, 1965); Annette Kolodny, *The Lay of the Land: Metaphor as Experience and History in American Life and Letters* (Chapel Hill: University of North Carolina Press, 1975); Philip J. Deloria, "Playing Indian"; Lora Romera, "Vanishing Americans: Gender, Empire, and New Historicism," *American Literature* 63 (1991), pp. 385–404.

30. Geoffrey Norman, "The Cherokee: Two Nations, One People," *National Geographic* 187 (5), pp. 72–97.

31. The historiographic pattern of equating the South with a biracial society continues, despite excellent attempts to challenge it by Verner Crane, Theda Perdue, Peter Wood, James Merrell, Charles Hudson, and others. Unfortunately, Indians also have been elided from the institutionalized discourses of "Southern Studies." Neither the graduate program at the University of North Carolina Chapel Hill nor the one at the University of Mississippi requires a course on Indians.

32. Joel Williamson, *Crucible of Race.*

33. Joseph Alexander Tillinghast, quoted in the *Charlotte Observer,* December 14, 1902.

34. Trudier Harris, *Exorcising Blackness: Historical and Literary Lynching and Burning Rituals* (Bloomington: Indiana University Press, 1984); Frank Shay, *Judge Lynch: His First Hundred Years* (New York: Ives Washburn Inc., 1938); Walter White, *Rope and Faggot: A Biography of Judge Lynch* (New York: Arno Press, 1969); Ida B. Wells-Barnett, *On Lynchings* (New York: Arno Press, 1969).

35. *Atlanta Constitution,* July 30, 1893; *Mobile Daily Register,* May 1, 1892.

36. Edward L. Ayers, *The Promise of the New South: Life After Reconstruction* (New York: Oxford University Press, 1992).

37. Joseph Roach, "Mardi Gras Indians and Others: Genealogies of American Performance," *Theatre Journal* 44 (1992), pp. 461–483; Samuel Kinser, *Carnival American Style: Mardi Gras at New Orleans and Mobile* (Chicago: University of Chicago Press, 1990).

38. William W. Quinn, Jr., "The Southeast Syndrome: Notes on Indian Descendant Recruitment Organizations and Their Perceptions of Native American Culture," *American Indian Quarterly* 14 (2) (1990), pp. 147–154; Green, "Tribe Called Wannabee," p. 46.

39. During winter 1995, several Alabama newspapers ran a feature story titled "Canoe Fight Instills Fear of Big Sam," a story that recounted for the millionth time how a white man named Sam Dale killed several Creeks in a canoe.

40. This scene is memorialized in a large mural displayed just beneath the dome of the State Capitol Building in Montgomery, Alabama, installed in 1930 with seven other scenes from Alabama history.

41. *Lakota Times,* October 30, 1991.

10

Florida Seminoles and the Marketing of the Last Frontier

Jay Mechling

Florida's Seminoles are an "invented" people in the special way culture critics in the late twentieth century write about "the invention of tradition." In the stories of their multiple inventions (sometimes by the Seminoles themselves, most often by whites) we find an intellectual lesson and a postmodern morality tale (of sorts). In this essay I examine the social construction of the Seminoles by historians, naturalists, travelers, novelists, and ethnographers, but especially by those who were "inventing" Florida for the tourist in the middle of the twentieth century. The Seminoles played a key symbolic role in the social construction of the meanings of Florida through tourism, and the touristic visit is the quintessential act in the modern search for "authenticity" and identity. The "discovery" of the Seminoles came very late in the history of the symbolic construction of American Indians, and the special circumstances of the Seminoles and of Florida combine to make this inquiry a special case study of the tension between the wild and the tame in American thought.

Of course, none of this is to say that there are not real people who call themselves "Seminole" or "Miccosukee" and who live their lives for their own sake, not as the projective material for others whose lives may be more confused or, at least, confused in a different way. But it is also true that there are real historical circumstances and real institutions that work to determine how a person constructs his or her life as a Seminole or a Miccosukee. The American Indian people and the rest of us are locked in a dialectical dance of interpreting each other, an interpretive dance in which even our own interpretations and performances of our "selves" are responding to our understanding of how the other is interpreting us.[1]

It is this tangle of interpretation that I am attempting to unravel in these pages. This essay is not an ethnography of the Seminole or Miccosukee people. Anthropologists and others have already created those realist narratives, which in the new model of culture criticism become "texts" for our analysis rather than scientific testimony about how the Seminole and Miccosukee "really live."[2] Nor does this essay offer a history of the Seminoles, a history still being written in rather traditional ways.[3] Rather, I examine a whole range of texts that purport to describe and interpret Florida's "Seminoles." And I use the term "Seminoles" to talk about both the Seminole and Miccosukee peoples, because the touristic imagination makes none of the distinctions the native people themselves would insist on making.

After recounting very briefly the historical circumstances that led to the public invention of Florida's Seminoles, I explain the symbolic importance of the landscape—the Everglades—in the construction of the meanings of the Seminoles. I then recount the three major stages in the interpretation of the Seminoles for tourists, the first two constructed by whites and the third by the Indians themselves. Finally, I offer a more general analysis of the importance of this case study.

Some Pertinent History

Florida has excited the white, European imagination since first contact.[4] After Ponce de León first landed in 1513, in search of the Fountain of Youth (as legend has it), explorers brought back tales of fantastic tropical flora and fauna. In European paintings and sculptures portraying the allegorical figure, "America," as one of the four continents, the alligator and the armadillo accompanied her as provocative icons of the wondrous beasts found in the New World.[5] The indigenous people of Florida—the Calusa during the Spanish period—were another sort of fauna symbolizing the wild and exotic, of a dangerous type; they mortally wounded Ponce de León in 1521. Killing the explorers seems only to have encouraged the Spanish missionaries, who established Spanish influence in Florida by midcentury. The Calusa paid for allying with the Spanish against the French and English, as the English continuously contested Spain's claims. Sir Francis Drake burned Saint Augustine in 1586 and John Davis returned in 1665 to burn again the city that had been rebuilt by the Spanish. By the early 1700s, one group (the Oconee) from the Southeastern Creek Confederacy of tribes moved south from Georgia into Florida, settling finally on the central Alachua prairie (south of Gainesville). The Muskogee, Creek people themselves, had a word, "Sim-in-oli" (also rendered "se-mi-no-lee"), which means "wild ones," that came to be attached to the Oconee and other Creeks who settled in Florida.[6] The English and their Creek allies pushed the Calusa into the Everglades, that great river of grass, and under British control (1763–1783) the Creeks were joined in Florida by runaway slaves and, near the end, by British refugees from the American Revolution.[7]

By the time naturalist William Bartram made his famous trip through Florida in 1774, the word "seminole" (Bartram's "Siminole") was common parlance for the Indians he came across and recorded as duly as he recorded his encounters with alligators and other Florida fauna. They "enjoy a superabundance of the necessaries and conveniences of life," wrote Bartram, "with the security of person and property, the two great concerns of mankind. . . . They seem to be free from want or desires. No cruel enemy to dread, nothing to give them disquietude, but the gradual encroachments of the white people."[8] Of course, things were to change. The loss of the American colonies led to England's surrendering Florida to Spain. The Creek wars of 1813–1814 brought more Creek refugees to Florida, including the Muskogee group. On the pretext of chasing runaway slaves, Andrew Jackson invaded Florida in 1818 and the result of this First Seminole War was that the territory fell under the control of the United States in 1821. The increasing pressure of white settlement led to the idea of relocating the Seminoles to a portion of the Louisiana Purchase that is now Oklahoma, but most Seminoles resisted. The great leader Osceola led the Second Seminole War (1835–1842), which scholars consider among the fiercest and bloodiest of all the Indian wars in the United States. General Thomas S. Jesup captured thousands of Seminoles, including Osceola, under a flag of truce. The prisoners were sent to Oklahoma, without Osceola (who died in prison), so by 1847 a census showed only 120 male Seminoles in Florida. "After the Third Seminole War, 1856–1858, no more than 150 Indians were left in the wild swamp area which no one else wanted."[9] But the Seminoles had never signed a surrender or peace treaty with the United States, a fact of much import in the later narratives about the people.

For several decades thereafter the Florida Seminoles lived in isolated camps. An executive order in 1911 created the first Mikasuki[10] reservation (eventually called the Big Cypress Reservation), joined soon by three other reservations at Brighton (the Cow Creek Seminole, who speak a Muskogee dialect), at Dania (Hollywood), and along the Tamiami Trail running from Miami across the Everglades to the west coast of the state. Thus, there are two language groups (the Muskogee-speaking Seminoles and the Hitchiti-speaking Miccosukee) spread across the reservations, but even this division does not capture the complexity of the groups and their relations. By some accounts, the Miccosukee who live along the Tamiami Trail (the "Trail Indians") are far more independent than the Miccosukee who have chosen to live on the Big Cypress Reservation.[11] And large numbers of other Seminoles continued to live in matrilineal and nuclear family "camps" off the reservations, a sign of the traditional independence of the Seminoles. Although the Seminole Tribe of Florida was incorporated in 1957 and the Miccosukee branch was incorporated as a distinct tribe in 1962, most Seminoles seem to regard these organizations less as governing bodies and more as agencies necessary for dealing with the governments of Florida and the United States.[12] By ethnographic and native accounts, it is the clan that matters most to the Seminoles, and the matrilineal patterns tie their loyalties to a narrow matrilineal or nuclear family "camp." Thus, the culture of the Seminoles made possible the most remarkable instition of all, the Seminole camp as touristic site. But before looking at the tourist sites interpreting the Seminoles, we must consider first the special landscape in which the Seminoles dwell.

The Everglades as the Last Frontier

Just as Frederick Jackson Turner was announcing the end of the frontier and wondering what effect that loss would have on American democratic institutions and traditions, other writers were introducing to the American public of the 1890s a "last frontier," the Florida Everglades. In this period, hunting and "exploring" clubs were an expression of the sort of "muscular Christianity" Theodore Roosevelt and others were championing, and the Everglades appears in some of this literature.[13] Adventure literature had found in the Everglades the perfect setting for "tests" of manhood, and in many of these stories men and boys softened by civilization find in the Everglades, the "last frontier," the rugged self-sufficiency their fathers experienced in the western frontier.

The Florida East Coast and other Florida railroads, the steamship lines, and the land companies created and encouraged a broad literature promising comfortable, safe experiences viewing a mysterious wilderness. Alanson Skinner, an assistant curator at New York's American Museum of Natural History, wrote an account in this vein. "Faster and faster the light of civilization creeps over the globe," he began.

> Africa, once an unknown wilderness, has been made a playground for naturalists and hunters; the lust for rubber has sent adventurers far into tropical America; both poles have been discovered; and yet, in South Florida, at the very threshold of civilization, is a vast swamp, the Everglades, which, up to very recently, has been traveled by white men only six times during the history of this continent.[14]

Every narrator writing about the Everglades slips into the same combination of awe and fear in describing this wild place. As late as 1947 an author wrote that the Everglades "have always been one of the unique regions of the earth, remote, never wholly known."[15]

Like other wilderness landscapes, the Everglades is contested terrain. Land developers saw great potential there if the swamp could be drained, and the history of the Everglades is in large part a history of the struggles between conservationists and developers. It was the digging of canals and the draining of vast stretches of the Everglades in the first decades of this century that changed the ecology of the landscape and ruined the natural subsistence base for the Seminoles. The massive slaughter of waterbirds for plumes to adorn turn-of-the-century hats and other fashions evoked still another conservationist movement. Through the efforts of conservationists across several decades, the Everglades National Park was created in 1947, but the tension between developers and conservationists continues. Indeed, the meaning of the Everglades as a mysterious wilderness depends in part on its juxtaposition against intensified versions of civilization, such as

Florida's Gold Coast of cities, hotels, and tourist attractions. That so desolate a wilderness exists a mere half-hour's drive from Atlantic beaches and modern hotels (no matter what the period) only heightens its mystery.

The Tourist Sites

It is useful to see the representation of the Seminoles as moving through three stages since the nineteenth century. In the first two of those stages, white America had control over the representations; in the third stage, the Seminoles "interpret back" by gaining control of their own representations, yet these self-representations seem trapped by the narrative conventions created in the first two stages.

At the outset, most narratives pictured the Seminoles as noble savages at one with nature. Many of the fiction and nonfiction books at the end of the nineteenth century counted the Seminoles as part of the fauna in the South Florida landscape. And the Seminoles' seclusion created an aura of mystery. "No tribe—or remnant of a nation, rather—," wrote one author, "has preserved its blood so free from contamination as this. Despite the changes and rude shocks which the war must have occasioned, the Seminoles have retained their old-time habits of speech, ceremonies, dress, and traditional rites of religion."[16] C. B. Cory wrote a long chapter on the Seminoles for his book on hunting and fishing in Florida, including a pieced-together, secondhand description of the important Green Corn Dance and a unique description of a manatee hunt. Like other writers, Cory noted the reliance of the Seminoles on the alligator for hides and meat, and the association of the Seminole with that liminal animal enhances the "wildness" of the Seminole.[17] Minnie Moore Willson, who worked with the Indian Rights Association of Philadelphia for the welfare of the Seminoles, was also a champion of conserving the birds and other treasures of the Everglades. In describing the Everglades as the "Least Known Wilderness in America," Willson noted that "here and there in the mysterious depths of the great Florida jungle live the 600 descendants of the bravest, purest blood American Indian—those patriots who refused to desert their country nearly a century ago and, escaping capture by blood hounds and bullets, hid themselves in the wilds of the tangled Everglade wilderness and were for years lost to the historian."[18] Willson presented a thoroughly romantic portrait of the Seminoles, wishing to preserve both those people and the Everglades from exploitation. A similarly romanticized view of the Seminoles also shows up in the boys' fiction of the early twentieth century.[19]

The first stage of the representation of the Seminoles saw them as usually noble embodiments of the wild, but the second stage began to set the Seminole apart from the wilderness and presented them as engaging the modern world on their own terms. Key to this stage was the creation of the commercial Seminole tourist camp. Some of the earliest turn-of-the-century postcards from Florida picture Seminoles in their "camps" (Figure 10.1). Adventurous tourists at first had to visit the Seminole camps out in the Everglades, but in 1914 an Irish immigrant, Henry

D.C.-281—Seminole Indians in the Heart of the Florida Everglades

Figure 10.1   *Postcard (1949) caption reads: "The Seminole Indians still use the primitive dug-out canoes in their contacts with other villages in the vast Everglades area. The waterway illustrated parallels the Tamiami Trail and offers a striking contrast between old and new methods of transportation."*

Coppinger, bought some land on the south bank of the Miami River, with thoughts of creating a commercial tropical garden. Several Seminole camps were located on Coppinger's land, so he asked the Seminoles to stay and become part of the tourist attraction, Coppinger's Tropical Gardens, Alligator Farm, and Seminole Indian Village. Along with the families in residence, other Seminole families would come in from remote camps to sell crafts and baby alligators to the tourists (Figure 10.2). The Coppinger family survivors insisted that eighteen-year-old Henry, Jr., was the first person to "wrestle" alligators for the tourists' entertainment and that it was he who taught the Seminoles alligator wrestling.[20] This could easily be true, as alligator wrestling never was a "tradition" of the Seminoles, except as a "tradition" invented for the tourists and first performed by Seminoles at Musa Isle.

In 1919 John A. Roop, the owner of the Musa Isle Grove, a successful fruit shipping and tourist attraction begun in 1907, established a Seminole village that survived for nearly fifty years as a tourist attraction.[21] Like Coppinger's, Musa Isle's Seminole village inhabitants displayed craft techniques for the tourists, sold the crafts as souvenirs, and wrestled alligators to the anxious delight of white tourists watching a wild man wrestle a wild reptile. Five Seminole families made Musa Isle their home, and many other families came through the village for brief visits.

A handsomely printed and illustrated booklet, *Musa Isle,* explained that the "fast-disappearing Seminoles still live at this beauty spot in their primitive way, just as they lived hundreds of years ago before their white brethren set out to con-

Figure 10.2 *Postcard (c. 1940s–1950s) caption reads: "Seminole Indian Village at Tropical Hobbyland, N.W. 27th Avenue and 15th Street, Miami, Florida. These thatched huts, with the exception of being fireproofed, are exact duplicates of a typical Seminole village located in the Everglades. The thatched roof sheds tropical showers, and the open construction is very practical for a tropical climate."*

quer the Everglades and develop Florida. Their modes of living and cooking have not varied."[22] Mixed with descriptions of Seminole customs and rituals are descriptions of the Florida alligator and its habits. Again, the symbolic pair—Seminole and alligator—signal the wildness of the Seminoles, and a conventional image on postcards from the commercial camps is the Seminole subduing the alligator (Figure 10.3). As denizens of a touristic site, the Seminole families at Coppinger's Tropical Gardens (later renamed Tropical Hobbyland) and at Musa Isle were expected to display their authentic "lifestyle." One historian wrote:

> The Mikasuki Seminoles' lifestyle in the tourist attraction, followed much the same effortless schedule as it did in the Indians' Everglades environment. The men at both Coppinger's and Musa Isle involved themselves periodically in hewing canoes. Craftwork and clothing were produced by the women. Men also produced crafts. . . . In fact, there is little difference between the daily activities in a Tamiami Trail camp . . . and those in the tourist attraction camps of Miami.[23]

By 1930 the two villages had become so central to the lives and economy of the Miccosukee Seminoles that over half of them "resided in a tourist attraction for varying lengths of time" that year.[24] Inevitably, some critics (including the Seminole agent, James L. Glenn) saw the Seminole village displays as "degrading" and "demoralizing." Especially troubling to some was the Seminoles' practice of

Figure 10.3 *Postcard caption reads: "Alligator wrestling. Henry Nelson, world's champion alligator wrestler, gives daily exhibitions of this ancient Seminole sport, at Tropical Hobbyland Indian Village, N.W. 27th Avenue and 15th Street, Miami. The private Tropical Hobbyland contains fifty alligators, and a dozen crocodiles, yet Henry will go into the water with them entirely unharmed."*

requesting or accepting tips from tourists. Alligator wrestlers depended heavily upon the tips, money thrown into the alligator pit at the end of a show. In a report to the Office of Indian Affairs in the Department of the Interior, the author singled out the commercial villages for special invective and recommended that the government cut off the health care and rations "of all Indians who accept this demoralizing employment."[25]

A third significant Seminole village included as part of a tourist attraction enterprise arose in central Florida, at Ross Allen's Reptile Institute at Silver Springs. (Figure 10.4). Silver Springs itself had been a tourist destination since the 1870s, and commercial glass-bottom boats began showing tourists the crystalline springs in the 1890s. A rugged entrepreneur, Allen moved to Ocala in 1929 to create an attraction centering around his herpetological interests. Originally Allen established only exhibits of snakes, alligators, and assorted wild animals, but in 1935 the Seminole colony at Silver Springs became part of the institute and several families established permanent residence there.[26]

Naturalist and writer Wilfred T. Neill relied upon Allen's institute both for information and sponsorship. Neill wrote a solid, scientifically respected book on alligators, based in part upon the research that had been undertaken at Silver

Figure 10.4 *Postcard (c. 1940s–1950s).*

Springs.[27] But Neill was also a popularizer of scientific knowledge, and his book *The Story of Florida's Seminole Indians* (1956) was written for the Florida tourist or native seeking a readable, entertaining, yet informed account of the Seminoles. Neill devoted a brief chapter to "The Silver Springs Seminoles," beginning with the point that the members of the colony "demonstrate that the Indians can become successful and respected members of a community and yet retain their own ways which mean so much to them" (p. 117). The Seminoles, he pointed out, had modern sanitary conveniences in addition to their traditional chickees. Many were Baptists. The men were not paid for being in residence; rather, the men earned income through labor at Silver Springs. The women and children received small wages for being in residence, but the sale of crafts was a significant source of income. "The handicrafts are derived from the Seminoles' own culture," Neill was careful to say; "these Indians are not set to making Alaskan totem-poles, Sioux war-bonnets, Kiowa teepees, or Algonkin canoes" (p. 118). The Seminoles are free to come and go. Neill concluded:

> In short, the Silver Springs Seminoles lead a good, well-rounded life. They have a steady income, ideal working hours and conditions, plenty of wholesome recreation, medical attention when necessary, spiritual guidance, and freedom to live as they wish. They are clean, honest, and well-mannered. And most important, they maintain their dignity and self-respect; they are well adjusted to a way of life combining the best features of white and Indian culture. (p. 118)

By the mid-1950s, then, the second stage in the representation of the Seminoles had matured. The Seminoles were now portrayed as noble children of the swamp, but also as people who could pick and choose from modern conveniences without jeopardizing the virtues of their traditional ways. One author noted, for example, that more and more Seminoles were enjoying motion pictures and were socializing more with white people.[28] The iconography of postcards during the 1950s began to feature Seminoles dressed in traditional costume but using modern appliances, like sewing machines, refrigerators, and electric stoves.[29] Perhaps most emblematic of the 1950s view was Joe Panther, the Seminole teenager who was the central character in a series of adolescent novels by Zachery Ball. Joe lives with his family at the Musa Isle village, occasionally visiting the Everglades to hunt and hone his native instincts; but he also moves easily in the world of the white man, gaining employment as a mate on a commercial game-fishing boat.[30]

By the 1960s, the increasing sense of Native American civil rights led simultaneously to the demise of the commercial villages and to the emergence of a third stage in the representation of the Seminoles. Not to be outdone by the white entrepreneurs, the Seminoles themselves decided to create an "authentic" camp site at their Dania Reservation near Hollywood. Although the reservation is as modern in its architecture as any in the surrounding Hollywood community, the tribe created an "Okalee Indian Village," "where the old life has been reconstructed for visitors."[31] The village was more a dead museum of the material culture of the Seminoles than a living museum or exhibition of traditional ways.

The Seminoles' representation of themselves entered a new phase in January 1989, when the Tribal Council chartered the Ah-Tha-Thi-Ki Museum (the Museum of the Seminole Tribe of Florida). When I visted the temporary museum in September 1993 (it had been open only a year), the small space displayed some of the artifacts and signage that will find an eventual home in a permanent museum to be built on the Big Cypress Reservation. The museum aims at interpreting Seminole history, customs, and crafts, and the models and artists' renderings of the planned museum suggest that it will be an attractive and modern cultural museum.

The temporary museum sits on the site of the now-abandoned Okalee Dania village, at the busy intersection of State Road 7 and Stirling Road. Despite the good intentions of the tribe, the museum's current location highlights the representational dilemma facing the Seminoles. Adjacent to the museum is a "Native Village," a small cluster of shops and other businesses that tap into conventional iconography having little to do with the Seminoles. The visitor must look hard for the "traditional" Seminole crafts—dolls, sweet-grass baskets, and patchwork clothing—hidden in a cluttered jungle of American Indian arts and crafts from everywhere but Florida. Here Navajo turquoise jewelry mixes with crafts from Central America. But down the street, things get even more complicated, for the largest signs within sight of the museum announce the two things that bring people to the Dania Reservation these days—tax-free tobacco products and gambling. A strip mall across the street from the large bingo palace lures tourists with a giant cement tepee, a housing form signifying "Indian" without regard to the specifics of Seminole culture. A gift shop nearby is filled with drums, tomahawks, spears, and other gawdy souvenirs that, again, signify the generic "Indian" to the tourists who may know no better. The museum sat empty that day, poor competition for whatever commercial versions of "Indianness" tourists were seeking. As I talked with the young man keeping watch over the museum and selling books and other materials from the small counter, he lamented the lack of interest in Seminole history and culture. Looking out toward the bingo hall, he told me that the people the tribe had hired to run the gambling for them were cheating the tribe—one more example, he said, of the bad luck of the Seminoles.

The next morning I began driving west along the Tamiami Trail, in search of the other great effort of the Florida Indians to interpret themselves. The Miccosukee Tribe has built a Miccosukee Culture Center and Indian Village about twenty-five miles west of Miami. The Miccosukee have attempted to combine the old conventions of representation with the new, but it is mainly the old that dominate. After buying my ticket in the modern, air-conditioned gift shop, I followed my "Information and Guide Map" through the gate and into a reconstructed village of thatched, open chickees. The printed guide explained that

> Our people never settled in one community like the Indians on reservations in the West. Miccosukees have always been rather independent. We stayed to ourselves in the Everglades for about a hundred years, resisting efforts to make us like everybody else. But when the highway, Tamiami Trail, was built in the 1930s, we started to accept some of the new world's concepts.
>
> In 1962 we were federally recognized as an Indian Tribe, thus separating Miccosukee from the Seminole Tribe. Our tribe now has complete education, health and public safety departments, which combine appropriate aspects of Indian and non-Indian practices.

Past the chickees showing how Miccosukee families live, cook, eat, and make traditional crafts, I found the Miccosukee Museum (founded in 1983), a modest but modern, air-conditioned museum displaying the material culture and early history of the Miccosukee and Seminoles, as well as the natural history of the Everglades. The museum was a refreshing break from a village that could have been Musa Isle in the 1950s, but a return to the outside brought me to the alligator pens and the alligator wrestling pit. The self-guided tour ends with the gift shop again, where Miccosukee clothing and beadwork mingle with other American Indian arts and crafts.

As I left the culture center and Indian village, I was struck by how trapped the Miccosukee seemed by the older conventions of representing the Seminoles. Control over the representation had changed hands, but otherwise there was little difference I could detect between this commercial village and the Musa Isle I recalled from my childhood in the 1950s and could see in the printed and visual materials from the 1920s through the 1940s. The Miccosukee were "getting themselves up" for the tourists in an old manner, and as I drove away I wondered if the Seminole Museum at Big Cypress would be any more successful in breaking away from the older visual and performance formulas. Had the Seminoles and Miccosukee offered a counterinterpretation of their cultures and their everyday lives? Had they really spoken back to nearly a hundred years' worth of white representations? What would it mean, even, to offer a counterinterpretation in public space?

Authenticity and Identity

The Seminoles are not the only indigenous American people to be incorporated into tourism, but the Seminole case offers some very interesting texts and puzzles for our thinking about matters of authenticity and the cultural representation of otherness. There are many themes running through the visual and verbal narratives about the Florida Seminoles, but I want to tease out just a few of these themes to see what this case tells us.

The Seminoles were an invention from the outset. As we have seen, the word "Seminole" gathers under one name a heterogeneous assemblage of Calusa remnants, Creek people, and others. The Seminoles identify primarily with clan and the isolated household, choosing to identify themselves as "Seminole" only on occasions when the people need to be presented or represented to others. The Seminoles, therefore, were constructed largely by white writers and commercial entrepreneurs for white audiences, sometimes with the collaboration of the indigenous people. The Seminoles provided rich projective material for the white imagination, and if we treat the touristic narratives as projective narratives, we can see what the Seminoles offered the white audience.

The white audience loved the "wildness" of the Seminoles. Framing this wildness, of course, was the symbolism of the Everglades. The "wildness" of the Seminoles made appropriate their display as a feature of the natural history of the Everglades and of Florida. In all three of the tourist Seminole villages operated from 1914 to the early 1960s, the village was a touristic site in the middle of a narrative about Florida wildlife. The Seminoles inhabited the Eden-like "tropical gardens" built by Coppinger; they were situated among the tropical animals and foliage of Musa Isle; and they were a stop on the guided tour of Ross Allen's Reptile Institute at Silver Springs, coming just between the demonstration of harmless snakes and the wild animal exhibit. These tourist attractions assumed the narrative, interpretive authority of natural history museums, exhibiting the wild people in the reproduced camp, leading their everyday lives. The guidebooks and postcard captions always emphasized that these Seminoles were "living just as they do in the wild country of the Florida Everglades."[32] One postcard caption explained: "The Seminole Indians who make the Florida Everglades their home are a strange and unique race. They are skillful fishermen and good hunters; wear a distinctive costume of horizontal striped material and are probably the most simple, primitive people living in the United States." The Edenic metaphor implied in most, and drawn explicitly in some, of the tourist attractions and in the touristic narratives included the notion that the Seminoles, unlike most other Americans, lived amid an abundance of food and in a comfortable climate. This view enters even the ethnographic literature.

And lest the tourist assume that the Seminoles on display were now tamed, no longer wild, many of the narratives for tourists emphasized the fact that the Seminoles never surrendered to the United States. A 1957 pictorial history book for tourists was entitled *The Unconquered Seminole Indians*,[33] and the caption on the address side of a postcard postmarked in 1953 read: "The only 'Indian Nation' that has not signed a Peace Treaty with the U.S.A. still carries on in primitive fashion the tribal lure of its ancestors in the Everglades, Florida."

Still, there were problems with this representation. The touristic imagination could see how the Seminoles maintained their "primitive" status out in the camps buried deep in the Everglades, but how was that possible in the tourist villages (which, it was said, had all the modern sanitary conveniences)? Indeed, the ethnographers and the Seminoles were asking the same question, first as increasing numbers of tourists visited the Everglades sites, and then as a new cross-state toll road ("Alligator Alley") brought traffic dramatically closer to the Big Cypress Reservation. The very incorporation of the tribes was meant by the leadership to enable them to address the question of the "modernization" of the Seminoles.

Buried not very deeply in this binary opposition between "primitive" and "modern" is an unexamined notion of "authenticity."[34] Consider a few examples. Alligator wrestling, as noted, was not an authentic Seminole custom. Alligators played a part in the economy of the Seminoles, more for the sale value of the hides than for the meat. Wrestling alligators for entertainment was an invention of white entrepreneurs, who encouraged the Seminoles to engage in this activity in the tourist attractions. Men like Coppinger and Allen knew instinctively, I think, that the symbolism of having a Seminole wrestle the threatening reptile was far more powerful than the sight of a white man engaged in the same struggle. For the Seminole men, alligator wrestling provided lucrative tips for work that was relatively easy and safe, despite appearances. A Seminole alligator wrestler interviewed in 1980 explained that alligator wrestling and snake handling actually went against tribal custom, but the money overcame these cultural taboos.[35] This "invented tradition" became part of the Seminole way of life, if we are willing to say (as I am) that life in the tourist villages constituted a Seminole way of life.

Louis Capron, who wrote both for the popular and the scholarly audience, provides another useful example of the dilemmas of "authenticity." Capron documented the Green Corn Dance, the most important Seminole seasonal ritual ceremony, and wrote of such technological adaptations as use of the sewing machine, the phonograph, and the automobile. The airboat had replaced the dugout canoe to such an extent that Capron and his *National Geographic* photographer asked ninety-year-old Charlie Cypress to build one last dugout canoe for their cameras, and that canoe was sent to the Smithsonian. But most symbolic for Capron was a change in the rattles used at the Green Corn Dance. "They used to be made of tortoise shells," he wrote for the *National Geographic* readers in 1956: "The women, who wore 12 to 16 on each leg, jerked them with a rhythm that gave cadence to the dance. . . . The modern substitute gives a clearer insight into the changing Seminole character than a thousand words. Evaporated milk cans, pierced with nail holes and containing a few beads or hard seeds, have almost replaced the shells. The result, though completely devoid of glamour, is much more effective."[36] There was the dilemma. The Seminoles' value as projective material for the white imagination lay primarily in the Seminoles' remaining wild and primitive. White Americans have always needed the "otherness" of the indigenous people as part of their own ethnosemiotic process of self-definition. Sometimes that native's otherness has been negative, but far more often the whites have imagined a Native American who leads an enviable, authentic life, more in touch with nature and with vital experience. For indigenous people to show any sign of abandoning their "authentic" culture for modern ways threatens their value as "the Other."

Thus, one line of popular and anthropological thinking worries about the loss of authentic Seminole traditions. Neill's chapter on the Silver Springs Seminoles assures the reader that the Seminoles are selling only authentic crafts, not the more generic "Indian" crafts sold at other tourist attractions. But what if they had sold southwestern jewelry, as they do now in Dania? A new line of reasoning among folklorists and anthropologists discards the notion of "authenticity" and the static view of culture implied by that term. Work on the effects of tourism upon native arts and crafts shows a complex dialectic that leads us to view culture as processual and dynamic. There are too many cases where crafts made originally for the tourist trade become incorporated as "traditional" in a Native American culture.[37] One oral historian discovered this process at Musa Isle:

> During the 1930's, the craft of manufacturing "tom-toms" was introduced at Musa Isle by an Indian from Arizona. . . . He instructed the Florida natives on how to paint Southwestern Indian motifs and portraits on the drums. Davis obtained green calf skins and cured them into rawhide for the drum heads. The drums were a major seller. . . . Additional exotic crafts were introduced at Musa Isle in 1932 by the wife of the new operator of the attraction, Nellie Campbell, who introduced the concept of "peace pipes" made from the large stand of bamboo growing on the attraction property. Mrs. Campbell also created an interest in developing new forms of beadwork.[38]

The worries of Neill, Capron, and other salvage ethnographers reflect the narrow conditions under which indigenous cultures serve the symbolic needs of white audiences.

Although the Seminole tourist attractions began as early as 1914, the true heyday of this touristic site was the 1950s, so it is useful to ask what these narratives about the Seminoles offered middle-class, white tourists in that decade. Leading an "authentic" life had become extremely problematic for the middle class in the

1950s. Anxiety about the bomb was enough, but many Americans were anxious about the effect of their affluence. Immersed in a commercial culture that increasingly defined the self through the objects and lifestyles one consumed, middle-class Americans worried about conformity and about the effects of this affluence upon fundamental American values, such as individualism.

The Seminoles served well as examples of people who could maintain their independence and individuality while living in 1950s America. They were unconquered, proud people, but they also lived in the small, nuclear units familiar to the white middle class. The tourist villages demonstrated clearly that the Seminoles could adopt modern sanitation facilities, sewing machines, automobiles, airboats, and television and still maintain something like an authentic, traditional way of life.

Finally, we might ask whether the tourist attractions and promotional materials were "good" for the Seminoles, who often collaborated in these enterprises. Certainly from the 1930s on there were criticisms of the tourist villages from physicians, members of the clergy, and Indian welfare groups. Two historians of Musa Isle and of Coppinger's Tropical Gardens offer a different view. Their interviews with some of the white and Seminole veterans of the tourist attractions suggest that the Seminoles living in the villages had an attitude different from their white "protectors." The draining of the Everglades and a host of other social and economic forces were drastically narrowing the economic options for the Seminoles in the 1920s and 1930s, and money was good in the camps. The Seminoles interviewed in the early 1980s had fond memories of life in the villages.[39] "It is this author's opinion," wrote one historian, "that the Indian families who were the most active in the tourist attractions, were [and continued to be] among the most traditionally oriented Indians in Florida, and their families continue to uphold a traditional, yet progressive, lifestyle."[40] Significant leaders of the 1950s, 1960s, and 1970s emerged from the tourist villages, noted this historian, arguing that the Seminoles preferred the economic self-sufficiency of the commercial attractions to the programs offered by federal Indian agencies.

These are Seminole memories mediated through white narratives. Perhaps the Was it good for the Seminoles? question is the wrong one to ask. Certainly Patsy West's phrase, "a traditional, yet progressive, lifestyle," seems itself another text of the 1950s projection of white anxieties upon the Seminoles. We have no unmediated narratives from the Seminoles about life in the commercial villages, but we would not know what to do with them even if they were available. What if our ideal informant said, "Yes, it was strange growing up as part of a tourist exhibit, but we did not have many economic options and we led pretty good lives there"? Is this "bad faith" masking complicity? To make that judgment we would have to assume for ourselves a privileged position of knowledge incompatible with the ethnosemiotic perspective. The Is it good for the Seminoles? question may belong to the view of culture in which "authenticity" is still an issue and a desideratum. The Seminole case helps us see how pointless such questions are and forces us to ask completely new questions about our own lives and the cultural encounter with otherness.

Notes

I wish to thank the directors and staffs of the special collections at the University of Miami, the F. K. Yonge Library of Florida History at the University of Florida, and Florida State University for their friendly and generous assistance in the archival work for this essay. A faculty research grant from the Davis Division of the Academic Senate of the University of California supported this research.

1. See E. Dean MacCannell, "Ethnosemiotics," *Semiotica* 27 (1979), pp. 149–171.

2. The classic ethnographies—such as William C. Sturtevant's "The Medicine Bundles and Busks of the Florida Seminoles," *Florida Anthropologist* 7 (1954), pp. 31–70 and Merwyn S. Garbarino's *Big Cypress: A Changing Seminole Community* (Prospect Heights, Ill.: Waveland Press, 1972)—employ a rhetoric shared by most ethnographies until "the crisis of representation" caught up with anthropology in the late 1960s. See the critical essays collected in James Clifford and George E. Marcus, eds., *Writing Culture: The Poetics and Politics of Ethnography* (Berkeley: University of California Press, 1986).

3. See, for example, Edwin C. McReynolds, *The Seminoles* (Norman: University of Oklahoma Press, 1957), Harry A. Kersey, Jr., *The Florida Seminoles and the New Deal, 1933–1942* (Boca Raton: Florida Atlantic University Press, 1989), and James W. Covington, *The Seminoles of Florida* (Gainesville: University Press of Florida, 1993).

4. Harry A. Kersey, Jr., *The Seminole and Miccosukee Tribes: A Critical Bibliography* (Bloomington: Indiana University Press, 1987) provides an indispensable guide to the literature.

5. Hugh Honour, *The New Golden Land: European Images of America from the Discoveries to the Present Time* (New York: Pantheon, 1975).

6. Wilfred T. Neill, *The Story of Florida's Seminole Indians* (St. Petersburg, Fla.: Great Outdoors, 1956), p. 8, and Louis Capron, "Florida's 'Wild' Indians, the Seminole," *National Geographic Magazine* 123 (1956): 816.

7. Garbarino, *Big Cypress*, p. 8.

8. William Bartram, *Travels of William Bartram*, ed. Francis Harper (1791; reprint New Haven: Yale University Press, 1958), p. 134.

9. Garbarino, *Big Cypress*, p. 12.

10. "Mikasuki" was the spelling long sustained by anthropologists and others, but the people themselves use "Miccosukee," which is now used by scholars as well.

11. See James W. Covington, "Trail Indians of Florida," *Florida Historical Quarterly* 58 (1979), 37–57; Covington, *Seminoles of Florida;* and Peter Matthiessen, *Indian Country* (New York: Penguin Books, 1984).

12. Capron, "Florida's 'Wild' Indians," p. 831.

13. See, for example, F. A. Ober, *The Knockabout Club in the Everglades* (Boston: Estes and Lauriat, 1887); Charles E. Whitehead, *The Camp-Fires of the Everglades, or Wild Sports in the South* (Edinburgh: L. D. Douglas, 1891); C. B. Cory, *Hunting and Fishing in Florida* (Boston: Estes and Lauriat, 1896); Wilmer M. Ely, *The Boy Chums in the Forest; or, Hunting for Plume Birds in the Florida Everglades* (New York: A. L. Burt Company, 1910); and A. W. Dimock, *Be Prepared; or, the Boy Scouts in Florida* (New York: Grosset and Dunlap, Publishers, 1912).

14. Alanson Skinner, "Across the Florida Everglades," *Atlantic, Gulf and West Indies Steamship News,* 7 (October 1915), p. 5.

15. Marjory Stoneman Douglas, *The Everglades: River of Grass* (New York: Rinehart and Company, 1947).

16. Ober, *Knockabout Club,* p. 102.

17. Jay Mechling, "The Alligator," in *American Wildlife in Symbol and Story,* ed. Angus K. Gillespie and Jay Mechling (Knoxville: University of Tennessee Press, 1987), pp. 73–98.

18. Minnie Moore Willson, *Snap Shots from the Everglades of Florida* (Tampa, Fla.: Tampa Tribune Publishing Co., 1917), p. 3.

19. See, for example, Wilmer M. Ely, *The Boy Chums Cruising in Florida Waters; or, the Perils and Dangers of the Fishing Fleet* (New York: A. L. Burt Company, 1914) and his *The Boy Chums in the Florida Jungle; or, Charlie West and Walter Hazard with the Seminole Indians* (New York: A. L. Burt Company, 1915).

20. Dorothy Downs, "Coppinger's Tropical Gardens: The First Commercial Indian Village in Florida," *Florida Anthropologist* 34 (4) (1981), pp. 225–231.

21. Patsy West, "The Miami Indian Attractions: A History and Analysis of a Transitional Mikasuki Seminole Environment," *Florida Anthropologist* 34 (1981), pp. 200–224.

22. James Lowther Berkebile, *Musa Isle: Stories About the Seminoles, Alligators, and Florida's Most Noted Indian Trading Post* (Augusta, Ga.: Phoenix Printing Company, 1926), p. 5.

23. West, "Miami Indian Attractions," p. 205.

24. Ibid., p. 207.

25. Roy Nash, *Survey of the Seminole Indians of Florida* (Washington, D.C.: United States Department of Interior, Office of Indian Affairs, 1932), p. 81.

26. Neill, *Story of the Seminole Indians,* p. 117.

27. Wilfred T. Neill, *The Last of the Ruling Reptiles: Alligators, Crocodiles, and Their Kin* (New York: Columbia University Press, 1971).

28. William C. Emerson, *The Seminoles: Dwellers of the Everglades* (New York: Exposition Press, 1954).

29. I disagree with the interpretation offered by Alison Devine Nordstrom, who argues in an exhibition catalog essay that these images show the separation of the Seminole from the new technology and that the "Indian's authenticity is affirmed by his immutability." Rather, I believe these images show not a "vanishing" culture but an adapting culture, one that preserves its authenticity in its ability to accommodate the new technologies. See her essay, "Some Photographs of Seminoles," in *Imag(in)ing the Seminole: Photographs and Their Uses Since 1880* (Daytona Beach, Fla.: Southeast Museum of Photography, Daytona Beach Community College, 1993).

30. Zachery Ball, *Joe Panther* (New York: Holiday House, 1950).

31. Louis Capron, "Florida's Emerging Seminoles," *National Geographic Magazine* 136 (1969), p. 727.

32. Wilfred T. Neill, *Ross Allen's Reptile Institute at Silver Springs* (Silver Springs, Fla.: Ross Allen Reptile Institute, n.d.), p. 19.

33. Irvin M. Pleithman, *The Unconquered Seminole Indians* (St. Petersburg, Fla.: Great Outdoors, 1957).

34. There is a considerable scholarly literature on the tourist's search for "authenticity." The reader should begin with E. Dean MacCannell's books, *The Tourist: A New Theory of the Leisure Class* (New York: Schocken, 1976) and *Empty Meeting Grounds: The Tourist Papers* (London: Routledge, 1992). Erik Cohen, in his essay "A Phenomenology of Tourist

Experiences," *Sociology* 13 (1979), pp. 179–201, attempts to find a middle ground between MacCannnell's view and those wholly critical of touristic experiences. Edward M. Bruner's essay, "Tourism, Creativity, and Authenticity," *Studies in Symbolic Interaction* 10 (1989), pp. 109–114, nicely and briefly summarizes current anthropological and folkloristic thinking about tourism and authenticity.

35. West, "Miami Indian Attractions," p. 207.

36. Capron, "Florida's 'Wild' Indians," p. 831.

37. See examples in the essays gathered by Nelson H. H. Graburn, ed., *Ethnic and Tourist Arts* (Berkeley: University of California Press, 1976) and by Valene L. Smith, ed., *Hosts and Guests: The Anthropology of Tourism* (Philadelphia: University of Pennsylvania Press, 1977).

38. West, "Miami Indian Attractions," p. 208.

39. Downs, "Coppinger's Tropical Gardens," p. 230.

40. West, "Miami Indian Attractions," p. 219.

11

Segregated Stories: The Colonial Contours of the Little Bighorn Battlefield National Monument

C. Richard King

In 1971, Alvin M. Josephy, Jr., visited the Custer Battlefield National Monument (as it was called then) in Montana with "some Indian friends." A Sioux family, a Southern Cheyenne man, and two Yakima youths accompanied the noted historian of the American West on a tour of the historical site, guided by a National Park Service ranger. "It was obvious," to Josephy that "they did not like what they were hearing. They kept glancing at each other as if they were not quite sure if it was all right for them to be there." His companions felt out of place, he argued, because the battlefield projected "a jaundiced, ethnocentric and therefore false view of the long struggle between themselves and the white invaders of their lands."[1] Over the past twenty-five years, the countless protests and other critical projects undertaken by Native American activists have been combined with efforts to modify and moderate retellings of the battle at the site. Specifically, activists worked toward the revision of exhibits and narratives so that they stress a clash of cultures instead of glorifying Custer, toward renaming of the battlefield, and toward the construction of a monument honoring Native Americans who participated in the conflict. But such efforts have done little to reduce the alienation that many Native Americans feel when visiting the Little Bighorn Battlefield National Monument. In fact, members of the Northern Cheyenne nation who were interviewed by Royal Jackson consider the site to be trivial and its renditions of the past to be false.[2] Even Crow interns working at the battlefield, with whom I spoke in summer 1994, had either rarely visited or had never been to the site prior to being employed by the National Park Service.

In contrast, during this period, Euro-American (non–Native American) visitors have continued to feel "at home" when touring the Little Bighorn Battlefield National Monument. To be sure, recent struggles over historical interpretation have troubled some of them, particularly Custer buffs, but most Euro-American tourists support efforts to present the battle as a complex clash of cultures, informed by perspectives from both sides of the conflict. Indeed, many Euro-American visitors, I would suggest, concur with Michael McCoy's assessment of the historical site: "So well has the National Park Service recreated the battle via displays, signs and tape recordings that you can almost see the action, hear the rifles repeating and soldiers and Indians screaming, and smell gunpowder lifting on the breeze."[3] For Euro-American visitors, then, contesting and perhaps altering the historical representations at the national monument, predicated as such criticism and potential changes are on objectivity, balance, and realism, would reinforce rather than undermine their imaginative re-creations and romantic renderings of the conflict.

The divergent sentiments and experience of Native Americans and Euro-Americans in relation to the Little Bighorn Battlefield National Monument derive from the ways in which the stories and structures fashioned at the historical site position them. More specifically, despite recent changes and continuing challenges, the persistence of this positioning emanates from the colonial contours of the monument. In reformulating the conflict, the signifying practices of exhibition, commemoration, and narration reproduce colonial categories and relations, enacting an intricate interplay of hierarchy, asymmetry, dominance, and difference. In examining the imperial recollections, or intersections of colonial practices and collective memories, that are emergent at the monument, I have brought together two largely isolated conceptual fields. Indeed, although works that study the production of the past in the present have highlighted the political technologies and historical struggles through which sociocultural identities and imagined communities materialize, with few exceptions such works have largely failed to address the ways in which public remembrances collude and collide with colonial discourses.[4] Even those studies attentive to the interconnections of power and signification in historical reproductions do not adequately examine the importance of imperial recollection in American culture.[5] Studies of the intersections of colonialism and culture in Africa and Asia have tended to neglect the contemporary United States, whereas those studies concentrating on American culture have all but ignored the ways in which mnemonic technologies shape American colonial contours.[6] In this chapter, I draw on ethnographic and archival research conducted during the summer of 1994 to explore the asymmetrical cultural histories and hierarchical relations produced at the monument through commemorative exclusion and segregated stories.

My examination of the Little Bighorn Battlefield National Monument differs from previous representations of the site in two significant ways. First, in place of the descriptive accounts common to both historical studies and tourist texts, I adopt an interpretive approach, questioning the accepted narratives that are constructed through memorialization, display, and historical representation. Second, in contrast with progressive readings, which either applaud modifications to the site acritically or unreflexively celebrate the multiple voices struggling to define its significance, I adopt a critical framework attentive to the connections of power and signification, tracing and challenging the persistence of imperial recollections at the site.

The Little Bighorn Battlefield National Monument

The Little Bighorn Battlefield National Monument, located on the Crow Agency in southeastern Montana, is composed of the Custer National Cemetery, the Little Bighorn Battlefield, the Reno-Benteen Battlefield, monuments to the slain and surviving U.S. soldiers, and a visitor center that contains a museum-bookstore as well as the archives and administrative offices. The National Park Service charges an admission fee, for which visitors receive a descriptive pamphlet and a brochure explaining the special programs offered daily. A road runs through the site, tracing a ten-mile loop that ushers visitors past the Custer National Cemetery and Visitor Center, then past Last Stand Hill and the monument to the U.S. soldiers, alongside the Little Bighorn Battlefield to the Reno-Benteen Battlefield, and back. Although tourists are invited to drive this route themselves, the National Park Service offers an hour-long bus tour. On the patio, at the southeast end of the visitor center, rangers and volunteers give programs or "patio talks," on the Plains Indians, the battle, the sociohistorical context, weapons and tactics, and the U.S. cavalry. To the east of the visitor center, in an area alongside the battlefield dubbed the amphitheater, two interpretive stations, one representing the U.S. cavalry and the other, the Plains Indians, provide hands-on, informal presentations on material culture, social life, and the battle. Visitors can ask questions of the rangers here, pretend to use weapons, and try on garments. Rangers are also usually stationed in front of the visitor center to answer questions.

The content and form of the histories currently produced at the Little Bighorn Battlefield National Monument emerge at the intersection of a number of complex sociohistorical processes. Most notably, commemoration, nationalism, tourism, and the resurgence of indigenous resistance have shaped the national monument and its retellings of the conflict.[7]

From 1877 to 1940, the Department of War administered a one-square-mile portion of battlefield, supplemented by a National Cemetery in 1879. Initially, the commanding officer of nearby Fort Custer was charged with the care of the battlefield; then, in 1894, an on-site superintendent assumed responsibility for the site.[8] Throughout this period, memorialization consolidated popular memory of the conflict. One year after the battle, in summer 1877, the bodies of the soldiers who had fallen were reburied on-site; Custer was reinterred in the National Cemetery at West Point; and a log monument to the event was erected by the

United States Army on the battlefield. Four years later, in 1881, a marble monument replaced the original wooden memorial. In 1930, the federal government purchased the Reno-Benteen Battlefield, five miles away from the supposed site of Custer's Last Stand, the battlefield's commemorative center. Although limited at first, tourism also affected the development of the battlefield during this period. From 1877 to 1894, picnicking at the battlefield was "a popular diversion for Army personnel" stationed at Fort Custer. Until the turn of the century, military officers, dignitaries, and celebrities, from Buffalo Bill Cody to Edward S. Curtis, frequently toured the historical site.[9] In the mid-1880s, the Chicago, Burlington, and Quincy Railroad laid track alongside the battlefield, quickly integrating the site into its guidebooks and marketing strategies, while also making it "accessible to the pilgrim" *en masse.*[10] Finally, during this period, anniversaries and reunions of Euro-American survivors attracted thousands of visitors to the battlefield.

In 1940, the battlefields, monuments, and national cemetery were transferred to the National Park Service and named the Custer Battlefield National Monument. Although the emergence of mass tourism and the rise of indigenous activism have profoundly affected the site, it has been, above all, the introduction and continual revision of official interpretive programs that has differentiated the National Park Service's administration from that of the War Department.[11] Throughout much of this period, official texts, interpretive programs, and museum exhibits were designed to be "accurate, tasteful, well-balanced, and significantly comprehensive."[12] Initially, professional interpreters, park rangers, and official guidebooks displaced local guides and pamphlets written by buffs.[13] Then, twelve years after the National Park Service assumed responsibility, and nearly thirty years after first being proposed, a historical museum and visitor center was dedicated on June 25, 1952. Although the museum concentrated upon, and even celebrated, Custer and his triumphal last stand at the expense of the sociohistorical context of the battle,[14] commentators praised its significance: "For both tourists and historians the museum gives life and added meaning to the silent stones outside."[15] Eight years later, the National Park Service renovated the museum, hoping to correct factual errors, balance historical accounts, and enhance the circulation of visitors through the gallery.[16] The museum was again renovated in 1986. Although the 1956 exhibits continued to constitute the core of historical displays, efforts were made to reframe the battle as a clash of cultures arising from a particular sociohistorical contest.[17] Changes in exhibitionary practices, according to some, derive from increased cultural sensitivity and reflect a recognition of past ethnocentrism.[18]

Pan-Indian political activism has not only sparked many of the National Park Service's recent reinterpretations, but it has also called into question the significance of these revisions. In fact, since the early 1970s, the dominant interpretations of the conflict at the Little Bighorn Battlefield National Monument have come under attack. Over the past twenty-five years, notable disruptions of the prevailing stories and structures fashioned at the site have included efforts to erect a cast-iron plaque memorializing indigenous combatants as part of the Trail of Broken Treaties on October 13, 1972; disruption of the centennial observances by American Indian Movement (AIM) protesters on June 25, 1976; and the placement of a plaque commemorating indigenous participants by George Magpie and AIM protesters on June 25, 1988.[19] Throughout this period, indigenous activists have argued quite forcefully that the site is ethnocentric and exclusionary, demanding that the National Park Service revise its historical representations and dedicate a monument to those Native Americans who participated in the conflict.[20] Although the activists' critical projects have not shattered the reproduction of imperial recollections at the Little Bighorn Battlefield National Monument, they have succeeded in renaming the battlefield, have altered the content and form of historical interpretation at the site, and have cleared the way for the construction of a memorial honoring Native American participants. Scandalized by these significant, if partial, revisions, individuals and organizations dedicated to orthodox interpretations have fought to rehabilitate heroic renderings of Custer, romantic renditions of the conflict, and triumphal accounts of the nation.[21] A letter to the editor of *National Parks* encapsulates the sentiments of this reactionary movement: "Putting up a monument at the Custer Battlefield to honor several thousand Indians who killed the 261 American soldiers is a wonderful idea. Maybe we can get the idea to spread. The Jews could put up a monument to the Nazi SS, the Armenians could put up a monument to the Turks, and the Irish could put up a monument to Cromwell."[22] Significantly, the collision of revisionary and reactionary ideologies has transformed the site into a cultural battleground. In spite of the continuing struggle over the presentation of the past, nearly four hundred thousand visitors tour the site annually. Hoping to respond to the indigenous critique and at the same time to ensure the continued interest of Euro-American tourists, the United States Congress recently approved changing the name of the memorial to the Little Bighorn National Monument and constructing a memorial to the participating Native Americans.

Commemorative Exclusions

Arguably the central attraction of Little Bighorn Battlefield National Monument is the monument to the members of the Seventh Cavalry killed in the battle atop Last Stand Hill (Figure 11.1). The remains of the soldiers are buried beneath the monument, although those of the officers have been removed and reinterred elsewhere. Well-manicured grass surrounds the monument and an interpretive sign explains the history of the site. At the center, overlooking the battlefield, a marker with an audio recording repeats a narrative of the battle whenever it is activated. On Last Stand Hill itself, headstones mark the positions where the bodies of Custer and about fifty of his men were found after the battle. All the marble markers are completely white, with a weathered, ivory hue, but the chevron of Custer's gravestone is black, highlighting who or what is the center of significance. A wrought-iron fence

Figure 11.1 *Monument to Seventh Cavalry soldiers killed in the Battle of the Little Bighorn. Photo courtesy of Little Bighorn Battlefield National Monument.*

encircles the markers, presumably to protect them from souvenir hunters. In the distance, concentrations of markers imprint the rolling landscape, indicating where other members of the Seventh Cavalry, detached from Custer, fell in battle.

The monument atop Last Stand Hill inscribes national narratives, predicated on differential constructs: "In memory of the officers and soldiers who fell near this place, fighting with the 7th United States Cavalry, against Sioux Indians. On the 25th and 26th of June A.D. 1876." The monument establishes two hierarchies of memory. First, it delimits the imagined community (the United States) and its citizen-heroes (the white soldiers), while defining its limits (the frontier) and the alien-enemies who populated it (Indians). Celebrating the sacrifice of the Seventh Cavalry, as well as its implications for state and community, the monument produces (present) differential relations, subjectivities, and sociocultural formations through commemorative exclusions. The monument, in conjunction with the concentration of headstones placed in its shadow, then remaps the battle and its histories: "The spectacle" of the white male body "remaps the coordinates of the battlefield," erasing Native Americans and their political agency.[23] Second, the memorial atop Last Stand Hill formulates an internal commemorative hierarchy: "Bvt. Maj. Gen. G. A. Custer; Captains; Lieutenants; Asst. Surgeons; Soldiers; Arikaree [Arikara] Indian Scouts; Civilians." (The one African-American to die with Custer, translator Isaiah Dorman, is identified only by his first name.) Thus the monument arranges those who died for their country within rigid, hierarchical categories. Interestingly, however, it also literally assimilates the Arikara scouts who died with the Seventh Cavalry; joining with the forces of civilization against the savages along the frontier, they became good Indians worthy of recalling. Within the memorials at the monument, the complex constructions of the nation-state, the citizen subject, and the past demand the commemorative exclusion of the Native American combatants, as well as the hierarchical ordering of the American forces.

Beyond the assimilated Arikara scouts, the site memorializes only one other Native American. No more than one-fourth mile beyond Last Stand Hill, a little removed from the road, stands Lame White Man's marker—"Lame White Man Fell Near Here." In contrast to the stark headstones commemorating the U.S. forces, Lame White Man's marker is wood, not marble, painted brown with engraved lettering painted yellow. It is more like a road sign and other National Park Service road markers than a commemorative plaque. As the only memorial dedicated to the Native Americans slain in the battle and their triumphant compatriots, it highlights an additional absence crucial to the production of the past at the monument. This absence is a clear indication of the way in which the site works to erode Native American subjectivities as well as their victory, dissolving in many ways both the conflict and its historicity. At various places throughout the site, this absence is explained, either by guides or by markers. Some explanations say there is lack of knowledge about where Native American participants fell, while others say that "kinsfolk" removed the bodies of the dead. In the end, this lacuna effaces the presence of Native Americans, their participation, and their perspectives. This commemorative exclusion collapses the historical complexities surrounding the battle, with a play of personalities and patriotism replacing a serious engagement of past and present asymmetries, hierarchies, and differences.

Segregated Stories

Segregation brings to life the practice of the past at the monument. The narratives told throughout the site operate through a logic rooted in an implicit acceptance of separate and unequal stories; as a consequence, two isolated discourses arise from the same violent historical entanglement. Whereas the program discussing "The Road to the Little Bighorn" traces the shared sociohistorical context enmeshing Native American and Euro-American cultures, most of the "patio talks" focus on discrete sociocultural formations: either on the Plains Indians or on the United States Cavalry. A similar separation governs the interpretive stations; one addresses everyday life in the U.S. military and the other, Plains Indian culture. These distinct realities materialize through assemblages of clothing, weapons, and other objects: The former contains (masculine) garments, riding tack, arms, and equipment; the latter includes (masculine and feminine) garments, beadwork, moccasins, a lance, a shield, a bow, and arrows, displayed in front of a tepee. The museum is likewise segregated: on one side are objects associated with Native Americans, whereas on the other are those connected with the United States (cavalry).

Segregation, as the following discussion clarifies, cripples the histories and cultures encoded at the monument; the stories told are neither equivalent nor comparable. Whereas accounts of the indigenous peoples of the Great Plains collapse distinct imagined communities into a flat, bounded, and timeless cultural area, representations of America materialize through considerations of a subculture, that of the United States Cavalry. Moreover, this initial discrepancy derives from the different techniques of display used to present the past. Anthropological technologies fashion Native American culture, whereas historical technologies construct Euro-American culture.

Although the narratives told throughout the monument make visible the colonial contours of the site, the significance of these segregated stories becomes clearer by juxtaposing the U.S. Cavalry and Plains Indian programs. During the former program, the ranger conducting the tour I attended invited the visitors to conceptualize the late nineteenth-century cavalry by recalling their own families or relatives who lived then. He then stressed that the overall focus of the talk was the social world and everyday life, and he used replicas, examples from individual lives, and personal accounts. In contrast, the Plains Indian presentation addressed material culture, illustrated through replica of historical Crow artifacts (despite the fact that members of the Sioux and Cheyenne nations fought against Custer, whereas only a handful of Crows scouted for the U.S. military): clothing, arrows, a tobacco bag, a saddlebag, a breastplate, a choker, and moccasins. All were circulated with the exception of the arrow. In place of social life, modes of production and objects dominated. Instead of the specific examples and personal accounts used in discussing the the U.S. Cavalry, generalizations reigned in the Plains Indian presentation. Finally, differing modes of authentication were implemented. Whereas the cavalry presentation relied on replicas, historical accounts, individual examples, and intimate, imaginative connections, the Plains Indian talk depended on an ethnographic aura/area model and on the anthropological impulse to blur specificities into generalities, contemporary substitutions, and existential connection—the presenter began: "I'm an enrolled member of the Crow tribe."

As I have indicated, the museum is segregated—literally divided into two discrete texts, the Native American to the left and the Euro-American to the right. Opening with a painting titled *Fruitless Victory,* the exhibits comprising the Native American collection include a diorama called "Custer's Last Stand," a collection of "Indian Weapons," an array of objects representing "Indian Medicine," two cases devoted to "The Plains Indian" and a display of photographs, biographies, and personal effects describing the "Indian Scouts." The exhibits constituting the non-native collection, in contrast, begin with three cases tracing Custer's life, then offer a familiar rendition of the battle in display cases, labeled in succession "The Doomed Battalion," "Reno's Retreat," and "There Were Survivors," and conclude with a collection of "Cavalry Arms and Equipment."

In both content and form, the set of images, objects, and texts assembled within the museum narrates segregated stories about the battle, its participants, and its significance. Distinct discursive fields frame the Native American and Euro-American portions of the museum. Whereas the Native American exhibits depend upon the tropes of natural history and colonial-conventional anthropology, the Euro-American exhibits rely upon historical tropes. Consequently, the exhibit fashions Native Americans as people without history, mired in superstition, possessing *a* culture now extinct but observable in interesting, didactic, and ultimately flat objects.

In contrast, the non-native collection of images, objects, and texts sets Euro-Americans as the central players within the story of the battle, securing subjectivity and historicity, whereas Native American combatants occupy marginal roles. The cases concentrating on the Seventh Cavalry plot the story from the cavalry vantage point. The displays detailing Custer's life open the Euro-American portion of the museum, grounding the heroic story. Then the viewer observes in turn the demise of Custer's forces in "The Doomed Battalion" case (Figure 11.2), the diorama portraying Reno's Retreat, and the valiant fight of the remnants of the Seventh Cavalry in the "There Were Survivors" case. Not only does this narrative transform the cavalry combatants into historical actors, but it also presents them as heroes who demonstrated the ideals of honor, valor, and sacrifice. The dioramas, moreover, confirm the centrality of the Euro-American combatants in three ways. First, they concentrate on the actions of the soldiers; second, they depict the battle from their perspective; and third, in the "Custer's Last Stand" diorama particularly, they

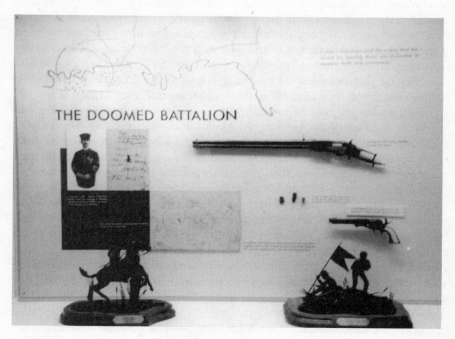

Figure 11.2 *"The Doomed Battalion" museum display case. Photo courtesy of Little Bighorn Battlefield National Monument.*

exclude Native American combatants almost entirely from view. Finally, biographical details subjectify members of the Seventh Cavalry. With the exception of a brief synopsis of the life of Sitting Bull at the entrance to the museum, Sioux and Cheyenne participants remain anonymous, without life histories and personalities. In contrast, the museum devotes immense space to examining Custer's career prior to the conflict, and even considers, if only briefly, the lives of the Native American scouts who accompanied the Seventh Cavalry.

Not only does the museum present Euro-American combatants as agents, it privileges them as knowing subjects. Indeed, at countless places the site reminds its visitors that the battle, particularly Custer's demise, remains a mystery. For example, a text in "The Doomed Battalion" case insists that although "Documents, field specimens, and the Indian accounts help piece together a part of the story . . . the complete story was lost with the battalion." Similarly, the diorama depicting "Custer's Last Stand" contends that because "No soldier survived to tell what actually happened, so this battle is one of the greatest mysteries of American history." Clearly, without white witnesses, "truth," "history," and "reality" remain obscured, partial, and even unknowable. By extension, the assemblage of images, objects, and texts in the museum suggests that Native American participants cannot tell us "what actually happened," that they cannot know the past; instead, they can only contribute to the master narratives of white history. The historiographical techniques utilized in the museum underscore this dichotomy.[24] The canons of history and archaeology map past patterns, codifying the range of possible and verifiable statements about the conflict. In contrast, with the exception of a solitary pictographic account of the conflict, the museum displaces Native American ways of knowing the past, devaluing the validity and significance of these techniques while confirming the position of the Euro-American witness, author, and agent.

The museum not only formulates the Euro-American as knowing subject and heroic agent, it also fashions the Native American as alien object. In contrast with the historical specificity in which it considers the subculture of the cavalry, the museum uses the cultural area concept to make sense of the Native American participants; that is, it assumes that cultures within a specific area (here, the Great Plains) share specific traits and characteristic cultural patterns.[25] On this foundation, it encapsulates "Plains Indian culture," using illustrative material objects and particular ethnological categories, namely warfare, cosmology, and daily life. Consequently, the museum glosses the polymorphous peoples of the Great Plains as a solitary sociocultural formation, with fragments of one nation becoming interchangeable with those of another. Thus, a mirror with ritual significance in the Cheyenne Sun Dance, a Sioux steel-pointed arrow, or a Sioux war club encode larger, unspoken narratives about social organization, supernatural beliefs, and subsistence.

Moreover, unlike the gallant Euro-American soldiers, the museum refers to the Native American combatants as "hostiles" and to their weapons as "dangerous."

The Native American exhibits, furthermore, concentrate on exotic aspects of culture, omitted from the Euro-American exhibits. While the "Indian Medicine" case purports to illuminate indigenous beliefs about the supernatural, it actually obscures them because it fails to contextualize or historicize them, presenting them instead as little more than a collection of curios (Figure 11.3). The Sioux and Cheyenne seem all the more exotic because the museum fails to relativize their practices through contrast with the magical and mystical beliefs of the Euro-American combatants. Equally problematic, the Native American exhibits focus on warfare and hunting at the expense of other everyday cultural practices, perpetuating the imperial nostalgia central to stereotypical representations of indigenous Plains peoples.

Finally, in contrast with the Euro-American portion of the museum, the Native American portion is ahistorical. It situates the cultures of the Sioux and Cheyenne "out of time," presenting them, on the one hand, as frozen, static specimens removed from the vicissitudes of time and, on the other hand, as teetering on the verge of extinction. Neither the war stories nor the biographies that solidify Euro-American subjectivities circulate within the Native American exhibits. Instead, the diverse peoples and nations of the northern Plains are reduced to an "ancient way of life," which simultaneously collapses their distinct histories and denies them coexistence with their Euro-American counterparts.

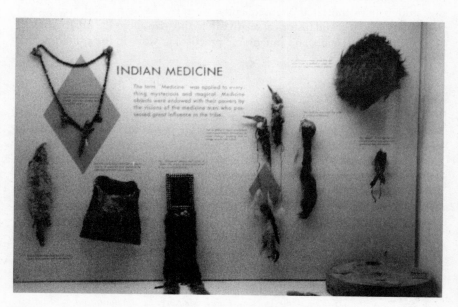

Figure 11.3 *"Indian Medicine" museum display case. Photo courtesy of Little Bighorn Battlefield National Monument.*

Conclusions

Clearly, the intersections of collective memories and colonial discourses at the Little Bighorn Battlefield National Monument have significant implications. Perhaps most important, they call attention to the lasting imperial imprint on contemporary U.S. culture, emphasizing that America's relationship with colonialism neither ends with the conclusion of the Revolutionary War, or even the Wounded Knee Massacre, nor is it limited to imperial designs, military campaigns, or marketing strategies in the periphery. In the preceding pages, I have offered a glimpse of the colonial contours of American culture and have documented the ways in which the signifying practices of narration, exhibition, and memorialization animate difference and domination. More specifically, I argue that the local patterns and precepts of imperial recollection that emerge at the Little Bighorn Battlefield National Monument construct asymmetrical histories, incommensurable cultures, and hierarchical relations. Although my ethnographic example only hints at the diverse ways in which empire, nation, culture, and remembrance collude, collide, contest, and circulate among American cultures, it highlights the importance of further anthropological investigations of the signifying practices articulated at the intersections of colonialism and culture in the contemporary United States. Because America is a colonial culture constantly remaking itself through remembrance, its mnemonic practices are much more diverse and complex than previous studies have indicated. Consequently, we must move beyond critiques of imperialist nostalgia and historical relativism to theorize about the intricate interplay of colonial practices and mnemonic practices at work in the contemporary United States.[26]

Notes

A National Science Foundation Summer Research Grant financed my investigations at the Little Bighorn Battlefield National Monument during summer 1994. This paper would not have been possible without the efforts and insights of the Little Bighorn Battlefield National Monument staff, especially Kitty Deernose. Moreover, the ideas, advice, and encouragement of Nancy Abelmann, Edward M. Bruner, Patricia Clark, Zephyr Frank, Marcie Gilliland, William Kelleher, Charles R. King, David Prochaska, Charles F. Springwood, and Steve Vaughn have greatly enhanced this paper.

1. "The Custer Myth," *Life* 71 (1) (July 2, 1971), pp. 49, 55.

2. *An Oral History of the Battle of the Little Bighorn from the Perspective of the Northern Cheyenne Descendants,* vol. 1 (Washington, D.C.: Government Printing Office, 1987), pp. 18, 69, 109.

3. Michael McCoy, *Montana: Off the Beaten Path* (Old Saybrook, Conn.: Globe Pequot Press, 1993), pp. 100–101.

4. See John Bodnar, *Remaking America: Public Memory, Commemoration, and Patriotism in the Twentieth Century* (Princeton: Princeton University Press, 1992); James Fentress and Chris Wickham, *Social Memory* (Oxford: Blackwell, 1992); John R. Gillis, ed., *Commemorations: The Politics of National Identity* (Princeton: Princeton University Press,

1994); Michael Kammen, *Mystic Chords of Memory: The Transformation of Tradition in American Culture* (New York: Vintage, 1993); George Lipsitz, *Time Passages: Collective Memory and American Popular Culture* (Minneapolis: University of Minnesota Press, 1990); and Barry Schwartz, "Social Change and Collective Memory," *American Sociological Review* 56 (1991), pp. 221–236.

5. See Michael L. Blakey, "American Nationality and Ethnicity in the Depicted Past," in *The Politics of the Past,* ed. Peter Gathercole and David Lowenthal (London: Unwin Hyman, 1990); Eric Gable, Richard Handler, and Anna Lawson, "On the Uses of Relativism: Fact, Conjecture, and Black and White Histories at Colonial Williamsburg," *American Ethnologist* 19 (1992), pp. 791–805; and Martha K. Norkunas, *The Politics of Public Memory: Tourism, History, and Ethnicity in Monterey, California* (Albany: State University of New York Press, 1993).

6. On colonial discourse see Patrick Brantlinger, *Rule of Darkness: British Literature and Imperialism, 1830–1914* (Ithaca: Cornell University Press, 1988); Nicholas Dirks, ed., *Colonialism and Culture* (Ann Arbor: University of Michigan Press, 1992); Lata Mani, "Contentious Traditions: The Debate on Sati in Colonial India," *Cultural Critique* 7 (1987), pp. 119–156; Timothy Mitchell, *Colonising Egypt* (Cambridge: Cambridge University Press, 1988); Edward Said, *Orientalism* (New York: Vintage, 1978); and Ann Laura Stoler, "In Cold Blood: Hierarchies of Credibility and the Politics of Colonial Narratives," *Representations* 37 (1992), pp. 151–189.

On the colonial contours of American culture see Amy Kaplan and Donald E. Pease, eds., *Cultures of United States Imperialism* (Durham, N.C.: Duke University Press, 1993); Catherine A. Lutz and Jane L. Collins, *Reading National Geographic* (Chicago: University of Chicago Press, 1993); and David Spurr, *The Rhetoric of Empire: Colonial Discourse in Journalism, Travel Writing, and Imperial Administration* (Durham, N.C.: Duke University Press, 1993).

7. See Edward T. Linenthal, "A Sore from America's Past That Has Not Yet Healed," in *Sacred Ground: Americans and Their Battlefields* (Urbana: University of Illinois Press, 1991), pp. 127–171 and his more recent "Committing History in Public," *Journal of American History* 81 (1994), pp. 986–991; Douglas C. McChristian, "In Search of Custer Battlefield," *Montana* 42 (1) (1992), pp. 75–76; Robert A. Murray, "Ghost-Herders on the Little Bighorn: The Custer Battlefield Story," Little Bighorn Battlefield National Monument Archives, 1981; Don Rickey, Jr., *History of Custer Battlefield* (Crow Agency, Mont.: Custer Battlefield Historical and Museum Association, 1967), and his condensed, more accessible essay, "The Establishment of Custer Battlefield National Monument," *Journal of the West* 8 (1968), pp. 203–216; and Robert A. Utley, "Whose Shrine Is It? The Ideological Struggle for Custer Battlefield," *Montana* 42 (1) (1992), pp. 70–74.

8. Rickey, *History of Custer Battlefield,* p. 67.

9. Ibid., p. 40.

10. Theodore Gerrish, *Life in the World's Wonderland* (Biddeford, Maine: Biddeford Journal, 1887), p. 409.

11. See Linenthal, "Sore from America's Past," pp. 127–171; and Linenthal, "Committing History in Public."

12. Rickey, *History of Custer Battlefield,* p. 121.

13. Ibid., p. 118.

14. Robert L. Hart, "Changing Exhibitionary and Sensitivity: The Custer Battlefield Museum," *First Annual Symposium of the Custer Battlefield and Museum Association, Hardin*

(Crow Agency, Mont.: Custer Battlefield Historical and Museum Association, 1987), pp. 34–53; Rickey, *History of Custer Battlefield*, p. 122; and Harry B. Robinson, "The Custer Battlefield Museum," *Montana* 2 (3) (1952), pp. 11–29.

15. Norman Maclean and Robert M. Utley, "Edward S. Luce," *Montana* 6 (3) (1956), p. 55.

16. Hart, "Changing Exhibitionary," pp. 37–38.

17. Hart, "Changing Exhibitionary," pp. 41–45.

18. Hart, "Changing Exhibitionary," and Linenthal, "Committing History in Public."

19. See *Trail of Broken Treaties: B.I.A. I'm Not Your Indian Anymore* (Rooseveltown, N.Y.: Akwesasne Notes, 1973), p. 6; Michael J. Koury, ed., *Custer Centennial Observance, 1976* (Fort Collins, Colo.: Old Army Press, 1978); and Linenthal, "Sore from America's Past."

20. Frank Del Olmo, "Activists' Plaque at Little Bighorn Honors 'Patriots' Who Beat Custer," *Los Angeles Times*, July 4, 1988, p. 124; and Linenthal, "Sore from America's Past."

21. Linenthal, "Sore From America's Past"; Michael Wayne Sarf, "Russell Means on Custer Hill," *American Spectator* 21 (December 1988), pp. 32, 34; see also almost any issue of the *Little Bighorn Associates Newsletter*, 1988–1995.

22. Edwin E. Rosenblum, untitled letter to the editor, *National Parks* 63 (3/4) (1989), p. 7.

23. Amy Kaplan, "Black and Blue on San Juan Hill," in *Cultures of United States Imperialism*, ed. Amy Kaplan and Donald E. Pease (Durham: Duke University Press, 1993), p. 223.

24. Eric Gable and Richard Handler, "The Authority of Documents at Some American History Museums," *Journal of American History* 81 (1994), pp. 119–136.

25. Richard Scaglion, "The Plains Culture Area Concept," in *Anthropology of the Great Plains*, ed. W. R. Wood and Margot Liberty (Lincoln: University of Nebraska Press, 1980), pp. 23–34.

26. On imperialist nostalgia, see Renato Rosaldo, "Imperialist Nostalgia," in *Culture and Truth: The Remaking of Social Analysis* (Boston: Beacon Press, 1989), pp. 68–87; and Pemina Yellow Bird and Kathryn Milun, "Interrupted Journeys: The Cultural Politics of Indian Reburial," in *Displacements: Cultural Identities in Question*, ed. Angelika Bammer (Bloomington: Indiana University Press, 1994), pp. 3–24; for more on relativism, consult Gable, Handler, and Lawson, "On the Uses of Relativism."

12

A War of Words: How News Frames Define Legitimacy in a Native Conflict

Cynthia-Lou Coleman

When a mining company attempted to dig a copper mine near Ladysmith, Wisconsin, during the early 1990s, the firm met with opposition from American Indians who use the area for hunting, fishing, and gathering. The Lac Courte Oreilles band of the Chippewa (Ojibwa) Nation argued that the mine would negatively impact the natural resources of the region and that treaty law protected the nation against technological and ecological encroachment. The Lac Courte Oreilles band was joined by grassroots environmentalists and the Sierra Club in opposing the Flambeau Mining Company, bringing claims to public attention via mass media channels and seeking legal methods to prevent the mine's construction.

In this chapter, I examine how claims made by mining opponents and supporters were presented in news accounts during an eighteen-month period. I argue that claims do not emerge in news stories without first being reinterpreted, or "framed." Framing may embody a variety of structures that essentially repackage information en route from claims maker to news reader or viewer.[1] Some argue that framing entails a sort of ideological massaging of information.[2] In the copper-mine case study, news frames delegitimized the mining opponents, painting them as irrational outsiders. Opponents included Native tribes, environmental organizations, grassroots citizens groups, and elected officials. On the one hand, American Indians, when featured in mainstream news accounts, were treated as "the other,"[3] as spiritually mysterious and embracing antitechnology and antiprogressive values. On the other hand, the agency charged with overseeing the mine's environmental impact (the Wisconsin Department of Natural Resources [DNR]) was presented in mainstream accounts as the arbiter of technical rationality.[4] The mining company also embodied rationality, truth, progress, democracy, and legal justice.

Frames that appeared to dominate news coverage of the mining issue included (1) conflict frames, (2) progress frames, (3) technological and scientific frames, (4) cyclical values frames, and (5) legitimation and delegitimation frames. These will be discussed in detail in the body of the chapter. Before embarking on how these frames were presented by Wisconsin news media, I present a brief overview of the copper-mine conflict, followed by an explanation of the methods used to conduct the study.

Background of the Controversy

The effort to establish the Flambeau Mine, which occupies a forty-acre site in rural Wisconsin, was officially launched in 1987 when the Salt Lake City–based Kennecott Copper Company filed a notice of intent to begin the lengthy permit process. Kennecott, whose parent organization is Rio Tinto Zinc (considered the world's largest mining company),[5] spent the next several years working with staff at the DNR, the agency charged with overseeing the environmental assessment of the mine. The final environmental impact report was released in 1990, followed by a public hearing held in July in Ladysmith. Hearings were covered widely by the press and broadcast media, and claims makers used the opportunity as a forum for debate and protest. Six months after the summer hearings, the court examiner approved the mine permits.

In opposing the permits, the Chippewa claimed that establishing the mine would violate fundamental treaty rights. Like many Indian nations, the Chippewa had entered into agreement with the U.S. government that certain land areas would be held in reserve, for Indian use, in exchange for granting the United States title to the lands.[6] The Lac Courte Oreilles band filed an appeal with the DNR's Division of Hearings and Appeals, charging that locating the mine in the region would hinder tribal rights to hunt, fish, and gather resources there. The appeal failed, and the Chippewa abandoned the treaty rights argument. Tribal leader Gaiashkibos told a public gathering that the legal fight over treaty rights would be prohibitively expensive.[7]

A new legal avenue opened in summer 1991 when the DNR acknowledged that endangered species (most notably a particular freshwater clam) had been found in the Flambeau River, where the mine's wastewater would be discharged. The Lac Courte Oreilles joined the Sierra Club in filing a lawsuit to block the mine, claiming the DNR had improperly issued mining permits. A court injunction was issued in August 1991, and the DNR was required to revise its environmental impact statement and address the issue of endangered species. Construction at the mine was temporarily halted.

The Chippewa victory was short-lived, however. A second judge ruled that the DNR had faithfully discharged its duties and that the mine posed no threat to the purple warty-back clam. Construction on the mine resumed.

The key proponents of establishing the mine included the Flambeau Mining Company; the Ladysmith Chamber of Commerce; civic, business, and real estate leaders; some politicians; and citizen support groups. Those opposing the mine included the Lac Courte Oreilles and other Indian bands and neighboring Indian nations, treaty rights organizations, environmental organizations such as the Sierra Club and the Wisconsin Greens, citizen groups, and selected politicians. Although professing an unbiased and apolitical view, the DNR was also a key player, as were the court systems, state elected officials, and the news media.

Methodology of the Study

The greatest amount of news coverage occurred during the public hearings and legal disputes. The height of coverage was in the summer months of 1990 and 1991, and I chose an eighteen-month period for the study, from March 1990 through August 1991. Ten newspapers from different-sized Wisconsin communities were selected, along with five advocacy publications.[8] The mainstream newspapers represented a range of publishers and communities, whereas the nonmainstream newspapers advocated Indian, environmental, mining, or "counterculture" interests.

In all, 571 news stories on the mine were found in the fifteen newspapers. Only news stories were selected, and letters to the editor, cartoons, and opinion pieces were discarded. Three coders assessed each story for claims made by mine proponents and opponents (claims were first ascertained by examining literature and speeches from each activist group).[9]

In opposing the mine, for example, the Rusk County Citizens Task Force asserted in its newsletter that the mine company would act like a "thief in the night," robbing the region of its precious wealth. Coders looked for mentions of robbery, stealing, theft, and so on, in addition to metaphors such as "thief in the night." Metaphors effectively convey meaning by packing multiple messages into one phrase. By referring to the mining company as a "thief in the night," the phrase carries with it images of theft, burglary, secrecy, and stealth. In effect, the metaphor contains multiple messages.[10]

An example of implied theft is illustrated in an article from the weekly *Ladysmith News*. The issue carried a page-one story on the master hearing, and the top section of page two was devoted to an article titled "Native Americans Oppose Copper Mine." This story recounts testimony made by Indians at the hearing, quoting speakers concerned with treaty rights, environmental pollution, and the actions of the mine company.[11] (It is noteworthy that the story on Native concerns is physically separated from the cover story about the hearing. Native voices are given a measure of space, but their concerns are set apart rather than given equal or simultaneous treatment.)

One speaker accused the mine company of theft, charging that "they are threatening to take what's not theirs." Another Indian added that "greedy companies are trying to make a profit." Tribal leader Gaiashkibos concurred, noting that "their only concern is profit and loss."

In addition to claims of theft and greed, opponents charged that the Wisconsin government system was flawed and that publics had been deceived. Gaiashkibos warned that the hearing was "all greased. . . . If you look at the way the Legislature has been duped over the last 20 years, they have been had in terms of changing the mining laws."[12] Others accused state officials of collusion. Native spokesman Walt Bresette told the *Wisconsin State Journal* that the state and mining companies had a "sweetheart relationship."[13]

Framing the Claims

Media Selection of Sources

Mining opponents and supporters alike used the mass media to voice their claims in the public arena. Recall, however, that claims were filtered through a variety of structural and ideological lenses before they were framed in press accounts. For example, some sources were likely to be interviewed by reporters, whereas others were given limited access to media channels. Not surprisingly, mainstream government, including state, city, and county sources, constituted roughly one-half (53 percent) of all sources quoted in mining news stories. Mining officials made up 16 percent of all sources quoted, whereas Indians accounted for only 9 percent. Mass-media researchers have noted that bureaucratic sources are much more likely to be interviewed and treated as credible than sources outside the mainstream culture, which tend to be ignored and delegitimized.[14]

Conflict Frames

Journalistic norms and structures also constrain news, thus shaping claims makers' reality into a news reality.[15] For example, the Wisconsin mining issue was largely framed as a conflict between proponents and opponents. Conflictive reporting is typical in such social struggles, particularly when issues are waged in court.[16] Reporting on the mine became heavily conflictual, with warlike metaphors punctuating mainstream coverage. The issue was described as a fight, battle, and skirmish. By framing the mining issue in battle terms, a powerful metaphor emerged—that of historic wars between Indians and the U.S. government. Such images continue to resonate in current-day discourse, evoking imagery that is reminiscent of the battles that resulted in divestment of Indian lands, resources, and culture.[17] The conflict frame is an important feature in this case study for several reasons: First, it pits two opposing sides against one another—hardly surprising in normative news discourse. But such coverage tends to be limited to simplistic, two-sided arguments rather than presenting a historical or social context. Second, readers are reminded of Indians in the context of the battlefield—where the outcome is predictable.

Thus conflictive framing resonates with stereotypical images, in which Indians are depicted as losers in military and cultural battles.

An example of the battle metaphor is illustrated by a feature story by Rogers Worthington in the Madison-based *Wisconsin State Journal.* Worthington described the dispute in the following warlike terms:

> (Ladysmith, Wis.) You can pick up a newsletter here called The Flambeau News, which speaks glowingly of a proposed 32-acre hole to be dug at the edge of town. Or you can pick up The Real Flambeau News, which portrays it as an awful idea.
>
> Such is the war of words between the Flambeau Mining Co. and the Rusk County Citizens Action Group in this northwest Wisconsin town of 3,800. Kennecott Copper Co., which owns Flambeau, promises it will operate one of the most ecologically sensitive mines ever. While this has won over some in Ladysmith, it has not swayed everyone.
>
> "I've seen what happens to a community around a metal mine of any kind," said Roscoe Churchill, leader of the citizens group and a longtime mining opponent. "You always have degradation of the air, with blasting and crushing, and you always have groundwater contamination." But the local feud has far bigger implications, says a loose statewide coalition of environmentalists, Chippewa Indians and academics. They fear Ladysmith would be a foot in the door for a major mining incursion into northern Wisconsin's pristine woods—much like those that have scarred terrain in northern Minnesota and Upper Michigan.[18]

This author used terms such as "war of words", "won over", "opponent", "local feud," and "incursion" in telling the Ladysmith story. But he was not alone in his conflictive description.

Warlike symbolism peppered a sizable story about a mine rally in the *Superior Evening Telegram,* a smallish daily newspaper based north of Ladysmith. The following excerpt is from an article titled "Mining Proposals Drawing Fierce Opposition": "The 74-year-old Churchill, of rural Ladysmith, was at the head of the march, in the front lines—as usual—of an environmentalism vs. development battle that has lasted 16 years." Churchill himself embraced war language, noting: "We've been fighting too long and we believe in what we are fighting for."[19]

Clearly the mine controversy evoked battle images partly due to the legal—and hence, adversarial—framework. The reporting on the court hearings also engendered conflictive coverage, as the following lead paragraph from an Associated Press story illustrates: "Ladysmith (AP)—A proposed open-pit copper mine along the Flambeau River in northern Wisconsin will face a court fight now that a state hearing examiner has granted permits for the project, environmentalists say."[20] Responding to the court's decision to approve the mine, another wire story framed the Chippewa perspective in combative terms, beginning with the following headline: "Indian Leader Blasts Ladysmith Mine Issue." The article continued, "Hayward (AP)—The leader of the Lac Courte Oreilles band of Chippewa Indians has lashed out at a decision by a state hearing examiner to approve all permits needed for a copper and gold mine in Rusk County. . . . 'This is a black day for the people of Wisconsin who share our reverence for the natural beauty and value of the northern woodlands,' Gaiashkibos said Tuesday."[21] No context for the story is given—has the tribal leader issued a news release or held a press conference? Yet the battle lines are clearly drawn through the framing of the story.

Two months after the court decision to approve the copper mine, a story appeared announcing that the tribe had decided against filing a lawsuit on the grounds of treaty rights violation (although the tribe did, in fact, join the Sierra Club months later in bringing an injunction against the mine after endangered species were discovered at the site). And although the news story avoided battle metaphors, it instead painted the Chippewa in primitive hues, heading the article with: "Chippewa Won't File Mine Suit; Express Views by Spearfishing." The article text read: "Chippewa Indians apparently are trading their legal pads for spears to show their opposition to Flambeau Mining Company's open pit copper and gold mine south of Ladysmith. . . . The Lac Courte Oreilles band of the Chippewa Indians, which has decided not to file a lawsuit to stop the Flambeau Mine, announced that it may spear Lake Holcombe this spring to draw attention to its opposition to the mine."[22] By characterizing the Indians as "trading legal pads for spears" the story suggests that atavistic implements are favored over modern methods—are Indians perhaps primitive? This symbolism is linked to the concept of social progress, another frame heavily used by reporters covering the dispute.

Progress Frames

Another recurrent theme surrounding the mine was illustrated by the metaphor of progress. Like conflict, progress encompasses a host of images and meaning steeped in American narrative traditions. Progress, for example, has been used to justify the forced removal of indigenous peoples from their homelands. As one government agent observed in the 1880s: "As long as Indians live in villages they will retain many of their old and injurious habits [but once removed to] individual lands or farms . . . [they] will begin their real and permanent progress."[23] Progress was also used to metaphorically elevate the fortune of the town of Ladysmith with the promise of jobs and cash. One reporter described the mine construction as "the sound of progress."[24] Moreover, the Flambeau Mining Company entwined progress with the concept of partnership (the company as trusted neighbor and friend) and adopted the slogan 'Partnership in Progress,' which decorated publications, buttons, and bumper stickers. Similarly, those criticizing Indians and environmentalists characterized them as antiprogressive and backward. One Ladysmith resident charged that opponents were both primitive and regressive: "They'll lead us back to the Stone Age."[25] The metaphor of progress also carries great symbolic meaning in that it resonates with the dominant values of moving ahead, success, and change: Progress is qualitatively good. The mining company clearly aligned itself with progress, bringing the community along as a "partner in progress." In contrast, Natives and environmentalists were depicted as primitive ("Stone Age"). Progress is closely linked with the concepts and underlying values of science and technology, a third important frame.

Technological and Scientific Frames

The copper-mine issue was frequently presented in news stories as an issue enfolded in a technological and scientific framework, which shows a rationalistic view.[26] Coverage touched on technological advances in mining, and proponents argued that modern mining practices limit ecological damage. A component of the rationalistic view is that the opinions of scientific experts (and the more, the better) carry a great deal of weight. According to the mining company: "Literally dozens of experts in the field of geology, hydrology, geological engineering and water resources management have applied their skills to testing the various components of the Flambeau Mining project . . . [concluding] that the project will not endanger public health, safety or welfare."[27] A similar stance was reflected by staff at the DNR, although the technology argument was wrapped around legal and regulatory issues. In other words, the DNR was charged with ensuring that the Flambeau Mine would meet current technological standards (only limited amounts of pollutants could be dumped in the river, for example) and that discussion of ethics or values was inappropriate. The project supervisor at the DNR, Robert Ramharter, explained at a public lecture that the permit process was not "an ethical or moral or qualitative decision" and that the DNR had "no position on mining."[28]

Opponents of the mine argued strenuously, however, that the permit process was indeed an ethical matter. And although Ramharter claimed that ethical judgments were detached from the purview of the DNR, values are embedded into the regulatory process—although they are not always obvious. For example, at the heart of the mining issue is the value of appropriate land use. Mining is thus valued and deemed appropriate, judging from the regulatory language. One DNR document stated that "following mining, if no other *better* use of the project area would be approved, the mining facilities would be dismantled and the land graded, vegetated and restored" (emphasis added).[29] This statement reveals the underlying value that land should be used for purposes that are deemed progressive.

Environmentalists and Native Americans argued, however, that the scientific precautions surrounding mining were not fail-safe. One opposition group noted that "contamination is bound to occur no matter how wisely a mine is designed or how diligent the operators are" and that "there is no proven cost-effective technology for successfully preventing or mitigating such pollution."[30] Tribal leader Gaiashkibos accused the regulatory agency of valuing technology over environmental concerns, noting "the white man almost worships technology as a god."[31]

Reporters, however, failed to illuminate the contest over values. Although the DNR claimed its judgments were value free, the regulatory process did indeed reflect values—values that are so ingrained we accept them as natural and normative.

Yet, the news media never questioned the DNR's position as being value free, although Indians and environmentalists were clearly portrayed as value driven.

Cyclical Values Frames

Chippewa cultural values, as expressed by Native voices in this controversy, often reflected a reciprocal relationship between humans and the ecosystem—a reciprocity that W. LaDuke has called cyclical thinking.[32] These dependencies and cyclical relationships are evidenced in some of the Chippewa literature. One brochure characterized Western values as incorporating domination over the land and animal species, while articulating Native values as cyclical and interdependent: "A keen sense of the interdependence of people, animal and plant life reach deep into the tradition and lifestyle of the Ojibwa people . . . we believe in the circle of life. We believe that all returns to its source; that both good and bad return to the place where they began . . . if care is not used when the circle is begun, then the hurts along the way will be received in the end. Such is the belief of the true Ojibwa."[33]

Some researchers have generalized Indian values of land as communally based.[34] One researcher noted that Indian values are based on natural and supernatural attachments to the land, whereas white settlers viewed land as a commodity: "Land as commodity is rooted in the freehold tenure of English law that makes land easily alienable, and in the capitalist idea of speculative value . . . in this sense, [land] is monetary and is established in the marketplace."[35] When such notions compete in public arenas, however, Indian values tend to be relegated to a lesser status and delegitimized.[36] J. G. Jorgensen noted that "nonmonetary aspects of Indian . . . values are treated informally and casually by the courts, by industries and by federal agencies."[37] We see the same pattern in news coverage of the Ladysmith case study.

Legitimation and Delegitimation Frames

Another theme that appeared throughout news coverage on the copper mine elevated some claims and contenders and thus relegated others to an inferior status. Delegitimating tactics were fairly subtle; perhaps the most noteworthy example came from the Flambeau Mining Company, which claimed ownership of "the facts." In doing so, the company thus accorded itself the role as possessor of the facts and the truth, and anyone who disagreed was therefore irrational or a liar. A disagreement over *values* therefore became a dispute over *facts*. An important document prepared for the press by the mining company was titled "A Closer Look at the Facts" and refuted "misrepresentations, distortions or misstatements" made, principally, by the opposition.[38] This type of delegitimation was carried through in the mining company newsletter, which provided mining officials with a forum for disputing opponents' claims. After one contentious court hearing, an article reporting the response of vice president Larry Mercando quoted him as saying, "'I've said all along that any objective person who studied all the facts would have to conclude that this mine will be environmentally sound . . . I'm embarrassed for them,' Mr. Mercando commented, shaking his head, 'I certainly believe they are entitled to their opinions, but it was pretty embarrassing when someone asked them to defend their position on the basis of facts and they couldn't.'"[39] Mercando's characterization of the opposition as irrational and uninformed was also noted in mainstream news accounts: "Mercando said mining opponents were using 'opinions and fear' in an effort to confront 'experts and facts' and referred to a number of anti-mining petition statements as 'inaccurate, misleading . . . yes, lies.'"[40]

Conclusions

By claiming ownership of the facts, the mine company positioned itself in a hierarchically elevated post. The company represented Western progress, scientific truth, the "facts," and democratic values. The newsletter produced by the company was inserted in the town paper, the *Ladysmith News,* and mailed to Gulf War servicemen and servicewomen from northern Wisconsin. By identifying itself with the war overseas, the Flambeau Mining Company demonstrated the core values of patriotism and democracy. And by linking the mine organization with patriotism, the company implied that anyone disagreeing with its position was *un*patriotic, and *un*-American. Moreover, mine spokesmen equated the Ladysmith operation with democratic values and in one court hearing argued that anyone who disagreed was therefore undemocratic and unlawful. In effect, democratic, scientific, and technological values merged: "'This isn't a question of whether or not we build the mine,' Mercando said. 'It's a question of whether or not a handful of people can frustrate the will of the majority, and equally important, it's a question of whether public policy and environmental regulations are going to be based on science and technology, or on misinformation, threats and intimidation.'"[41]

Another critical component of mass media framing was the alignment of facts and rationality surrounding the technological dispute over the mine. Whereas Indians and environmentalists argued that "the technology doesn't exist that will clean up the mine,"[42] the DNR and mine officials argued that technology could safely harness nature by extracting minerals from the earth using scientifically proven, modern-day methods. Opposing views tended to be portrayed by scientists and regulators as irrational. Mining spokesmen discounted the opposition as undemocratic and antiprogressive—values that were cast as being complementary. Finally, mining supporters tended to characterize the opponents as rabble-rousers and outsiders, while Indian values were presented as outside the mainstream and mysterious. When Indians were invited to express their views in press accounts (and recall that these views represented only 9 percent of all sources quoted), these opinions were framed in conflictual language, thus characterizing the battle as between "us" and the "other." Such battle images reflect longstanding stereotypes of United States–Native American interaction, in which battles over land and cultural values historically favored the more powerful invader.

Similarly, Native views were often separated from mainstream views in physical terms: Several news stories from Chippewa perspectives were treated as sidebar elements of more central stories, thus again separating "us" from the "other." And Indian values were regarded as primitive or mysterious, relegated to a lesser status than values that echoed progress, science, technology, and rationality. Such "cultural" views are illustrated in an article by Mary Jo Kewley in the *Wausau Daily Herald*, with this headline: "Band Opposes Mine on Spiritual Grounds." Indian values are linked to a mysterious religion and are thus spiritual rather than rational:

> Chippewa spiritual leader Eugene Begay believes taking from the Earth—as mining would do—creates an irreparable imbalance.
>
> "You are taking from Mother Earth that which was to be there for a purpose," said Begay, a Lac Courte Oreilles elder. "We give homage to the environment. You cannot remove things from the environment because Mother Earth is alive."
>
> The Lac Courte Oreilles Chippewa are outspoken opponents of Kennecott Corp.'s proposed copper mine at Ladysmith. Begay said he would never agree to any mining operation in the ceded territory because it is an affront to traditional Chippewa values.
>
> Begay's beliefs are rooted in the teachings of the Grand Medicine Lodge, the spiritual community founded in Anishinabe (Chippewa) tradition.
>
> "The main reason for the signing of the treaties was to perpetuate the spiritual way of life of the Anishinabe people," he said.

The mine company's vice president was quoted in the same story as dismissing the relevance of treaty rights and noted, "We own the land and we own the mineral rights."[43] This has the effect of dismissing outright the spiritual claim—a claim that is inextricable from treaties that protect the ceded territories.

Yet, the mine company co-opted "Indian" values. In making an appearance at the master hearing, the attorney for the Flambeau Mining Company adopted a conservationist ethic and linked the mine project to—of all people—Chief Seattle: "We too come before you, Mr. Schwarz, as stewards of the earth. It is our hope that by the end of this hearing, you, as well as the concerned citizens who have questioned the environmental integrity of this project, will realize that under Wisconsin's law environmental stewardship and mining are not conflicting endeavors." The attorney then dismissed charges that the company would destroy the Flambeau River and the Ladysmith community, predicting the company will "march through history arm-in-arm with Chief Seattle, Gandhi, Rachel Carson and Martin Luther King." The attorney successfully wrapped spirituality, conservationism, civil rights, democracy, self-governance, and stewardship into one package—the Flambeau Mine.[44]

Thus the news frames that emerged in the community conflict surrounding construction of a copper mine in Ladysmith, Wisconsin, legitimized and endorsed the values of progress, technical and rational approaches to problem-solving, and democratic values. Those who disagreed with such values—values framed by the mining company and the DNR as "facts"—were discounted as irrational and emotional outsiders. Values such as cyclical relationships were seen as vague and oppositional to technoscientific attitudes.

When reporters package these views in news accounts, the typical scenario is one of conflict, in which pro- and anti-mining sources face off with each other in an ideological duel. I argue that dominant views that embrace progress, democracy, and technological solutions are accepted as normative and rational. Views that are considered cultural, such as cyclical relationships, are framed in the news as less legitimate than technorational views. Scant attention is given to a critical analysis of such technorational values; they are simply accepted as correct and valid.

Notes

I appreciate and acknowledge support for this research from Professor Sharon Dunwoody and the Center for Environmental Communication and Educational Studies at the University of Wisconsin at Madison. I also received encouragement and financial support from the Lynn Reyer Dissertation Fund at the University of New Mexico and the Osage Tribal Education Committee.

1. See, for example, W. A. Gamson and A. Modigliani, "Media Discourse and Public Opinion on Nuclear Power: A Constructionist Approach," *American Journal of Sociology* 95 (1) (1989) pp. 1–37; T. Gitlin, *The Whole World Is Watching: Mass Media in the Making and Unmaking of the New Left* (Berkeley: University of California Press, 1980); E. Goffmann, *Frame Analysis: An Essay on the Organization of Experience* (New York: Harper and Row, 1974); J. Hartley, *Understanding News* (London: Routledge, 1982).

2. Gitlin, *Whole World Is Watching;* Hartley, *Understanding News.*

3. M. Omi and H. Winant, *Racial Formation in the United States: From the 1960s to the 1980s* (London: Routledge, 1986).

4. A. Plough and S. Krimsky, "The Emergence of Risk Communication Studies: Social and Political Context," *Science, Technology, and Human Values* 12 (3/4), pp. 4–10.

5. A. Gedicks et al., *Land Grab: The Corporate Theft of Wisconsin's Mineral Resources* (Madison, Wis.: Center for Alternative Mining Development Policy, 1982); "Midwest Treaty Network," n.d., in-house technical report.

6. V. Deloria, *The Indian Affair* (New York: Friendship Press, 1974).

7. Center for Resource Policy Studies and Programs, 1991, University of Wisconsin at Madison. Videotape series from lectures, titled "Mining in Wisconsin."

8. Mainstream newspapers included the *Wisconsin State Journal, Milwaukee Journal, Wausau Daily Herald, Superior Evening Telegram, Chippewa Herald Telegram, Eau Claire Leader-Telegram, Ladysmith News, Hayward-Sawyer County Record, Rice Lake Chronotype,* and *Phillips Bee.* Advocacy press included *News from Indian Country, Masinaigan, Shepherd Express, Green Net,* and *Flambeau News.*

9. The author is grateful to fellow coders Benami Bacaltchuk and Jan Lathrop for their assistance and support.

10. M. Edelman, *The Symbolic Uses of Politics* (Urbana: University of Illinois Press, 1967); G. Lakoff and M. Johnson, *Metaphors We Live By* (Chicago: University of Chicago Press, 1980).

11. "Native Americans Oppose Copper Mine," *Ladysmith News,* July 19, 1990, p. 2A.

12. "Ladysmith Hearing to Focus on Mining Permits," *Superior Evening Telegram,* July 16, 1990, p. 1.

13. "Mining Digging Up Controversy," *Wisconsin State Journal,* March 4, 1990, p. 15A.

14. See, for example, D. Berkowitz and D. W. Beach, "News Sources and News Context: The Effect of Routine News, Conflict, and Proximity," *Journalism Quarterly* 70 (1), pp. 4–12; M. Fishman, *Manufacturing the News* (Austin: University of Texas Press, 1980); D. L. Lasorsa and S. D. Reese (1990). "News Source Use in the Crash of 1987: A Study of Four National Media," *Journalism Quarterly* 67 (1), pp. 60–71; H. Molotch and M. Lester, "Accidental News: The Great Oil Spill as Occurrence and National Event," *American Journal of Sociology* 81 (2), pp. 235–260; B. B. Ringer and E. R. Lawless, *Race, Ethnicity, and Society* (London: Routledge, 1989); P. J. Shoemaker, "Media Treatment of Deviant Political Groups," *Journalism Quarterly* 61, pp. 66–75, 82; C. Smith, "News Sources and Power Elites in News Coverage of the Exxon Valdez Oil Spill," *Journalism Quarterly* 70 (2), pp. 393–403; T. A. Van Dijk, *Communicating Racism: Ethnic Prejudice in Thought and Talk* (Newbury Park, Calif.: Sage Publication, 1987).

15. E. Herman and N. Chomsky, *Manufacturing Consent: The Political Economy of the Mass Media* (New York: Pantheon, 1988).

16. C. N. Olien, P. J. Tichenor, and G. A. Donohue, "Role of Mass Communication," in *Needs Assessment: Theory and Methods,* ed. D. E. Johnson et al. (Ames: Iowa State University Press, 1987), pp. 66–88; R. J. Griffin and S. Dunwoody, *Press Coverage of Risk from Environmental Contaminants,* United States Environmental Protection Agency, CR-817599-01-0, Washington, D.C., 1992.

17. C. L. Coleman, "Science, Technology, and Risk Coverage of a Community Conflict," *Media, Culture, and Society* 17, pp. 65–79.

18. "Mine vs. Environment: Ladysmith Split over Proposed Copper Mine," *Wisconsin State Journal,* May 21, 1990, p. 1A.

19. "Mining Proposals Drawing Fierce Opposition," *Superior Evening Telegram,* February 23, 1991, p. 17B.

20. "Ladysmith Mine Permits Okayed," *Superior Evening Telegram,* January 16, 1991, p. 1.

21. "Indian Leader Blasts Ladysmith Mine Issue," *Superior Evening Telegram,* January 23, 1991, p. 21.

22. "Chippewa Won't File Mine Suit; Express Views by Spearfishing," *Ladysmith News,* March 14, 1991, p. 1.

23. D. McNickel, *Native American Tribalism* (London: Oxford University Press, 1973), p. 81.

24. "Mine Construction Sounds Like Progress to Some," *Wausau Sunday Herald,* August 18, 1991, pp. 1A, 4A.

25. "Use Extreme Caution Before Reneging on Mine Pact," *Ladysmith News,* October 4, 1990, pp. 1, 3.

26. Coleman, "Coverage of a Community Conflict."

27. "A Closer Look at the Facts," Flambeau Mining Company Document, no. 34, 1990.

28. Center for Resource Policy Studies and Programs, 1991.

29. "Cumulative Impacts of Mining Development in Northern Wisconsin," Wisconsin Department of Natural Resources Fact Sheet, March 1991.

30. R. Churchill, "Declaration of Independence," Rusk County Citizens' Task Force, n.d.

31. "Gaiashkibos Bridges Two Worlds," *Wisconsin State Journal,* March 11, 1990, pp. 1A, 16A.

32. W. LaDuke, "A Society Based on Conquest Cannot Be Sustained: Native Peoples and the Environmental Crisis," in *Toxic Struggles: The Theory and Practice of Environmental Justice,* ed. R. Hofrichter (Philadelphia: New Society Publishers, 1993), pp. 98–106.

33. Great Lakes Indian Fish and Wildlife Commissions brochure, n.d.

34. J. G. Jorgensen, "Land Is Cultural, So Is a Commodity: The Locus of Differences Among Indians, Cowboys, Sod-busters, and Environmentalists," *Journal of Ethnic Studies* 12 (3), pp. 1–21; LaDuke, "Society Based on Conquest."

35. Jorgensen, "Land Is Cultural," p. 4.

36. C. L. Coleman, "An Examination of the Relationship of Structural Pluralism, News Role, and Source Use with Framing in the Context of a Community Controversy," Ph.D. diss., University of Wisconsin, Madison; G. H. Landsman, "Indian Activism and the Press: Coverage of the Conflict at Ganienkeh," *Anthropological Quarterly* 60 (3), pp. 101–113.

37. Jorgensen, "Land Is Cultural," p. 18.

38. "Closer Look at the Facts."

39. "Mining Opposition Witnesses Admit They Never Fully Read," *Flambeau News,* August 9, 1991, p. 1.

40. "Use Extreme Caution."

41. "Mining Official Says Opposition Won't Cave In to Protesters," *Wausau Daily Herald,* July 11, 1991, p. 1B.

42. Wisconsin Resources Protection Council brochure, n.d.

43. "Band Opposes Mine on Spiritual Ground," *Wausau Daily Herald,* July 16, 1990, p. 4A.

44. "Contested Mine Hearing Progressing Slowly," *Ladysmith News,* July 26, 1990, p. 1A.

13

Going Indian: Discovery, Adoption, and Renaming Toward a "True American," from *Deerslayer* to *Dances with Wolves*

Robert Baird

While lying there listening to the Indians, I amused myself with trying to guess at their subject by their gestures, or some proper name introduced. . . . It was a purely wild and primitive American sound, as much as the barking of a chickaree, and I could not understand a syllable of it. . . . I felt that I stood, or rather lay, as near to the primitive man of America, that night, as any of its discoverers ever did.

—Henry David Thoreau[1]

As soon as possible after my arrival, I design to build myself a wigwam, after the same manner and size with the rest. . . . and will endeavour that my wife, my children, and myself may be adopted soon after our arrival. Thus becoming truly inhabitants of their village, we shall immediately occupy that rank within the pale of their society, which will afford us all the amends we can possibly expect for the loss we have met with by the convulsions of our own. According to their customs we shall likewise receive names from them, by which we shall always be known. My youngest children shall learn to swim, and to shoot with the bow, that they may acquire such talents as will necessarily raise them into some degree of esteem among the Indian lads of their own age; the rest of us must hunt with the hunters.

—J. Hector St. John Crevecoeur[2]

With thanks to the Blackfoot tribe who adopted me.

—Leslie A. Fiedler[3]

Taken together, the three epigraphs above are good examples of a very old, and still ongoing, process of the American imagination: the White discovery of, and the renaming and adoption into, the tribal society of the American Indian. "Going Indian" describes an imaginative mythopoeic process, recurring often enough in American history, letters, and media to merit more attention, especially after the apparent resurrection and further development of this gesture in Kevin Costner's tremendously popular *Dances with Wolves.* This film was released too long after any other great epic Western to be anything but a boondoggle—or so we thought, until "Costner's folly" was seen by millions and had won seven Academy Awards.

A traditional ideological goal in American literature and film has been the search for Americanness. Crevecoeur's third letter as an American farmer was titled "What Is an American," and his famous melting-pot response was lengthy and detailed, testifying to the seriousness with which the question was met. Tautologically, the defining American characteristic has been the attempt to define the American character. It is the question itself—indeed, that the question has been open for so long—that marks this nation as unique. One answer to the question of national identity proposes that the original inhabitants of North America represent "True Americans," whose character deserves emulation. *Dances with Wolves* accepted this not-new proposal and sought to convince modern motion-picture audiences that only by going backward into history, back into tribalism, could the American hero hope to go forward.

D. H. Lawrence argued that Europeans "came to America for two reasons: 1. To slough the old European consciousness completely. 2. To grow a new skin underneath, a new form. This second is a hidden process."[4] Leslie Fiedler praised Lawrence's insight, suggesting that

> He knew something . . . which we are born not knowing we know, being born on this soil . . . that the essential myth of the West and, therefore, of ourselves . . . [is] the myth of Natty Bumppo and Chingachgook. Here is, for us—for better or for worse, and apparently forever—the heart of the matter: the confrontation in the wilderness of the White European refugee from civilization and the "stern, imperturbable warrior."[5]

This meeting, Fiedler noted, occasioned two possible outcomes: "a metamorphosis of the WASP into something neither White nor Red" or "the annihilation of the Indian."[6] Although the latter option was the most frequently chosen path of story makers for the "penny dreadfuls" and nickelodeons, the metamorphosis of White into Red developed rapidly in the 1950s with the "sympathetic Western," and it is in *Dances with Wolves* that the myth reached its culmination and logical end.

Three famous theories help explain how a motion picture of the 1990s would, first, attempt a big-budget dramatization of the going-Indian myth and, second, reach an appreciative audience in the process. The first theory is Claude Levi-Strauss's notion that myths and narratives reconcile cultural contradictions and bring opposing forces and values together. With the going-Indian myth, the contradiction is between nature and industry; hunting and agrarianism; innocence and decadence; manifest destiny and the sacred homeland. Thus, *Dances with*

Wolves is a cinematic myth that addresses still-unresolved traumas and contradictions of American history, as well as current contradictions between industrialism and environmentalism, tribal society and industrial society, the melting-pot theory and ethnic pride movements.

The second theory was propounded by R.W.B. Lewis in *The American Adam,* wherein the author described the historical development of the idea of a new American hero who would be "emancipated from history, happily bereft of ancestry, untouched and undefiled by the usual inheritances of family and race."[7] That the American continent triggered images of the Garden of Eden among European immigrants has been ably documented by many scholars. But the Garden of Eden was not empty, and for those uncomfortable with the demonization of native inhabitants of this continent, the American Indian provided a ready-made Adamic figure. The American Adam and Garden of Eden myths were easily transposed into American Westerns and musicals, including the mythic and cinematic forerunner of *Dances with Wolves,* Delmer Davies's *Broken Arrow* (1950), considered the first of the sympathetic Westerns of the 1950s. This film traces the transformation of an Indian fighter (played by Jimmy Stewart) into a man who befriends Cochise, marries an Apache maiden, and fights to establish some truce between the land-hungry settlers and the Apache. The American Adam undercurrent is manifested in *Broken Arrow* during a pastoral honeymoon scene that takes place on the banks of a wild pond. Stewart and the Apache maiden Morning Star have just been married. Stewart is reclining beside the still waters as the camera follows Morning Star, who walks majestically toward her lover, then lies in his arms:

Morning Star: "You are asleep?"
Stewart: "No . . . I'm quiet because I'm so happy. I'm afraid if I open my mouth my happiness will rush out in a funny noise like, Ya-hoo!"
Morning Star: "What does that mean? It is an American word?"
Stewart: "Uh huh. I think it was a word made by Adam when he opened his eyes and saw Eve."

The dream of Pocahontas cannot last too long, however, and even in this first sympathetic western, Morning Star dies before the last reel. In contrast to the deluge of conventional Westerns, *Broken Arrow* was, for its time, the most pointed liberal critique of manifest destiny and the sad history of relations between Indians and Whites.

The third theory comes from Sigmund Freud's limited work with the "family romance," in which he attempted to account for certain fantasies of young children who denied their literal parentage in favor of more noble, imaginary mothers and fathers.[8] Freud claimed, in *Der Familienroman der Neurotiker,* that all young people must break with their parents at some point—that each generation must break with the previous one. A family romance might be created in response to various motivations, for example, to compensate for loss of parental love, or because of fear of breaking the incest taboo or with realization of parental fallibility.

This theory suggests a psychological mechanism that can account for the success of those narratives wherein the white protagonist goes Indian. Working on the personal and collective psychological levels, the romance of Native American parentage would satisfy the wish for a return to the Garden of Eden, where strong and noble parents live in an environment of abundance and harmony, free of the decay, pollution, and anxiety of industrial society. Crevecoeur's epigraph was written during the troubled context of the American Revolution, when the author found himself pulled between British allegiance and colonial rebellion. His romance of living with the Indians was never enacted in reality, but it was exactly the tale of the noble savage that Europeans would find appealing.[9]

Elizabeth Stone provides evidence that modern, adult Americans have engaged in family romances of Indian ancestry. In a study of the psychological dynamics of family stories, Stone interviewed Black and White Americans who claimed Indian ancestry even against rather conclusive evidence to the contrary. In spite of the truth of a family's history and the Indian's oppression and negative stereotyping in our culture, Stone found a number of Americans who claimed Indian blood in the manner that others would pridefully recall European royalty or illustrious Puritan ancestry. It is "the idea of the Indian," "a powerful symbol, especially since World War II," that Stone found in American literature from Ernest Hemingway to Ken Kesey, an idea "suggestive of our mourning for our lost pre-industrial Eden."[10]

These three theories offer a rudimentary dynamic in which *Dances with Wolves* can be seen to function as mythical *narrative* (Levi-Strauss) among the *collective conscious* (Freud) and in the context of American *history* (Lewis). As such, this dynamic helps contextualize historical and fictional prototypes of the going-Indian myth in *Dances with Wolves*.

Thoreau and Russell Dance with Wolves

Thoreau was, Leslie Fiedler believed, "at his mythological core an Indian himself, at home in the unexplored regions where women flinch," and Fiedler added that Thoreau himself claimed that "all poets are Indians."[11] Thoreau's Walden adventure strikes me as a case study on the limits on how far a Harvard man can go Indian, and although Thoreau never entertains the notion of becoming a "squaw-man," the "idea of the Indian" infuses every page of *Walden*. At one point in his masterpiece, Thoreau mused: "My days were not days of the week, bearing the stamp of any heathen deity, nor were they minced into hours and fretted by the ticking of the clock; for I lived like the Puri Indians, of whom it is said that 'for yesterday, to-day, and to-morrow they have only one word, and they express the variety of meaning by pointing backward for yesterday, forward for to-morrow, and overhead for the passing day.' "[12] Besides the explicit reference to living "like the Puri Indians," I also like the notion here of near timelessness, so central to any mythological state, as well as the privileging of the Indian lifestyle in contrast with the rush to keep European time. Although Thoreau drew no special attention to it when he mentioned it, the story of the naming of Walden Pond, the naming of Walden in *Walden,* offers evidence, both literary and historic, of the claim "the Indian" holds not only on the American landscape, but on Thoreau's and our imaginations: "My townspeople have all heard it in their youth, that anciently the Indians were holding a pow-wow upon a hill here ... and while they were thus engaged the hill shook and suddenly sank, and only one old squaw, named Walden, escaped, and from her the pond was named."[13] Thoreau best shows where he has been and where he would like to go in *The Maine Woods,* where he admitted, "One revelation has been made to the Indian, another to the white man. I have much to learn of the Indian, nothing of the missionary. I am not sure but all that would tempt me to teach the Indian my religion would be *his* promise to teach me his."[14]

Thoreau never wrote the great work on the Indian he had been planning. His notebooks, though, were full of carefully collected details of native dress and behavior. Most important, his greatest book may have captured more of the "idea of the Indian" than any scientific work he could have written.

Although he called himself an illustrator,[15] Charles M. Russell is, along with Frederic Remington, the most famous of the Western artists. Russell, who began life as the son of a wealthy St. Louis family, eventually lit out for the territory of Montana.[16] As a painter, sculptor, and writer, Russell focused his attention on the lifestyles of cowboys, trappers, desperadoes, and Indians, all of which he captured in his seemingly simple, rough-hewn style. In a 1922 painting of a squaw man titled, "When White Men Turn Red," Russell depicted a leather-clad, mounted White man descending into a river valley with his two Indian wives, three horses, and four dogs. Russell has poured a luminous golden sunlight over the distant mountain range and lower sky of this painting, and this golden sidelight outlines his figures, the effect being boldly romantic and serene. In commentary accompanying this painting in his *Remington and Russell,* Brian W. Dippie noted that "Russell himself had felt the lure of Indian life and knew that he, like several of his cowboy friends, would have been quick to take an Indian wife had the right woman come along."[17] Dippie mentioned a short story from Russell's *Trails Plowed Under,* titled "How Lindsay Turned Indian." In this tale, Russell related how, as a young boy, Lindsay ran off from a mean stepfather (a fictional "literalization" of Freud's family romance?) to eventually find himself following a tribe of Piegan Indians, as he had nowhere else to turn. After meeting the rearguard of the traveling Piegans, the young Lindsay uses his magnifying glass to light the pipe of the Piegan chief. Of course, for a people who worship the sun, this is no small feat, and the chief intones, "The grass has grown twice since my two sons were killed by the Sioux ... my heart is on the ground; I am lonesome, but since the sun has sent you, it is good. I will adopt you as my boy ... Child of the Sun, it is good."[18] Much like Lieutenant John J. Dunbar, in *Dances with Wolves,* Lindsay's important transition comes with his first buffalo hunt. In both cases the adopted Whites get their first kill, eat the fresh liver of their killed animal, and consider that moment as the important point of no return in their going Indian: "My boy . . . that's been sixty-five years ago as near as I can figure. I run buffalo till the whites cleaned 'em out, but that's the day I turned Injun, an' I ain't cut my hair since."[19]

The hunt has long been an initiation ritual for many different groups, and the buffalo-hunt scene and subsequent feast in *Dances with Wolves* mark Dunbar's almost complete assimilation into the tribe, shown by his trading of pieces of his cavalry blues for Indian gear; his winning over of Wind-in-His-Hair (who was earlier a strong doubter of Dunbar's intentions toward the tribe); and his participation in the culturally important role of storyteller, when Dunbar recounts his own hunting feat over and over to the tribe's great enjoyment. In short, the buffalo hunt's central position in Plains tribe culture would have made it the perfect path, both fictionally and historically, for any non-Indian to follow if he sought access to the flesh-and-bone existence of a tribe (Figure 13.1).

Getting Past the Massacre

Ever since Mary Rowlandson's Captivity Narrative (first published in 1682), any White seeking to go Indian has had to confront "the massacre." The historical and

Figure 13.1   *Lt. John Dunbar (Kevin Costner), Kicking Bird (Graham Greene), and other Sioux scout out a herd of buffalo in the film* Dances with Wolves. *Photo, Ben Glass, copyright 1990 Orion Pictures Corporation. All rights reserved.*

mythic power of the massacre is so pervasive that it seems all Westerns that deal with the confrontation of White and Red must address this issue in some manner.

An interesting negotiation of the massacre occurs in *Broken Arrow,* in which Jimmy Stewart's character saves his own life by having aided a wounded Cheyenne boy. When Stewart and the young boy are eventually surrounded by a group of warriors, the grateful young Cheyenne successfully pleads for Stewart's life with the menacing warriors. But when a group of unsuspecting Whites interrupt the Cheyenne just as they are about to release Stewart, he is bound and gagged and forced to watch the resulting massacre. He must witness as well the torture of three White survivors of the battle—two are "crucified" and one is buried up to his neck, smeared with cactus pulp, and eaten by ants. Later in the film Stewart must pass through the civilized, industrial equivalent of the Indian massacre nightmare—the lynching—when his own society tries to string him up for his defense of the Indian; he is only saved at the last minute, with the rope already around his neck. Stewart's near-lynching by the townspeople, like Dunbar's beating at the hands of his fellow Cavalrymen in *Dances,* signifies the one side of the cultural dialectic that the hero must pass through in order to prove his commitment to the synthesis of cultural contradiction. The binding and gagging of Stewart is evocative of the deep psychological chasm that the modern liberal conscience must negotiate between the archetypal Massacre and the Noble Indian; that is, atrocities of history cannot be erased but must be witnessed, then passed through. Although sometimes suppressed, historical atrocities will, when they eventually force their way into cultural narratives, be dichotomized into the poles of evil aggressors and innocent victims; sometimes this dichotomy is inverted, as when the good (morally or historically justified) Indians attack the U.S. Cavalry in *Dances with Wolves* and in the made-for-television *Son of the Morning Star.*

Arthur Penn's "progressive" Western *Little Big Man* begins with (what else?) a massacre of the family of the young Jack Crabb. However, the film, and Thomas Berger's book upon which it is based, cannot exhaust the psychic energy and mythic trauma of the massacre with this single bloodletting. Therefore, following the general reversal of the Western tale we find throughout *Little Big Man,* Penn gives us another slaughter by inverting the conventions of the massacre, presenting Custer's infamous "battle" with the Cheyenne beside the Washita River. This time the cavalry does the massacring.

Almost twenty years after the sympathetic Western *Little Big Man,* the even more sympathetic *Dances with Wolves* cannot circumvent the massacre, and in fact, includes three massacres, one of which is told as a flashback of Stands-with-a-Fist (a White adopted by the Lakota Sioux, who becomes Dunbar's wife). The Stands-with-a-Fist flashback is as distilled and powerful an embodiment of the massacre trauma as has ever been presented by Hollywood. Shot in soft focus and at sunset, the scene begins, slow-motion, as an idyllic view of a rustic farm and cabin; two frontier families are eating outdoors on a large table when ominous looking Pawnee warriors ride slowly in on horseback, their faces painted in bilious blues and bloody reds. At first it seems a peaceful meeting of the two cultures, but then a tomahawk flies through the air, and the scene takes on added poignancy as the edit returns us to the horrified gaze of the young witness and, by a film dissolve, to the still-haunted Stands-with-a-Fist.[20]

The third massacre in *Dances* transforms the horror associated with that depiction into the Hollywood-sanctioned celebration of dispatching the badmen—the U.S. Cavalry. Dunbar has been captured by the cavalry as a renegade and is being taken by wagon in shackles to a frontier prison. When the Lakota attack and kill Dunbar's tormentors, one realizes that—even with ninety years of Hollywood history turned on its head—we have here the same cheer for the good guys; the skillful and precise application of violence in order to right the world; the promise of "regeneration through violence," which Richard Slotkin has so eloquently elaborated upon.

Another strategy for resolving the historical trauma and contradiction of the massacre is, through sleight of hand, to present viewers with a tribe of Noble Savages (The Sioux in *Dances* and the Cheyenne in *Little Big Man*), and then with a tribe of just plain old-fashioned savages (the Pawnee in both films). This strategy has the function of addressing White historical fear and guilt within the same narrative, providing a way in which a *fiction* can remain simultaneously *true* to contradictory emotional responses to history.

Renaming

In *A Man Called Horse,* Lord Morgan (Richard Harris) is captured by a band of Sioux in 1825. Yellow Hand decides to save this strange White man for a slave of some sort and, after tying a rope around his neck, proceeds to ride Morgan like a horse before the other laughing warriors of the raiding party. Taken back to the Sioux camp, Morgan is mistreated until he eventually earns the Sioux's respect through his endurance, his slaying of attacking Shoshone braves, and his successful completion of the Sun Dance ritual. Although never explicitly mentioned in the film, Morgan's Indian name itself is transformed from the beast-of-burden connotations of that word to the more noble connotations for *horse* one would expect from a horse culture. *Little Big Man*'s young Jack Crabb (Dustin Hoffman) gets his name from old Chief Lodgeskins (Chief Dan George), who gives Jack his name—Little Big Man—by way of a story the old chief tells the rather short young man to inspire his confidence. Later, Jack kills a Pawnee during a war party and further strengthens his bond to the tribe, eventually becoming a squaw man in more ways than one.

In *Dances with Wolves*, Lieutenant John J. Dunbar is named, at first without his knowledge, by his Sioux brothers who have seen him "dancing" with his "pet" wolf, Two Socks. Dunbar had been trying to get Two Socks to return to his fort as he rode out to the Indian camp, but the wolf would playfully snap at his heels when Dunbar tried to chase him back. The Indians watched in the foreground of the shot, incredulous that a White man could have such a relationship with a wild animal. This scene in the film is presented with no fanfare, narration, or dialogue that signifies its tremendous importance to the film's mythopoeic task. Thus viewers take Dunbar's frolic with Two Socks as just another day-in-the-life event for John Dunbar, that is, as natural and spontaneous. Because viewers do not hear the Lakota warriors name Dunbar and because they already know the title of the film, the scene achieves two brilliant effects. First, the renaming scene is one of the most calculated moments of the film, yet it comes off as an utterly natural occurrence (accentuated by being filmed in long shot and soft focus, with a PBS nature-documentary style). Second, Costner, in effect, lets every viewer rename Dunbar with his Lakota name, since the scene plays sans dialogue or even gesture from the Lakota. This has the effect of making filmgoers active participants in the sacred ritual of renaming a man into nature and the tribe.

Although this renaming fits nicely with the standard Hollywood story convention of depicting an *evolving* character, this infrequent, but telling, tendency says more about American romantic concepts of the Indian and the natural than it does about Hollywood storytelling. This renaming of a White man with a natural name and his shedding of his European name is the quintessential American myth—the self-made man rediscovering both America and, most important, his own true self in the process. Freed from the oppressive yoke of European tradition, self-made even to his name (founder of his self—the task of Walt Whitman's *Leaves of Grass*), this character of literature and film has, after two hundred years, become only more solidified in our consciousness. From a string of names with no "direct relation to the universe"—Natty Bumppo, Lewis Henry Morgan, Lord Morgan, Jack Crabb, and John Dunbar—emerge Indian names, true names: Leather Stocking/Deerslayer/Hawkeye; Tayadaowuhkuh; Horse; Little Big Man; Dances-with-Wolves. European interest in Indian names did not develop solely from fictional romances of the noble savage; the real contrast between Indian naming and European naming sparked the imaginations of many explorers, trappers, and immigrants who sought to communicate and understand that first task of language, naming.

The naming process in Indian cultures was an apparently less rigid and legalized endeavor than modern-day Americans are accustomed to. A Cheyenne boy might, after returning from his first successful war party, be named after his "most outstanding predecessor."[21] In the Sioux tribe, a young man could be given a new name upon initiation into one of the important warrior or police societies of the tribe, and a "town crier" (a poor old man hired by the boy's father) might be asked to announce to the village the boy's new name.[22] Birth as well as death were occasions for naming in Sioux society, and the dead would be given, after the proper rituals were observed, a "spirit name," by which they would be called from that moment on.[23] After the birth of one Sioux girl who was given twenty-two hand-crafted cradles from friends and family, she was named in such a way as to memorialize this impressive gift-giving: They-Love-Her. Children could be named after an important grandparent, a father's military exploits, or "in reference to a dream he had experienced."[24] If those sources were not enough, a Sioux child might even gain a name from a *winkte*. A Sioux young man who could not or did not want to join in the hunt or war party adopted the female role of *winkte*, or transvestite; the *winkte* was both respected for his supernatural powers and feared for his transgression of the sexual taboos. Blue Whirlwind discusses the *winkte's* naming function within the tribe: "There is a belief that if a winkte is asked to name a child, the child will grow up without sickness. My grandson was given the name Iron Horse when he was three days old by a winkte, and I gave him a horse. Fathers will go to the winkte and flirt with him. Whatever the winkte says will become the secret name and this he will name the child. Winkte names are often unmentionable and therefore are not often used. Girls never had winkte names."[25] Since an Indian might begin life with a pet name, take a formal name at the age of six, and be renamed for every important achievement or event of later life, the federal government sought to stabilize things with the imposition of a single Christian name at census times: From elaboration to consistency, from poetry to legalese.

Indian names gain in appeal through their correspondence between the bearer and experience. Indian names develop out of the life of the tribe or the individual. Modern names are, at best, in honor of some favored relative, at worst a name one's parents felt "sounded nice." Few refer "directly to the universe" in any Emersonian way. Like Adam's naming of the animals, the taking of an Indian name is the earning of a moniker that has grown spontaneously out of one's life and character in the archetypical Garden. Indian names seem something the poet-Indian can respect as living language, not fossilized nomenclature. Indeed, how many of us can say that we have earned our names? Or say what it is they mean?

Dances and the Developing Myth

As I heard my Sioux name being called over and over, I knew for the first time who I really was.

—from the diary of John J. Dunbar

Dances with Wolves seems to me to be the latest, most important development in this mythopoeic founding of the "onley real American."[26] It is a different myth than the one Fiedler called the "anti-feminist" myth, in which the runaway male flees from the White woman to his native, dark-skinned companion. Lieutenant John J. Dunbar marries Stands-with-a-Fist, a White survivor of the massacre, who has nearly forgotten her first family and language. *Dances with Wolves* accomplishes, I think for the first time in our American imagination, the transmigration of the White family unit into the mythical hunting ground of the Indian. By the end of the film, Dances-with-Wolves and Stands-with-a-Fist have already transfigured into buckskins, the Sioux language, the Sioux way. Edward D. Castillo, a Native American academic, has written an excellent review of *Dances with Wolves* that explores many of the same issues analyzed here. Castillo has asserted that

Dances is "really about the transformation of the white soldier Lt. John Dunbar into the Lakota warrior Dances with Wolves."[27] Recalling Dunbar's hope to "see the frontier . . . before it's gone," Castillo noted: "That simple childlike desire touches an unspoken yearning in many Americans, young and old."[28] His words "childlike desire" recall Freud's family romance as well as the wish-fulfillment aspect of *Dances*. Even more interesting is this passage in Castillo's essay: "While exchanging parting gifts, Dances with Wolves tells Kicking Bird, 'You were the first man I ever wanted to be like. I will not forget you.' Indians know that no white man or woman can become Indian, but many of us hope those who have learned of our cultures and appreciate their unique humanity will be our friends and allies in protecting the earth and all of her children."[29]

Since *Dances with Wolves* starts with Lieutenant John J. Dunbar near death on a Civil War operating table and never once flashes back to any fictional family or past, Dunbar's line to Kicking Bird—"You were the first man I ever wanted to be like"—becomes illustrative of a close adherence to the imaginative logic of the family romance. Through a brief examination of only some of the material, this chapter has shown how the generic logic of the family romance was embossed in *Dances with Wolves* with the American Adam myth and the historical legacy of Native American cultures. In retrospect, one should be surprised neither at *Dances with Wolves'* enthusiastic reception nor at the many modern Americans who found going Indian a still viable trail to follow through the American imagination.

Postscript: (The Return of) *Dances with Wolves*

During the November "ratings sweeps" of 1993, ABC broadcast a new, expanded version of *Dances with Wolves*. At fifty minutes longer than the original, the new *Dances* exploited the television Western miniseries formula that worked so well with *Lonesome Dove*. The new *Dances* was originally composed by Costner and producer Jim Wilson for foreign distribution and simply reintegrated footage originally trimmed for the American theatrical release. As can be expected, much of the footage simply expanded on plot, characters, and themes in the original American version. A few additions bridge minor gaps in the narrative and flesh out issues that might have puzzled some original viewers. The crazy Major Fambrough, who sends Dunbar on his "knight's errand" is shown, through added footage, to be certifiably insane. The environmental destruction theme is pushed even further in a number of additions and in one wholly new scene. One addition has the slothful mule driver Timmons littering as he crosses the prairie, tossing a tin can to the ground as Dunbar registers the appropriately modern reaction of indignation. The horror of Fort Sedgewick's polluted pond grows through the addition of animal carcasses and by witnessing Dunbar having to swim into the pond, bandanna over nose, to struggle with the wet dead weight of the animals before he burns them. The wholly new scene of environmental devastation occurs when Kicking Bird and Dunbar journey alone to the sacred Sioux mountains

(Kicking Bird: "The animals were born here.") but find instead an ominous silence and the remnants of a hunting camp strewn with animal corpses and empty whisky bottles. The mystery surrounding the prior inhabitants of Fort Sedgewick is also settled. Before Dunbar reaches the deserted fort: The last of the fort's troops are shown cowering in their caves until their officer assembles them, commends them for staying after the others deserted, and suggests they mount an orderly mass desertion with, "The army can go to Hell!" The new version also fleshes out a few of the minor characters. Two Socks, Dunbar's friendly wolf, gets much more on-screen time, and the trio of young Sioux boys that includes Smiles-a-Lot turn up in a number of scenes of "teenage" drama and hijinks: last-minute jitters before the unsanctioned raid on Dunbar's horse, a vigorous but denied attempt to join the men during the buffalo hunt, and a foiled prank to close the smoke flap on the tepee of the honeymooning Dances-with-Wolves and Stands-with-a-Fist. The inversions of cultural prejudice occasionally seen in the original film are seconded with one more quite pointed gibe that takes place during the massacre of Timmons. A Pawnee brave starts to take Timmons's quilt for a trophy until he sniffs it suspiciously, throws it on the ground in disgust, and cleans his hands with dirt. On a more romantic note, the new film elaborates on the courtship between Dances-with-Wolves and Stands-with-a-Fist, including Dances's need to rely on tribal gifts of horses and clothing in order to purchase his new bride, in the traditional Sioux way, from her father-guardian, Kicking Bird.

But the most substantial difference between the new and original versions of *Dances* involves the night scene just before the buffalo hunt. In the original film, this scene is one long take that lasts for only twenty-eight seconds. The Sioux camp appears in the background, ponies in the middle ground, and Dunbar, resting on his bedroll, is stretched out in the foreground, his voice-over narration intoning: "As they celebrated into the night, the coming hunt, it was hard to know where to be. I don't know if they understood, but I could not sleep among them. There had been no looks, and there was no blame. There was only the confusion of a people not able to predict the future." One assumes simply that Dunbar is finding some time alone before the next day's big hunt. In the expanded version, however, the scene contains two minutes of footage and twenty-five shots that change not only the meaning of this single scene but imbue the entire film with a greater moral complexity. The scene begins with Dunbar riding into camp with a small band of warriors. A large fire is burning in the center of camp as the Sioux dance around it. Dunbar holds back and sizes up the situation. He notices a wagon, filled with buffalo hides. His voice-over narration explains things:

> It was suddenly clear now what had happened, and my heart sank as I tried to convince myself that the white men who had been killed were bad people and deserved to die, but it was no use. I tried to believe that Wind-in-His-Hair and Kicking Bird and all the other people who shared in the killing were not so happy for having done it, but they were. As I looked at the familiar faces I realized that the gap between us was greater than I could ever have imagined.

The narration accompanies a building intimacy of shot scales, growing closer to the dancing Sioux as well as including Dunbar's reaction shots. Two crucial insert shots provide gory emphasis: a severed white man's hand tied in rope and hanging over the flames of the campfire; a long blonde scalp at the end of a pole, reflecting the reddish glow. This unexpurgated scene then ends with the same thirty-second shot and voice-over found in the original; but now Dunbar's comment about not being able "to sleep among them" takes on a pointed meaning. The scene in the original *Dances,* then, is literally a repression of the novel and the shooting script, a repression of the massacre.[30]

Whereas the other material in the film merely expands and explains themes already extant in the first release, this reincorporated material marks a radical addition, I should say a *return,* to the film. While trimming *Dances* to a tight (!) 181 minutes kept the film distributable and positioned for Oscar contention, Costner might have deflected a great deal of subsequent criticism that his Sioux were too wholesome by keeping just this one moment of unbridgeable cultural difference in the original film. (He might also have included, as the new film does, another moral complication of the Sioux: A brief scene early in the narrative makes it clear that Stands-with-a-Fist's husband died, not while defending the tribe from the marauding Pawnee, but during a raid *on* the Utes, explicitly undercutting the assumption the first film may have given that *these* Sioux practice only defensive tribal warfare.) This is not to deny *Dances'* radical inversion of the Western. Whereas *The Searchers* turns on a White man's obsessive attempts to find and retrieve a White woman from her tribal life, *Dances,* at midpoint, gives us a White cavalry officer who returns a White woman to her tribal life as a simple matter of course. But what I find so interesting is how the latest model in the progressive Western cannot live by genre inversion alone, but rather ends up negotiating, deflecting, and ultimately retrieving the massacre. Neither version of *Dances,* I think, is the definitive, authoritative edition—the "director's cut." Multiple versions of narratives, sometimes, betray tensions not so easily written off as just more of the same. Thus, I think we have two films now: *Dances with Wolves,* and *(The Return of) Dances with Wolves.*

Notes

An earlier version of this essay was published as "Going Indian: In and Around *Dances with Wolves,*" in *Michigan Academician* 25 (1993), pp. 133–146. Reprinted with permission.

1. Henry David Thoreau, *The Maine Woods* (New York: Harry N. Abrams, 1989), pp. 184–185.

2. J. Hector St. John Crevecoeur, *Letters from an American Farmer* (Gloucester, Mass: Peter Smith, 1968), p. 225.

3. Leslie A. Fiedler, *The Return of the Vanishing American* (New York: Stein and Day, 1968), epigraph preceding the title page of this book.

4. D. H. Lawrence, *Studies in Classic American Literature* (New York: Viking Press, 1923), p. 53.

5. Fiedler, *Return of the Vanishing American,* p. 167.

6. Ibid., p. 24.

7. R.W.B. Lewis, *The American Adam: Innocence, Tragedy, and Tradition in the Nine-teenth Century* (Chicago: University of Chicago Press, 1955), p. 5.

8. Sigmund Freud, *The Standard Edition of the Complete Psychological Works of Sigmund Freud* (London: Hogarth Press, 1959), vol. 9, pp. 236–241.

9. Richard Slotkin, *Regeneration Through Violence: The Mythology of the American Frontier, 1600–1860* (Middletown, Conn.: Wesleyan University Press, 1973), p. 263. Slotkin's book is an exhaustive examination of American myth, with brilliant work on the "Indian-ization" theme.

10. Elizabeth Stone, *Black Sheep and Kissing Cousins: How Our Family Stories Shape Us* (New York: Penguin Books, 1988), p. 131.

11. Fiedler, *Return of the Vanishing American,* p. 106.

12. Henry David Thoreau, *The Illustrated Walden: With Photographs from the Gleason Collection* (Princeton: Princeton University Press, 1973), p. 112.

13. Ibid., p. 182.

14. Ibid., p. 248.

15. Charles M. Russell, *Trails Plowed Under* (New York: Doubleday, 1935), p. xx.

16. Harold McCracken, *The Charles M. Russell Book: The Life and Work of the Cowboy Artist* (Garden City, N.Y.: Doubleday, 1957), pp. 13–36.

17. Brian W. Dippie, *Remington and Russell* (Austin: University of Texas Press, 1982), p. 156.

18. Russell, *Trails,* p. 139.

19. Russell, *Trails,* p. 144.

20. Men are not the only ones to gain an Indian name. The historical figure Virginia Dare, who was the first European child born in the new world and disappeared in 1587 with the rest of Sir Walter Raleigh's colony, has presented a puzzling mystery to historians ever since her disappearance. In a children's book titled *Virginia Dare: Mystery Girl* (New York: Bobbs-Merrill Co., 1958), part of a series called Childhood of Famous Americans, Augusta Stevenson created a fictionalized conclusion to Virginia's story. Given the problems of presenting a children's story that must deal with the massacre, Stevenson seems to have followed the mythical tradition, giving Virginia an adoptive tribe and an Indian name: White Flower.

21. E. Adamson Hoebel, *The Cheyennes: Indians of the Great Plains* (New York: Holt, Rinehart and Winston, 1960), p. 94.

22. Royal B. Hassrick, *The Sioux: Life and Customs of a Warrior Society* (Norman: University of Oklahoma Press, 1964), pp. 18–19.

23. Ibid., p. 303.

24. Ibid., p. 313.

25. Ibid., pp. 134–135.

26. Charles M. Russell left a number of comments concerning his vote for the true American. In a 1914 letter to Judge Pray, Russell used pen, ink, and watercolor to depict a rather forlorn, mounted Indian. Handwritten beside the brave, Russell inked, "This is the onley [sic] real American. He fought and died for his country. Today he has no vote, no country, and is not a citizen, but history will not forget him"; from Janice K. Broderick, *Charles M. Russell: American Artist* (St. Louis: Jefferson National Expansion Historical Association, 1982), p. 84. Russell expressed much the same sentiment in another letter to Joe

Scheurle, possibly around 1916: "The Red man was the true American. They have almost gon [sic]. But will never be forgotten. The history of how they fought for their country is written in blood, a stain that time cannot grind out"; from *Good Medicine: The Illustrated Letters of Charles M. Russell* (New York: Doubleday, 1929), p. 127.

27. Edward D. Castillo, review of *Dances with Wolves, Film Quarterly* 44 (summer 1991), p. 16.

28. Ibid., p. 19.

29. Ibid., p. 20.

30. Michael Blake's novel (*Dances with Wolves* [New York: Fawcett Gold Medal Book, 1988]) makes Dunbar's cultural anxiety even more apparent than the expanded film does. Some relevant passages: "Suddenly it was clear as a cloudless day. The skins belonged to the murdered buffalo and the scalps belonged to the men who had killed them, men who had been alive that very afternoon. White men. The lieutenant was numb with confusion. He couldn't participate in this, not even as a watcher. He had to leave." (p. 167). The scene concludes with Dunbar racked with existential anxiety over his indeterminate place in the world: "More than anything he wanted to believe that he was not in this position. He wanted to believe he was floating toward the stars. But he wasn't. He heard Cisco lie down in the grass with a heavy sigh. It was quiet then and Dunbar's thought turned inward, toward himself. Or rather his lack of self. He did not belong to the Indians. He did not belong to the Whites. And it was not time for him to belong to the stars. He belonged right where he was now. He belonged nowhere. A sob rose in his throat. He had to gag to stifle it. But the sobs kept coming up and it was not long before he ceased to see the sense in trying to keep them down" (pp. 167–168).

14

"Her Beautiful Savage": The Current Sexual Image of the Native American Male

Peter van Lent

From cigar-store icon to cowboy's sidekick, the Native American male has played a wide variety of roles in popular culture. Given this range of interpretation, it is not surprising that he has eventually turned up as a full-fledged sex symbol.[1] As popular culture continues to provide increasingly stronger expression for social creativity, the emergence of the American Indian male as "stud" will most likely be recorded as a moderately significant development. This topic is worth exploring since it leads to certain unexpected conclusions about the image of Native men and about contemporary sexuality itself.

Few actualities in any category of culture spring forth spontaneously. The current image of the Native American male as sexy has grown out of earlier archetypes. Our dominant culture can tuck away inside its burden of guilt such horrors as the image of a "bloodthirsty savage, often crazed, seeking vengeance or just malicious fun."[2] In past centuries, the vision of violent sexuality was pretty standard treatment of Native men in popular genres such as the Indian captivity narratives. Today, however, Native American men are most often portrayed as sexual in "good" ways. Two familiar labels come to mind: those of "Noble Savage" and "Fearless Warrior."

Both these archetypes have been competently studied as cultural phenomena, but reviewing several key concepts produces helpful reference points. On the "noble" side is a good deal of the residue of Romanticism; according to the typical formula, Native Americans derive their nobility from being close to the primal forces of life, that is, close to nature and the natural state of things. American Indians are vestiges of an original human form—the way we all were before being

211

corrupted by civilization. Traditional Native values are said to resound with a moral purity lost to most of us. American Indians seek to live in harmony with nature, not to exploit it. They are depicted as gentle and trusting with each other and others. When threatened, however, they courageously defend themselves and that which is theirs. If we add qualities of loyalty, strong spirituality, and taciturn self-possession, the stereotype is pretty much complete. It is a durable image, this noble Indian, and it can be found at many moments and at all levels of Western culture—in the French novels of Vicomte Chateaubriand, in the ponderous beat of Henry Wadsworth Longfellow's *Hiawatha*, and in the rash of "Native American films" so popular in the final years of this century. In "Oochigeas," his musical tribute to an Indian couple, the Acadian singer, Roch Voisine, evokes a particularly poignant image of the pre-Columbian ideal:

> Here's a story I've been told
> About a child of 12 years old
> Breathing life to young trees falling
> Before the barbed wire on the plain
> Before the white man ever came.[3]

The "Fearless Warrior" image is a bit more complex. This character type overlaps with the courageous defender mentioned above, but it is less passive, less blissful, and less benign. This archetype is strongly visual. Media presentations have conditioned us to picture a young male on a horse, his bare chest streaked with war paint, wearing a full-feathered warbonnet; he is situated above the horizon on a bluff, waving a feathered spear either in defiance of an enemy or in a gesture of exhortation urging his companions on to battle.

The last appearance of the character Wind-in-His-Hair in the film *Dances with Wolves* draws heavily from this classic representation (see Figure 14.1). In the film's final scene, just as John Dunbar/Dances-with-Wolves and his wife are leaving the encampment of the band of free Sioux with whom they have been living, the voice of Wind-in-His-Hair comes resounding down from a rocky cliff above the village. He shouts a farewell homage to his white companion: "Dances-with-Wolves, I am Wind-in-His-Hair. Do you see that I am your friend? Can you see that you will always be my friend?" As the camera pans up to the outcropping, we see the Sioux warrior on horseback wielding a spear and yelling his defiant pledge of friendship at fate, the U.S. cavalry, and all the forces that have severed his friendship and will soon end his way of life.

There is a blending, or at least a common denominator, of other male images in the archetypes mentioned above. In the dust whirls of a thousand Indian war parties we see the shadows of the Roman legionnaire, the musketeer, the buccaneer, the frontiersman, the U.S. Marines storming the beach. In short, this male image is cut from the age-old fabric of the epic hero. And, here is an essential fact: From time immemorial, the human psyche, most often the female psyche, has been conditioned to see this type of dashing, bold, undaunted, hell-bent, angry, im-

Figure 14.1   *Rodney Grant as Wind-in-His-Hair, from* Dances with Wolves. *Photo, Ben Glass, copyright Orion Pictures Corporation. All rights reserved.*

petuous, and brave man as sexual. With all due respect to contemporary feminist sensibilities that would advocate a kinder, gentler image, the qualities of physical strength, action, and determination still largely define the erotic ideal of the male of our species.

As the example of Wind-in-His-Hair shows us, however, there is more to the heroic formula than glorious victories and swashbuckling sexuality. Deeply embedded in the mystique of the fearless warrior is an air of tragic destiny, the potential for defeat and death. Victory has never been a sine qua non for heroism; it is enough to fight the good fight. Like Roland, the Lone Ranger, and countless others, the personal history of our Native American warrior is often clouded by an ominous fatalism. Yet he is even the more appealing for this. This heroic dimension appears more clearly in a second familiar representation of the Native American warrior that has been reproduced innumerable times in material culture and obviously has a great deal of popular appeal. Juxtaposed against the spear-waving fighter evoked above is the image in a sculpture titled *End of the Trail,* first created by James Fraser and reinterpreted by several other artists since. The sole character is an exhausted, beaten warrior slumped over on his equally weary horse. No longer is the feathered spear raised in defiance. Instead, it hangs down from war-weary arms and points to the ground. What rivets us is not pathos, not the sadness of a warrior who has lost his fight. Rather, this defeated warrior stirs in all who see him an age-old surge of caring and affection, an almost physical attraction. A faithful fighter, he wins over the heart of a father or brother who would rush to help him dismount and would gently lead him to rest and protection. Courageous yet vulnerable, he stirs in the female mind the age-old response of being needed and providing comfort. Even at the end of the trail, the fearless warrior, with all his depressive weariness, is irresistibly appealing.

The examples of Native American male sexuality in this study all derive their attraction from the basic elements of these archetypes. Some are the heroes of popular romantic novels, often called supermarket fiction, of which a favorite subgenre has been dubbed "Indian romances," since the principal male character is almost invariably of Native heritage. Other Native hunks are to be found in the visual representations on greeting cards or wall decorations. Finally, there are the recent films that deal with indigenous cultures and are now referred to as "Native American films." Wherever we find them, these forms all fulfill a certain formula of sexiness linked to past archetypes and are carefully crafted to present a sexual image that is very much in keeping with contemporary taste. Most Native male characters are placed in a traditional setting, often close to nature. Nearly all of them are decent, good men. They are all shown as gentle and loving in one way or another, but they all are warriors at heart. To some degree each one of them is vulnerable, even victimized; some are murdered. And, finally, let us not forget the physical. In fact, let us begin with it, since the most immediately appealing quality that all these young men share is that they are very, very handsome.

Physical Appeal

Physical attraction has always been the primary force in eros. Realizations such as "she's just another pretty face," or "he's just a brainless hunk" come later, often much later. It is facial and corporal beauty that first awakens an amorous response. The physical attraction of American Indian men as they are depicted in popular culture today is a complicated bit of imaging. In a sense, the creators want to have their [beef]cake and eat it, too. In one respect, the cliché of "exotic" good looks is exploited. Native heroes all have glistening, coppery skin and long, raven-black hair; they smell of cedar and pine needles, and they usually wear little more than a breechclout. An oil painting by Ozz Franca reproduced on a greeting card printed by the Leanin' Tree Company offers a perfect example of this representation (Figure 14.2). The subject's long black hair, feathered headband, bare and heavily mus-

Figure 14.2   The Model, *painting by Ozz Franca, reproduced on a greeting card in the Indian Heritage Series, by Leanin' Tree, Inc. Copyright Leanin' Tree.*

cled torso are classic. High cheekbones and oriental eyes give his face an exotic cast, but the elongated nose and face are curiously Caucasian, and this leads us to an important fact. In current popular culture the exoticism of the Native male is always carefully controlled. For example, most of the heroes of the Indian romance novels are of mixed blood—"half-breeds"[4] (Figure 14.3). This convention provides a safety net against several sexual pitfalls. First, it checks the exotic image from

Figure 14.3   *Cover of recent Indian romance novel. Copyright Leisure Books. Courtesy Dorchester Publishing Co.*

being too alien and keeps it well within the bounds of "tall, dark and handsome."[5] Second, it also avoids any squeamishness about miscegenation on the part of the reader. Since the hero is half-white, the romantic-sexual bond is not truly interracial and, once again, "the half-breed's" appearance can be quite comfortably Caucasian. In the words of one romance author: "Bronson could pass as a white man."[6] In fact, in the novel in which this phrase occurs, the major plot line involves the white heroine's rejection of her husband once she discovers that he is half Native American. She had not guessed this fact from his appearance alone.

The issue of nudity or near-nudity has proven to be a bit unruly. The representation of Native Americans without clothes is a very old tradition. Even during the age of exploration the earliest narratives and accompanying sketches drew considerable attention to the Natives' scant clothing or total lack of it. The captive narratives of the eighteenth century frequently mention nudity among the "savages." This theme was carried through into the nineteenth century, at which point it was often accompanied by heavy moral condemnation of such immodesty. The Native Americans' disregard for clothing was supposedly clear proof that they were inferior and primitive. No doubt many Victorians clucked their tongues and voiced disapproval as they studied the pictures of Native nudity. It may not be too cynical to assume that many of them were meanwhile feasting their eyes on images of a Native woman's breasts or the voluptuous musculature of an Indian brave. Thus, even when presented in the guise of moralizing, appreciation of the unclothed body of Native Americans has a long history.

Contemporary filmmakers are by no means unaware of the physical appeal of Native male actors. *The Last of the Mohicans, Map of the Human Heart,* and *Children of the Dust* all include scenes of partial male nudity. Even the Disney Studios' *Squanto,* which aims at an early adolescent audience, arranges key action sequences in which the principal actor, Adam Beach, takes several rolls, thereby losing any effective covering of his derriere by his breechclout.

One of the frequently mentioned attributes of the Native male's physical appearance is the sparsity of body hair. This is to the liking of more than one romance novel heroine: "'Everything you do pleases me,' she murmured, reaching a hand to his hairless, broad chest . . . 'I love you so, Yellow Thunder.'"[7] Another heroine has become so accustomed to her Native lover's body that her first contact with a white man in a long time causes her some surprise: "His hands were pale as his face, covered with curling, reddish hairs. Not smooth and brown like Nokona's hands."[8] In one episode of the Canadian television series *North of Sixty,* a Native male prostitute also makes an appropriate reference: "Middle-aged white guys . . . like Indians 'cause their skin's so smooth." Like Native nudity, a lack of body hair was mentioned in early travel accounts, but it seems to be a rather recent trend to consider this trait so very attractive. Perhaps the body-building movement of the 1980s and 1990s with its fixation on clearly outlining each bulging muscle has made hairless chests (and other parts) fashionable. It may not be going too far to link the admiration for unhairy Native males to the "androgynous appeal" that critics have attributed to current box-office idols. However, this association is not sustained by many descriptions of the Native male physique that emphasize rugged, physical strength: "Her hands wandered lovingly over his hard-muscled flesh. His chest was as solid as a rock wall, his arms and legs were long, corded with muscle."[9] Furthermore, there is nothing ambisexual about the sharply defined facial features so often attributed to American Indian heroes: "His face gleamed in the sun, so hard, so chiseled, skin into bone, that it looked carved from stone."[10] Hawk noses, high cheekbones—none of this suggests the pliant curvaceousness often associated with ambiguous sexuality. Just as Caucasian features serve as a check on exoticism, perhaps unhairiness keeps the strong-featured, hard-bodied Native males from appearing too primitive, too overwhelmingly wild. In this case, though, human physiology supports the aesthetic choice: Men of Oriental origin do tend to have less body hair than those of other races.

It has been determined to this point that there is a marked similarity in the physical descriptions of our heroes in question. However, there are two Native men whose images are enjoying a good deal of current popularity and who are not "marketed" in the ways encountered thus far. The appeal of the film characters portrayed by Graham Greene is widely acknowledged. This actor consistently evokes praise for his portrayals of Native men such as Kicking Bird in *Dances with Wolves* and Walter Crow Horse in *Thunderheart*. Yet, at first glance, these characters do not fit our mold. Graham Greene is not young, and although no one would dispute the fact that he is a nice-looking man, no one would call him a "Native hunk" either. His appeal lies in more subtle characteristics. Equally appealing, but again not really "stud material," is the Navajo police officer, Jim Chee, in Tony Hillerman's mystery novels. Granted, Chee is young, and the author even goes so far as to describe him as good-looking,[11] but little attention is devoted to this character's appearance. Thus, we must be careful at this point not to be blinded by bronze pecs and wind-blown hair. Chee and Greene's characters cannot be written out of our sexual formula. They are attractive and appealing men, less due to physical appearance than personal qualities. Greene's characters are lauded by critics for their understated good humor and forthright honesty. Chee is strongly appealing to readers because he is a decent young man who is struggling sincerely to grow and succeed despite the confusion created by his bicultural life. It appears that what a man *is* can make him just as irresistible as how he looks.

Sexiness of Character

To begin this discussion let us return to the painting reproduced on the greeting card. Given the feathered headband, the beaded necklace, and the Indian print blanket, one would expect the title of this painting to be something like *Buffalo Thunder* or *Flying Arrow*. In other words, the title would most likely indicate that this is a portrait and would show the Native custom of selecting human names from nature or from cultural objects. However, the painting is called *The Model*. There are two conclusions to be drawn from this surprising title. First, it gives conscious recognition to the current popularity of the Native male image. This painting is not retrospective after all. By identifying him as a model, the artist implies that this Native man earns his living from his attractiveness and the fact that his look is "in." The second conclusion is even more significant. As noted above, "the model" is not wearing a western-style shirt, cowboy boots, and jeans. Today, when the Indian man is depicted in his sexual mode, he is most often transferred back to the past, a time of a traditional lifestyle. Almost without exception the Indian romances take place in the nineteenth century.[12] Nearly all of the current Native American movies and made-for-television movies deal with historical events and Native characters from the past. The basic story of *Thunderheart* is contemporary, but in order to find his true identity, the principal male character must delve far back into his family history. Perhaps Jim Chee is once again the exception to the pattern. Hillerman mentions the sexual attraction of white female students to Native men in a present-day university setting: "Chee recognized the look. . . . He had seen it . . . often among Anglo coeds enrolled in Native American Studies courses. . . . Chee had concluded early that their interest was more in Indian males than in Indian mythology. Their eyes asked if you were really any different from the blond boys they had grown up with."[13] However, even Chee's character relates directly to the past due to his fidelity to Navajo tradition and his efforts to perpetuate the ancient role of the *yataalii*, a singer of traditional songs used in Navajo religious ceremonies.

Today's popular Native males are also appealing because they often play the roles of the "good guys." In the plots of Indian romances, the white males are often drunkards and dirty, whereas the Native men are close to the healthful, healing powers of nature. Narrative passages frequently describe them bathing in a lake or river. In the recent film version of *Last of the Mohicans,* the Europeans are shown as liars and as unfaithful to their promises, as in the case of the attack on the British retreat from Fort William Henry. Native Americans, by contrast, are depicted as true to their word. Native males consistently display loyalty to their people and culture, whereas many white men are depicted as loyal only to their own greed. Even in their finest moments, most whites in the Native American films are driven by a sense of manifest destiny. They invade traditional Indian lands with no hesitation, feeling that technological superiority gives them the right to break treaties and to ignore the territorial needs of these "uncivilized" Natives. The Indian characters, on the other hand, continually show great respect and consideration for others. One romance heroine acknowledges her lover's compassion even in the face of her own obstinacy: "She could give her heart to this tender warrior who ministered to her despite her refusal to serve him."[14] Another hero never fails to return with generosity a kindness he was once shown: "He often gave his share of the hunt to the old woman who had stepped forward and intervened in his behalf. Her husband was old and unable to hunt, so she was dependent on others to provide her lodge with meat."[15] The Native hero's positive interaction with others is often described as gentleness and tenderness, especially when he is relating to children and women. The "Indian proverb" printed inside the *Model* card reads: "Nothing is so strong as gentleness; nothing so gentle as real strength." The readers of one romance novel are told, "the gentleness in his dark eyes was surely why Juliana had trusted him."[16] A greeting card frequently found on the shelves of Indian reservation gift shops shows an Indian father seated on the ground stirring a campfire while his child snuggles close to his chest (Figure 14.4). The message inside the card says that what makes a man great is "the things he does for everyone."

In one of the better-written passages from a romance novel, a stereotypical heroine is wrestling with her conflicting feelings of cultural repulsion and physical attraction to the Native hero. While she is secretly observing him teaching a young boy how to throw a knife, the child accidently wounds his teacher in the leg. The heroine is terrified for the child but then amazed when the older Comanche simply stanches the blood from the cut and calmly goes on instructing the boy in knife usage. She begins to feel very differently about this man who can be "sensitive to the feelings of a child."[17] Although the image of the Native male relating affectionately to children is pleasant and reassuring, there are those who

Figure 14.4   Where Eagles Soar, *painting by Marilyn Bendell, reproduced on a greeting card in the Indian Heritage Series by Leanin' Tree, Inc. Copyright Leanin' Tree.*

would question whether it is sexy. In response, one need only mention the popularity of a theme depicted on posters sold frequently in novelty stores for mounting on dorm-room and other walls. The photo on the poster shows young, attractive males, usually partially nude, holding totally nude infants in their arms. This item of material popular culture is infamous for its photographic treatment of male beefcake, and its use of the male-with-child motif points to a strong romantic reaction.

The issue of male commitment to love relationships is a sore point in American culture today. Almost daily the media make disconcerting announcements such as "the number of fatherless homes in the United States has never been so high." Surely the image of the loving, child-oriented, Native male, described by the critic Angela Aleiss as "so devoted to family,"[18] is a healthy relief from this constant parade of male deficiency. In fact, in most of the Indian romances, it is the Native hero who feels unwavering amorous devotion to the white heroine, who, in turn, struggles with the problem of commitment. Likewise, in Barbara Kingsolver's *Animal Dreams,* the female narrator puts a new gender twist on the old "love 'em-and-leave-'em" structure as she repeatedly delays any commitment to her handsome Apache lover, who struggles with feelings of being sexually objectified:

"I don't know what you want from me," I said.
"I want more than I'm getting. More than sex."
"Well, maybe that's all I have to offer."
He still waited.
"Lloyd, I'm just here till next June. You know that. I've never led you on."[19]

Although it should not be implied that indigenous culture should "exist to serve the white in some way,"[20] it might be safe to say that the popularity of the current Native male image may help to address a perceived social problem, at least by providing a fantasy answer to that problem. In popular culture, at any rate, American Indian lovers and fathers are portrayed as men who commit.

If the spirits of Cochise, Geronimo, and countless other Native heroes are aware of this study so far, they are probably not pleased. Too much emphasis on good looks, tenderness, and love dilutes the image of the brave and courageous warrior. The score must be evened up, for indeed the survival of tough men in a violent time is a vivid part of the mystique of the Indian image. Even the most saccharine of Indian romance novels propels its male heroes onto the warpath at some point, and the display of bravery, strength, and determination is consistent with the epic mode described thus far. Occasionally, the violent passages have an almost lyric undertone: "The Indian sprang to his feet and whirled to see her, all in one graceful movement as though he was dancing in a dream. His eyes flashed wild and hot, straight into hers. His face, dark and hard as the iron in her hands, held a look so fierce that it stopped her heart."[21] The recent movie version of *Geronimo* wins the highest marks for action and battle scenes, but the other Native American films are not far behind. There are occasional Indian bad guys, but mostly, the Native heroes pit their courage against white enemies and right makes might, at least in popular culture, for they emerge from the dust of battle as invincibly romantic, if not always victorious.

There are some unsettling questions raised by current Native male characterization. To begin with, placing the Native male hero in a historical past and depicting him as basically "good" is distressingly ironic. These decent, honorable characters are living fictionally in a time when the actual dominant culture considered American Indians anything but "good." Indeed, the infamous words of General Sheridan in the nineteenth century, about the only "good" Indian being a dead one still ring in our ears.[22] In the formal tradition, the novels of Scott Momaday and other Native American writers present Native male characters who are contemporary, not historical. They also differ from the dominant stereotype in that their characters often display disturbing and thought-provoking realities. Should we deduce from the lack of stable, well-integrated contemporary Native male characters that the "noble savage"—for so long a symbolic vestige of lost purity—has himself undergone the corruption and demoralization of modern civilization? Should we rework the familiar phrase to say, "the only good Indian is a historical Indian?" Or, even worse, to extend the "stereotype of the vanishing Indian" noted by Peter Beidler, can it be that the Native American as a racial group is extinct, having been "biologically and culturally absorbed into the dominant white culture?"[23] Finally, is popular culture guilty of denying an urgent reality simply to opiate the masses, in this case with romanticism? Reverting to past images and refusing to face present realities is certainly the theme of David Bradley's painting *Sleeping Indian,* in which the reclining Native male's traditional dress and bow and arrows contrast eerily with the symbols of modern technology in the background (Figure 14.5). Yet, to answer yes to this last question, at least, would be making too harsh a judgment on a sphere of cultural activity that serves society in its own way, with its own resources. To see this, let us consider the Native male characters more specifically in their fictional contexts.

Sexiness and Situation

He is dashingly handsome and has admirable qualities. Now, how do the works in which he figures involve the Native hero in situations where he displays attractive male behavior? Given the romantic preference for historical characterizations, it is appropriate that the Native male is most often found in a natural setting where he leads a traditional life and has ready access to Indian culture. Even the romance novel half-breeds have invariably been raised by their Native parent. Poor Squanto in the Disney film is hauled off to England and has some European adventures, but the main plot line here is how he will find his way back to North America, which he ultimately does.

When confronted with a desirable woman, popular Native heroes seldom fail to prove ardent lovers. The romance novels again provide pertinent examples in

Figure 14.5 Sleeping Indian, *painting by David Bradley, reproduced on a greeting card by Garfinkel Publications. Copyright 1994 Garfinkel Publications.*

frequent passages devoted to amorous activity that skirts the edges of soft porn. Descriptions of a Native male's throbbing "manhood" and the heroine's "silken depths"[24] and phrases such as "spilled his seed on her intimate parts"[25] are standard fare. In contrast, the subtly developed relationship between Uncas and Alice in the film *The Last of the Mohicans* is all the more touching. Similarly, although Jim Chee is not a virgin, his romantic pursuits of Mary Landon and later of Janet Pete always fall within the realm of restrained yet credible narrative.

The affectionate intimacy between Kicking Bird and his wife in *Dances with Wolves* leads to an important observation. Romance between married lovers has not had an extensive history in recent times. Ever since the Middle Ages, when the courtly love craze overtook Western culture, romantic art has been obsessed with eros, the sexual-romantic attraction between young, unmarried males and females. For seven hundred years, this amorous mode has pushed any other type of love story out of the picture. Indeed, when it was certain that Cinderella, Snow White, Sleeping Beauty, and innumerable others "got married and lived happily ever after," the story was over. Kicking Bird's loving marriage and other Native love relationships contribute to our study in two ways. They illustrate certain American Indian values, but they may also be indicative of a new direction in Western art: the return of the other loves.[26] It has been noted how the final vision of Wind-in-His-Hair evokes a stereotypically romantic male image. However, we must remember, perhaps with some surprise, that his endearing homage is paid to a male friend, thus to *philia,* or brotherly love, not to eros. In the same film, just minutes before the departure scene, a young Sioux, with tears streaming down his face, gives Dances-with-Wolves a farewell gift. The boy's emotion is clearly motivated by *storge,* or affection.[27] If, indeed, the treatment of love in art is changing, it would not be the first time that popular culture served as the harbinger of a new direction.

Of all the situations in which our heroes display their charms, the Native male as victim seems to be the most compelling. Naturally these men would encounter obstacles. This is the essence of a good story, whether it is conveyed literarily or visually. Art without tension has its place, but, honestly now, can a serene watercolor of Japanese koi or a greeting card showing an Indian father snuggling his son really compete with a frenzied hunting scene or that of a war party? Aesthetics has never denied that adventure and challenge are at the very heart of human experience. A curious fact is, however, that most of our popular narratives take the obstacle-tension formula one step further and depict the Native American male in situations of real suffering. Often, the suffering is physical: He is tied up for days on end, tortured, or in the case of Uncas, the next-to-the-last Mohican, murdered. Mental suffering is also common, and it often stems from racial prejudice due to mixed blood. One hero laments: "I was coldly informed that the Confederate States of America could win the war quite nicely without the help of any filthy, thieving half-breeds."[28] In the case of the half-breeds, the suffering is twofold since both whites and Natives discriminate against them.

Even when not directly focusing on racial differences, whites are consistently causing suffering for the Native people. The vision of Squanto returning to his village only to find that his loved ones have been wiped out by a European disease is particularly poignant. The lead male in *Thunderheart,* Ray Levoi, is victimized by an unscrupulous colleague and ultimately loses his job with the Federal Bureau of Investigation. Corby White in the television film, *Children of the Dust,* is rejected by the white woman he loves (and who loves him!) and is ultimately killed. Wind-in-His-Hair loses his close friend. The couple in *Map of the Human Heart* are separated forever. Even Jim Chee is abandoned by Mary Landon, who returns to her white family in the Midwest. The list of tragic situations is endless and constitutes its own Trail of Tears.

It is clear from these examples that, in addition to everything else, the Native male must be a victim if he is to fulfill his sexual role. Why? To a large extent, the answer lies in the familiar process of image control. Too triumphant a Native male would be beyond the realm of audience or reader response. These heroes must have a weakness, must not be too self-sufficient if they are to provide a sexual vision. Romance dictates some givens: The vulnerability cannot come from being ugly or being a "bad guy." However, showing the Indian man as the victim of undeserved suffering gives him a very approachable human dimension. There is suddenly room for reassurance, companionship, support—the things that are offered by love. Within the realm of sexual love, the male as victim evokes a uniquely feminine response, a combination of the maternal and the erotic—the urge to comfort, to heal, to caress. One romance heroine is able to acknowledge this bond between victimization and eros: "She moaned softly as his tongue slid over her lips . . . This was what she had wanted, had needed since the first time she saw him in the Apache camp, a prisoner, badly wounded. He had stirred something deep within her."[29]

Once again we see the narrowly crafted path that the Native American sexual male must tread in popular culture. He must be tender and loving, yet a bold warrior, exotically handsome but not too alien, a good man, but prey to the evil of others. Yet, thanks to popular culture, he is the latest sex symbol of the twentieth century, succeeding the cowboy, the space wanderer, the detective, and others. In fact, being associated with Native maleness has become such a trend that it crops up at times when it might not be entirely expected. In one of his last novels, *Last of the Breed,* Louis L'Amour created a hero who is "part Sioux and part Cheyenne,"[30] who, due to his involvement in a military fiasco, must escape across the Bering Strait, retracing the migration of his ancient ancestors. Tristan, the character created by Brad Pitt in the film *Legends of the Fall,* has been raised in close contact to a Native family, and he displays the influence of this upbringing at certain points in the film. In the television series *Dr. Quinn, Medicine Woman,* the male lead, Byron Sully, has a close, adoptive relationship with the local Cheyenne. Even "dirty" jokes deal with Native male sexuality to some degree. The following twist on the familiar riddle pattern was told recently to the author at a bar near the St. Regis Mohawk Reservation (called *Akwesasne,* in the Mohawk language) in northern New York state:

Question: What does a Hopi man have that is long and hard?
Answer: His name.

Conclusion

Thus, American society welcomes the Native male hero, in the same way as we welcome other characters such as the emergency room physician and the emergency medical technicians who respond to 911 calls. Perhaps the recent proliferation of the images of sensitively effective yet vulnerable men points to a desire to resuscitate the masculine gender. Is American society seeking an antidote to the bumbling, male ignoramuses whose image has been all too prevalent in recent decades? Media advertising, usually for some household product, is especially guilty in this regard. Countless commercial messages have reveled in showing an inept male being belittled by an overbearingly informed woman because he has made a stupid purchase or has bungled some domestic procedure. But even more than the medical rescuers perhaps, the Native male is the perfect hero to rehabilitate the masculine mode and to symbolize the male ideal as we pass to the new millennium. Until recently, American popular culture was vacillating in its portrayal of heroes. Traditional preferences brought forth the Sylvester Stallone–Bruce Willis–type "men of action" character, and certainly this structure has predominated in all popular genres throughout the twentieth century. Yet, contemporary values demand a more sensitive, loving male image. If he is carefully created, popular culture's new Indian male satisfies both these current societal profiles. Loving him—a minority and a victim of much that we regret—makes American dominant culture feel less guilty. Handsome in a way that is trendy, worthy of admiration, consistent with codes of bravery and commitment, he is irresistibly attractive. In the preface to his book *The White Man's Indian,* Robert Berkhofer, Jr., states that "white interest in the American Indian surges and ebbs with the tides of history."[31] Thus the dominant culture's image of the Indian has constantly been made and remade in response to that culture's changing preoccupations. The current image of the Native American male owes its surge of popularity not so much to cultural whimsy as to the fact that he is responding to specific and significant needs of the dominant segment of our society.[32]

Notes

1. Title quotation is from Fabio, *Comanche* (New York: Avon Books, 1995).
2. Robert F. Berkhofer, Jr., *The White Man's Indian: Images of the American Indian from Columbus to the Present* (New York: Vintage Books, 1979), p. 98.
3. *Oochigeas,* Les Editions R.V. International, compact disk STR CD 3105, 1993.

4. For a chart showing the racial identity of heroes and heroines in a sample of numerous Indian romances, see Peter G. Beidler, "The Contemporary Indian Romance: A Review Essay," *American Indian Culture and Research Journal* 15 (4) (1991), pp. 97–125.

5. This expression is actually used verbatim in Fabio, *Comanche*, p. 4.

6. Ibid., p. 56.

7. Cassie Edwards, *Savage Sunrise* (New York: Leisure Books, 1993), p. 214.

8. Genell Dellin, *Comanche Rain* (New York: Avon Books, 1995), p. 328.

9. Madeline Baker, *Apache Runaway* (New York: Leisure Books, 1995), p. 313.

10. Dellin, *Comanche Rain*, p. 24.

11. See Martin Greenberg, ed., *The Tony Hillerman Companion* (New York: Harper Collins, 1994).

12. Beidler, "Indian Romance," p. 98.

13. Tony Hillerman, *People of Darkness* (New York: Harper and Row, 1980).

14. Fabio, *Comanche*, p. 203.

15. Baker, *Apache Runaway*, p. 151.

16. Edwards, *Savage Sunrise*, p. 259.

17. Dellin, *Comanche Rain*, p. 63.

18. Angela Aleiss, "Le Bon Sauvage: *Dances with Wolves* in the Romantic Tradition," *American Indian Culture and Research Journal* 15 (4) (1991), p. 92.

19. Barbara Kingsolver, *Animal Dreams* (New York: HarperCollins, 1990), p. 182.

20. Stelio Cro, *The Noble Savage: Allegory of Freedom* (Waterloo, Ontario: Wilfrid Laurier University Press, 1990). Quoted in Sandy Greer, "The Noble Savage," *Winds of Change* (spring 1993), p. 92.

21. Dellin, *Comanche Rain*, pp. 18, 19.

22. Hillerman himself refers to this quote in *People of Darkness*, p. 7.

23. Beidler, "Indian Romance," p. 101.

24. Fabio, *Comanche*, p. 406.

25. Ibid., p. 211.

26. At the time of this writing, a current box-office hit is the film *Rob Roy*, which includes numerous scenes depicting physical romance between married lovers.

27. For a brilliant treatment of those differing love structures, see C. S. Lewis, *The Four Loves* (New York: Harcourt Brace, 1960).

28. Fabio, *Comanche*, p. 306.

29. Baker, *Apache Runaway*, p. 268.

30. Louis L'Amour, *Last of the Breed* (New York: Bantam Books, 1986), p. 9.

31. Berkhofer, *White Man's Indian*, p. xiii.

32. An interesting discussion of this need to reestablish a more substantial masculine image can be found in R. William Betcher and William S. Pollock, *In a Time of Fallen Heroes* (New York: Guilford Press, 1993).

15

Cultural Heritage in *Northern Exposure*

Annette M. Taylor

On one of his regular visits to *Northern Exposure*'s fictional town of Cicely in the real state of Alaska, traditional healer Leonard Quinhagak seeks expressions of the "collective unconscious of white culture."[1] He hopes to discern the "curative powers" in white people's fables, such as those that permeate Native American stories and legends. By uncovering the wisdom and moral lessons in such tales, he believes he will be better able to help the white people in his practice, who, he says, "are starting to assimilate." In his interviews with Cicely's European descendants, which he conducts with the formality of a scientific survey, he hears high-school tales of insects in hair-sprayed, beehive hairdos, rats disguised as fried chicken, and escaped psychopaths clamping their hooks onto cars parked on lovers' lane. "And then what?" Leonard asks. "How does the character's story impact your life? Are you aware of the story's influence in your daily activities?" The storytellers are baffled; they know of no deep meaning.

Disappointed, Leonard concludes that the white culture's stories, rather than providing clues to spiritual and physical health, only tend to make people feel worse. "White people don't seem concerned at all about using mythology to heal themselves," he says. At the end of the episode, however, Leonard finds the "white medicine" he was looking for. He observes that Native American character Ed Chigliak, who had been suffering from stress and a loss of confidence, begins to feel better by watching Orson Welles's *Citizen Kane*. Ed immerses himself in the movie, analyzing not only the story but its relation to the real life of the real star. Film can be "magic," Leonard says to Ed. "It seems to have cured you."

The intertextual tapestry of representations and misrepresentations, ironies, and incongruities concerning "other" cultures in real life and in popular culture presented on America's prime instrument of enculturation is nothing short of delicious. More than being just a twisted commentary on the impact of the media's cultural portrayals upon collective and disparate societies, however, this 1993 episode of the popular and award-winning CBS series also symbolizes the variant cultural plays in *Northern Exposure* itself. The clash of cultures is, after all, the primary focus of this series, as creators Joshua Brand and John Falsey have said. By considering Native American culture as one of those "cultures," *Northern Exposure,* when it premiered in summer 1990, became the first television series in fifteen years to feature Native American characters in regular, prominent roles.[2] The show is set apart by its willingness not only to defy the familiar stereotypes but also to reject the easy antistereotypes.

When the creators of *Northern Exposure* assigned "Indians" as the indigenous people of their town of Cicely, Alaska, they cleverly avoided the risk of cliché. After all, Americans, whose impression of Alaska has been formed primarily by Jack London tales and Walt Disney films, might have expected "Eskimos" in igloos. By denying viewers the obvious, *Northern Exposure*'s creators found a unique opportunity to recast popular culture imagery of Native Americans not only in one arena but in two—the western frontier and the northern frontier.

To many people—indoctrinated by Hollywood associations of buckskin and feathers, mysticism and Mother Earth, drunken fools and trusty servants—the term "Indian" remains inextricable from such fabrications. Indians are still defined by what they are not, namely, white European Americans. As Robert F. Berkhofer, Jr., has pointed out, Indians must reject their culture in order to be considered like everyone else.[3] Indians who remain faithful to their heritage and traditions cannot, by definition, be part of the larger society. In either case, native people face but one end: annihilation and obliteration.

By contrast, *Northern Exposure* casts its native population as alive, well, and flourishing, part of the dominant white society and modernity, yet still practicing traditional ways. The Native American culture in Cicely complements rather than contradicts the Judeo-Christian, European-based culture, and its people are complex personalities that majority audiences can relate to.

Like all popular culture, however, *Northern Exposure* suffers gaps and contradictions, which simultaneously lend it power and popularity.[4] The text fosters messages of goodness in cultural diversity and community—arguably the preferred, constructed meaning of the series. The show, as popular culture, also invites audience participation, and viewers can delight in bringing to episodes their own wisdom, values, and morals. This openness of the text, which allows what John Fiske calls "guerrilla" readings, in turn makes accessible the opposing codes of native people's inevitable annihilation. It is ironic, therefore, that the dominant ideology of *Northern Exposure,* which tends to counter the negative stereotypes of Native American culture, is vulnerable to contradictory meaning and validates the messages it seeks to supplant.

Television Images of Native Americans

In the late 1950s and early 1960s, television offered as many as twenty-eight Westerns per week, including *The Lone Ranger, Cheyenne, Wagon Train,* and *Gunsmoke.* People remember all of those black-and-white tales as detailing the lives of cowboys and Indians. In actuality, most Westerns focused on the cavalry, sagebrush heroes, honorable gunslingers, father figures, and rich settlers. The "red devils" may have provided dramatic tension, but they only occasionally surfaced above the horizon.[5]

Like feature films, television confined Native Americans to a handful of tribes and cultures and then redrafted them to suit popular conceptions.[6] Screen Indians belonged only to Plains tribes, spoke the same language, dressed in the same clothes, and practiced the same religion. Native American characters filled well-established, and now well-documented, roles: They were noble but doomed leaders, drunken or pathetic fools, trusty servants or treacherous villains. Even as friendly sidekicks, they were marginalized—Tonto always remained to the side of the Lone Ranger and rarely said anything.

Throughout the history of television, Native Americans have been featured as the lead characters in only about a half-dozen series, four of which confined them to the past and, in so doing, affirmed their annihilation.[7] The first series, *Brave Eagle,* which ran one season during 1955–1956 on CBS, boldly suggested the historical mistreatment of Native Americans, as a Cheyenne chief tried to safeguard his homeland from the oncoming settlers. Given that viewers knew the settlers would eventually take the land and confine natives to reservations, the underlying message of the show was doom. The following season, *Hawkeye and the Last of the Mohicans* ran in syndication and featured James Fenimore Cooper's characters. Set in the 1750s in New York State, the series related the escapades of Nat "Hawkeye" Cutler and his Indian blood brother, Chingachgook, as they helped the pioneers to settle and the army to quash "the constant Huron uprisings."[8] The show's premise clearly fosters the dichotomy between righteous whites, who move forward into the future, and mostly evil indigenous people who try to block progress.

Cheyenne, an ABC series from 1957–1963, told tales of frontier scout Cheyenne Bodie, a man of Cheyenne descent trained in the ways of both Native American and European American cultures. Cheyenne might be found one week working as a scout for a wagon train or another week working on ranch, but he was always working to assimilate.

Law of the Plainsman, which ran on NBC from 1959–1962, offered the most fantastic premise. A fourteen-year-old brave in Arizona, about to scalp a wounded army captain, inexplicably relents and nurses the soldier back to health. The captain adopts the supposedly nameless boy, christening him Sam Buckhart. Sam eventually goes to Harvard, then becomes a lawman in New Mexico. Like Cheyenne or Hawkeye, Sam served the larger society in trying to calm angry natives.

It took Burt Reynolds, himself of Native American descent, to bring a modern-day Native American to the small screen in a lead role. The 1966 ABC series, *Hawk,* featured a half-Iroquois New York City police lieutenant, who worked nights for the district attorney's office. The series did not deal with Native American issues or identity—unless Hawk's talent to see in the dark was supposed to be characteristic of his ethnicity.[9] The series lasted only three months.

Seven years later, television tried again. Launched during the 1974–1975 season on ABC and pulled after only three months, *Nakia* featured a modern-day Navajo working as a sheriff's deputy in rural New Mexico. Deputy Nakia Parker supposedly found his loyalties divided between his traditional ways and modern police practices,[10] but whatever cultural conflicts Nakia had were relegated to subplot, since programming guides only mention the usual crime fare of murders, kidnappings, and thefts.[11]

For the next fifteen years, Native American television characters slipped into obscurity, despite the counterculture interest in Native American philosophy and artistry, the rise in pro-Indian Hollywood movies, and the "red power" political movement. By the early 1970s, when the popularity of Westerns had waned, Native Americans' representation on television dropped to a mere 0.3 percent of all TV characters. Compared to all other ethnic groups, they were more likely to be involved in violence, were the least likely to be innocent victims, and were rarely associated with any discernible profession.[12]

Conspicuous by their virtual absence on television are Alaska Natives. Alaska's history would seem to have all the elements for a good "Western"—indigenous peoples, outside invaders, and conflict over the rich natural resources. The three major gold rushes to Alaska and the neighboring Canadian Yukon around the turn of the century provide all the drama of any Wild West story. But the gold rushes were stories of the new Americans, not Alaska Natives.

Alaska Natives escaped Hollywood treatment—many would say mistreatment—in part because of their distance from the rest of the country, which made them unfamiliar and invisible. In addition, conflicts between Alaska's indigenous peoples and outsiders over land, resources, and sovereignty have been pitched mostly on Capitol Hill and in the courts, rather than in armed combat. Except for a few battles during the Russian occupation days, Alaska Natives never warred with the invaders and never posed a significant threat.

The Tlingit Indians of the archipelago of southeast Alaska, who had won several battles early on against the Russians, were forced to share Alaska's southern panhandle by the early 1800s. The Tlingits nevertheless escaped outside dominance and maintained their way of life by playing the Russians and Americans off against each other in the trading business. The mainland of Alaska, home to Inupiat and Yuit Eskimos and Athabaskan Indians, was simply too cold, too bleak, and too dark to appeal to many non-natives. The Aleuts of the Alaska Peninsula and Aleutian Islands were not so lucky. Enslaved and nearly exterminated by the

Russians, they continued to suffer under the United States. In one of the most egregious examples of tyranny, the U.S. government kept the Pribilof Islands Aleuts in a state of virtual servitude until 1984.[13]

Whereas tribes in the lower forty-eight states have suffered from genocidal policies almost continually since the late 1700s, Alaska Natives, with exception of the Aleuts, were virtually ignored by the government until the late 1880s. Only then did a nearly century-long, government-sanctioned policy of eradicating native religions, languages, and cultures begin, instituted primarily through the education of Alaska Native youth in faraway boarding schools. Nevertheless, Alaska Native distinctive traditions, cultures, and subsistence lifestyles have survived, in part because of these peoples' hold on the land. After legally thwarting construction of the 800-mile-long trans-Alaska pipeline that the federal government and oil industry desperately wanted, Alaska Natives in 1971 signed their first treaty and land settlement claim with the U.S. government. They were awarded about 40 million acres, in addition to other lands of cultural significance—about 11 percent of the land mass—and $1 billion. With those funds, Alaska Natives, who now comprise about 16 percent of the state's population, have created both cultural nonprofit organizations and for-profit businesses to maintain their independence.

The image most Americans have of Alaska and its people, despite their rich and varied history, comes primarily from documentaries, such as *Nanook of the North* (1922), *Eskimo* (1934), *The Alaskan Eskimo* (1953), and Disney nature films, along with a handful of feature films, such as *The White Dawn* (1974) and *White Fang* (1991). Only four TV shows, including *Northern Exposure,* have been situated in Alaska. The first, *The Alaskans,* ran on ABC during the 1959–1960 season and told the story of three hustlers who settle in Alaska during the gold rush days. The following year, the gold rush was also the theme of NBC's short-lived series, *Klondike.* Neither program dealt with natives or native culture, nor did ABC's 1974 crime drama, *Kodiak,* which was canceled after only four episodes.

Thus, television for the most part has eliminated distinctions among real Native American peoples and cultures in both the lower forty-eight states and Alaska. The overall message, whether in a turn-of-the-century or a modern-day setting, is that Indians who retain cultural identity are doomed and assimilated Indians always abandon their people.

In *Northern Exposure,* then, television offers the first truly successful series to prominently feature Native American characters as normal, functioning human beings within modern society. Whereas *Hawk* tried to assimilate its Native American into the dominant culture and *Nakia* stressed an irreconcilable conflict between two cultures, *Northern Exposure* attempts to portray Native culture as complementary to the dominant culture. And, most unusual for TV in general, the majority culture in Cicely is better for the influence of the native culture. Equally significant, the native characters on *Northern Exposure,* although part of an ensemble cast, are integral to the very fabric of the show (Figure 15.1).

Figure 15.1 *The cast of* Northern Exposure, *including Elaine Miles as Marilyn (lower-right corner) and Darren E. Burrows as Ed (upper-left corner). CBS publicity photo.*

Northern Exposure and the Western Genre

Northern Exposure is based on the premise of a young Jewish doctor from New York being forced to live in Alaska to work off his medical school loans, which were financed by the state. Dr. Joel Fleischman had hoped to serve his time in Anchorage but instead finds himself in Cicely, a village of 839 persons. Weekly episodes relate the experiences of the foreigner and the rooted inhabitants of the frozen backcountry. Many of Cicely's residents are Native American, as suggested by the crowd scenes, although seven of the nine leading characters are from predominantly white communities in the lower forty-eight states and Canada.

Northern Exposure in many ways mimics the classic Western and its clash of cultures. *Northern Exposure* has civilization meeting primitivism, social structure encountering anarchy, scientism confronting naturalism in the ultimate Western frontier. The difference here is that characterizations of the characters continually change, depending on the scriptwriters' and the viewers' imaginations.

As a principal character for the first five seasons, Fleischman was the well-bred and educated, urbane citizen of New York City, entering the nascent wilderness town of Cicely. If *Northern Exposure* were a creature of the 1950s and 1960s, a superior Fleischman would force an inferior, indigenous population of Cicely to adapt to his ways or get out of the way. He would be a Marcus Welby in the Big Valley, nursing the spiritually deprived to moral health. The town's menfolk, meanwhile, would be a bonded group of manly cowboys, respecting the doctor hero as they would a trail boss or wagon master. The "girls"—and they would be girls no matter what their age or experience—would be adoring, submissive, flighty, fidgety, or meddling.[14] The status of the Indians would depend on how well they behaved. All those Indians in The Brick, the town's bar-restaurant, would have to be closely watched, however, since everyone knows that liquor and Indians are a lethal combination.

Just as the real Alaska is a place where people can and do reinvent themselves, so *Northern Exposure* is a show that reinvents Western-genre characters and relationships. Maurice Minnifield, the Ben Cartwright of the program with his wealth and power, assumes the role of a buffoon who hides his loneliness and sentimentality. The town's radio disc jockey, ex-con, and Alaskan Adonis, Chris "In the Morning" Stevens, is the town's spiritual guide, waxing eloquent on great philosophers and poets. Holling Vincouer, old adventurer and shootist, holsters his weapons and settles down contentedly with a business, young wife, and baby. Although they tend to maintain a definitional connection to men, the women are self-reliant and assertive. Maggie O'Connell, the former debutante who is expected to get the hero, à la *Guys and Dolls,* is a bush pilot who has loved and lost too many times. Young Shelly Tambo Vincouer, the ditsy blonde bombshell, has the expected purity of heart but also a wealth of common sense and self-esteem. Ruth-Anne Porter, the occasionally meddling and self-righteous store owner, remains a respected elder despite suffering occasional confusion. These are complex characters rather than strictly good guys or bad guys.

The "hero" in *Northern Exposure* is the antithesis of the classic Western's true American hero: Fleischman is Jewish and of Russian descent. Although he claims to represent progressivism and civilization, viewers soon see that his vision is narrow and his behavior rude. By contrast, Cicely's "natives," which include both indigenous and European descendants, are tolerant and respectful. They are open to all possibilities: to dead lovers coming back as malamutes, to truth and justice arising from democratic discussion, to wisdom dispensed by 250-year-old spirits, to love. They are gentle people with clear moral vision and enough common sense to seek help when they lose that vision. Unlike other Western heroes, Fleischman changes, or "notices the light," as he says at the end of the 1993–1994 season, and he becomes part of the society he found.

When actor Rob Morrow, who plays Fleischman, announced his intent to leave the show as of February 1995, two new characters were brought in early in the 1994–1995 season—Dr. Philip Capra, a willing émigré to Cicely from Los Angeles, and his wife, Michelle Shadowski Capra, who quietly suffers the transplant. To Phil, Cicely is "the America we've been looking for." To Michelle, "It's like stepping back in time." The "outsider" theme of *Northern Exposure* and its clash of cultures continues with these newcomers. As with Fleischman, the dramatic tension is internal as the new foreigners become transformed by Cicely's people, culture, and environment.

Some elements of the old Western genre bleed into *Northern Exposure*'s principal Native American characters as well. Ed Chigliak—film buff, novice filmmaker, shaman-in-training, bag boy, paperboy, and general lackey—sometimes comes across as the "crazy Indian," a bit slower than the non-natives; akin to *Gunsmoke*'s Festus, he lends comic relief to the busy, burdened town leaders. Marilyn Whirlwind, Dr. Fleischman's (and later Dr. Capra's) office manager and receptionist, is lovely and loyal and speaks wisely in clipped phrases. She is a kind of female Tonto to Fleischman's Lone Ranger. In the old Westerns, Ed and Marilyn might be considered "civilized" since, by outward appearances, they seem to live like the white man. Consequently, they would be tolerated by the majority community, allowed to be in town rather than being relegated to reservation or subplot.

As viewers have seen, however, these are also complex characters. Marilyn Whirlwind is nobody's Tonto. She scrubs the examining room, holds her tongue, and maintains tranquility, but the audience knows she is in charge. In every conflict of wills or ways between Fleischman and Marilyn, Marilyn wins. By the twenty-seventh episode, in the 1991–1992 season, Fleischman has admitted that he depends on Marilyn, trusts her judgment, and considers her a partner. When he thinks he might be dying and then discovers that Marilyn knew the lab reports said otherwise but did not tell him, he goes into a momentary rage. He quickly stops and looks at Marilyn. She says nothing. He nods: "Right, you're right. Got it." Fleischman finally "hears" Marilyn and what she has been teaching him.

Marilyn's influence also extends to the other townspeople. When Maurice tries to launch a multi-million-dollar ostrich farm venture—with Marilyn's ostriches—and take most of the profit, Marilyn negotiates the better deal and lays down the rules. When Holling goes off on a bender, moping about his insignificant life, she is the only one in town who can get him to return home.

Although she is a woman of few words, Marilyn is not stoic like Tonto. Marilyn registers a range of emotions and attributes. She was noticeably angry when

Holling, during an early mayoral election, implied that all native people voted alike. She was obviously in love with the silent "Flying Man," who visited Cicely when the circus bus broke down. She can be warm and generous, impatient and calculating. She has outwitted both Fleischman and Maurice, but she has also charmed them.

The audience has seen Marilyn as a normal and average woman who loves her family, eats at a dinner table, goes to work, and tries to be a decent human being. Marilyn adheres to cultural traditions, just as Christians celebrate Christmas and Jews mark Hanukkah. During the annual Raven Pageant in a 1991 December episode, Marilyn told the real-life Alaska Native myth about how the raven brought light to the world. The portrayal displayed all the respect that would appear in a scene of a Christian telling the story of the birth of Jesus. Although Marilyn can be annoyingly stereotypical when she slips into the role of wise, saintly chief, any tendency toward stereotyping her as Earth Mother is muted by the fact that Marilyn cannot exclusively claim wisdom and righteousness. Chris Stevens, as well as Ruth-Anne, also share such gifts.

Although the character Ed Chigliak may talk like a space cadet, he is nobody's fool. He tends to be a half beat behind, but that is due more to his age and innocence than to his IQ, which was touted at a high of 180, although it seemed to have declined a bit by the 1992–1993 season. Realizations "hit" Ed like a tap on the shoulder or an unexpected kiss on the cheek. He lives in the moment, delights in the everyday, looks at the moon and sees a bunny rabbit. He, too, defies the stereotypes, not only because his skewed world view so often makes sense but also because he shares so many traits with the more worldly and experienced Shelly.

Ed, an orphan, has found a way to merge the traditional and contemporary and settle into majority and minority cultures without suffering a split personality. He is like his mentor, the recurring character Leonard Quinhagak, a shaman who respects, learns, and uses modern medical techniques. Ed has a strong affinity for Native American philosophy and spirituality, as becomes evident when he is called to shamanism at the start of the 1993–1994 season. Even before he began his training, he paid close attention to spirits and held a deep respect for his elders. He also appreciates his American citizenship, takes his voting rights seriously, and studies American history in preparation for his first election. A child of the late twentieth century, he is a media junkie and knows everything and anything that has to do with filmmaking. His passion is the very medium that has so distorted the image of Native Americans. And so, unlike the Indians of John Ford's Westerns, Ed is not a relic of the past but is of a new generation with a bright future.

Northern Exposure takes Native Americans seriously and views native culture as a viable and beneficial companion. It celebrates both the similarities and differences of all peoples and cultures and lauds the value of the culturally diverse community. Popular culture's longtime schism between Indians and everyone else, between wilderness and civilization, between tradition and science is acknowledged but dismissed. The treatment is not unlike that of Cicely's townspeople to Fleischman's temper tantrums; they do not preach, but rather ignore him until he gets over it and learns better.

Northern Exposure uses the fantastic to play with the point. In one episode, Leonard seeks to update his modern medical knowledge by observing Fleischman, who initially dismisses Leonard's practices as quackery. When Shelly comes to the doctor with a rash, Fleischman diagnoses it as an allergic reaction but cannot identify the cause. He sends Shelly home with an ointment, which fails to work. Later, Leonard talks to Shelly about her childhood and then suggests that she is shedding her skin to be reborn. Shelly finds the explanation quite reasonable and returns home to molt. Upon learning of Leonard's diagnosis, Fleischman is livid. When he calms down, Leonard talks to him rationally. Eventually, Fleischman admits to his own limitations: If he cannot be certain of the accuracy of his diagnosis, then he cannot be certain of the error of Leonard's. The episode ends with new, pink skin for Shelly and growth for Fleischman.

Northern Exposure's Ambivalent Cultural Identity

Northern Exposure's Brigadoon-like dreaminess, with stories that slip and slide between the possible and impossible, lends the program its appeal. Unfortunately, this elusiveness also extends to the program's Native American identity. The issue is not simply whether the program is factual but whether it is a fair representation of the people and cultures it capitalizes upon. Clearly, it is not. Although every non-native, regular character since the first season has had an identifiable family, cultural, or religious background, Ed and Marilyn for most of their tenure in Cicely have been generic "Indians."[15] Ed finally identified himself as Tlingit at the end of the program's fourth season in 1993, but scriptwriters offered no description of these Alaska Natives. More than a year later, Marilyn's cultural heritage still remained unclear. The absence of defined cultures for Ed and Marilyn has effectively put their ancestors into Hollywood's buckskins and feathered bonnets.

"Indian" is not a term commonly used in Alaska, even though it is an accepted anthropological name for one of the three major ethno-linguistic groups of Alaska Natives. Instead, Alaska's Indians are Athabaskans, Tlingits, Haidas, or Tsimshians, or they are identified by location, as with the Tanana River Athabaskan Indians. The differences among them in lifestyle, religious practices, and language are quite profound.

Alaska's Indians, like the Inuit and Aleuts, developed diverse cultures to suit the different environments and resources in their home regions. Athabaskans, whose cousins are the Apache and Navaho, years ago lived in small bands in the Alaska interior and traveled often over great distances in search of food. Today, many continue to live in the interior in some fifty-five cohesive villages with populations well under three hundred. They still travel far to survive, now to urban centers for seasonal jobs to earn cash to buy what they cannot make or hunt on their own. They are known for their tolerance of others and their adaptability, which is evident in the customs and technology they have routinely borrowed from other cultures.[16]

Tlingits, because of the rich fisheries literally at their door, historically settled in permanent villages and developed complex social structures, elaborate ceremonies, and highly refined styles of art, most notably the black form-lines of animals representing clan crests or stories. These are the people of the totem poles, bentwood boxes, ocean-going canoes, Chilkat robes, button blankets, and potlatch memorials. Many Tlingits continue to live in southeast Alaska in small villages that depend largely on fish, game, and timber, as well as art.[17]

To generalize either culture is risky. Culture is a process, continually redefining itself as it is reshaped by present experiences. Culture is largely negotiable by the different groups within it who have different standards of measurement. What it means to be "Tlingit" or "Athabaskan" differs among those who follow conservative and traditionalist leaders, those who follow progressive leaders, and those who have adopted a European-American worldview. In any case, however, Alaska Native identity generally varies according to family, clan, village, group of villages, linguistic group, and race.[18]

Despite the variances among real Alaska Natives, *Northern Exposure* dilutes native identity to one generic form. Marilyn comes simply from "Marilyn's tribe," and Ed comes from "Ed's tribe," which for nearly four years remained anonymous. Although refusing to name the cultural base for Cicely, *Northern Exposure* has nevertheless progressively appropriated a Tlingit culture. Since the premier episode, the town has featured totem poles, which are *only* found among the Tlingits and Haidas, and various artwork and artifacts in the Tlingit black, form-line style. However, Cicely is positioned in the Alaska interior, home primarily to Athabaskans in real life. Although *Northern Exposure* has avoided placing its town in a specific location, all geographic references since the premiere have put Cicely north of Anchorage. By the 1994–1995 season, Cicely had shifted west and seemed very close to being in a traditionally Inupiat Eskimo area. Creating a Tlingit identity for an Alaska interior village is akin to fabricating a Canadian town in Mexico or identifying New Yorkers as the majority population of Louisiana: It is ridiculous.

To add to the cultural confusion, Marilyn Whirlwind early in the series wore a Cayuse–Nez Percé costume during a powwow attended by six-foot-tall Crows—novice actors from Montana. Marilyn then performed a dance characteristic of the Washington-Idaho area Native Americans. The implication to the viewing audience was that the powwow, dress, and dance were Alaskan when, in fact, they are not. Then, at the end of 1991, Marilyn suddenly and silently seemed to adopt the ways of Chilkat Tlingits. During the community Christmas pageant, she wore a Chilkat robe and danced under an archway of classic Tlingit design. She told the raven myth, a common Alaska Native story of the creation, but then missed the Tlingit distinction of a second raven and failed to clarify that the raven is not a deity in any Alaskan culture.

Since then, Marilyn has suggested that she might be Athabaskan since her grandfather, Emery Whirlwind, came from the Alaska interior. But in an episode about Emery's adventures with Princess Anastasia of Russia and Lenin, Emery appeared to be more like Daniel Day-Lewis in *The Last of the Mohicans* than any Alaska Native. He also used resources more commonly associated with Inuit, for example, seal gut and whalebone. Marilyn thus has floated in a tribe of "any Indian," slipping dangerously close to clichés. An "Indian" on television today without a tribe, language, religion, culture, or occupation is hardly distinguishable from the homogenized Indians of the old TV Westerns. In the realm of TV, Marilyn might just as well be a Cheyenne in Navajo dress practicing the rites of the Hopis.

Long without any moorings, Ed has already lapsed into the role of stereotypical sidekick in some episodes and New Age spiritual wonder in others. More and more often, he has served as Fleischman's or Maurice's servant, even though his tendency to wander makes him unreliable and obviously less obedient than Tonto or Daniel Boone's companion, Mingo. Whatever promise Ed's newfound cultural identity at the end the 1992–1993 season held for improving popular conceptualizations of Native Americans was dashed when Tlingits were defined only in terms of their "dying language."

Although "Athabaskan" and "Haida" have been dropped into characters' conversations during the 1993–1994 and 1994–1995 seasons, these words have been used without description or definition. Just as "tribe" has no meaning to Alaska Natives, the names of Alaska Native groups used in *Northern Exposure* have no meaning to most American viewers.[19] By failing to distinguish Alaska Native cultures, they have been subsumed by *Northern Exposure*'s producers and writers under the tribes of the lower forty-eight states. The series has diluted these cultures and glossed them with the Hollywood stereotypes that Alaska Natives had long managed to escape.

The popularity of made-for-TV movies, such as *Son of Morning Star,* and Hollywood movies, most notably *Dances with Wolves* and *Last of the Mohicans,* which strove to be authentic at least in terms of language and dress, has opened the door to more realistic portrayals of Native Americans as distinct cultures, groups, and individuals. Some critics have argued, however, that these movies found popular acceptance only because they focused on the past and perpetuated the noble savage image now being called "the new Custerism."[20] Popular culture generally avoids contemporary real-life Native Americans and Native American issues because of national collective guilt about government policies of genocide. Guilt makes people feel bad, and people who feel bad do not feel like spending money. And the purpose of television, after all, is to sell products.[21]

Northern Exposure showcases Indians but can avoid provoking guilt because the series deals with Alaska Natives, about whom most Americans know little. Simultaneously, the show offers a certain degree of absolution by being benevolent toward all "Indians" without provoking a dichotomy between native and European American cultures. Unlike the 1970s anti-Westerns, *Northern Exposure* does not reverse the stereotype. The whites might act stupidly or irrationally, but they are not evil. Because the series ignores contemporary issues about jobs, environment, land use, education, and subsistence in the real Alaska bush, viewers can easily escape into a frontier fantasy, albeit one that twists the old formulas so that no one is really a bad guy.

It is ironic that although cultural distinctions are minimized, cultural differences drive the series. Ed, Marilyn, and Leonard are not simply characters who happen to be Native American. Rather, they are characters who, largely because of their cultural heritage and worldview, have impact on the action and on other characters. *Northern Exposure* is interesting because it plays with the issue of who is being acculturated. Leonard suggests that the outsiders are the ones being assimilated, but the text also allows non-native audiences to assimilate the natives without being distracted by too many cultural differences. Natives in *Northern Exposure* are like the Judeo-Christian, Eastern and Western European descendants, who are like the Native Americans. Ed, Shelly, and Maurice; Marilyn, Chris, and Maggie; and even Leonard and Joel are linked both by their similarities and their differences. They complement and contradict. They are mirrors—alike, but not quite.

Northern Exposure moves in and out of expected, idealized, and commonplace meanings; meanings flow into each other, and the resulting blend both affirms and denies the original ideologies. This is the pleasure of popular culture. However, the contractions and inadequacies of *Northern Exposure* allow too much room for error as viewers try to sort the representation from the reality. Unlike the situation with police or private-eye shows, most viewers have no real experience or factual information they can use to compare or counter the stylized images of Alaska Natives and fill in the gaps left in the text. The clichés can too easily slip into everyday-life consciousness, and audiences begin to believe that all Alaska Natives talk to spirits, fly like eagles, and guard their homes with totems.

Conclusion

Northern Exposure is not a documentary or history lesson about Alaska Natives. Nevertheless, television and other media need to consider minority groups in more realistic, accurate terms. Television would never consider giving Cajuns Russian accents, putting Islamic women in bikinis, or portraying former President Ronald Reagan as a Rhodes scholar. *Northern Exposure* would never have Joel Fleischman praying in a Catholic Church or confuse the moviemaking styles of Ed Chigliak's favorite directors. Yet television does distort and distill Native American groups to just such an extent. Dismissing *Northern Exposure*'s treatment of Alaska Native cultures as innocent, poetic license only perpetuates the five-centuries-old attitude that native cultures are unimportant and insignificant. By minimizing their significance and simultaneously distorting their image, television compounds the insult.

Northern Exposure tries, on the one hand, to battle the myths by bringing Native Americans into the present and proclaiming them, first of all, to be alive. Rather than melting the native culture into the dominant European American culture, the show attempts to applaud its distinctions. Rather than stressing those distinctions as points of conflict and alienation, the show attempts to view them as complementary. The show avoids the villainy, shuns the helpless-victim act, and gingerly skirts the morally superior and noble savage portrayals. The characters are complex, with good and bad traits. Even Ed has lied. The actors really are Native American (most of them from tribes in the lower forty-eight states), and the characters speak normally and lead average lives. The show is a gigantic step forward in treating a minority group as a part of the world rather than as separate from it or in constant conflict with it. In some ways, *Northern Exposure* begins to rescue the term "Indian" from the connotations perpetuated in the old Westerns.

On the other hand, for all the cultural displays and signals of multicultural acceptance, *Northern Exposure* fails to escape its racist antecedents. The Native Americans here are as displaced as the non-native characters who move into Cicely from Canada and the United States. Whereas the non-natives at least have prior homes, the Alaska Natives are dispossessed of their land, as well as their identity. *Northern Exposure* has snatched bits and pieces of Native American folklore, artistry, and impressions and merged them with bits and pieces of Alaska Native culture to create something new. The show celebrates the composite, but ends up co-opting native culture.

Incorrect images, whether kind or evil, become naturalized through popular culture. They seep into our subconscious, temper our personal attitudes and reactions, and influence government policies and even Supreme Court decisions. The distortion, in the case of Alaska Natives, cannot be easily disputed by facts readily available from viewers' daily experience. Without accurate information to counter and replace the old images of "Indians," audiences are left with manufactured impressions. Until ignorance is confronted, Native Americans will never completely escape the old Custerism and will remain shapeless and ultimately invisible to the dominant culture.

Notes

1. This episode was first broadcast on November 8, 1993.

2. Before *Northern Exposure*, *Twin Peaks* had the Native American character Deputy Hawk. However, his role was not integral to the series, and he was not featured consistently week to week. The same applied to the native character on the short-lived program *Nurses*. *Walker, Texas Ranger*, whose lead character is part Native American, premiered after *Northern Exposure*, on April 24, 1993. Walker's cultural heritage is most obviously displayed through his relationship with his Uncle Ray, played by the Native American actor Floyd Red Crow Westerman.

3. Robert F. Berkhofer, Jr., *The White Man's Indian: Images of the American Indian from Columbus to the Present* (New York: Vintage Books, 1979).

4. See, for example, John Fiske, *Understanding Popular Culture* (New York: Routledge, 1989), pp. 103–127.

5. See, for example, Ralph Brauer and Donna Brauer, *The Horse, the Gun, and the Piece of Property* (Bowling Green, Ohio: Bowling Green University Popular Press, 1975); Hal Himmelstein, *Television Myth and the American Mind* (New York: Praeger, 1984), pp. 164–180; Rita Parks, *The Western Hero in Film and Television: Mass Media Mythology* (Ann Arbor, Mich.: UMI Research Press, 1982), pp. 125–154; Jane Tompkins, *West of Everything* (New York: Oxford University Press, 1992), pp. 7–10.

6. See, for example, Alfonso Ortiz, "The Dark Side of the Moon—Images of the Indian and the American Dream," Charles Charropin Memorial Lecture, Rockhurst College, Kansas City, April 1977. Ortiz found that all Native American imagery comes from a mere five sources, with Sioux imagery dominating.

7. This figure comes from numerous books and articles on the subject, especially the following: Tim Brooks and Earle Marsh, *The Complete Directory to Prime-Time Network TV Shows: 1946 to Present* (New York: Ballantine Books, 1992); Vincent Terrace, *The Complete Encyclopedia of Television Programs: 1947–1976*, 2 vols. (New York: S. S. Barnes and Company, 1976).

8. Ibid., vol. 1, pp. 342–343.

9. Ibid., vol. 2, p. 342.

10. Ibid., p. 133.

11. See *TV Guide* (September–November 1974).

12. See Mauricio Gerson, "Minority Representation in Network Television Drama, 1970–1976," *Mass Communication Review* (fall 1980), p. 11; Bradley S. Greenberg and Carrie Heeter, "Television and Social Stereotypes," in Joyce Sprafkin, Carolyn Swift, and Robert Hess, eds., *Rx Television: Enhancing the Preventative Impact of TV* (New York: Haworth Press, 1983), pp. 37–52; and John F. Seggar, Jeffrey K. Hafen, and Helena Hannonen-Gladden, "Television's Portrayals of Minorities and Women in Drama and Comedy Drama, 1971–1980," *Journal of Broadcasting* 25 (summer 1981), p. 284.

13. For a history of U.S. government policy toward Pribilof Aleuts, see Dorothy Knee Jones, *A Century of Servitude: Pribilof Aleuts Under U.S. Rule* (Landham, Md.: University Press of America, 1980).

14. Brauer and Brauer, *Horse, Gun, and Property*, pp. 188–191.

15. From the first season, *Northern Exposure*'s writers have identified Fleischman as a New York Jew. Maggie O'Connell, despite her Irish name, is a rich Protestant from Grosse Pointe, Michigan. Shelly Tambo Vincouer is a poor Catholic from Saskatoon, Saskatchewan, Canada. Chris Stevens of Wheeling, West Virginia, came from a broken home, served time in a state penitentiary, and has adopted an eclectic blend of religious and mythical beliefs. Holling Vincouer, of royal French ancestry, grew up on a farm in Quebec, and Maurice Minnifield of Tulsa, Oklahoma, is primarily a child of the military, having enlisted at the age of sixteen. Ruth-Anne Porter's background is less clear; but she raised her sons in Seattle and was more gratified by one son's choice to live in poverty as a poet than by her other son's career in Wall Street.

16. See, e.g., Richard K. Nelson, *The Athabaskans: People of the Boreal Forest* (Fairbanks: University of Alaska Museum, 1983); and James W. Vanstone, *Athapaskan Adaptations:*

Hunters and Fishermen of the Subarctic Forests (Arlington Heights, Ill.: Harlan Davidson, 1974).

17. See, for example, Nora Marks Dauenhauer and Richard Dauenhauer, eds. (1994), *Haa Kusteeyi, Our Culture: Tlingit Life Stories* (Seattle: University of Washington Press, 1994); Nora Marks Dauenhauer and Richard Dauenhauer, eds., *Haa Tuwunaagu Yis, for Healing Our Spirit: Tlingit Oratory* (Seattle: University of Washington Press, 1990).

18. See Dauenhauer and Dauenhauer, *Haa Kusteeyi, Our Culture;* and Tom Kizzia, *The Wake of the Unseen Object: Among the Native Cultures of Bush Alaska* (New York: Henry Holt and Company, 1991).

19. Tribes are political delineations. Native Alaskan groups historically have not been bound by shared leadership or laws; rather, they tend to be grouped by clans. Since the 1930s, however, some groups have joined together to increase their bargaining clout in Washington, D.C., and have called themselves "tribes."

20. See, for example, Wayne Michael Sarf, "Oscar Eaten by Wolves," *Film Comment* 27 (6) (1991), pp. 62–70; David Seals, "The New Custerism," *Nation,* May 13, 1991, pp. 634–639.

21. See, for example, Todd Gitlin, *Inside Prime Time* (New York: Pantheon Books, 1983), pp. 226–228; Jerry Mander, "What You Don't Know About Indians," *Utne Reader* (November/December, 1991), pp. 70–72.

16

Not My Fantasy: The Persistence of Indian Imagery in *Dr. Quinn, Medicine Woman*

S. Elizabeth Bird

For a century and a half, media depictions of male American Indians have alternated between two main images: the ignoble savage (Indian as wild, marauding beast) and the noble savage (Indian as close to the land, spiritual, heroic, virtuous—and doomed).[1] Both views have existed in all kinds of popular manifestations, from dime novels and Wild West shows to movies and television. In popular movies, although both images have existed alongside each other for years, the noble savage has gradually gained ascendancy over the ignoble savage, especially since the 1960s.[2]

Until the 1950s, TV programming, like film, presented American Indians as brutal savages, whose role en masse was to attack wagon trains, scalp settlers, and terrorize white women. Alternatively, the individual Indian might appear as a trusty sidekick, like the Lone Ranger's Tonto. The noble savage image had less impact on television, although a few "progressive" Westerns, such as *The High Chaparral* in the late 1960s, tried to present Indians as human beings who had a right to the land they claimed. Once the TV Western went into decline at the end of the 1960s, producers came to ignore the Indian altogether.[3]

This changed with the growing tide of multiculturalism in the late 1980s and early 1990s. A defining moment arrived with the 1990 release of the movie *Dances with Wolves*, which was widely praised for its realistic depiction of Lakota Indian culture. "Authenticity," in terms of accurate historical detail in costume and language, began to replace such familiar practices as casting Whites in Indian roles and haphazardly mixing elements from any and all Native cultures. In the early

245

1990s, movies such as *The Last of the Mohicans, Thunderheart, Geronimo,* and *Squanto* continued a reevaluation of the American Indian, with none deviating appreciably from the now-established script of the Indian as noble, spiritual, and again, doomed.

Television at last woke up. Like moviemakers, TV producers are still reluctant to cast Native American actors in generic roles, but they have developed series that attempt to include Indian story lines and characters. One of these series was CBS's now-cancelled *Northern Exposure,* set in contemporary Alaska and featuring several Native characters.

The other series is *Dr. Quinn, Medicine Woman,* another CBS production. It features a crusading woman doctor in post–Civil War Colorado Springs, who each week does battle against sexism, racism, environmental pollution, and child abuse on the American frontier. Dr. Michaela Quinn, played by Jane Seymour, is aided by a smoldering frontiersman called Byron Sully, whose persona owes a clear debt to Daniel Day-Lewis's Hawkeye in *The Last of the Mohicans.* Although White, Sully has a close, perhaps adoptive, relationship with the local Cheyenne tribe and "knows their ways" (Figure 16.1). Quinn and Sully have had a slowly developing romance, which culminated in a wedding for the season finale in May 1995. *Dr. Quinn* was intended to be a family show, so even before her marriage Dr. Quinn had acquired a family in the form of three children, Brian, Colleen, and Matthew, whom she adopted after a friend conveniently died. The townsfolk include several strong, independent women; a male population of bigots and weaklings, who receive their comeuppance from Dr. Quinn on a weekly basis; and one African-American couple, who provide opportunities for Dr. Quinn to display her progressive fervor. Near the town is a Cheyenne village, peopled by largely anonymous Indians; there are no strong female Cheyenne characters, and the plots that feature Cheyenne usually focus on men.[4] The stories are melodramatic, predictable, and sentimental, but they have worked—the show became the most successful new series of the 1992–1993 season. It has remained popular ever since, proving extremely successful with a very valuable group—women of age 18–49.

In contrast to *Northern Exposure, Dr. Quinn* was savaged by the critics, who described it in terms ranging from "treacle" to "drivel . . . its every nuance calculated out of lowest-common-denominator concerns."[5] However, I find the series fascinating in its apparently successful yet uneasy mixture of liberal progressiveness with "traditional American values." The show can be read and critiqued from various perspectives: For example, it demonstrates a fairly strong, if ambivalent, feminist sensibility.[6] At the beginning of the 1994 season, it was one of only two dramatic programs that had a woman as its central character (the other was Angela Lansbury's *Murder, She Wrote*), and the show has been credited with making producers reevaluate the conventional wisdom that women actors cannot carry an hour-long drama.

However, I focus this essay on *Dr. Quinn*'s portrayal of the Cheyenne characters and how that portrayal is received by some White and Indian viewers. Although

Figure 16.1 *Occasionally Dr. Quinn has dressed in Indian clothing for story purposes. Here Joe Lando as Byron Sully and Jane Seymour as Dr. Quinn pose in front of a Cheyenne tepee. CBS publicity photo.*

the show's values are rooted in the 1990s, perhaps the most striking aspect of *Dr. Quinn* is how familiar the Indians are and how the long-established imagery persists today.

Representation of the Cheyenne

The producers of *Dr. Quinn* clearly intend to present a sympathetic, positive picture of American Indians, drawing heavily on *Dances with Wolves*. An adviser on Native American culture is credited, care has been taken to present accurate costumes and language, and the people are certainly not crazed savages. But are they people the audiences can care about? That is a more problematic question. The show frequently opens with a scene in the idyllic Cheyenne village, where the inhabitants wander to and fro wearing benign expressions of content. A few have names but have no real personalities, and no story lines focus on them directly. Rather, they function as plot devices to allow Michaela and Sully to make a point. Indeed, *Dr. Quinn* illustrates perfectly the point that the Indian of popular culture is a White creation that meets White needs.[7] The "Imaginary Indian," to use Daniel Francis's term, is a kind of generic cultural construction: "Through the prism of White hopes, fears, or prejudices, indigenous Americans would be seen to have lost contact with reality and have become "Indians," that is anything non-Natives wanted them to be."[8] Thus we see the alternation between archetypes—between Noble (doomed) Savage and Demonic (doomed) Savage, depending on which image suited the needs of a particular time period. For instance, as Indians "disappeared" in the East, the nonthreatening, noble Indian took over American popular culture, at least until the Indian wars of the late nineteenth century resurrected another archetype, the Wild Indian.

Dr. Quinn arrived on the scene after at least two decades of increasing romanticization of the Indian. The Cheyenne are presented as beautiful, serene, and spiritual, reflecting the 1990s fascination with New Age–tinged mysticism that has been the fastest-growing aspect of popular depictions of Indians since the counterculture embraced them in the 1960s. Stewart Brand succinctly describes this 1960s appeal, which, with the exception of drug use, sums up *Dr. Quinn*'s picture of the Cheyenne: "From a distance Indians looked perfect: ecologically aware, spiritual, tribal, anarchistic, drug-using, exotic, native, and wronged."[9]

Brand points out astutely that Indians looked perfect "from a distance": Popular culture has never been eager to get to know Indians as individuals. From early times, a convention has been to depict Indians in groups, as an aesthetic element in a picture or story that is not theirs. Francis describes landscape painting in which Indians "are seldom seen up close; rather they are figures in idyllic natural settings with no individuality . . . the Indian is merely part of the landscape."[10] The opening credits of *Dr. Quinn* recall this, as we see a montage of closeups of Michaela, Sully, their family, and other townspeople. A group of Cheyenne are photographed on horseback against the majestic Colorado landscape.

Even as we get closer to the Cheyenne, they are allowed little individuality. *Dr. Quinn's* ideal Indian is represented by Cloud Dancing, the village medicine man, who has a consistent role in the show as the representation of the Doomed Indian, a calm, noble person who never fights back and is grateful for the attentions of the heroic White individuals. In the 1990s, we recognize his pain, but ultimately we shrug our shoulders and say, What can we do? Cloud Dancing speaks English and argues for peaceful coexistence with the settlers, whose progress seems inevitable. The stoicism of the doomed Indian has a long history, as Robert Tilton points out in his discussion of nineteenth-century Indian romances: "Although they still have the potential for passionate actions, it is their antiquated, stoic acceptance of their individual fate and of the ultimate demise of their people that endeared these noble savages to white readers."[11] As the series progresses, Cloud Dancing suffers the loss of an unborn child because of his wife's malnutrition, the death of his adult son from saving Michaela's life, and finally, the death of most of his village, including his wife, at the hands of White soldiers. Yet his stoicism remains unshaken, and his main concern seems to be that his medical knowledge be passed on to Michaela so that it will not die with his people.

This stereotypical stoicism precludes both anger and humor, so the Cheyenne rarely show either. As Vine DeLoria points out, humor, which is a vital part of Indian life, has been wiped out by mainstream depictions, to the point that a picture of a laughing Indian looks "wrong" to White eyes.[12] As for anger, Indians who succumb to that are potentially unsettling and need to be shown as wrong. Even in *Dr. Quinn,* where the Wild Indian has largely been supplanted by the noble, spiritual Indian, the brutal savage is still present in the recurring image of the renegade "dog soldier." These Indians have not accepted White control, refuse to stay on the reservation, and use violent means to combat White people, raiding farms and destroying White property. Although occasional lip service is paid to the justness of their anger, the message is clear that these warriors are misguided. Sully, Michaela, and Cloud Dancing are frequently seen trying to persuade the friendly Indians to curb the dog soldiers' excesses. The renegades are clearly defined as deviant, out of control, and a challenge to the correct 1990s Imaginary Indian, who suffers all indignities with a stoic smile and an acknowledgment that really there are many good, kind White people who wish this had never happened.

The dichotomy between good and bad Indian is spelled out in a two-hour episode in which Michaela is kidnapped by a band of dog soldiers, led by a sinister warrior in an eye patch named, of course, One Eye. Cloud Dancing's son has joined the dog soldiers, having become grief-stricken and vengeful after his sweetheart died in an earlier typhus epidemic. As Michaela is held captive, One Eye lustfully begins to assault her, but she is saved by Cloud Dancing's son. The son later allows her to escape but only at the cost of his own life—One Eye kills him. It is a scenario as old as the Imaginary Indian himself: the "good Indian" sacrifices himself for the White hero. As Rayna Green puts it, the "good" Indian, "acts as a friend to the white man, offering . . . aid, rescue, and spiritual and physical comfort even at the cost of his own life or status and comfort in his own tribe to do so. He saves white men from 'bad' Indians, and thus becomes a 'good' Indian."[13] So while "bad Indians" are demonized and objectified as "other," "good Indians" also lose their subjectivity, becoming part of the White person's story.

All *Dr. Quinn*'s Cheyenne characters seem one-dimensional: Not one episode has focused on the individual problems of a Cheyenne or a Cheyenne family, whereas the African-American couple and many of the weak-willed townspeople have had episodes devoted to an exploration of their character. Rather, the Cheyenne are plot devices—they give a horse to Michaela so she can make the point that women can ride well; they describe their vision quest, not so that we can see a Cheyenne growing spiritually but so that Matthew can work out his adolescent angst. Thus, *Dr. Quinn* shows the typical colonialist pattern of appropriating aspects of Indian culture and giving them importance only if they meet White needs. A typical episode in this vein involved the problems of Loren Bray, the curmudgeonly, fiftyish storekeeper, who, in some kind of midlife crisis, decides to leave town and seek his fortune in Bolivia. Naturally he does not get far and is found in the woods by Sully, who persuades him to seek guidance from the Cheyenne. The episode climaxes with the Cheyenne leading Loren in a special dance they have created for him. Once again, they constitute exotic scenery for a White person's concerns.

Sometimes, the show displaces Indians completely while using their cultural experience to make a 1990s moral point. For instance, one episode featured an extended story about a woman who is the sole survivor of an army raid on her Cheyenne village. She is brought to town, where she faces the ignorance and racism of the local people, who call her a savage, try to bar her from the church, and so on. Although this story seems to offer a good chance to develop a Cheyenne character more fully, the producers avoid this by a careful decision—she is White and was merely raised Cheyenne. The message of the story—to show the cruelty of racism—is subtly inverted. The townspeople learn a lesson, as the young woman gradually becomes more "civilized," but that lesson is not that Indians are people, too, and should be treated as such. Rather, it is that they should have recognized from the outset that she was not *really* an Indian at all, so their contempt was misplaced. In fact the only role for real Indians in this story was to die—the woman's entire village, including her husband, has been wiped out by the army.

The show again avoids an extended treatment of an individual Indian's plight in an episode in which a Wild West show comes to town. Sully needs money to build the house for his marriage, and he is induced to perform in the show as a knife thrower. He is dressed in "Indian" costume and war paint and introduced with great fanfare as a "Wild Mountain Man Raised by Indians." When performance time comes, however, he can bear the humiliation no longer and walks out, decrying the cheapening of Indian culture. *Dr. Quinn*'s producers could have introduced a real Indian for both this role and the female survivor story—almost every week a "guest star" is featured whose personality becomes the focus of the episode. Yet when the opportunity arises to cast that role for an Indian, a White substitute is found. This has the continual effect of displacing the Indians as viable individuals with their own identity and stories, as if saying that viewers cannot expect to empathize with Indian problems unless they can see how Whites would suffer in that position. In fact, Sully's ongoing role is to stand in for the Cheyenne, so that their culture is represented, while they as people can be pushed into the background. After all, he is a better Indian than the Cheyenne, as is made abundantly clear in the opening scene of one episode, when he beats Cloud Dancing in a tomahawk-throwing contest.

Thus, the role of the Cheyenne is to provide an exotic, attractive backdrop for the heroes and, subtly, to suggest that they are willing to fade away in the face of White progress. As has already been shown, part of that role is to die, sometimes in great numbers, in order to move the plot along and showcase Michaela and Sully. The show has a knack for touching on some of the most horrific episodes in the history of Indian-White relations, yet nevertheless suggesting that everything really came out all right.

For example, in several episodes, the chief of the Cheyenne band is identified as Black Kettle, a real Colorado chief whose fate is known. In November 1865, three years before the time in which *Dr. Quinn* is set, the U.S. Third Cavalry under Colonel John M. Chivington charged Black Kettle's sleeping Cheyenne village at Sand Creek. Black Kettle, who had always maintained a peaceful relationship with the army, rushed from his tepee and raised a U.S. American flag, followed by a white flag. The cavalry ignored him and massacred over two hundred of the five hundred villagers. Black Kettle survived and continued to attempt to negotiate peace. In late 1868, the year in which *Dr. Quinn* is set, his band was attacked by George Armstrong Custer's forces, and Black Kettle and about one hundred other Cheyenne were killed. This engagement was known as the Battle of Washita, but it was actually a massacre much like that at Sand Creek.

Therefore, during the time the show is set, Black Kettle's village must have been demoralized and certainly distrustful of Whites, rather than being the serene group of noble people we see regularly on the show. While Sand Creek has received only passing mention, Washita was finally addressed in an episode broadcast late in the 1994–1995 season. This episode was revealing in the characteristic way it showed the massacre—not as a catastrophe for the Cheyenne, but as a trauma for Michaela Quinn. She fails to talk Custer out of attacking the Cheyenne, and eventually she and Sully, along with Cloud Dancing, come upon the village, completely wiped out, with everyone dead. Cloud Dancing's wife, Snowbird, dies in his arms. Everything from then on continues from Michaela's point of view. She withdraws from her family, blames herself for the massacre, and goes into a depression. Finally, Cloud Dancing comes to her and assures her it was not her fault, then spends several days passing on his medical skills to her, before leaving for South Dakota. Michaela returns to her family, and happiness reigns again.

Washita was the second two-hour special that focused on the Cheyenne—an episode from the previous season followed the same pattern. Again, the suffering of the Cheyenne functions mainly to contrast Michaela and Sully's nobility with the brutality of the U.S. army and the townspeople. In this show, Black Kettle has been involved in peace talks with the army and is persuaded to accept gifts of food and blankets as part of a settlement. Dr. Quinn helps persuade the Cheyenne to take the blankets, which turn out to be infected with typhus, and the Cheyenne begin to fall sick and die. This, however, becomes a side issue, because Michaela's adopted son Matthew also has typhus. On learning this, she leaves the Indians and runs to Matthew, who of course survives.

By the end of the episode, forty-five Cheyenne are dead, and yet somehow the show presents a happy ending, as the townspeople perform a pageant for George Washington's birthday. I have already mentioned the show's attempts to be both sensitive to the Cheyenne and also patriotic and "traditional," and this uneasy balance becomes positively contorted in the finale to this episode. The happy townspeople are picnicking while listening to the Declaration of Independence, read by homely Horace, the telegraph operator, dressed as Abraham Lincoln. As Horace reads, this dialogue ensues:

Horace.   He has endeavored to bring to the inhabitants of these frontiers, the merciless Indian savages . . .
Brian.   Is he talking about the Cheyenne?
Sully.   'Fraid so.
Horace.   . . . whose known rule of warfare is an undistinguished destruction of all ages, sexes, and conditions . . .
Michaela.   I've heard the Declaration read many times but I don't remember ever hearing that passage.
Sully.   It took living here and seeing the truth in order to see the lies.
Brian.   They lie about the Indians?
Michaela.   I'm afraid so, Brian; they lie to themselves. But this is still the greatest country in the World—

The show ends with a fireworks display playing over the rapt faces of the families in the park, the Indians elided for ever.

Watching Dr. Quinn

But what do viewers actually think about Dr. Quinn and its portrayal of the Cheyenne? We must remember that the critic's reading may not necessarily be shared by the audience; indeed, the professional reviewers' scathing opinions of Dr. Quinn are clearly ignored by its loyal fans. In a preliminary attempt to explore this question, I gave nineteen people (nine American Indians and ten non-Indians) copies of a videotape that included three episodes of Dr. Quinn, which they watched in their own time. They were then asked to write down their initial responses to the show, without being asked any specific questions. Next, four focus-group sessions, two for Indians and two for non-Indians, were held, at which they discussed the program.[14] Their responses demonstrate in real terms how the notion of the Imaginary Indian is indeed part of our (White) cultural landscape.

In the focus groups, we talked about many aspects of the show, apart from its treatment of the Cheyenne, and both Indian and White participants had some good things to say about it. Women of all ethnic backgrounds identified with Michaela, her adopted daughter, and many other female characters, who are clearly stronger than most of the men. The few participants who regularly watched the show were all women, who usually watched with their children. It was generally seen as a "sweet," family show and was compared with *Little House on the Prairie* or *The Waltons.* Men generally did not like the sentimentality or the tendency toward male bashing; they found it hard to identify with the weak male characters.

But there were clear differences in how the two ethnic groups perceived the Cheyenne characters. Most of the White participants thought the portrayal of the Cheyenne was accurate and positive. They did note that the people had little individuality; as one woman put it, "All they do is have these children mindlessly running in circles and everybody's always thanking Dr. Quinn. We have nothing else going on in this Cheyenne camp at all."[15] However, it was not an area that concerned them much. Some complained that the picture of the Cheyenne was simply too noble. One woman commented:

> Like when I was out in North Dakota, a lot of Indians, even though they were on the reservation and they were taken care of, they were always in the bar. I remember walking down to the tennis courts . . . and I would have to walk through the tunnel and . . . (it sounds racist but I'm not) there were always drunken Indians sleeping in the tunnels that you had to walk through to get down. They don't show that, they only show the good qualities in the Indian population.[16]

The more positive comments often reflected the traditional stereotype of the good, stoic Indian. For example, in one episode on the tape, Cloud Dancing is captured by Custer's forces. They imprison and mistreat him, at one point lining him up before a firing squad and then firing over his head. The White participants admired this and found it believable. As one woman said: "He didn't compromise . . . I think the audience was to perceive this as a Native American value and that's being true to your word and being willing to go to death."[17] Commented another, "I think, the way he was just quiet, yet . . . he was saying so much without saying anything verbally . . . you know, they're very . . . they can be very intense emotionally but able to suppress it and not show it."[18]

Most seemed to feel that contemporary Native Americans would like the portrayal, even if it was romanticized. As one woman said, "The popularity of becoming a Native American in some true spiritual sense is becoming very popular and very important."[19]

Some American Indians did like it—women particularly enjoyed the female roles. In an earlier study that used all-male focus groups to compare Indian and White interpretations of the movie *The Searchers,* JoEllen Shiveley found that middle-aged Indian men enjoyed the movie and identified strongly with the White hero, played by John Wayne.[20] Shiveley concluded that the structure of the movie and the cultural associations of "cowboy" with freedom and independence from modern culture led the Indian respondents to this identification, allowing them to enjoy the story in spite of its negative depictions of Indians: "The structure of oppositions that defines the heroes in a film seems to guide viewers' identification with the characters in the film and overrides any ethnic empathy."[21] In the same way, female Indian participants were able to identify with *Dr. Quinn*'s strong female characters: "Where that doctor was telling her that she's not good enough because she's a woman, and I know how that feels . . . I think my daughter would really like it because it shows that women can do stuff."[22]

Indian women, then, were somewhat torn between the appeal of the women characters and their simultaneous dismay at the bland and culturally inaccurate depictions of the Cheyenne. As an Ojibwa woman said, "What I notice in all these movies is that they always got the same kind of tepee, they're set up in the same way and the same horses." When watching one episode, she noticed that Dr. Quinn's daughter was helping treat Indian patients and found that unlikely: "I think it was in the second episode that young girl was doctoring that Indian woman, and I thought, Oh, get real, the Indians wouldn't let that happen."[23]

Indian men, on the other hand, did not find much to like. Sully is the only strong, male hero, and as I discuss later, he does not appeal to Indian men. Shiveley points out that the Indians in her study were middle-aged and living on reservations, where "traditional" Western movies were very popular. However, when Shiveley discussed Westerns with Indian college students, "The heightened ethnic awareness . . . interferes with, or overrides, their responses to the Western so that they do not get caught up in the structure of oppositions in the narrative."[24] Two of the older men in my study mentioned that when they were growing up, they "rooted for the cowboys" too, although rarely any longer, whereas younger men found this option impossible.

Thus, both Indian men and women were offended by the lack of attention to Cheyenne individuality: "They're caricatures and they're not human beings with their own language, their own thoughts, their own feelings, and . . . they come and go in order for her to save them or in order for her to make some great moral statement."[25] In Shiveley's study, whereas Whites saw Westerns as historically authentic, Indians did not; the same difference appeared here. Whites were impressed by the care with costumes and so on, whereas Indians found the cultural details phony: "They seemed to wander around in really beautiful, I mean purple dyed smoked buckskin which just amazed me . . . I thought: Oh jeez, this is really corny. And they're supposed to be living near the town. That is so divorced from anything that supposedly happened, I mean by the time those towns came in they were already half starved out."[26]

One group debated the very use of the title "medicine woman," which seems to have been used by the producers as a catchphrase. The American Indians found this problematic—No, Dr. Quinn could not be a medicine woman and would never be seen as one: "They would have known and respected that she might have the cure for smallpox or something . . . but it would not be the same kind of respect that they might give one of their spiritual leaders . . . they can't put them two names in the same context."[27] Another agreed that the producers misunderstood Native attitudes to healing: "There's something missing when you imply to an Indian person 'medicine woman.' And what's missing is the ceremony that goes along with healing. Because we know how powerful [is] the placebo effect . . . their mind, their spirit, they have to be an active participant in their own healing . . . Much more than what's implied by the term 'medicine woman' in that movie."[28]

Clearly what shows here is a sense of "ownership" about Native culture that is irrelevant to White viewers but that means a great deal to Indian viewers. Authenticity, and with it the ability to identify with the show's premise, is more than a matter of getting the costumes right. Indian participants needed to talk about specific aspects of the portrayal of Indian characters and their frustration with it, whereas to White viewers the issue of Indian representation was of much less interest than, say, the perceived unfairness of gender representations.

In some other respects, the Native participants clearly disagreed with the conclusions of the White respondents, for instance, in their reaction to the character of Sully. White men did not particularly like Sully, seeing him as too perfect and too "hunky." However, they recognized his type from their stock of popular cultural images, pointing to the "going-Indian" theme from *Dances with Wolves* and other movies: "I can't think of one (movie) that there hasn't been this White guy that has somehow been part of their culture."[29] "I think he was a trapper. . . . You see them in Westerns you know, the deal with the Indians they do, back and forth. They go up, shoot a bear and trade the bear skin either way."[30]

White women liked Sully a lot, as the producers clearly intended them to. "He's this magical guy who lives two lives."[31] "He stands up for the women and he stands up for the blacks and he stands up for the American Indians and, you know, he's always doing the right stuff. The 'ideal'—he doesn't exist of course in real life, but the ideal man."[32]

Indian viewers found Sully much more problematic. His role as a "stand-in" Indian was very clear to them—the fact that through him Indian concerns could be introduced without actually having to develop real Indian characters. "You've got this quasi-Fabio lookalike as the love interest . . . Looks like a model and once in a while he goes out and hangs out with dog soldiers, which seems rather strange to me."[33] "Here's another White person fixing the Indians."[34] Although Sully's persona fits smoothly into the White repertoire of Western images, it has no place in Indian culture. As one Indian put it, "I mean, I know a lot of old stories and stuff, my ancestors past, I can't ever recall one where anyone talked about a long-haired, light-skinned, hairy guy that helped out my tribe."[35] But, he laughingly added, "I know people like that nowadays." For Sully fits perfectly a contemporary, Indian-defined stereotype—the "wannabee," who claims Native ancestry and appropriates Indian culture and identity.[36]

The difference between Indian and White perceptions was illustrated in other ways. Whereas Whites admired the stoic endurance of the imprisoned Cloud Dancing, several Indians were angered by it, arguing that the Cheyenne was presented as defeated and unable to act. The African-American blacksmith was allowed to fight back by refusing to make chains for the Indian prisoner, and White characters used clever trickery to free him. But Cloud Dancing did nothing: "His manhood was suppressed. All the way through the whole film it showed that. The black man had a choice, the Indian didn't have a choice . . . he was in chains . . . he was under guard . . . His dignity was violated: They put him up against a firing squad and they didn't kill him."[37] Another man agreed: "I didn't like that part, I would have went off, I could have seen anger, but he just walked down, put his head down, made him look pitiful, you know. That kind of pissed me off, that part."[38]

Popular culture theorists often talk about "resistant readings" of television texts—some viewers will interpret a TV show in ways that the producers do not expect, in ways that might empower them.[39] Others have argued with this, saying that although audiences may interpret the meaning of the story differently, they still "read" the narrative in the same way, since the power to define the story still remains with the producers.[40] Thus, Celeste Condit argues, "I detect little fundamental inconsistency with the denotations processed by the viewers; instead it is the *valuation* of these denotations, and the attached connotations that viewers draw upon, which becomes important."[41] The difference in these valuations is clear in the contrast between Indians' and Whites' interpretations of the imprisonment scenes. Both saw Cloud Dancing as powerless and silent, taking no action to change his situation. For Whites, this illustrated perfectly their model of the strong, stoic Indian, who endures brutality without flinching and accepts his inevitable fate with dignity. For Indians, it illustrated equally well the way that their people have been brutalized, humiliated, and deprived of all dignity. The contrast could not be more stark.

At times, Indian viewers did offer readings of *Dr. Quinn* that were genuinely "resistant," that is, rather than being angered and dismayed by the perceived negative imagery, they were able to turn it around and derive pleasure from it. One episode on the tape opens with a sequence on the reservation in which Snowbird, Cloud Dancing's wife, gives Michaela a horse in return for her medical help. She explains that everyone in the village thinks the horse is hopelessly untrainable, but "she'll run for me, and I know she'll run for you." Clearly the intended reading is to show how well-respected Dr. Quinn is. Several Indian viewers, however, saw this as another irritating example of the subservience of the Indians: "It made the Cheyenne almost look dependent upon the services she offered and they didn't have ways to heal themselves."[42]

But one Ojibwa respondent gave an alternative reading: "American Indians long, long time ago, treated white people like they were, not a mystery, but they were more or less something as an oddity. So when you were an oddity in the culture, you were set aside, and you were given things." He illustrated this by equating Dr. Quinn's rather ambiguous "female medicine man" role with the special role many Native groups gave to homosexuals or cross-dressers, mentioning that they were often respected, but regarded with a little awe. He decided that the Cheyenne woman who gave the horse may have placed Dr. Quinn in a similar role: "With that woman, my feeling was, she thought, I'll just accept this. If I give her this horse, she'll get the hell out of here. I mean it was a no-good horse, that was a give-away from the American Indian point of views, give her a rotten horse. Was it out of respect? Maybe it was. Maybe she figured she's such a good medicine woman, let her tame this damn thing."[43]

Nevertheless, oppositional readings like this were quite rare. As Condit points out, "oppositional and negotiated readings require more work of viewers than do dominant readings."[44] The Ojibwa viewer who framed the above reading indicates the difficulty of doing so: "That is how I rationalized it or justified what was taking place in front of me. Trying to assign some good . . . I was looking for positive things."[45] Similarly, the Indians in Shiveley's study clearly found enough in traditional Westerns to make these films a valued part of their popular culture. But, especially as their sense of ethnic identity increases, minorities who feel alienated from the dominant message of the culture are likely to simply turn off, rather than do the work of trying to find an empowering alternative message. As Condit concludes, "Hence, the trade-off among what marginal audience groups want, what other audience groups want, and what the producers are willing to give them as a compromise may still retain a great deal of control for producers and dominant groups."[46]

Conclusion: The Persistence of Fantasy

It seems White culture cannot let go of its ingrained images of American Indians. Ultimately, *Dr. Quinn* seems to be very successful in taking familiar, recognizable aspects of the traditional Imaginary Indian and adapting them to a 1990s "family show." Stuart Hall points out that popular culture genres do not remain static but are constantly "transformed," reworking what came before so that "from one period to another, they come to stand in a different relation to the ways working people live and the ways they define their relations to each other, to 'the others' and to the conditions of life."[47] *Dr. Quinn* is similar to other shows that preceded it, like *Little House on the Prairie,* in that it plays on the same set of images about the family, the frontier, and the American melting pot. Yet the audience has indeed changed "the way [these shows] define their relations to each other," and that is reflected in, for example, popular genres that feature radically different attitudes toward gender roles. Women now have much greater power as both audiences and producers to bring about these transformations. Yet the "relations . . . to 'the others'" still persist, because "the others," in this case American Indians, have had very little power to produce a transformation.

Certainly, things have changed, in many ways for the better, and *Dr. Quinn* reflects this. *Dr. Quinn* is 1990s-sensitive, playing on the sense of guilt that many White people feel about the treatment of Native peoples. As Francis writes, "Sympathetic regret or retrospective outrage are the feelings these movies seem most likely to evoke. In a sense, Indian movies have never been about Indians at all. They have been about White concerns: White guilt, White fear, White insecurity."[48]

This guilt is made explicit in a scene after the typhus epidemic, when Cloud Dancing is allowed a rare moment of anguish. Sully approaches him as he mourns by the riverside:

Sully.   Cloud Dancing, I'm sorry. I'm sorry for bringing them blankets and for believing the army. I'm sorry for everything my people are doing to yours.
Cloud Dancing.   The spirits tell me my anger is good, my hate is not. There are good men, there are bad men. You're a good man, Sully, you're still my brother.
(They embrace.)

At the same time that *Dr. Quinn* goes along with notions of White guilt, it equally clearly allows White audiences to see the destruction of Indian culture as both inevitable and as somehow accidental. The show holds on to the "renegade" image, for example, because it helps assuage guilt: After all, some of the Indians drove us to it, helping to bring about their own destruction. Thus there were good and bad guys on both sides, and the bad things happened because of bad guys like Custer and the renegades, but good guys like Michaela and Sully are really who we are. As an Indian focus-group participant put it, the show frames things so "you can look at somebody like Custer as an evil person, but the fact was that it was a deliberate policy . . . these things were institutional."[49]

In other words, the show presents everything as an individual matter rather than as something systematic. We clearly get the impression that good people could have prevented these things; in fact, it almost lulls us into thinking they actually did. So everything is really fine, and maybe the Indians love us all after all. George Lipsitz argues that frequently the key to the success of popular genres is that they resonate with familiarity, yet put a new twist on old images: "These folk retentions survived because of their appeal as narratives, but also because they marshaled the resources of the past as part of defining identity in the present."[50] The mountain man, the stoic and renegade Indians, the pious preacher, the reformed prostitute, even the energetic, educated White woman who signals progress, are all familiar cultural staples.[51] Even the guilt is not new, just more sharply felt.

Westerns, even family TV versions like *Dr. Quinn,* feel "authentic" to White audiences—a myth that is "an affirmation of their own social experience."[52] Because the Western does not represent a cultural myth for Indians, it is "inauthentic," in a way that goes far beyond the details of costume or artifacts. Perhaps, as an Ojibwa man explained, media forms like television, rooted as they are in the conventions and stereotypes of the past, cannot provide the kind of myths that work for minorities: "I think what's coming up now is virtual reality experience rather than just one dimension. We're going to have something more than T.V., where . . . our people will win the game . . . That's the thing of the future."[53]

Frederic Jameson argues that popular culture texts can represent "our deepest fantasies about the nature of social life, both as we live it now, and as we feel in our bones it ought rather to be lived."[54] As an Ojibwa participant described it, *Dr. Quinn* is indeed a fantasy, with a lot of appealing qualities. But, she said, "I think this was the way the White people of today would have liked for it to have been. I don't think it was my fantasy."[55]

Notes

1. Images of female American Indians have their own, related characteristics, tending to alternate between the noble "princess" and the subservient-to-the-savage "squaw." See Rayna Green, "The Pocahontas Perplex: The Image of Indian Women in American Culture." *Massachusetts Review* 16 (4) (1975), pp. 698–714.

2. See Michael T. Marsden and Jack Nachbar, "The Indian in the Movies," in *Handbook of North American Indians: History of Indian-White Relations,* vol. 4, ed. Wilcolm E. Washburn (Washington D.C.: Smithsonian Institution Press, 1988), pp. 607–616.

3. See Chapter 15 in this volume, Annette Taylor, "Cultural Heritage in *Northern Exposure,*" for a summary of television's treatment of American Indians.

4. This may seem surprising, given that, in general, the female characters are much stronger than the males. However, I believe it reflects the fact that the Indian stereotypes that are most current today are male stereotypes, rather than the older "princess" and "squaw" images.

5. See John J. O'Connor, "It's Jane Seymour, M.D., in the Wild and Wooly West," *New York Times,* February 4, 1993, p. B5; Richard Zoglin, "Frontier Feminist," *Time,* March 1, 1993, pp. 63–64.

6. Bonnie J. Dow presents an excellent analysis of the "tensions between utopian and ideological functions" related to feminism in *Dr. Quinn.* Some of the same tensions are apparent in the treatment of American Indians. See the chapter on "Postfeminism, Nostalgia, and Domestication of the Television Western in *Dr. Quinn, Medicine Woman,*" in Dow's forthcoming book, *Prime Time Feminism: Television, Media Culture, and the Women's Movement Since 1970* (Philadelphia: University of Pennsylvania Press, forthcoming).

7. See Robert F. Berkhofer, Jr., *The White Man's Indian: Images of the American Indian from Columbus to the Present* (New York: Vintage Books, 1979); Daniel Francis, *The Imaginary Indian: The Image of the Indian in Canadian Culture* (Vancouver, British Columbia: Arsenal Pulp Press, 1992).

8. Francis, *Imaginary Indian,* p. 5.

9. Stewart Brand, "Indians and the Counterculture, 1960s–1970s," in Washburn, ed., *Handbook,* p. 570.

10. Francis, *Imaginary Indian,* p. 25.

11. Robert S. Tilton, *Pocahontas: The Evolution of an American Narrative* (Cambridge: Cambridge University Press, 1994), p. 56.

12. Vine DeLoria, Jr., *Custer Died for Your Sins: An Indian Manifesto* (Norman: University of Oklahoma Press, 1988).

13. Rayna Green, "The Only Good Indian: The Image of the Indian in American Vernacular Culture." Ph.D. diss., Indiana University, 1974, p. 382.

14. The 19 respondents (8 women and 11 men) were all undergraduate or graduate students at the University of Minnesota, Duluth. They ranged in age from 19 to 43, with an average age of 30. In order to protect identities, I will refer to individuals by number when quoting them, then give their gender, self-defined ethnicity, and age on first reference.

15. Participant 7, female, white, 31.

16. Participant 2, female, white, 30.

17. Participant 1, female, white, 29.

18. Participant 6, female, Caucasian, 25.

19. Participant 6.

20. JoEllen Shiveley, "Cowboys and Indians: Perceptions of Western Films Among American Indians and Anglos," *American Sociological Review* 57 (1992), pp. 725–734.

21. Ibid., p. 728.

22. Participant 12, female, Alaska Native, 42.

23. Participant 13, female, Anishinabe (Ojibwa), 38.

24. Shiveley, "Cowboys and Indians," p. 732.

25. Participant 14, male, Sami Lapp/Cree, 30.

26. Participant 14.

27. Participant 15, male, Ojibwa/Caucasian, 19.

28. Participant 11, male, Ojibwa-Anishinabe, 43.

29. Participant 10, male, white, 26.

30. Participant 4, male, white, 30.

31. Participant 6.

32. Participant 7.

33. Participant 14.

34. Participant 17, male, American Indian, 42.

35. Participant 15.

36. See Rayna Green, "The Tribe Called Wannabee: Playing Indian in America and Europe," *Folklore* 99 (1) (1988), pp. 30–55, for a discussion of the phenomenon in contemporary culture.

37. Participant 17.

38. Participant 19, male, American Indian, 25.

39. See, for example, John Fiske, "Meaningful Moments," *Critical Studies in Mass Communication* 5 (1988), pp. 246–251, and *Television Culture* (New York: Methuen, 1987); Henry Jenkins, *Textual Poachers: Television Fans and Participatory Culture* (New York: Routledge, 1992); David Morley, *Family Power and Domestic Leisure* (London: Comedia, 1986); Andrea Press, *Women Watching Television* (Philadelphia: University of Pennsylvania Press, 1991), and many others.

40. See, for example, my conclusion in S. Elizabeth Bird, *For Enquiring Minds: A Cultural Study of Supermarket Tabloids* (Knoxville: University of Tennessee Press, 1992).

41. Celeste M. Condit, "The Rhetorical Limits of Polysemy," *Critical Studies in Mass Communication* 6 (2) (1989), p. 107, emphasis added.

42. Participant 15.

43. Participant 17.

44. Condit, "Limits," p. 109.

45. Participant 17.

46. Condit, "Limits," p. 110.

47. Stuart Hall, "Notes on Deconstructing the Popular," in *People's History and Socialist Theory*, ed. Raphael Samuel (London: Routledge, 1981), p. 228.

48. Francis, *Imaginary Indian*, p. 107.

49. Participant 14.

50. George Lipsitz, *Time Passages: Collective Memory and American Popular Culture* (Minneapolis: University of Minnesota Press, 1990), p. 115. See also my essay, S. Elizabeth Bird, "Cultural Studies as Confluence: The Convergence of Folklore and Media Studies," in *Popular Culture Theory and Methodology*, ed. Harold E. Hinds, Jr. (Bowling Green, Ohio: Popular Press, forthcoming). See also Jesus Martin-Barbero, *Communication, Culture, and Hegemony* (Newbury Park, Calif.: Sage Publications, 1993).

51. Robert Berkhofer points out that "In the Western formula, lawlessness and savagery must recede before the vanguard of white society, of which the town and particularly the educated White woman are the prime symbols" (*White Man's Indian*, p. 97).

52. Shiveley, "Cowboys and Indians," p. 733.

53. Participant 11.

54. Frederic Jameson, "Reification and Utopia in Mass Culture," *Social Text* 1 (1979), p. 147.

55. Participant 13.

17

Moo Mesa: Some Thoughts on Stereotypes and Image Appropriation
Theodore S. Jojola

What can you expect from filthy little heathens?
The whole race is like a curse . . . Their skins hellish
red . . . They're only good when they are dead!

—*from the song "Savages" in* Pocahontas

By the turn of the last century, "playing Indian" had became a national obsession. National organizations such as the Boy and Girl Scouts of America appropriated Indian folklore for their mainstay activities, and even adults participated in their own fantasy pageants. Annually, for example, the Smoki People—"white men and women from all walks of life of Prescott, Arizona"—reenacted the Hopi Snake Dance as well as other "ancient, mystic rites and ceremonies" of the southwestern Indians.[1]

The most recent wave of sports hysteria also attests to the problem of popular revisionism. Team mascots such as the Redmen, the Redskins, the Seminoles, the Braves, the Scalpers, the Utes, and the Chiefs continue to dominate the media. Far from benign, the mascots have been personified through idiotic characters such as Willie Wampum (Marquette University), Chief Noc-A-Homa (Atlanta Braves), and Chief Iliniwek (University of Illinois). These, in turn, have given way to demeaning gestures such as the infamous "tomahawk chop." Together, they perpetuate outmoded stereotypes rather than the purported "positive and heroic" stature of American Indians.

Other commercial images such as the Mazola Indian maiden, the Mazda Navajo jeepster, and the Santa Fe railway chief continue to ply the trade of the

public mystique. The so-called Santa Fe artistic style as well as New Age environmentalism, mysticism, and spirituality have dominated the mass market to an
even greater extent. "Tribalism" becomes transformed into a vogue lifestyle for the
social elite. Fakes, opportunists, and the medicine-show people continue to in-
doctrinate the unwary.

As a matter of fact, the depiction of the Indian became a sustaining industry in
popular culture. In the Hollywood industry, movies about Indians abounded,
even though story lines were accomplished largely through the casting of non-
Indian actors. Beginning with the 1968 Civil Rights movement, however, some
advances were made in reversing the stereotypical images of American Indians.
Incidents such as the 1969 occupation of Alcatraz Island, the takeover of the Bureau of Indian Affairs headquarters in 1972, and the 1973 Federal Bureau of Investigation confrontation at Wounded Knee, South Dakota, by Indian activists
served to bring attention to the plight of contemporary Indians.

Eventually, many elements of these important struggles were simply forgotten.
Even with the onset of liberal guilt, public sympathy gradually moved away from
the contemporary struggles of native people and toward a revisionist history of
American colonialism. Such was the case with the Best Motion Picture of 1990,
Dances with Wolves—an overly romantic portrait of Lakota Sioux life just before
the Sioux are massacred. In 1995, the revisionist history continues with the Disney animation film, *Pocahontas*. Based on half-truths, the character of Pocahontas
is woven into a contemporary context; the film is an Indian-princess, ecofeminist
fantasy that represents yet another appropriation with appeal for the mainstream
masses.

Pocahontas represents one genre of image making that has been overlooked in
the light of other media. More often than not, animation is discounted as a rather
innocuous form, principally because it is intended as entertainment for children.
When animation is used in the context of cartoon, its role becomes even more
submerged. As a whole, humor is not taken seriously. But as I was to find out, animation turns out to be surprisingly complex. Not only is it a very malleable
medium, it is not constrained by the need to depict real events and situations.
Rather, fantasy is the norm, and roles can be elaborated upon to express any type
of sentiment or situation. Perhaps the only limitation upon the proliferation of
this form is the fact that the costs of its production are exorbitant. Frame upon
frame must be hand-rendered, making it a labor-intensive industry of both fact
and fancy.

The Wild West C.O.W.-Boys of Moo Mesa

This chapter is drawn from my firsthand experience in working within this
medium. Early in 1992, I was contacted by the Division of Children's Programs at
ABC-TV regarding a concept in development for a new animated cartoon called
The Wild West C.O.W.-Boys of Moo Mesa.[2] The story was based on the depiction of

CowTown, a small southwestern mesa-top community whose human residents had been replaced by their domesticated animals and their menagerie of desert companions after a mysterious incident with a falling comet, a result of a catastrophic solar accident that changed the otherwise grazing bovines into humanized animals. The cartoon situations depicted the daily episodes of the cometized animals trying to cope with their new human abilities. All of the cast of characters were framed in the classic style of a B-grade Western movie, with humor reminiscent of Gary Larson's *Far Side* cartoon series.[3]

The target audience for these characters was the kindergarten set. Although the series was developed as a Saturday morning ABC-TV cartoon, there were great pains taken to make the series more reminiscent of the 1950s children's club shows. Children could subscribe to *Moo Mail,* the publication of the children's fan club. Episodes were purposely developed with the intent of reinforcing moral values drawn out of the situations the stories portrayed. These moral values were usually presented as a "code of the West." These, in turn, were the guiding credos for the actions of the various characters, especially the three main bovine characters—Cowlorado, Marshal Moo Montana, and the Dakota Dude—who were charged with enforcing the law of the town (Figure 17.1).

One of the proposed characters, however, was totally out of sync with the concept of the show. Because the concept appropriated the standard cowboys-and-Indians fare, it was necessary to include an Indian sidekick. Unfortunately this sidekick, Geronimoo, had come packaged as an outrageous terror-bull with a Mohawk-style haircut, chiseled out of the likes of the quintessential Indian savage. The primary objection to this image arose from concern for the kindergarten audience. Given this most impressionable age—one where children have trouble distinguishing between cartoon fiction and reality—a savage cow would have played directly into an unacceptable stereotype. It was destined to repeat hundreds of

Figure 17.1   The C.O.W.-Boys of Moo Mesa.

stereotypical cartoon characters; the only missing elements were the "ughs," the "grunts" and the incessant tom-tom beating that would doubtless have accompanied the portrayal of this character (Figure 17.2).

The design of the character was based on the classic B-grade Western Hollywood stereotype of the Apache warrior, Geronimo. The action-figure toy was masked with feathers and war paint, animal-tooth necklace, bow and arrow, chopping tomahawk, and G-string and was embossed in red-hued plastic; the proposed character was reminiscent of the worst Indian stereotype. His depiction was as follows:

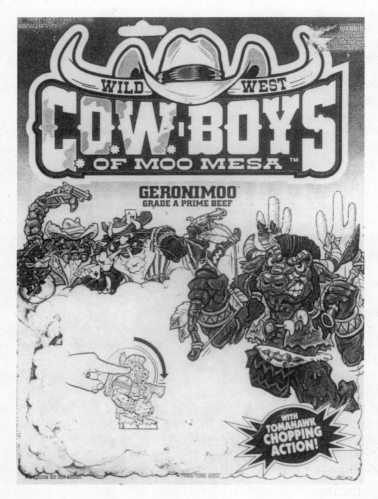

Figure 17.2   *Geronimoo, packaged as an action-figure toy.*

Geronimoo is a strong silent Native American COW-boy, sometimes mysterious and always unflappBULL. He is totally in tune with nature, and his mystical powers are UDDERLY amazing. With a magic ritual that he learned from his father, Chief Grazin' Bull, Geronimoo can cure a bad case of hiccups and make it rain at the same time. He never allows himself to be BULLied by others, but always searches for a peaceful solution when locked in the horns of a serious Bully brawl.[4]

But, whoa there, little doggie! The task seemed innocent enough—recreate a cartoon character by reforming a critter varmint for the kiddy set. This was the daunting instruction leveled at me after an initial screening committee for ABC's Division of Children's Programs rejected the sketch concept of Geronimoo. What follows is a frame-by-frame account of how this character was revised.

Scrutinizing CowTown and Moo Mesa

Without the blessing of the review committee, the concept of Geronimoo was as good as dead. The original request, which was forwarded for my consideration, was to see if I could or would concur with the proposed changes for a revised character. Because the Geronimoo character was unacceptable, a new character named Phil Thomas was forwarded for consideration.

Pueblo culture itself is replete with a long and deep-abiding tradition of story-telling. This is nowhere more true than in Isleta Pueblo, where I was born and raised. And if this character was to be revised in a fashion that was consistent with my own culture, this included a revamp of the name as well. As a matter of fact, I was fortunate to have been weaned at a time when the story tradition was still very active. My maternal grandfather was especially versed in this skill, and he imbued me as a child with stories of animals who were characters in the timeless story plots and situations created by their distinct personalities. At the inception of my critique of Phil Thomas, I proposed that his name be changed. The name of my maternal grandfather, the storyteller, was José Rey Papuyo, but everyone in our family knew him as J.R.: "This [Phil Thomas] is not a common name in Puebloland. I would recommend, José Rey, which is very common. This is his formal name when he is introduced to strangers, but hardly anyone knows him by that. Instead, all his friends call him by his initials, J.R."[5]

I attempted after that to turn the characterization of Phil Thomas into a persona that was typified by my own grandfather. It was a rather straightforward task on my part, although it became obvious as the collaboration ensued that mainstream perceptions of native people were lacking a bona fide cultural context. The verbatim "conversation" that follows is formed of extracts taken from the ABC "Bible" (cartoon-speak for the script) and my responses to it, which are presented in the italicized passages.

ABC.   PHIL THOMAS is the fourth member of the gang and a bit of an erratic satellite.
   Phil is so tuned in that he's, well, a little tuned out. A close brush with the shard has

made Phil a bit more "sensitive" than the others to the random cause and effect of events on Moo Mesa. Because of this, Phil has embraced a more encompassing cosmology.

Jojola.   *J.R. is philosophical in disposition. He has a very profound sense of the past and the incident with the comet accentuated his intuition. He can anticipate actions shortly before they happen (sort of like Radar on M.A.S.H.) and the other C.O.W.-Boys are continuously baffled by this ability. In the end, J.R. always takes consolation by telling the others, "I told you so." All the other human-animals consider him somewhat eccentric. On the other hand, all the other nonhumans consider him normal. His cosmology is different from all the others. It is drawn from recollections from his ancestors of the first world who were equal with the animals and who at that time used to eat and talk with the animals.*

ABC.   The truth is, Phil is a little more clued in to natural rhythms than the other C.O.W.-Boys and has an incredible positive attitude. He's just a bit unreliable. It's hard to figure out just when Phil is onto something or when his internal wires may have become crossed a little. Phil is intensely serious about his vision, though, and teaches respect for everything around him.

Jojola.   *The truth is, J.R. has a different sense of time. Whereas all the other C.O.W.-boys are linear in their thinking and sense of time, he is totally cyclical in his reasoning and in his sense of time. It is the period of the day and not a watch that drives his actions. When he's not around and the dudes are in a pickle, it forces them to try and reconstruct what J.R. would have done or if J.R. had said anything before that they can use as clues to help them out.*

ABC.   Phil's got an unconsciously green thumb and he knows a lot about Mesa flora and fauna. He's always making some strange plant into a meal. Phil is a popular C.O.W.-Boy but that's because most people think he's joking when he's dead serious. It's never clear whether Phil is just a master punster or a brilliant visionary.

Jojola.   *Unlike his cow-counterparts, J.R. is a vegetarian. He detests moo juice but has a penchant for sarsaparilla. None of the plants are strangers to J.R. He knows which can be eaten and which can be used for medicine. He saves the seeds of the fruits he eats and he's always planting them somewhere else.*

The consequent sketch of Phil Thomas, however, suffered from other fatal stereotypes. Dressed in the fashion of a Keystone Cop, Phil Thomas sported the attire, hair braids, and stance of a Plains Indian (Figure 17.3). The drawing was certainly not reminiscent of the character sketch the writers had intended; instead, it was rather on the bullish side. Compared with his sidekicks, he seemed rather formal and aloof. Nevertheless, it was a dramatic improvement over Geronimoo.

The relationship of the C.O.W.-Boys to Phil Thomas appeared to appropriate the classic synergy of the cowboy to the Indian sidekick motif, reminiscent of Tonto and his downplayed relationship to the hero, the Lone Ranger:[6]

ABC.   Phil doesn't ride with the C.O.W.-Boys all the time but he does know Moo and the boys are the Good Guys because they're always helping him and his tribe.

Jojola.   *Stay away from 'injun,' 'feathers,' 'tepees,' and 'tribe.' The Good Guys are always welcome at their Pueblo. They are always seeking their advice and they both help each other out of their various predicaments. J.R.'s intuition always makes him appear at the right time, especially when the C.O.W.-boys are in serious trouble. At other times he is al-*

Figure 17.3 *Early draft of Phil Thomas character, showing Plains Indian characteristics.*

most impossible to find, and J.R.'s family always sends the C.O.W.-Boys on a wild goose chase with their directions, which are crystal clear to them but as clear as mud to the C.O.W.-boys.

ABC. Phil is always giving Moo and the boys refuge, showing them shortcuts or reporting things that are happening out in the wild. When Phil does ride with the C.O.W.-Boys, he's a helpful ally—especially since he never gets lost.

Jojola. J.R. never takes a shortcut. He always leads the C.O.W.-Boys along paths that are more complicated than they could be and he loses them often because he is much swifter than they are. J.R. is always looking for new things to discover or new plants to cultivate. He's a recycler, as well. He will pack newly found items even at the expense of wasting time or making the travel more burdensome for his comrades. That's why he prefers riding a buckboard or walking, instead of a horse.

It became obvious that the character profile was being swayed toward a Pueblo Indian image, perhaps in anticipation or in response to my initial feedback as a Pueblo Indian. The bottom line, however, was that there were major inconsistencies between the Plains image of Phil Thomas and the implied and potentially offensive attributes of his persona as proposed in the profile:

ABC.   Phil lives outside of town in a hillside community of cave dwellings and ladders. The life there is a little different than CowTown—part Indian pueblo, part New Age commune.

Jojola.   The town where J.R. lives is an Indian Pueblo. Through his gadgetry, the Pueblo has been transformed into a New Age commune. The one- and two-story adobe Pueblo has been transformed so that it has both ladders and solar greenhouses. It also has solar arrays and windmills. It is built at the mouth of a large canyon by a natural mountain stream. Toward the back and in the canyon wall are cliff dwellings that were the homes of his ancestors. Occasionally, when times get troublesome, they sometimes retreat there.

ABC.   Phil has a family and they are all self-actualized. Dinner at Phil's is like dinner at someone's house who's gone back way beyond nature. Phil doesn't understand the games town folk play and why they live in those weird buildings. Because of his unique perspective, Phil sees through the veils of society but he is a bit too trusting. He's a bit like Cowlamity in this way, but not as militant.

Jojola.   The village is bursting at the seams with boisterous children. They are naturally curious about visitors and love to play jokes on them. J.R.'s family is composed of an extended family. His grandfather as well as a couple of close cousins live with his immediate family. The house is not very complicated nor is his family. Simplicity of lifestyle is the rule in the house. There is always more than one activity going on in the house.

Moreover, it was necessary to revamp the "shaman" aspects of the character and to make the personality more consistent with the temperament of native people. Being a "hippie madman" and a "New Age" cowboy simply did not lend itself to a more wholesome southwest character. In particular, the flavor of this New Age profile was also potentially ripe for abuse.

ABC.   He's the New Age C.O.W.-Boy—repeatedly seeing patterns in nature where there may or may not be any, reverently treating objects like they have personalities and frequently purporting to be in contact with phantom spirits.

Jojola.   These are not 'phantom' spirits—they are the spirits of his ancestors.

ABC.   He's part shaman and part hippie madman continually spouting *koan*-like utterances of intuitive brilliance or confusing passages of absurdist blither.

Jojola.   He is eccentric, but he is not a shaman (this depiction is potentially offensive). He loves to spin conundrums, which sometimes makes him an irritant, especially when the others are looking for quick answers and quick solutions.

Given the lack of a Pueblo presence in the cartoon world, it was necessary to reconstruct the character in its entirety. After a series of discussions that resulted in rejecting Phil Thomas, it was proposed that a new character be formulated that was more, well, indigenous to the Southwest and to mold its appearance directly on Pueblo culture:

ABC.   Phil sees Moo as a good spirit but a little stiff and out of touch with his inner calf. He likes Dakota and is always amazed at how quickly that steer works through his emotional problems. Phil thinks Cowlorado is always joking, constantly laughing at the kid even when the kid is trying to be deadly serious. And Phil is always welcome at The Tumbleweed. He's kind of like family there and is a surrogate father to Annie and Cody.

Jojola.   Do not use the imagery of the saguaro cactus—it's not indigenous to Puebloland. If you insist on using this imagery, then attribute it to J.R.'s idiosyncrasies. He bought the plants off a journeyman and planted them all over Moo Mesa, where they now flourish. As for 'the Single Injun Plains,' rename it the 'Single Antelope Plains.' Also, the 'giant tepee house' in Tumbleweed is a stereotype—something like a giant Santa Fe–style hotel would be OK.

ABC.   Phil thinks the Code of the West is a fine way to live but why have codes?

Jojola.   J.R.'s favorite code is When the cows come home, it's time to hit the Hay!

My grandfather was of the unique cohort of individuals who had an intuitive grasp of mechanics. The common joke in our extended family was that "J.R. could fix anything with baling-wire." In addition, he was born before the turn of the century and represented the last of the "old-timers" in the community. He moved in his own time and space. He became the perfect motivation for the new character.

ABC.   Phil has an intense interest in primitive science and technology and is always pulling contraptions he's invented out of his pouch to aid in investigations and battles. He should've patented his burlap telescope. Sometimes Phil's inventions work and sometimes they cause more problems than they were supposed to solve. Many times, Phil's inventions can only be worked by Phil and it is quite amusing to see the other try.

Jojola.   'Primitive science' is not an acceptable description. Rather, he has a maniacal curiosity for new gadgets and gizmos. In fact, this is his one major personality flaw. He is easily duped by any snake-oil seller and he never seems to learn his lesson when it comes to buying worthless gadgets. He's the kinda guy who'll stand transfixed in front of a veg-a-matic demonstration or the home-buyers network, oblivious to anything else or anyone else around him. Oftentimes, he will pull out these gadgets, which are intended to be revolutionary but which don't often work. When they don't work he often fixes them so they do, but the solution is so esoteric that he is the only one that can make it work. He uses only three types of weapons: a rabbit stick (sort of like a boomerang), an atl-atl (spear thrower), and a sling (which he arms with cactus berries).

It was natural to begin the reconstruction of Phil Thomas with what was already familiar. Not all elements were to be discarded, but it was apparent that a new profile had to be elaborated. It should be noted, however, that the imaging of Pueblo Indians in cartoons historically has not been a very lucrative business. With few exceptions, such images have escaped the cartoonist's pen. One exception was a series called *Canyon Kiddies*, which was later dubbed *Canyon Country Kiddies*, by Jimmy Swinnerton.[7] This regular feature was popularized in *Good Housekeeping* magazine from May 1922 through September 1938.[8] In these cartoons, the commonsense lifeways of the Hopi and Navajo Indians of Arizona were depicted through the wide-eyed innocence of their children. The series is noteworthy in that it did not defer to the usual acrid warwhoop and face paint depiction typified by the comic strip series *Tumbleweeds*.[9] Instead, it made a fair, albeit simplified, representation of the region and its cultures.

Another, more contemporary, attempt was made at depicting Hopis in a Marvel Comics edition of "NFL SuperPro" in 1992. Titled "The Kachinas Sing of

Doom," this infamous episode was voluntarily recalled by the publisher after the Hopi government and its religious leaders protested the depiction of the unmasking of Kachinas in the story.[10] Even more recently, a native Zuni Pueblo artist, Phil Hughte, broke officially into the ranks of the profession with the cartoon depictions of the anthropologist Frank Hamilton Cushing and his impact on Zuni culture.[11] Originally compiled as forty-three paintings, the cartoon collection of Hughte was drawn in a style reminiscent of Mort Walker's *Beetle Bailey* cartoon strips but with depictions that are directly related to Zuni culture.[12]

Therefore, J.R.'s based-on-fact profile needed to be transferred to a cartoon sketch. And, once again, it became necessary to dig into the inventory of animal personae for possible ideas. The folk stories of Isleta Pueblo were filled with them, and this rich cultural source seemed to be the perfect trove for a good match. Southwest desert animals were diverse and varied, and besides cometized cows, there could be a few indigenous species integrated as well.

The first of these concepts was based on a well-known Isleta folk-legend creature whose name was "big head," or antelope-boy.[13] Legend has it that the human community repatriated this fleet-footed human after hunters spotted him suckling on an antelope in the middle of a herd. His prowess was well regarded in the native community and the fact that he was often portrayed as a hero who employed ingenious solutions was consistent with the profile of J.R. Ultimately, a new mock-up was drafted and submitted for consideration:

> *Jojola.* Unlike the other C.O.W.-Boys, J.R. should depict an indigenous animal of the mesa—cows were brought to the New World by the non-natives, you know. Perhaps an antelope (see attached sketch)? This antelope is relatively neutral in Pueblo cosmology but is admired for its speed, cunning, and prowess. The antelope is also equally at home in the foothills or grazing in the plains and, typically, is known in real life to mingle among cows for camouflage! These attributes can be personified, including the fact that, unlike its cow counterparts, it is a vegetarian. His favorite expression is Is that so? (Figure 17.4).

After further consideration, it was decided that the visual was simply too complex for both the animation and the child's mind. Other animals were considered until a determination was made that a buffalo could suit the purposes of the cartoon sketch much better. There was a solid consensus among the collaborators of Moo Mesa. The other natural association that proved positive was the juxtaposition of the non-native domestic cow alongside the American bison.

The concept proved fruitful. A series of original sketches were exchanged, with each successive rendering becoming progressively better (Figure 17.5, 17.6, 17.7). My input consisted of refining the cultural details of the humanoid buffalo and was particularly focused on toning down the "hulky" attributes of the character. My intention was to make the character more affable and personable, compared to the other rough-and-tumble C.O.W.-Boys, while building a distinctive and Pueblo-like persona.

Rather significantly, each new sketch entailed making some of the nuances of Pueblo habits and customs more culturally specific. Particular attention was given

Figure 17.4   *Phil Thomas in his antelope incarnation.*

to the distinctive shirt, sash, and boots of the character. Another concern was the manner in which the hair was coiffed. In order to assist the graphic illustrators, examples of Pueblo men were sent to the artists, and from these, new character profiles were created. In some instances the efforts paid off, whereas in other cases, the images regressed. One particularly noteworthy disaster was the redepiction of J.R. as a rather Amish-looking kind of buffalo! (Figure 17.8).

In the end, a number of compromises were incorporated into the sketch of J.R. Basically, many of J.R.'s original features were stylized to conform with the other C.O.W.-Boys. In particular, his face was softened and the complex lace patterns of the Isleta shirt were simplified, resulting in a ribbon-shirt-like garment. The shell pendant simply became a diamond lapel shape. As was later explained to me, many of these decisions were made in order to provide a simple illustrative format for the animators (Figure 17.9).

Conclusion

J.R. was an appropriation in the revised sense. For me, as a native collaborator on the project, J.R. represented a unique revision from a native's perspective.

Figure 17.5   *First version of J.R. as a Pueblo character.*

Although many elements of the persona were compromised in the final production, I became increasingly aware of the other considerations that had to be weighed as the depictions of the character emerged. The representations of dance, song, and mystical traditions, for example, became problematic. At the same time that I felt it was important to portray reality, I also had a sense of uncertainty about whether such depictions might reveal too much about the Pueblo culture. There was an interesting see-sawing set of considerations that had to be weighed both in the light of Pueblo cultural etiquette and because I was acutely aware of the secretive aspects of Pueblo society.

The initial image of Phil Thomas represented a depiction of the Indian from a predominantly non-native perspective and was driven by popular non-native ideals of Native American life and customs. Hence the archetypes of tepees and saguaro cactus subconsciously crept into what was to be a Pueblo landscape. Both the Phil Thomas character and the backdrop were a whimsical fabrication of odds and ends intended to portray Native America.

Even after the creation of J.R., it remained to be seen whether all this work really resulted in a notable shift from the usual American Indian stereotyping.

Figure 17.6 *Second draft of J.R.*

Did my input as a native person really make any difference, and could collaboration between natives and non-natives prove to be useful and constructive? This is an important question with implications for contemporary Native America and the deconstruction of the American Indian stereotype.

The development of the J.R. character in *Moo Mesa* is an interesting example of collaboration between native and non-native producers and image makers. Geronimoo was the pure stereotype, done in isolation and detached from native reality. Typifying the fierce "Indian" and warlike savage, the persona was antithetical to contemporary Native America. It certainly is not an image that would be considered wholesome for little children, and its depiction was rightly assessed as being offensive to native people. But it represents the foundation from which most depictions of popular mainstream culture emerge, and such representation continues even with supposedly more "enlightened" productions like Disney's *Pocahontas*.

As long as indigenous imagery and thought continue to be preempted by non-indigenous people—in isolation—the interpretation will be fundamentally equivocal. The stereotype of the Indian long ago diverged from the reality of contemporary

Figure 17.7   *Third draft of J.R.*

tribal people. The themes have been exhausted, and there is little chance for any more innovation and meaning to develop from such static images. The task, therefore, is to stop Indian stereotypes from being perpetuated.

In the face of the exotic and primitive, outsiders draw on their own preconceptions and experiences to selectively appropriate elements of the "Indian." The consequent image may be a subjective interpretation, the purpose of which is to corroborate the outsider's viewpoint. I refer to this process as revisionism, and more often than not, it entails remaking native people by divorcing them from their own social and community realities.

Native people have resented being cast into stereotypes. They are rejecting being placed into roles that serve to reaffirm the mainstream's perception of their communities. As a result of new successes in diversifying their economies—especially through Indian gaming—many native communities have now begun to regulate their own tourist enterprises and museums. This is a relatively new phenomenon, and it places the issues of image making squarely on their own shoul-

Figure 17.8 *J.R. with his Amish look.*

ders. As "insiders," how much cultural information will they be willing to divulge and under what pretext?

At the same time, whether the dominant image is the warbonneted, face-painted, and buckskin-clad "chief" or the erotic Indian princess, the irony is that many native people continue to cater to such images. There is no consensus among Indian people—many native communities are divided and factionalized over the exploitation of their own cultural images. Although attempts have been made by some tribes to regulate the use of sacred images and symbols, other tribes and individuals have made a profitable enterprise of playing the stereo-typed Indian.

Nonetheless, unless direct roles in the image industry are sought by native people, the process of stereotyping by outsiders will continue. Native people need to infuse the diversity of their own cultures into such image making; they need to become ar-ticulate in terms of those elements that represent their own cultures and traditions. This will take patience, since the task is to counter generations of distortions that

Figure 17.9   *Final version of J.R.*

have been accepted in the mainstream as truths. Playing Indian should no longer be a one-sided game. If native people are to make a significant impact on this front, then they have to reappropriate and revise their own roles, basing that revision on their own context and understanding of their traditions. They have to become directly involved, so that their native voice becomes dominant.

As for *Moo Mesa*, the indications of success in revising such imagery in favor of the Native American populace came in a rather unexpected manner. In the "First Cowllector's Item" of the Archie Comics Series, J.R. was cast in a rather auspicious way.[14] The plot revolved around the discovery of a dinosaur in CowTown. But the most significant aspect of this encounter was not the change from the norm of the Indian savage. Instead, J.R. was revealed to be the keeper of books—a librarian with scientific curiosity to boot. I would venture to say that this depiction, in itself, ultimately did justice to the memory of my grandfather and to native people in general.

Notes

I wish to acknowledge the efforts of the production crew for *Moo Mesa* in this cartoon collaboration, including Nancy Tuthill and Linda Steiner, of the ABC TV Children's Programs Division; and Mitch Schauer and Ray Lee of Gunther Wahl Productions, Inc. I also want to note that all opinions and scholarship are solely my own and do not necessarily reflect the opinions of ABC TV or its affiliates.

1. Quotes from the program notes of the 28th Annual Smoki Ceremonials at Prescott, Ariz., August 14, 1949.

2. *The Wild West C.O.W.-Boys of Moo Mesa* was a creation of Ryan Brown by R. E. Bee, Inc., and syndicated by the division of Children's Programs, ABC-TV. The first episode premiered late in 1992 in a prime Saturday morning cartoon slot. The enterprise was expanded beyond that with the publication of a series by Archie Comic Publications and the merchandising of toys by Hasbro, Inc. The program had relatively short-lived success, lasting only a few seasons.

3. *The Far Side*, by Gary Larson, Universal Press Syndicate.

4. Description from Geronimoo, Cowboy figurine back cover. Distributed by Hasbro, Inc., Pawtucket, R.I., 1991. The original sketch of Geronimoo was identical to this figurine. Despite all the efforts to revise and discard this original image, the figurine was packaged for merchandizing in its original form and distributed after the cartoon became popularized. Estimating from the copyright date, this occurred before the fact.

5. The dialogue represents statements from the "Bible"—*Wild West C.O.W.-Boys of Moo Mesa*, 1992—with my responses in italics.

6. It is rather ironic that the Native American actor Michael Horse, who portrayed Tonto in the movie remake of the *Lone Ranger*, was to be the voice of J.R.

7. Swinnerton published the best of these cartoons in a publication titled *Canyon Country Kiddies* (New York: Doubleday, 1923).

8. Harold G. Davidson, *Jimmy Swinnerton: The Artist and His Work* (New York: Hearst Books, 1985), p. 104.

9. Tom K. Ryan, syndicated by North American Syndicates, Inc.

10. "The Kachinas Sing of Doom," in "NFL SuperPro" *Marvel Comicbooks* 1 (6) (March 1992).

11. *A Zuni Artist Looks at Frank Hamilton Cushing: Cartoons by Phil Hughte* (Zuni, N. Mex.: Pueblo of Zuni Arts and Crafts, A:shiwi A:wan Museum and Heritage Center Publication, 1994).

12. See Ted Jojola, "Exhibition Reviews: A Zuni Artist Looks at Frank Hamilton Cushing: Cartoons by Phil Hughte," *Museum Anthropology* 19 (1) (1995).

13. A variant of the tale of the antelope-boy can be found in Elsie Clews Parsons's study of Isleta Pueblo, *How They Began to Race for the Sun*, 47th Annual Report of the Bureau of American Ethnology (Washington, D.C.: Smithsonian Institution, 1929–1930), p. 386.

14. "Valley of the Thunder Lizard," in "The Wild West C.O.W.-Boys of Moo Mesa," *Archie Comics* 1 (March, 1993).

18

What Does One Look Like?

Debra L. Merskin

The world knows us by our faces. . . . When our caras *do not live up to the "image" that the family or community wants us to wear and when we rebel against the engraving on our bodies, we experience ostracism, alienation and shame.*

—Gloria Anzaldua[1]

Soul and face and body, words and action contribute to our identity. We invent ourselves. We are invented by others. I'm not sure what I look like; I just know I don't look like "one," at least according to cultural definitions of what constitutes "Indianness" (see Figure 18.1).

"You wouldn't know it by looking at you!"
"You are? Really? That's wild!"
"Oh yeah, I can see it in your face! Do you color your hair?"

Let me tell you something about myself. First, about my parents. They met at a tavern in Muskegon, Michigan. He was a struggling young accountant; she worked in a bakery. He came from Chicago as a child. His parents were Polish—hardworking, honest, deliberate people. They had immigrated to the United States with their parents. They were fair-haired and fair-minded.

Her parents? The trail is less direct. She came from the Arkansas Ozarks in the 1930s. Cherokee. Tsalagi. My mother's "formal" education ended in the sixth grade. She was needed at home to cook and clean for her mother, two older brothers, and an abusive father. It was bad to be black and it was worse to be Indian. The water fountains didn't exist that my mother's people were allowed to drink from. Signs were posted "Whites only," "Blacks," and "No Indians Allowed!"

Figure 18.1   *What does one look like? Portrait of the author, Debra L. Merskin, who is half Cherokee, half Polish.*

The Cherokee family moved from Hot Springs to the mountains, quietly farmed, and quietly buried their ethnicity with the first planting.

For as long as I can remember, stories of poverty and shame colored our conversations. There is a rich oral tradition in these mountains that weaves fanciful yarns and practical prose. Very little is written. Very few could write. Many more stories were kept hidden, identities concealed. My mother's stories of growing up in the South of the 1930s have survived, though without any tangible evidence of the past, such as photographs, diaries, or letters.

There were several attempts to draw my family into native culture. My grandmother tells me of the time that a group of Indians was traveling through the countryside. A woman asked her, "Why don't you come with us to Oklahoma and claim your share?" It was hard to hide. In 1961, when I was three years old, my mother and her brothers did just that—set off to find out what this homesteading was all about. The stake was land in Oklahoma that the U.S. government was willing to give the Cherokee for homesteading. My mother came back in disgust. It was better, she said, to remain in the hills, without heat or plumbing, than to accept this offering. She came back with something else as well. She presented me with a pair of tiny beaded moccasins, instructing me to keep them safe, to hide them away.

My mother lived with a great deal of shame. Shame about what she looked like, shamed by her lack of school-learning and her life. I wasn't her first baby. She carried a heavy burden. So heavy that I felt the weight, too. When given a choice to be raised in the white society of my father or in my mother's mountain community, I chose white. It seemed safer. It was. I have her face and his hair. It's the hair that does it, you see. You can't be fair-haired and be an Indian. It's not allowed, at least according to white standards. It's too confusing. "Passing" is threatening. Definitions of appropriate physical appearance form a specific function in American society, created to service the status quo by keeping things orderly. If a person varies from what's considered to be the standard, it confuses things.

No one has ever asked if I have white blood. People often assume I am white— only white. That's understandable. All the information we're given in society would lead anyone to believe that based on how I look, that's all there is to me. So, OK, we don't have the time to inquire. Anyway, who would? Isn't it obvious? No. People base these assumptions on their own experiences. If they've met one, they've met them all. Maybe you don't notice because you've never had to. When you see a white person in the subway or the supermarket, do you ever feel a tug, an impulse to go up to that person and say, "Are you white? You are? What's it been like for you?"[2]

There are particular physical characteristics attributed to "Indianness"—coarse, straight black hair; ruddy complexion; high cheekbones; a pronounced nose. Indians have a propensity to wear loincloths and buckskin, feathers in the hair, and lots and lots of beads. Indians, of course, can't hold their liquor; they have a mean streak, are oversexed or lazy. Europeans first associated America with the Indian woman. Pocahontas. Sacagawea. Women are either the Land O'Lakes maiden— Sue Bee–honey types, seductive and sensual, women of the earth—or the asexual roly-poly Marilyn-type squaw.[3] These are images from the past. These are also the limiting images of the present, as modern-day Indians are not permitted to exist side-by-side with whites, existing only in cultural representations of the past.

The images also apply to mixed-race women—perhaps even more so. Although genes fall where they may, even those with mixed parentage are expected to look like one. But I don't. As a mixed-blood woman I am suspect, walking a narrow trail between worlds. It's ironic: I carry the blood of oppressor and oppressed. Sometimes the combination burns in my veins. Not fitting a stereotype carries its own kind of burden, but being invisible carries its own kind of pain.

There is a sense of racial dishonesty associated with claims of Indianness. Certainly there have been those individuals who hopped on the diversity bandwagon, having suddenly discovered Indian grandmothers. Wannabees. This results, more than ever, in a cultural pressure to *prove* it. I only know that I am what I am— proud. I ask for nothing from others. Nothing, that is, except acceptance.

I've made some shy attempts to reach into this part of myself. My own visions of what I should look like/be/do/see/ cloud my eyes. At gatherings I'm afraid somehow I'm wrong, that I'll have to defend myself for something I don't understand, for something I'm looking to reclaim.

Ten years ago my mother died, and along with her, some validation of my feelings. My aging grandmother occasionally tells stories of what it was like before.

But soon there will be no one left to tell the tales. No one wrote it down. I'd like to share in that remembering. I can look at my tiny moccasins, twirl the little beads around, but I can never, ever, wear them.

> What are you?
> What a strange combination!
> I've heard of that. I've just never met one.
> Doesn't it bother you, what people might think?
> You don't look like one.
> What does *one* look like?

Notes

1. Gloria Anzaldua, ed., *Making Face, Making Soul: Creative and Critical Perspectives by Women of Color* (San Francisco: Aunt Lute Foundation, 1990), p. xv.

2. Claire Huang Kinsley, "Questions People Have Asked Me: Questions I Have Asked Myself," in *Miscegenation Blues,* ed. Carol Camper (Toronto: Sister Vision, 1994), p. 118.

3. Marilyn is a character on the CBS television program *Northern Exposure.* Squaw: "An Algonquian word for a married or mature woman that later became a demeaning term for all Indian women, Algonquian or not." In Rayna Green, *Women in American Indian Society* (New York: Chelsea House Publishers, 1992), p. 14.

Bibliography

"Across Arizona." (1990). In *The West: A Collection from Harper's Magazine*. New York: Gallery Books.

Ahern, W. H. (1983). "'The Returned Indians': Hampton Institute and Its Indian Alumni, 1879–1893." *Journal of Ethnic Studies* 10 (4):101–124.

———. (1986). "'To Kill the Indian and Save the Man': The Boarding School and American Indian Education." In L. Remele, ed., *Fort Totten: Military Post and Indian School, 1867–1959*. Bismarck: State Historical Society of North Dakota.

Akens, H. M., and V. P. Brown. (1967). *Alabama Heritage*. Huntsville, Ala.: Strode.

Albers, P. C., and W. R. James. (1984). "Utah's Indians and Popular Photography in the American West: A View from the Picture Post Card." *Utah Historical Quarterly* 52 (winter):72–91.

Aleiss, A. (1991). "Le Bon Sauvage: *Dances with Wolves* in the Romantic Tradition." *American Indian Culture and Research Journal* 15 (4):91–95.

Alger, W. R. ([1877] 1972). *Life of Edwin Forrest, the American Tragedian*. 2 vols. Reprint, New York: Benjamin Blom.

Annual Report of the Board of Indian Commissioners to the Secretary of the Interior for 1905. (1906). Washington, D.C.: Government Printing Office.

Annual Report of the Commissioner of Indian Affairs to the Secretary of the Interior for the Year 1881. (1881). Washington, D.C.: Government Printing Office.

Anzaldua, G., ed. (1990). *Making Face, Making Soul: Creative and Critical Perspectives by Women of Color*. San Francisco: Aunt Lute Foundation.

Atal, Y. (1981). "The Call for Indigenization." *International Social Science Journal* 33: 189–197.

Ayers, E. L. (1992). *The Promise of the New South: Life After Reconstruction*. New York: Oxford University Press.

Badger, J. E., Jr. (1876). *Left-Handed Pete, the Double Knife: Or, the Princess of the Everglades*. New York: Beadle and Adams.

Baine, R. M. (1992). "Notes and Documents: Myths of Mary Musgrove." *Georgia Historical Quarterly* 76 (2):428–435.

Baird, G. W. (1891). "General Miles's Indian campaigns." *Century Magazine*, July, 351–370.

Baker, R. S. (1905). "Lynching in the South." *McClure's*, 24 January, 302.

Ball, Z. (1950). *Joe Panther*. New York: Holiday House.

Ballantine, B. et al. (1993). *The Native Americans*. Atlanta: Turner Publishing.

Banks, Rosemarie K. (1993). "Staging the 'Native': Making History in American Theatre Culture, 1828–1838." *Theatre Journal* 15 (4) (December):461–486.

Barry, K. (1993). *Reflections: Ephemera from Trades, Products, and Events*, vol. 1. Brattleboro, Vt.: Iris Publishing.

——. (1994). *Reflections: Ephemera from Trades, Products, and Events,* vol. 2. Brattleboro, Vt.: Iris Publishing.

Bartram, W. ([1791] 1958). *Travels of William Bartram,* ed. Francis Harper. Reprint, New Haven: Yale University Press.

Beidler, P. G. (1991). "The Contemporary Indian Romance: A Review Essay." *American Indian Culture and Research Journal* 15 (4):97–125.

Berkebile, J. L. (1926). *Musa Isle: Stories About the Seminoles, Alligators, and Florida's Most Noted Indian Trading Post.* Augusta, Ga.: Phoenix Printing Company.

Berkhofer, R. F., Jr. (1979). *The White Man's Indian: Images of the American Indian from Columbus to the Present.* New York: Vintage Books.

Berkowitz, D., and D. W. Beach. (1993). "News Sources and News Context: The Effect of Routine News, Conflict, and Proximity." *Journalism Quarterly* 70 (1):4–12.

Betcher, R. W., and W. S. Pollack. (1993). *In a Time of Fallen Heroes.* New York: Guilford Press.

Bhabha, H. (1983). "The Other Question: The Stereotype and Colonial Discourse." *Screen* 24 (6):18–36.

——. (1991). "Conference Presentation." In P. Mariani, ed., *Critical Fictions.* Seattle: Bay Press.

——. (1994). *The Location of Culture.* London and New York: Routledge.

Bingham, A. (1970). *Mashpee: Land of the Wampanoags.* Falmouth, Mass.: Kendall Printing Co.

Bird, S. E. (1992). *For Enquiring Minds: A Cultural Study of Supermarket Tabloids.* Knoxville: University of Tennessee Press.

——. (1994). "Is That Me, Baby: Image, Authenticity, and the Career of Bruce Springsteen." *American Studies* 35 (2):39–58.

——. (In press). "Cultural Studies and Confluence: The Convergence of Folklore and Media Studies." In *Popular Culture Theory and Methodology,* ed. H. E. Hinds, Jr. Bowling Green, Ohio: Popular Press.

Blackman, M. B. (1980). "Posing the American Indian." *Natural History* 89 (10) (October):68–74.

Blake, M. (1988). *Dances with Wolves.* New York: Fawcett Gold Medal Book.

Blakey, M. L. (1990). "American Nationality and Ethnicity in the Depicted Past." In P. Gathercole and D. Lowenthal, eds., *The Politics of the Past.* London: Unwin Hyman.

Bodnar, J. (1992). *Remaking America: Public Memory, Commemoration, and Patriotism in the Twentieth Century.* Princeton: Princeton University Press.

Bordwell, D., J. Staiger, and K. Thompson. (1985). *The Classical Hollywood Cinema: Film Style and Mode of Production to 1960.* New York: Columbia University Press.

Boughton, W. A. (1947). *Everglades Adventure.* Boston: Bruce Humphries.

Bourne, R. (1990). *The Red King's Rebellion: Racial Politics in New England, 1675–1678.* Oxford: Oxford University Press.

Brand, S. (1988). "Indians and the Counterculture, 1960s–1970s." In *Handbook of North American Indians: History of Indian-White Relations,* vol. 4, ed. W. E. Washburn. Washington, D.C.: Smithsonian Institution Press.

Brannon, P. A. (1921a). "Macon County: Present Day Place Names Suggesting Aboriginal Influence." *Arrow Points* 5 (1):5–9.

——. (1921b). "Tallapoosa County: Present Day Place Names Suggest Aboriginal Influence." *Arrow Points* 5 (6):104–108.

———. (1922). "Alabama Postoffice and Stream Names, 1922." *Arrow Points* 6 (1):3–7.

Brantlinger, P. (1988). *Rule of Darkness: British Literature and Imperialism, 1830–1914.* Ithaca: Cornell University Press.

Brauer, R., and D. Brauer. (1975). *The Horse, the Gun, and the Piece of Property.* Bowling Green, Ohio: Bowling Green University Popular Press.

Broderick, J. K. (1982). *Charles M. Russell: American Artist.* St. Louis: Jefferson National Expansion Historical Association.

Brooks, T., and E. Marsh. (1992). *The Complete Directory to Prime-Time Network TV Shows: 1946 to Present.* New York: Ballantine Books.

Brown, J.S.H., and M. Matthews. (1993). "Fair Wind: Medicine and Consolation on the Berens River." *Journal of the Canadian Historical Association* 4:55–74.

Brownlow, K. (1979). *The War, the West, and the Wilderness.* New York: Alfred A. Knopf.

Bruner, E. M. (1989). "Tourism, Creativity, and Authenticity." *Studies in Symbolic Interaction* 10:109–114.

Calloway, C. G. (1992). *North Country Captives.* Hanover, N.H.: University Press of New England.

Camper, C., ed. (1994). *Miscegenation Blues.* Toronto: Sister Vision.

Capron, L. (1956). "Florida's 'Wild' Indians, the Seminole." *National Geographic Magazine* 123:819–840.

———. (1969). "Florida's Emerging Seminoles." *National Geographic Magazine* 136:716–734.

Carter, J. et al. (1984). *Eyewitness at Wounded Knee.* Lincoln: University of Nebraska Press.

Castillo, E. D. (1991). Review of *Dances with Wolves. Film Quarterly* 44:14–23.

Catlin, G. (1841). *North American Indians, Being Letters and Notes on Their Manners, Customs, Written During the Eight Years Travel Amongst the Wildest Tribes of Indians in America,* vol. 1. Edinburgh: J. Grant.

Churchill, W., N. S. Hill, and M. J. Barlow. (1979). "An Historical Overview of Twentieth Century Native American Athletics." *Indian Historian* 12 (4):22–32.

Clifford, J., and G. E. Marcus, eds. (1986). *Writing Culture: The Poetics and Politics of Ethnography.* Berkeley: University of California Press.

Clinton, T. (1921). "Emigration of the Creek Indians, 1836–37." *Arrow Points* 3 (6):3.

Coates, K., and F. McGuinness. (1985). *Pride of the Land: An Affectionate History of Brandon's Agricultural Exhibitions.* Winnipeg, Manitoba: Peguis Publishers.

Cockran, D. (1962). *The Cherokee Frontier, 1540–1783.* Norman: University of Oklahoma Press.

Cohen, E. (1979). "A Phenomenology of Tourist Experiences." *Sociology* 13:179–201.

Coleman, C. L. (1994). "An Examination of the Relationship of Structural Pluralism, News Role, and Source Use with Framing in the Context of a Community Controversy." Ph.D. diss., University of Wisconsin, Madison.

———. (1995). "Science, Technology, and Risk Coverage of a Community Conflict." *Media, Culture, and Society* 17:65–79.

Coleman, M. (1993). *American Indian Children at School: 1850–1930.* Jackson: University of Mississippi Press.

Colin, S. (1987). "The Wild Man and the Indian in Early 16th Century Book Illustration." In C. F. Feest, ed., *Indians and Europe.* Herodot, Netherlands: Rader Verlag.

Condit, C. M. (1989). "The Rhetorical Limits of Polysemy." *Critical Studies in Mass Communication* 6 (2):103–122.

Cooper, J. F. (1962). *The Last of the Mohicans.* New York: Signet.

Corner, G., ed. (1948). *The Autobiography of Benjamin Rush: His "Travels Through Life" Together with His Commonplace Book for 1789–1813.* Princeton: Princeton University Press.

Cory, C. B. (1896). *Hunting and Fishing in Florida.* Boston: Estes and Lauriat.

Covington, J. W. (1979). "Trail Indians of Florida." *Florida Historical Quarterly* 58:37–57.

———. (1993). *The Seminoles of Florida.* Gainesville: University Press of Florida.

Crevecoeur, J.H.S. (1968). *Letters from an American Farmer.* Gloucester, Mass.: Peter Smith.

Cro, S. (1990). *The Noble Savage: Allegory of Freedom.* Waterloo, Ontario: Wilfrid Laurier University Press.

Darrah, W. (1977). *The World of Stereographs.* Gettysburg, Pa.: W. C. Darrah, Publisher.

Dauenhauer, N. M., and R. Dauenhauer, eds. (1990). *Haa Tuwunaagu Yis, for Healing Our Spirit: Tlingit Oratory.* Seattle: University of Washington Press.

———. (1994). *Haa Kusteeyi, Our Culture: Tlingit Life Stories.* Seattle: University of Washington Press.

Davidson, H. G. (1985). *Jimmy Swinnerton: The Artist and His Work.* New York: Hearst Books.

Dellin, G. (1995). *Comanche Rain.* New York: Avon Books.

Deloria, P. J. (1994). "Playing Indian: Otherness and Authenticity in the Assumption of American Indian Identity." Ph.D. diss., Yale University.

Deloria, V. (1974). *The Indian Affair.* New York: Friendship Press.

———. (1988). *Custer Died for Your Sins: An Indian Manifesto.* Norman: University of Oklahoma Press.

Dench, A. E. (1915). *Making the Movies.* New York: Macmillan.

Derrida, J. (1980). *Of Grammatology.* Baltimore: Johns Hopkins University Press.

———. (1986). "Difference." In M. Taylor, ed., *Deconstruction in Context.* Chicago: University of Chicago Press.

Deutelbaum, M. (1983). "Structuring Patterning in the Lumière Films." In J. Fell, ed., *Film Before Griffith,.* Berkeley: University of California Press.

Dimock, A. W. (1912). *Be Prepared: or, the Boy Scouts in Florida.* New York: Grosset and Dunlap, Publishers.

Dippie, B. W. (1982). *Remington and Russell.* Austin: University of Texas Press.

———. (1982). *The Vanishing American: White Attitudes and U.S. Indian Policy.* Lawrence: University Press of Kansas.

Dirks, N., ed. (1992). *Colonialism and Culture.* Ann Arbor: University of Michigan Press.

———. (summer 1913). *The Rodman Wanamaker Expedition of Citizenship to the North American Indian: Address of the President of the United States and Other Messages.* Department of Library Services, Special Collections, American Museum of Natural History.

———. (summer and autumn 1913). *The Purpose and Achievements of the Rodman Wanamaker Expedition of Citizenship to the North American Indian.* Department of Library Services, Special Collections, American Museum of Natural History.

Dixon, J. K. (1909). *Wanamaker Primer on the North American Indian.* Philadelphia: Wanamaker Originator.

———. (1913). *The Vanishing Race.* New York: Doubleday Page and Company.

Dorris, M. (1993). *Working Men.* New York: Henry Holt.

Douglas, M. S. (1947). *The Everglades: River of Grass.* New York: Rinehart and Company.

Dow, Bonnie. (Forthcoming). *Prime Time Feminism: Television, Media Culture, and the Women's Movement Since 1970.* Philadelphia: University of Pennsylvania Press.

Downs, D. (1981). "Coppinger's Tropical Gardens: The First Commercial Indian Village in Florida." *Florida Anthropologist* 34 (4):225–231.

Doxtator, D. (1992). *Fluffs and Feathers: An Exhibit on the Symbols of Indianness, a Resource Guide.* Rev. ed. Brantford, Ontario: Woodland Cultural Centre.

Drinnon, R. (1980). *Facing West: The Metaphysics of Indian Hating and Empire Building.* Minneapolis: University of Minnesota Press.

Edelman, M. (1967). *The Symbolic Uses of Politics.* Urbana: University of Illinois Press.

Edmunds, D. (1983). *The Shawnee Prophet.* Lincoln and London: University of Nebraska Press.

Edwards, C. (1993). *Savage Sunrise.* New York: Leisure Books.

Edwards, E., ed. (1992). *Anthropology and Photography.* New Haven: Yale University Press.

Ellis, E. S. (1899). *Osceola, Chief of the Seminoles.* New York: E. P. Dutton.

Ely, W. M. (1910). *The Boy Chums in the Forest; or, Hunting for Plume Birds in the Florida Everglades.* New York: A. L. Burt Company.

———. (1914). *The Boy Chums Cruising in Florida Waters; or, the Perils and Dangers of the Fishing Fleet.* New York: A. L. Burt Company.

———. (1915). *The Boy Chums in the Florida Jungle; or, Charlie West and Walter Hazard with the Seminole Indians.* New York: A. L. Burt Company.

Emerson, W. C. (1954). *The Seminoles: Dwellers of the Everglades.* New York: Exposition Press.

Fabio. (1995). *Comanche.* New York: Avon Books.

Fentress, J., and C. Wickham. (1992). *Social Memory.* Oxford: Blackwell.

Ferguson, R. et al., eds. (1990). *Out There: Marginalization and Contemporary Culture.* Cambridge: MIT Press.

Fiedler, L. A. (1968). *The Return of the Vanishing American.* New York: Stein and Day.

Fishman, M. (1980). *Manufacturing the News.* Austin: University of Texas Press.

Fiske, J. (1987). *Television Culture.* London: Methuen.

———. (1988). "Meaningful Moments." *Critical Studies in Mass Communication* 5: 246–251.

———. (1989). *Understanding Popular Culture.* New York: Routledge.

Fleming, P., and J. Luskey. (1986). *The North American Indians in Early Photographs.* New York: Harper and Row.

Foucault, M. (1980). *Power/Knowledge: Selected Interviews and Other Writings, 1972–1977.* New York: Pantheon Books.

Fowler, D. D., and C. S. Fowler, eds. (1971). "Anthropology of the Numa: John Wesley Powell's Manuscripts on the Numic Peoples of Western North America, 1868–1880." *Smithsonian Contributions to Anthropology* 14.

Francis, D. (1992). *The Imaginary Indian: The Image of the Indian in Canadian Culture.* Vancouver, British Columbia: Arsenal Pulp Press.

Freire, P. (1990). *Pedagogy of the Oppressed.* New York: Continuum Press.

Freud, S. (1959). *The Standard Edition of the Complete Psychological Works of Sigmund Freud.* London: Hogarth Press.

Gable, E., and R. Handler. (1994). "The Authority of Documents at Some American History Museums." *Journal of American History* 81:119–136.

Gable, E., R. Handler, and A. Lawson. (1992). "On the Uses of Relativism: Fact, Conjecture, and Black and White Histories at Colonial Williamsburg." *American Ethnologist* 19:791–805.

Gamson, W. A., and A. Modigliani. (1989). "Media Discourse and Public Opinion on Nuclear Power: A Constructionist Approach." *American Journal of Sociology* 95 (1):1–37.

Garbarino, M. S. (1972). *Big Cypress: A Changing Seminole Community.* Prospect Heights, Ill.: Waveland Press.

———. (1989). *The Seminole.* New York: Chelsea House Publishers.

Gardner, J. C. (1983). *An Annotated Bibliography of Florida Fiction, 1801–1980.* St. Petersburg, Fla.: Little Bayou Press.

Gates, H., ed. (1985). *Race, Writing, and Difference.* Chicago: University of Chicago Press.

Gedicks, A. et al. (1982). *Land Grab: The Corporate Theft of Wisconsin's Mineral Resources.* Madison, Wis.: Center for Alternative Mining Development Policy.

Geertz, C. (1973). "Thick Description: Toward an Interpretive Theory of Culture." In C. Geertz, *The Interpretation of Cultures.* New York: Basic Books.

Geller, P. (1994). "Creating Corporate Images of the Fur Trade: The Hudson's Bay Company and Public Relations in the 1930s." In J.S.H. Brown, W. J. Eccles, and D. P. Heldman, eds., *The Fur Trade Revisited: Selected Papers of the Sixth North American Fur Trade Conference.* East Lansing: Michigan State University Press.

Gerrish, T. (1887). *Life in the World's Wonderland.* Biddeford, Maine: Biddeford Journal.

Gerson, M. (1980). "Minority Representation in Network Television Drama, 1970–1976." *Mass Communication Review* (fall):10–16.

Gifford, J. (1911). *The Everglades and Other Essays Relating to Southern Florida.* Miami, Fla.: Everglades Land Sales Co.

Gillis, J. R., ed. (1994). *Commemorations: The Politics of National Identity.* Princeton: Princeton University Press.

Gitlin, T. (1980). *The Whole World Is Watching: Mass Media in the Making and Unmaking of the New Left.* Berkeley: University of California Press.

———. (1983). *Inside Prime Time.* New York: Pantheon Books.

Godsell, P. H. (1934). *Arctic Trader: The Account of Twenty Years with the Hudson's Bay Company.* New York: Putnam's Sons.

Goetzmann, W. (1966). *Exploration and Empire: The Explorer and the Scientist in the Winning of the American West.* New York: W. W. Norton.

Goffmann, E. (1974). *Frame Analysis: An Essay on the Organization of Experience.* New York: Harper and Row.

———. (1979). *Gender Advertisements.* New York: Harper and Row.

Good Medicine: The Illustrated Letters of Charles M. Russell. (1929). New York: Doubleday.

Graburn, Nelson H. H., ed. (1976). *Ethnic and Tourist Arts.* Berkeley: University of California Press.

Green, R. (1974). "The Only Good Indian: The Image of the Indian in American Vernacular Culture." Ph.D. diss., Indiana University.

———. (1975). "The Pocahontas Perplex: The Image of Indian Women in American Culture." *Massachusetts Review* 16 (4):698–714.

———. (1988). "The Tribe Called Wannabee: Playing Indian in America and Europe." *Folklore* 99 (1):30–55.

———. (1992). *Women in American Indian Society.* New York: Chelsea House Publishers.

Greenberg, B. S., and C. Heeter. (1983). "Television and Social Stereotypes." In J. Sprafkin, C. Swift, and R. Hess, eds., *Rx Television: Enhancing the Preventative Impact of TV*. New York: Haworth Press.

Greenberg, M., ed. (1994). *The Tony Hillerman Companion*. New York: HarperCollins.

Greer, S. (1993). "The Noble Savage." *Winds of Change* (spring):89–92.

Griffin, R. J., and S. Dunwoody. (1992). *Press Coverage of Risk from Environmental Contaminants*. United States Environmental Protection Agency, CR-817599-01-0, Washington, D.C.

Gross, B. D. (1985). "Edwin Forrest, *Metamora*, and the Indian Removal Act of 1830." *Theatre Journal* (May):181–191.

Grounds, R. (1995). *Tallahassee and the Name Game*. Ph.D diss., Princeton Theological Seminary.

Guha, R., and G. Spivak, eds. (1988). *Selected Subaltern Studies*. New York: Oxford University Press.

Gurnee, C. G. et al. (1990). "Substance Abuse Among American Indians in an Urban Treatment Program." *American Indian and Alaska Native Mental Health Research* 3 (3):17–26.

Habermas, J. (1984). *The Theory of Communicative Action*. Vol. 1, *Reason and the Rationalization of Society*, Thomas McCarthy, trans. Boston: Beacon Press.

———. (1988). *On the Logic of the Social Sciences*. Cambridge: MIT Press.

Hall, S. (1981). "Notes on Deconstructing the Popular." In *People's History and Socialist Theory*, ed. R. Samuel. London: Routledge.

Harmon, A. (1990). "When Is an Indian Not an Indian? The 'Friends of the Indian' and the Problems of Indian Identity." *Journal of Ethnic Studies* 18 (2):95–123.

Harris, T. (1984). *Exorcising Blackness: Historical and Literary Lynching and Burning Rituals*. Bloomington: Indiana University Press.

Harrison, G. B. (1889). *Edwin Forrest: The Actor and the Man*. Brooklyn, N.Y.: Brooklyn Eagle Book Printing Dept.

Harrison, L. R. (1912). "The Bison-101 Headliners: Critical Review of the New York Motion Picture Company's Series of Two-Reel Subjects." *Motion Picture World*, 27 April, 320–322.

Hart, R. L. (1987). "Changing Exhibitionary and Sensitivity: The Custer Battlefield Museum." *First Annual Symposium, Custer Battlefield and Museum Association, Hardin*. Crow Agency, Mont.: Custer Battlefield Historical and Museum Association.

Hartley, J. (1982). *Understanding News*. London: Routledge.

Harvard Encyclopedia of American Ethnic Groups (1980). Cambridge: Harvard University Press.

Hassrick, R. B. (1964). *The Sioux: Life and Customs of a Warrior Society*. Norman: University of Oklahoma Press.

Hatley, M. T. (1989). "The Dividing Paths: The Encounters of the Cherokees and the South Carolinians in the Southern Mountains, 1670–1785." Ph.D diss., Duke University.

Hawkins, B. (1980). "A Sketch of the Creek Country in the Years 1798 and 1799." In *Letters, Journals, and Writings of Benjamin Hawkins*, vol. 1, ed. C. L. Grant. Savannah, Ga.: Beehive Press.

Herman, E., and N. Chomsky. (1988). *Manufacturing Consent: The Political Economy of the Mass Media*. New York: Pantheon.

Hertzberg, H. W. (1971). *The Search for an American Indian Identity.* New York: Syracuse University Press.

Hillerman, T. (1980). *People of Darkness.* New York: Harper and Row.

Himmelstein, H. (1984). *Television Myth and the American Mind.* New York: Praeger.

Hinsley, C. M. (1979). "Anthropology as Science and Politics: The Dilemmas of the Bureau of American Ethnology, 1879 to 1904." In W. R. Goldschmidt, *Uses of Anthropology.* Washington, D.C.: American Anthropological Association.

———. (1991). "The World as Market-place: Commodification of the Exotic at the World's Columbian Exposition." In I. Karp and S. B. Lavine, eds., *Exhibiting Cultures: The Poetics and Politics of Museum Display.* Washington, D.C.: Smithsonian Institution Press.

Hoebel, E. A. (1960). *The Cheyennes: Indians of the Great Plains.* New York: Holt, Rinehart and Winston.

Holm, B., and G. I. Quimby. (1980). *Edward S. Curtis in the Land of the War Canoes: A Pioneer Cinematographer in the Pacific Northwest Coast.* Seattle: University of Washington Press.

Holmes, O. W. (1859). "The Stereoscope and the Stereograph." *Atlantic Monthly,* June, 738–748.

Honour, H. (1975). *The New Golden Land: European Images of America from the Discoveries to the Present Time.* New York: Pantheon.

Hooper, J. J. (1993). *Adventures of Captain Simon Suggs, Late of the Tallapoosa Volunteers; Together with "Taking the Census" and Other Alabama Sketches.* Tuscaloosa: University of Alabama Press.

Hulme, J. (1990). *The Enlightenment and Its Shadows.* New York: Routledge.

Hutchinson, T. ([1764] 1936). *The History of the Colony and Province of Massachusetts-Bay,* vol 1, ed. L. Mayo. Reprint, Cambridge: Harvard University Press.

Hutton, L. (1891). *Curiosities of the American Stage.* New York: Harper and Brothers.

Hyer, S. (1990). *One House, One Voice, One Heart: Native American Education at the Santa Fe Indian School.* Santa Fe: Museum of New Mexico Press.

Irving, W. (1854). "Philip of Pokanoket." In *The Works of Washington Irving.* 10 vols. London: Henry G. Boker.

Jacknis, I. (1984). "Franz Boas and Photography." *Studies in the Anthropology of Visual Communication* 10:1.

———. (1992). "George Hunt, Kwakiutl Photographer." In E. Edwards, ed., *Anthropology and Photography.* New Haven: Yale University Press.

Jackson, R. G. (1987). *An Oral History of the Battle of the Little Bighorn from the Perspective of the Northern Cheyenne Descendants.* 3 vols. Washington, D.C.: Government Printing Office.

Jacobs, W. R. (1972). *Dispossessing the American Indian.* New York: Scribner's.

James, G. W. (1902). "The Snake Dance of the Hopis." *Camera Craft* 1 (1) (November): 3–10.

Jameson, F. (1979). "Reification and Utopia in Mass Culture." *Social Text* 1:130–148.

JanMohamed, A. (1985). "The Economy of Manichean Allegory: The Function of Racial Difference in Colonialist Literature." In H. L. Gates, ed., *Race, Writing, and Differences,* Chicago: University of Chicago Press.

Jay, R. (1987). *The Trade Card in Nineteenth-Century America.* Columbia: University of Missouri Press.

Jefferson, J. (1889). *The Autobiography of Joseph Jefferson.* New York: Century Co.

Jenkins, H. (1992). *Textual Poachers: Television Fans and Participatory Culture.* New York: Routledge.

Johnson, W. F. (1891). *Life of Sitting Bull and the History of the Indian War of 1890–91.* New York: Edgewood.

Jojola, T. S. (1995). "Exhibition Reviews: A Zuni Artist Looks at Frank Hamilton Cushing: Cartoons by Phil Hughte." *Museum Anthropology* 19 (1):54–56.

———. (1995). "Some Preliminary Notes on *Pocahontas.*" *American Indian Libraries Newsletter* 18 (1) (fall 1995):1–3.

Jones, D. K. (1980). *A Century of Servitude: Pribilof Aleuts Under U.S. Rule.* Landham, Md.: University Press of America.

Jones, E. (1988). *Native Americans as Shown on the Stage, 1753–1916.* Metuchen, N.J.: Scarecrow Press.

Jones, Sally L. (1992). "The Original Character of Edwin Forrest and his American Style." Ph.D. diss., University of Toronto.

Jordan, P. L. (1992). *Premier Contact—Premier Regard.* Marseilles: Musées de Marseille.

Jorgensen, J. G. (1984). "Land Is Cultural, So Is a Commodity: The Locus of Differences Among Indians, Cowboys, Sod-Busters, and Environmentalists." *Journal of Ethnic Studies* 12 (3):1–21.

"The Kachinas Sing of Doom." (1992). In "NFL SuperPro," *Marvel Comicbooks* 1 (6) (March).

Kammen, M. (1993). *Mystic Chords of Memory: The Transformation of Tradition in American Culture.* New York: Vintage.

Kaplan, A., and D. E. Pease, eds. (1993). *Cultures of United States Imperialism.* Durham, N.C.: Duke University Press.

Karp, I., and S. B. Lavine, eds. (1991). *Exhibiting Cultures: The Poetics and Politics of Museum Display.* Washington, D.C.: Smithsonian Institution Press.

Kehoe, A. B. (1983). *The Ghost Dance: Ethnohistory and Revitalization.* New York: Holt, Rinehart and Winston.

Kersey, H. A., Jr. (1987). *The Seminole and Miccosukee Tribes: A Critical Bibliography.* Bloomington: Indiana University Press.

———. (1989). *The Florida Seminoles and the New Deal, 1933–1942.* Boca Raton: Florida Atlantic University Press.

Kingsolver, B. (1990). *Animal Dreams.* New York: HarperCollins.

Kinser, S. (1990). *Carnival American Style: Mardi Gras at New Orleans and Mobile.* Chicago: University of Chicago Press.

Kinsley, C. H. (1994). "Questions People Have Asked Me: Questions I Have Asked Myself." In *Miscegnation Blues,* ed. Carol Camper. Toronto: Sister Vision.

Kivlahan, D. et al. (1985). "Detoxification Recidivism Among Urban American Indian Alcoholics." *American Journal of Psychiatry* 142 (12):1467–1470.

Kizzia, T. (1991). *The Wake of the Unseen Object: Among the Native Cultures of Bush Alaska.* New York: Henry Holt and Company.

Kolodny, A. (1975). *The Lay of the Land: Metaphor as Experience and History in American Life and Letters.* Chapel Hill: University of North Carolina Press.

Koury, M. J., ed. (1978). *Custer Centennial Observances, 1976.* Fort Collins, Colo.: Old Army Press.

Kreyling, M. (1988). "Southern Literature: Consensus and Dissensus." *American Literature* 60 (1) (March):83–95.

Krippendorff, K. (1980). *Content Analysis: An Introduction to Its Methodology.* Newbury Park, Calif.: Sage Publications.

Krouse, S. A. (1987). "Filming the Vanishing Race." In J. Ruby and M. Taureg, eds., *Visual Explorations of the World: Selected Papers from the International Conference on Visual Communication.* Aatchen: Editions Heridot.

LaDuke, W. (1993). "A Society Based on Conquest Cannot Be Sustained: Native Peoples and the Environmental Crisis." In R. Hofrichter, ed., *Toxic Struggles: The Theory and Practice of Environmental Justice.* Philadelphia: New Society Publishers.

Lakoff, G., and M. Johnson. (1980). *Metaphors We Live By.* Chicago: University of Chicago Press.

L'Amour, L. (1986). *Last of the Breed.* New York: Bantam Books.

Landsman, G. H. (1987). "Indian Activism and the Press: Coverage of the Conflict at Ganienkeh." *Anthropological Quarterly* 60 (3):101–113.

Lasorsa, D. L., and S. D. Reese. (1990). "News Source Use in the Crash of 1987: A Study of Four National Media." *Journalism Quarterly* 67 (1):60–71.

Lawrence, D. H. (1923). *Studies in Classic American Literature.* New York: Viking Press.

Lears, J. (1994). *Fables of Abundance: A Cultural History of Advertising in America.* New York: Basic Books.

Lesley, C., ed. (1991). *Talking Leaves.* New York: Delta Books.

Levy, J. E., and S. J. Kunitz. (1974). *Indian Drinking: Navajo Practices and Anglo-American Theories.* New York: Wiley.

Lewis, C. S. (1960). *The Four Loves.* New York: Harcourt Brace.

Lewis, R.W.B. (1955). *The American Adam: Innocence, Tragedy, and Tradition in the Nineteenth Century.* Chicago: University of Chicago Press.

Lindsay, V. (1913). *The Art of the Moving Picture.* New York: Liveright.

Linenthal, E. T. (1991). "A Sore from America's Past That Has Not Yet Healed." In *Sacred Ground: Americans and Their Battlefields.* Urbana: University of Illinois Press.

———. (1994). "Committing History in Public." *Journal of American History* 81:986–991.

Lipsitz, G. (1990). *Time Passages: Collective Memory and American Popular Culture.* Minneapolis: University of Minnesota Press.

Lomawaima, K. Tsianina. (1993). "Domesticity in the Federal Indian Schools: The Power of Authority over Mind and Body." *American Ethnologist* 20:227–240.

———. (1994). *They Called It Prairie Light: The Story of Chilocco Indian School.* Lincoln: University of Nebraska Press.

Lutz, C. A., and J. L. Collins. (1993). *Reading National Geographic.* Chicago: University of Chicago Press.

Lyman, C. (1982). *The Vanishing Race and Other Illusions: Photography of Indians by Edward Curtis.* Washington, D.C.: Smithsonian Institution Press.

Lyotard, J. (1984). *The Postmodern Condition: A Report on Knowledge.* Minneapolis: University of Minnesota Press.

MacAndrew, C., and R. Edgerton. (1969). *Drunken Comportment.* Chicago: Aldine.

MacCannell, E. D. (1976). *The Tourist: A New Theory of the Leisure Class.* New York: Schocken.

———. (1979). "Ethnosemiotics." *Semiotica* 27:149–171.

———. (1992). *Empty Meeting Grounds: The Tourist Papers.* London: Routledge.

MacDonnel, D. (1986). *Theories of Discourse: An Introduction.* Cambridge: Basil Blackwell.

MacFarlane, W. G. (n.d.) *The Seminole Indians of Florida: Their Life and Customs in the Everglades: Florida Alligators.* Chicago: American Autochrome Co.

Maclean, N., and R. M. Utley. (1956). "Edward S. Luce." *Montana* 6 (3):51–55.

Malmsheimer, L. M. (1985). "'Imitation White Man': Images of Transformation at the Carlisle Indian School." *Studies in Visual Communication* 11 (4) (fall):54–75.

———. (1987). "Photographic Analysis as Ethnohistory: Interpretive Strategies." *Visual Anthropology* 1:21–36.

Mander, J. (1991). "What You Don't Know About Indians." *Utne Reader* (November/December):67–74.

Mani, L. (1987). "Contentious Traditions: The Debate on Sati in Colonial India." *Cultural Critique* 7:119–156.

Manzione, J. (1991). *"I Am Looking to the North for My Life," Sitting Bull, 1876–1881.* Salt Lake City: University of Utah Press.

Marsden, M. T., and J. Nachbar. (1988). "The Indian in the Movies." In *Handbook of North American Indians: History of Indian-White Relations,* vol. 4. Washington, D.C.: Smithsonian Institution Press.

Martin, J. W. (1991). *Sacred Revolt: The Muskogees' Struggle for a New World.* Boston: Beacon Press.

Martin-Barbero, J. (1993). *Communication, Culture, and Hegemony.* Newbury Park, Calif.: Sage Publications.

Mason, D. P. (1975). *Five Dollars a Scalp: The Last Mighty War Whoop of the Creek Indians.* Huntsville, Ala.: Strode.

Mason, Jeffrey. (1991). "The Politics of *Metamora.*" In *The Performance of Power,* ed. Sue-Ellen Case and Janelle Reinelt. Iowa City: University of Iowa Press.

Mason, P. G. (1990). "Deconstructing America." Ph.D. diss., Rijksuniversiteit Utrecht.

Mattiessen, P. (1984). *Indian Country.* New York: Penguin Books.

McBeth, S. (1984). "The Primer and the Hoe." *Natural History* 93 (8) (August):4–12.

McCannell, E. D. (1976). *The Tourist: A New Theory of the Leisure Class.* New York: Schocken.

———. (1992). *Empty Meeting Grounds: The Tourist Papers.* London: Routledge.

McChristian, D. C. (1992). "In Search of Custer Battlefield." *Montana* 42 (1):75–76.

McCoy, I. (1827). *The Practicability of Indian Reform: Embracing Their Colonization.* Boston: Lincoln and Edmands.

McCoy, M. (1993). *Montana: Off the Beaten Path.* Old Saybrook, Conn.: Globe Pequot Press.

McCracken, H. (1957). *The Charles M. Russell Book: The Life and Work of the Cowboy Artist.* Garden City, N.Y.: Doubleday.

McDowell, William, Jr., ed. (1958). *Documents Relating to Indian Affairs, May 21, 1750–August 7, 1754.* Columbia: South Carolina Archives Department.

McGee, W. J. (1904). "Strange Races of Men." *World's Work* 8 (1) (May):5185–5188.

McLoughlin, W. G. (1984). *Cherokees and Missionaries, 1789–1839.* New Haven: Yale University Press.

———. (1986). *Cherokee Renascence in the New Republic.* Princeton: Princeton University Press.

McNickel, D. (1973). *Native American Tribalism.* London: Oxford University Press.

McReynolds, E. C. (1957). *The Seminoles.* Norman: University of Oklahoma Press.

Mechling, J. (1987). "The Alligator." In *American Wildlife in Symbol and Story,* ed. A. K. Gillespie and J. Mechling. Knoxville: University of Tennessee Press.

Meek, A. B. ([1855] 1914). *The Red Eagle: A Poem of the South.* Reprint, Montgomery, Ala.: Paragon Press.

Mitchell, L. (1981). *Witnesses to a Vanishing America.* Princeton: Princeton University Press.

———. (1990). "William Richard Cross, Photographer on the Nebraska-South Dakota Frontier." *South Dakota History* 20:81–95.

Mitchell, T. (1988). *Colonising Egypt.* Cambridge: Cambridge University Press.

Molotch, H., and M. Lester. (1975). "Accidental News: The Great Oil Spill as Occurrence and National Event." *American Journal of Sociology* 81 (2):235–260.

Mooney, J. (1991). *The Ghost-Dance Religion and the Sioux Outbreak of 1890.* Lincoln: University of Nebraska Press.

Morgan, H. (1986). *Symbols of America.* New York: Viking Press.

Morley, D. (1986). *Family Power and Domestic Leisure.* London: Comedia.

Morris, R. C. (1994). *New Worlds from Fragments: Film, Ethnography, and the Representation of Northwest Coast Culture.* Boulder: Westview Press.

Morrison, T. (1993). *Playing in the Dark: Whiteness and the Literary Imagination.* New York: Vintage Books.

Moses, L. G. (1984). "Wild West Shows, Reformers, and the Image of the American Indian, 1887–1914." *South Dakota History* 14 (fall):193–221.

Mosher, J. (1985). *Liquor Legislation and Native Americans: History and Perspectives.* Berkeley Social (Alcohol) Research Group, Working Paper F 136. Berkeley: University of California.

Mourning Dove. (1990). *A Salishan Autobiography,* ed. J. Miller. Lincoln and London: University of Nebraska Press.

Murdoch, J. E. (1880). *The Stage.* Philadelphia: J. M. Stoddart and Co.

Murray, R. A. (1981). "Ghost-Herders on the Little Bighorn: The Custer Battlefield Story." Little Bighorn Battlefield National Monument Archives.

Musser, C. (1991). *Before the Nickelodeon.* Berkeley: University of California Press.

———. (1991). *High-Class Moving Pictures: Lyman H. Howe and the Forgotten Era of Traveling Exhibition, 1880–1920.* Princeton: Princeton University Press.

Namias, J. (1995). *White Captives.* Chapel Hill: University of North Carolina Press.

Nash, R. (1932). *Survey of the Seminole Indians of Florida.* Washington, D.C.: United States Department of Interior, Office of Indian Affairs.

Neill, W. T. (n.d.). *Ross Allen's Reptile Institute at Silver Springs.* Silver Springs, Fla.: Ross Allen Reptile Institute.

———. (1956). *The Story of Florida's Seminole Indians.* St. Petersburg, Fla.: Great Outdoors.

———. (1971). *The Last of the Ruling Reptiles: Alligators, Crocodiles, and Their Kin.* New York: Columbia University Press.

Nelson, R. K. (1983). *The Athabaskans: People of the Boreal Forest.* Fairbanks: University of Alaska Museum.

Noah, M. M. (1969). "She Would Be a Soldier." In R. Moody, ed., *Dramas from the American Theatre, 1762–1909.* Boston: Houghton Mifflin.

Nordstrom, A. D. (1993). "Some Photographs of Seminoles." In *Imag(in)ing the Seminole: Photographs and Their Uses Since 1880.* Daytona Beach, Fla.: Southeast Museum of Photography, Daytona Beach Community College.

Norkunas, M. K. (1993). *The Politics of Public Memory: Tourism, History, and Ethnicity in Monterey, California.* Albany: State University of New York Press.

Norman, G. (1995). "The Cherokee: Two Nations, One People." *National Geographic* 187 (5):72–97.

Ober, F. A. (1887). *The Knockabout Club in the Everglades.* Boston: Estes and Lauriat.

Odell, G.C.D. (1931). *Annals of the New York Stage.* Vol. 3. New York: Columbia University Press.

Olien, C. N., P. J. Tichenor, and G. A. Donohue. (1987). "Role of Mass Communication." In *Needs Assessment: Theory and Methods,* ed. D. E. Johnson et al. Ames: Iowa State University Press.

Omi, M., and H. Winant. (1986). *Racial Formation in the United States: From the 1960s to the 1980s.* London: Routledge.

Ong, A. (1987). *Spirits of Resistance and Capitalist Discipline.* New York: State University of New York Press.

An Oral History of the Battle of the Little Bighorn from the Perspective of the Northern Cheyenne Descendants. Vol. 1. (1987). Washington, D.C.: Government Printing Office.

Oriard, Michael. (1993). *Reading Football: How the Popular Press Created an American Spectacle.* Chapel Hill: University of North Carolina Press.

Ortiz, A. (1977). "The Dark Side of the Moon—Images of the Indian and the American Dream." Charles Charropin Memorial Lecture, Rockhurst College, Kansas City, April.

Parks, R. (1982). *The Western Hero in Film and Television: Mass Media Mythology.* Ann Arbor, Mich.: UMI Research Press.

Parrish, R. (1993). *The Dividing Line.* New York: Penguin.

Parsons, E. C. (1929–1930). *How They Began to Race For the Sun.* Forty-seventh Annual Report of the Bureau of American Ethnology. Washington, D.C.: Smithsonian Institution.

Pearce, R. (1965). *Savagism and Civilization.* Baltimore: Johns Hopkins Press.

Perdue, T. (1991). "Osceola: The White Man's Indian." *Florida Historical Quarterly* 70:475–488.

Phelps, H. P. (1972). *Players of a Century: A Record of the Albany Stage.* Albany, N.Y., 1880. Reprint, New York: Benjamin Blom.

Pickett, A. J. (1962). *History of Alabama, and Incidentally of Georgia and Mississippi, from the Earliest Period.* Birmingham, Ala.: Birmingham Book and Magazine Co.

Pleithman, I. M. (1957). *The Unconquered Seminole Indians.* St. Petersburg, Fla.: Great Outdoors.

Plough, A., and S. Krimsky. (1987). "The Emergence of Risk Communication Studies: Social and Political Context." *Science, Technology, and Human Values* 12 (3/4):4–10.

Pratt, R. H. (1964). *Battlefield and Classroom: Four Decades with the American Indian, 1867–1904,* ed. R. M. Utley. New Haven: Yale University Press.

Press, A. (1991). *Women Watching Television.* Philadelphia: University of Pennsylvania Press.

Query, J. (1985). "Comparative Admissions and Follow-up Study of American Indian and Whites in a Youth Chemical Dependency Unit on the Northern Central Plains." *International Journal of the Addictions* 3 (4):489–502.

Quinn, W. W., Jr. (1990). "The Southeast Syndrome: Notes on Indian Descendant Recruitment Organizations and Their Perceptions of Native American Culture." *American Indian Quarterly* 14 (2):147–154.

Ransome, J. B. (1838). *Osceola: Or Fact and Fiction: A Tale of the Seminole War.* New York: Harper and Bros.

Ray, A. J. (1988). "The Hudson's Bay Company and Native People." In *Handbook of North American Indians: History of Indian-White Relations,* vol. 4, ed. W. E. Washburn. Washington, D.C.: Smithsonian Institution Press.

Rickey, D., Jr. (1967). *History of Custer Battlefield.* Crow Agency, Mont.: Custer Battlefield Historical and Museum Association.

———. (1968). "The Establishment of Custer Battlefield National Monument." *Journal of the West* 8:203–216.

Ringer, B. B., and E. R. Lawless. (1989). *Race, Ethnicity, and Society.* London: Routledge.

Roach, J. (1992). "Mardi Gras Indians and Others: Genealogies of American Performance." *Theatre Journal* 44:461–483.

Roberts, T. (1991). "The Reconstruction of a Poet." *Mississippi Quarterly* 44 (spring): 203–207.

Robinson, H. B. (1952). "The Custer Battlefield Museum." *Montana* 2 (3):11–29.

Rogin, M. P. (1975). *Fathers and Children: Andrew Jackson and the Subjugation of the American Indian.* New York: Alfred A. Knopf.

———. (1987). *Ronald Reagan: The Movie, and Other Episodes in Political Demonology.* Berkeley: University of California Press.

Romera, L. (1991). "Vanishing Americans: Gender, Empire, and New Historicism." *American Literature* 63:385–404.

Rosaldo, R. (1989). "Imperialist Nostalgia." In *Culture and Truth: The Remaking of Social Analysis.* Boston: Beacon.

Rush, B. (1812). "An Account of the Vices Peculiar to the Indians of North America." In *Medical Inquiries and Observations upon the Diseases of the Mind,* ed. B. Rush. Philadelphia: Kimber and Richardson.

Russell, C. M. (1935). *Trails Plowed Under.* New York: Doubleday.

Said, E. (1978). *Orientalism.* New York: Vintage.

———. (1993). *Culture and Imperialism.* New York: Alfred Knopf.

Sanders, Lacey. (1991). "'Real Indians' at Red River: The Hudson's Bay Company's 250th Anniversary Pageant," Winnipeg.

Sanjek, R. (1993). "Anthropology's Hidden Colonialism: Assistants and Their Ethnographers." *Anthropology Today* 9 (2) (April):13–18.

Sarf, W. M. (1988). "Russell Means on Custer Hill." *American Spectator* 21 (12):32–34.

———. (1991). "Oscar Eaten by Wolves." *Film Comment* 27 (6):62–70.

Scaglioh, R. (1980). "The Plains Culture Area Concept." In *Anthropology of the Great Plains,* ed. W. R. Wood and M. Liberty. Lincoln: University of Nebraska Press.

Scherer, J. C. (1975). "You Can't Believe Your Eyes: Inaccuracies in Photographs of North American Indians." *Studies in the Anthropology of Visual Communication* 2 (2):67–79.

———. (1988). "The Public Faces of Sarah Winnemucca." *Cultural Anthropology* 3 (2) (May):78–204.

Schooling, W. (1920). *The Hudson's Bay Company, 1670–1920.* London: Hudson's Bay House.

Schwartz, B. (1991). "Social Change and Collective Memory." *American Sociological Review* 56:221–236.

Seggar, J. F., J. K. Hafen, and H. Hannonen-Gladden. (1981). "Television's Portrayals of Minorities and Women in Drama and Comedy Drama, 1971–1980." *Journal of Broadcasting* 25 (summer):277–288.

Shay, F. (1938). *Judge Lynch: His First Hundred Years.* New York: Ives Washburn.

Shiveley, J. (1992). "Cowboys and Indians: Perceptions of Western Films Among American Indians and Anglos." *American Sociological Review* 57:725–734.

Shoemaker, P. J. (1984). "Media Treatment of Deviant Political Groups." *Journalism Quarterly* 61:66–75, 82.

Simpson, A., and M. Simpson, eds. (1975). *Diary of King Philip's War, 1675–1676,* by Colonel Benjamin Church. Tiverton, R.I.: Lockwood Publications.

Skinner, A. (1915). "Across the Florida Everglades." *Atlantic, Gulf and West Indies Steamship News* 7:5.

Slagle, L., and J. Weibel-Orlando. (1986). "The Indian Shaker Church and Alcoholics Anonymous: Revivalistic Curing Cult." *Human Organization* 45 (4):310–319.

Slotkin, R. (1973). *Regeneration Through Violence: The Mythology of the American Frontier, 1600–1860.* Middletown, Conn.: Wesleyan University Press.

Smith, C. (1993). "News Sources and Power Elites in News Coverage of the Exxon Valdez Oil Spill." *Journalism Quarterly* 70 (2):393–403.

Smith, V. L. (1977). *Hosts and Guests: The Anthropology of Tourism.* Philadelphia: University of Pennsylvania Press.

Spurr, D. (1993). *The Rhetoric of Empire: Colonial Discourse in Journalism, Travel Writing, and Imperial Administration.* Durham, N.C. and London: Duke University Press.

Stevenson, A. (1958). *Virginia Dare: Mystery Girl.* New York: Bobbs-Merrill.

Stewart, O. C. (1977). "Contemporary Documents on Wovoka, Prophet of the Ghost Dance in 1890." *Ethnohistory* 24 (3):210–225.

Stoler, Ann Laura. (1992). "In Cold Blood: Hierarchies of Credibility and the Politics of Colonial Narratives." *Representations* 37:151–189.

Stone, E. (1988). *Black Sheep and Kissing Cousins: How Our Family Stories Shape Us.* New York: Penguin Books.

Stone, J. A. (1969). "Metamora, or the Last of the Wampanoags." In *Dramas from the American Theatre, 1762–1909,* ed. R. Moody. Boston: Houghton Mifflin.

Sturtevant, W. C. (1954). "The Medicine Bundles and Busks of the Florida Seminoles." *Florida Anthropologist* 7:31–70.

Sundquist, E. (1993). *To Wake the Nations: Race in the Making of American Literature.* Cambridge: Harvard University Press.

Swinnerton, J. (1923). *Canyon Country Kiddies.* New York: Doubleday.

Szasz, M. C. (1977). *Education and the American Indian: The Road to Self-Determination Since 1928.* Albuquerque: University of New Mexico Press.

———. (1989). "Listening to the Native Voice." *Montana: The Magazine of Western History* 39 (3):42–53.

Takaki, R. (1993). *A Different Mirror: A History of Multicultural America.* Boston, Toronto, London: Little, Brown.

Taussig, M. (1992). *The Nervous System.* New York: Routledge.

Terrace, V. (1976). *The Complete Encyclopedia of Television Programs: 1947–1976.* 2 vols. New York: S. S. Barnes.

Terry, A. (1881). *Report of the Secretary of War.* Washington, D.C.: Government Printing Office.

Thoreau, H. D. (1973). *The Illustrated Walden: With Photographs from the Gleason Collection.* Princeton: Princeton University Press.

————. (1989). *The Maine Woods*. New York: Harry N. Abrams.

Thornton, R. (1986). *We Shall Live Again: The 1870 and 1890 Ghost Dance Movements as Demographic Revitalization*. Minneapolis: University of Minnesota.

————. (1991). "The Demography of the Trail of Tears Period: A New Estimate of Cherokee Population Losses." In *Cherokee Removal: Before and After*, ed. W. L. Anderson. Athens: University of Georgia Press.

Tilton, R. S. (1994). *Pocahontas: The Evolution of an American Narrative*. Cambridge: Cambridge University Press.

Titley, E. B. (1986). *A Narrow Vision: Duncan Campbell Scott and the Administration of Indian Affairs in Canada*. Vancouver: University of British Columbia Press.

Tompkins, J. (1992). *West of Everything*. New York: Oxford University Press.

Toulmin, S. (1990). *Cosmopolis: The Hidden Agenda of Modernity*. New York: Free Press.

Trachtenberg, A. (1989). *Reading American Photographs*. New York: Hill and Wang.

Trail of Broken Treaties: B.I.A. I'm Not Your Indian Anymore. (1973). Rooseveltown, N.Y.: Akwesasne Notes.

Twain, M. (1987). *Roughing It*. New York: Viking Penguin.

Utley, R. (1973). *Frontier Regulars: The United States Army and the Indian, 1866–1891*. Lincoln: University of Nebraska Press.

————. (1993). *The Lance and the Shield*. New York: Henry Holt.

Utley, R. A. (1992). "Whose shrine Is It? The Ideological Struggle for Custer Battlefield." *Montana* 42 (1):70–74.

"Valley of the Thunder Lizard." (1993). In "The Wild West C.O.W.-Boys of Moo Mesa," *Archie Comics* 1 (March).

Van Dijk, T. A. (1987). *Communicating Racism: Ethnic Prejudice in Thought and Talk*. Newbury Park, Calif.: Sage Publications.

Van Kirk, S. (1980). *Many Tender Ties: Women in Fur Trade Society, 1670–1870*. Winnipeg, Manitoba: Watson and Dwyer.

Vandenhoff, G. (1865). *An Actor's Note-Book; or, the Green-Room and Stage*. London: John Camden Hotten.

Vanstone, J. W. (1974). *Athabaskan Adaptations: Hunters and Fishermen of the Subarctic Forests*. Arlington Heights, Ill.: Harlan Davidson.

Vestal, S. (1957). *Sitting Bull: Champion of the Sioux*. Norman: University of Oklahoma Press.

Villanueva, M. (1989). "The Use of Alcohol in Pre-Colombian South America Native Cultures." Pacific Graduate School of Psychology.

Vizenor, G. (1978). *Word Arrows, Indians, and Whites in the New Fur Trade*. Minneapolis: University of Minnesota Press.

Waldman, C. (1985). *Atlas of the North American Indian*. New York and London: Facts on File.

Wallace, A.F.C. (1969). *The Death and Rebirth of the Seneca*. New York: Vintage Books.

Washburn, W. E., ed. (1988). *The Handbook of North American Indians: History of Indian-White Relations*, vol. 4. Washington, D.C.: Smithsonian Institution Press.

Watson, C. S. (1993). *From Nationalism to Secessionism: The Changing Fiction of William Gilmore Simms*. Westport, Conn.: Greenwood.

Watson, E. S. (1962). "Orlando Scott Goff, Pioneer Dakota Photographer." *North Dakota History* (January-April):211–215.

Watts, E. (1990/1991). "The Changing Critical Placement of Humor of the Old Southwest." *Mississippi Quarterly* 44 (winter): 95–103.

Weatherford, E. (1992). "Starting Fire with Gunpowder." *Film Comment* 28:64–67.

Weeks, P. (1990). "Post-Colonial Challenges to Grand Theory." *Human Organizations* 49 (3):239.

Wells-Barnett, I. B. (1969). *On Lynchings.* New York: Arno Press.

West, C. (1990). "The New Cultural Politics of Difference." In *Out There: Marginalization and Contemporary Cultures,* ed. R. Ferguson et al. Cambridge: MIT Press.

West, P. (1981). "The Miami Indian Attractions: A History and Analysis of a Transitional Mikasuki Seminole Environment." *Florida Anthropologist* 34:200–224.

Westermeyer, J., and J. Peake. (1983). "A Ten Year Follow-up of Alcoholic Native Americans in Minnesota." *American Journal of Psychiatry* 140 (2):189–194.

White, R. (1991). *The Middle Ground: Indians, Empires, and Republics in the Great Lakes Region, 1650–1815.* New York: Cambridge University Press.

White, W. (1969). *Rope and Faggot: A Biography of Judge Lynch.* New York: Arno Press.

Whitehead, C. E. (1891). *The Camp-Fires of the Everglades, or Wild Sports in the South.* Edinburgh: L. D. Douglas.

Wickman, P. R. (1991). *Osceola's Legacy.* Tuscaloosa: University of Alabama Press.

Williams, B. B. (1979). *A Literary History of Alabama: The Nineteenth Century.* Rutherford, N.J.: Fairleigh Dickinson University Press.

Williams, H. D. (1988). "The North Georgia Gold Rush." Ph.D. diss., Auburn University.

Williams, W. L. (1986). *The Spirit and the Flesh.* Boston: Beacon.

Williamson, J. (1984). *The Crucible of Race: Black-White Relations in the American South Since Emancipation.* New York: Oxford University Press.

Wilson, C. R. (1989). "History and Manners." In *Encyclopedia of Southern Culture,* ed. C. R. Wilson and W. Ferris. Chapel Hill: University of North Carolina Press.

Willson, M. M. (1917). *Snap Shots from the Everglades of Florida.* Tampa, Fla.: Tampa Tribune Publishing Co.

Wimsatt, M. A. (1989). *The Major Fiction of William Gilmore Simms: Cultural Traditions and Literary Form.* Baton Rouge: Louisiana State University Press.

Winkler, A. M. (1968). "Drinking on the American Frontier." *Quarterly Journal of Studies on Alcohol* 29:413–445.

Wissler, C. (1912). "The Catlin Paintings." *American Museum Journal* 12 (3) (March): 89–93.

———. (1922). *The American Indian: An Introduction to the Anthropology of the New World.* New York: Oxford University Press.

Woodbury, L. J. (1963). "Death on the Romantic Stage." *Quarterly Journal of Speech* 49 (1):57–61.

Wooster, R. (1988). *The Military and United States Indian Policy, 1865–1903.* New Haven: Yale University Press.

Yellow Bird, P., and K. Milun. (1994). "Interrupted Journeys: The Cultural Politics of Indian Reburial." In *Displacements: Cultural Identities in Question,* ed. A. Bammer. Bloomington: Indiana University Press.

Young, M. (1988). "Racism in Red and Black: Indians and Other Free People of Color in Georgia Law, Politics, and Removal Policy." *Georgia Historical Quarterly* 73 (fall):492–518.

Zinn, H. (1980). *A People's History of the United States.* New York: Harper and Row.

"A Zuni Artist Looks at Frank Hamilton Cushing: Cartoons by Phil Hughte." (1994). Zuni, N. Mex.: Pueblo of Zuni Arts and Crafts, A:shiwi A:wan Museum and Heritage Center Publication.

About the Book

One hundred members of NatChat, an electronic mail discussion group concerned with Native American issues, responded to the recent Disney release *Pocahontas* by calling on parents to boycott the movie, citing its historical inaccuracies and saying that "Disney has let us down in a cruel, irresponsible manner." Their anger was rooted in the fact that, although Disney had claimed that the film's portrayal of American Indians would be "authentic," the Pocahontas story the movie told was really white cultural myth. The actual histories of the characters were replaced by mythic narratives depicting the crucial moments when aid was given to the white settlers. As reconstructed, the story serves to reassert for whites their right to be here, easing any lingering guilt about the displacement of the native inhabitants.

To understand current imagery, it is essential to understand the history of its making, and these essays mesh to create a powerful, interconnected account of image creation over the past 150 years. The contributors, who represent a range of disciplines and specialties, reveal the distortions and fabrications white culture has imposed on significant historical and current events, as represented by treasured artifacts such as photographic images taken of Sitting Bull following his surrender, the national monument at the battlefield of Little Bighorn, nineteenth-century advertising, the television phenomenon *Northern Exposure,* and the film *Dances with Wolves.*

Well illustrated, this volume demonstrates the complacency of white culture in its representation of its troubled relationship with American Indians.

About the Contributors

Robert Baird, who has worked as a postproduction sound and picture editor on twelve motion pictures, including Alan Rudolf's *Trouble in Mind* (1985), is completing his dissertation at the University of Illinois, using cognitive psychology to address spectatorship and affect in horror-thriller threat scenes.

S. Elizabeth Bird is associate professor of anthropology and humanities at the University of Minnesota, Duluth. She is author of *For Enquiring Minds: A Cultural Study of Supermarket Tabloids* (1992) and has published numerous articles and book chapters in cultural studies, folklore, and mass communication.

John Bloom, visiting assistant professor of American Studies at Dickinson College, holds a doctorate in American Studies from the University of Minnesota. As a Fellow with the American Council of Learned Societies, he conducted research on athletics at federally operated boarding schools for Native Americans, 1890–1950.

Cynthia-Lou Coleman studied news coverage of the Flambeau Copper Mine in Wisconsin print media as part of her doctoral work at the University of Wisconsin at Madison. She continues to explore health and risk-communication issues that affect Native Americans. An enrolled member of the Osage (Oklahoma) Nation, Coleman is assistant professor in the School of Journalism and Mass Communication, University of Oregon, where she teaches communication.

Bonnie Duran, of Opelousas-Coushatta heritage, is assistant professor in the Department of Family and Community Medicine, University of New Mexico. She holds a doctorate in public health from the University of California at Berkeley, has worked in public health research and education with Native Americans for twenty years, and is author (with Eduardo Duran) of *Native American Post-Colonial Psychology* (1995).

Peter Geller is postdoctoral fellow in history at the University of Winnipeg, having recently completed his doctorate at Carleton University, Ottawa. He has published several papers on the uses of film and photography by the state, missionaries, and the Hudson's Bay Company in representing the Canadian north from 1920–1939.

Frank Goodyear, doctoral student in American Studies at the University of Texas at Austin, is researching and writing on the cultural role played by photography in the opening up and development of the American West.

Alison Griffiths is a doctoral candidate in the Department of Cinema Studies at New York University, completing a dissertation on the origins of ethnographic film from the silent era. Her previously published work includes essays on national and cultural identity in minority broadcasting.

Theodore S. Jojola, of Isleta Pueblo Indian ancestry, is chair of the Native American Studies Program and associate professor of planning at the University of New Mexico. He holds a doctorate from the East-West Center, University of Hawaii, and is researching the role of image in sustaining tribal community development.

Sally L. Jones, American by birth, holds a doctorate from the University of Toronto, Graduate Centre for Study of Drama. Her thesis, *The Original Characters of Edwin Forrest and His American Style,* won the University's Clifford Leech prize in 1992 as outstanding thesis on drama. A performer and director, she has taught theater history at Ryerson University, Toronto, and at Queen's University.

C. Richard King, doctoral candidate in anthropology at the University of Illinois at Urbana-Champaign, is conducting research on colonialism and culture, gender and sexuality, the history of anthropology, social theory, and Native American studies. His essay in this volume is part of his dissertation, "Imperial Recollections: The Colonial Contexts and Postcolonial Predicaments of Narrating the Native American Past in the Contemporary United States."

Joel W. Martin is associate professor of American studies and religious studies at Franklin and Marshall College. He is the author of *Sacred Revolt: The Muskogees' Struggle for a New World* (1991). Born and raised in Opelika, Alabama, he has published several articles related to the study of cultural contact in the Southeast.

Jay Mechling, professor of American Studies at the University of California at Davis, received his graduate degrees in American civilization from the University of Pennsylvania. The author of over seventy essays and book chapters, he is completing books on the Boy Scouts and on Florida in the American imagination; he and his wife (Elizabeth Walker Mechling) are at work on a book on nuclearism in American culture.

Debra L. Merskin, of Cherokee descent, is assistant professor in the school of Journalism and Mass Communication, University of Oregon and holds a doctorate from Syracuse University. Her research concerns the representation of women and minorities in the media, especially the use of personal advertisements in the daily press, a subject related to her background in the Florida advertising business.

Jeffrey Steele is professor of English at the University of Wisconsin at Madison. He is author of *The Representation of the Self in the American Renaissance* (1987) and *The Essential Margaret Fuller* (1992), as well as of numerous articles on literary figures Walt Whitman and Margaret Fuller and other aspects of American literature.

Annette M. Taylor, who for many years was a daily newspaper reporter in Montana and Alaska, is assistant professor of journalism at the University of Dayton in Ohio, where she teaches news, feature and public relations writing, media law, and publication design. She is working on her dissertation in American Culture Studies at Bowling Green State University.

Peter van Lent, who is partly Mohawk, is associate professor at St. Lawrence University, New York, where he serves as faculty coordinator for the undergraduate extension program at Akwesasne, the nearby St. Regis Mohawk Reservation. He has published widely in literature and folk culture, and recent projects include *The Hidden Heritage,* a book on the French folk culture of New York state, and a bilingual edition of the French and Indian War documents at Fort Ticonderoga. He holds a doctorate from Stanford University.

Index

Abbott, F. H., 86
Abe Loebenberg's Arcade Clothing House, 48, 49
Adams, John, 30
Advertising
  American Indians used in, 45–63, 263
  contemporary portrayal of men in, 226
Affectionate intimacy, 224
African Americans
  advertising images using, 47, 48
  at Custer's Last Stand, 172
  Indians contrasted with, 139
  post–Civil War treatment of, 140, 141
  racial stereotypes of, 45–46
  television's portrayal of, 250, 256
Agate, Frederich Styles, 23
Ah-Tha-Thi-Ki Museum, 158
AIM. *See* American Indian Movement
Alaska Natives, 232–233, 236–242, 244(n19)
Alaskan Eskimo, The (film), 233
Alaskans, The (TV series), 233
Alcatraz Island occupation, 264
Alcohol
  colonial discourse and, 112, 113–114, 118–119
  drunken Indian stereotype and, 113, 114–115, 121, 125, 235
  indigenous discourse and, 117–119
  legislation prohibiting sale of, 117
  political economy of, 115–117
  temperance movements and, 118–124
Alcohol treatment programs, 125, 128(nn 50, 51)
Aleiss, Angela, 221
Aleut Indians, 232–233, 238
Alger, William, 18

Allen Theater, 72
Alligator wrestling, 154, 156, 161
American Adam, The (Lewis), 197
American Anthropologist, 83
American Indian: An Introduction to Anthropology, The (Wissler), 80, 92
American Indian Movement (AIM), 171
American Indians
  advertising images using, 45–63, 263
  Alaska Natives as, 232–233, 236–242
  alcohol use and, 111–125
  cartoon stereotypes of, 263–278
  on *Dr. Quinn, Medicine Woman* (TV series), 246–259
  early cinematic representations of, 79–92
  federal boarding schools for, 97–99
  going-Indian myth and, 195–207
  Haskell Homecoming and, 101–109
  Hudson's Bay Company depiction of, 65–75
  Little Bighorn Battlefield National Monument and, 167–178
  media news framing involving, 181–191
  on *Northern Exposure* (TV series), 229–230, 233, 234–242
  photographic narratives of, 29–41
  physical characteristics of, 281–284
  school sports and, 97, 99–101, 105–106
  sexual appeal of male, 211–226
  in southern history, 129–145
  stereotyped images of, 2–6
  suppression of native customs among, 74, 77(n33), 102
  television images of, 231–233, 245–248
  temperance movements among, 118–124

theatrical recreations of, 13–24
  tourism and, 153–163
American Museum of Natural History, 82,
  84, 89, 91, 152
American Revolution, 139–140
Anger, 249
Animal Dreams (Kingsolver), 221
Anniversary Brochure, Hudson Bay
  Company, 65, 68, 75(n1)
Annual Conference of Indian Missionary
  Workers, 102
Antebellum period (1831–1861),
  134–140
Anthropology
  American Indian studies in, 83–84
  ethnographic filmmaking and, 80–92
  tourism and, 161–162, 178
Anzaldua, Gloria, 281
Arbuckle Brothers Coffee, 58–59, 60–61
Archetypes
  of American Indian male, 211–214, 221
  noble vs. demonic savage, 248, 249–250
  See also Stereotypes
Arikara Indians, 172–173
Assimilationism, 74, 84, 98, 119, 120–121,
  123, 133–134, 233, 241
Associated Press, 185
Athabaskan Indians, 232, 238, 239, 240
Athletics. *See* Sports
Atkins, Edmond, 116
Atlanta Braves, 144–145, 263
Austen's Oswego Bitters, 51, 52
Ayer's Cherry Pectoral, 55

Bacon Rind, 104
BAE. *See* Bureau of American Ethnology
Bailey, Dix & Mead's photographic
  Western, 33–41, 42(n4)
Bailey, Joshua Bradford, 30, 32–33,
  42(n13)
Baird, G. W., 29–30
Baird, Robert, 10, 195
Ball, Zachery, 158
Banks, Rosemarie K., 19
Bartram, William, 150–151
Battles
  of Horseshoe Bend, 133, 143–144

of the Little Bighorn, 31, 84, 85, 105,
  168, 171–172
  of Tippecanoe, 58, 123
  of Washita, 251, 252
  See also Massacres
Beach, Adam, 217
Beadle, Erastus, 30
Beaver magazine, 65, 69, 75
Beetle Bailey (Walker), 272
Begay, Eugene, 190
Beidler, Peter, 222
Bendell, Marilyn, 220
Bentzoni, Charles, 31, 37, 38
Berger, Thomas, 201
Berkhofer, Robert, Jr., 3, 7, 82, 83, 104,
  226, 230, 261(n51)
Bhabha, Homi, 112, 126(n6)
Bierstadt, Albert, 36
Big Cypress Reservation, 151, 158, 161
Bill Nye's History of the United States, 6,
  118
Bird, S. Elizabeth, 1, 245
Blackfoot Indians, 104, 105
Blackfoot Reservation, 86
Black Hawk, 19, 58
Black Hawk War, 58–59
Black Kettle, 251, 252
Black Maria film studio, 81
Blacks. *See* African Americans
Blake, Michael, 209(n30)
Bloom, John, 8, 97
Bloomers, 108
Blue Whirlwind, 204
Boarding schools
  for Alaska Natives, 233
  federal establishment of, 97–99,
    110(n18)
  sports participation by Indians in,
    99–101, 109
Board of Indian Commissioners, 110(n18)
Boas, Franz, 89
Boone, Daniel, 240
Border-crossers, 131–132
Bosomworth, Thomas, 130
Bradley, David, 222, 223
Bradley's Super-Phosphate of Lime, 52–53,
  54

Brady, Matthew, 25(n22)
Brand, Joshua, 230
Brand, Stewart, 248
Brave Eagle (TV series), 231
Bresette, Walt, 184
British-Indian relations, 145(n6)
Broken Arrow (film), 197, 201
Brotherly love, 224
Brown, Ryan, 279(n2)
Buffalo Bill. *See* Cody, Buffalo Bill
Buffalo hunt, 199–200
Bureau of American Ethnology (BAE), 81, 83
Bureau of Indian Affairs, U.S., 46, 102, 264
Burke, Charles H., 101–102
Burrows, Darren E., 234
Bush, W. Stephen, 89–91

Calusa Indians, 150
Camera Craft, 81
Canyon Country Kiddies (Swinnerton), 271, 279(n7)
Capellano, Antonio, 2
Capron, Louis, 161–162
Carlisle Indian Industrial School, 97, 99, 106
Carlisle Plaza Mall mural, 97, 98, 100
Cartier, Jacques, 115
Cartoon stereotypes, 264–278
Casinos, 5–6, 158–159, 276
Cass, Lewis, 16
Castillo, Edward D., 204–205
Catlin, George, 82, 83, 135
Center for Substance Abuse Prevention, 128(n51)
Century Magazine, 29
Character sexiness, 218–222
Chateaubriand, Vicomte, 212
Cherokee Indians, 133–134, 141, 142–143, 281
Cheyenne (TV series), 231
Cheyenne Indians, 98, 167, 176, 177, 202, 203
    television's portrayal of, 246, 248–257
Chicago Tribune, 32
Chiefing, 141
Children of the Dust (TV film), 217, 225

Children's cartoons, 264–278
Chilocco Indian School, 108–109
Chippewa Indians. *See* Ojibwa Indians
Chivington, John M., 251
Christianity
    "civilization" of Indians through, 102, 133
    Native American Church and, 124
    suppression of Indian rituals and, 102
Church, Benjamin, 14
Churchill, Ward, 100
Cinderella, 3
Cinema. *See* Films
Citizen Kane (film), 229
Citizenship, U.S., 102–103
Civility, as colonial ideology, 114
"Civilization" of Indians
    Christianity and, 102, 133
    See also Assimilationism
Civil Rights movement (1968), 264
Civil War
    antebellum period of, 134–140
    southern representation of Indians following, 140–142
Cochise, 221
Cody, Buffalo Bill, 30, 40, 41, 43(n21), 46, 81, 84, 94(n20), 170
Coleman, Cynthia-Lou, 9, 181
Collective memory, 110(n11)
Collier, John, 108
Colonial discourse
    civility and, 114–115
    defined, 112, 126(n6)
Colonialism
    alcohol use and, 115–117
    cultural memories and, 168, 178
    defined, 112
    revisionist theories of, 264
    television's portrayal of, 250
    See also Imperialism
Comanche Indians, 123
Commercialism
    of Indian stereotypes in advertising, 45–63, 263
    of Little Bighorn Battlefield National Monument, 167–178
    of Seminole Indians, 153–163

Condit, Celeste, 256, 257
Confederate secession, 139–140
Conflict frames, 182, 184–186
Conscientizaçao, 125
Continental Film Company, 88
Cook, Captain James, 115
Cooper, James Fenimore, 13, 135, 231
Coppinger, Henry, 153–154
Coppinger's Tropical Gardens, Alligator
    Farm, and Seminole Indian Village,
    154, 155, 160, 163
Corn Planter, 120
Cory, C. B., 153
Costner, Kevin, 196, 200, 203, 205
Crabb, Jack, 201
Crazy Horse, 29
Cree Indians, 122
Creek Indians, 133, 140, 143, 151
Crevecoeur, J. Hector St. John, 195, 196,
    198
Crockett, Davy, 137
Cross, William R., 30, 31, 32–41, 42(n12)
Crow Agency, 169
Crow Indians, 84, 85, 174
Crow Reservation, 84, 85
Cultural imperialism. *See* Imperialism
Curtis, Edward, 31, 79, 86, 88–91, 170
Custer, George, 41, 56, 58, 84, 85, 169, 170,
    171–172, 174–176, 251, 258
Custer Battlefield National Monument,
    167, 170
Custer National Cemetery, 169
Customs
    Christian missionary suppression of, 102
    government suppression of, 74, 77(n33)
    journalistic description of, 107–108
    See also Rituals
Cyclical values frames, 182, 188
Cypress, Charlie, 161

Dale, Sam, 147(n39)
Dances with Wolves (film), 7, 10, 196–207,
    212, 213, 218, 224, 240, 245, 248, 255,
    264
    expanded version of, 205–207
Dances with Wolves (novel by Michael
    Blake), 209(n30)

Dancing
    ethnographic filming of, 81–82
    government suppression of, 74
    journalistic description of, 107–108
    Seminole tourism and, 161–162
Dania Reservation, 158
Dare, Virginia, 208(n20)
Davies, Delmer, 197
Davis, John, 150
Dawes Act (1887), 46, 62, 98, 109(n1)
Day-Lewis, Daniel, 240, 246
DeGraff, William H., 42(n12)
Delegitimation frames, 182, 188–189
de León, Ponce, 150
Deloria, Philip J., 139
DeLoria, Vine, 249
Demonic Savage archetype, 248
Dench, Ernest Alfred, 91–92
Department of Indian Affairs, Canada,
    73
Department of Natural Resources (DNR),
    181, 182, 183, 187–188
Deutelbaum, Marshall, 81
Diamond Lawnmowers, 53, 55
Diary of King Philip's War (Church), 14
Dispossessing the American Indian (Jacobs),
    116
Dix, George P., 30, 32–33, 42(n13)
Dixon, Joseph K., 79, 84–86, 88, 89, 92
Dixon, W. K. L., 81
DNR. *See* Department of Natural
    Resources
Dog soldiers, 249
Doomed Indian archetype, 248, 249
Dorman, Isaiah, 172
Dove, Mourning, 62
Drake, Samuel, 14
Drake, Sir Francis, 150
Dr. Quinn, Medicine Woman (TV series),
    10, 225, 246–259
    survey of responses to, 252–257,
    260(n14)
Drunken Indian stereotype, 9, 113,
    114–115, 116, 121, 125
Dunbar, John J., 199, 200, 202–207, 212
Duran, Bonnie, 8–9, 111
Duryeas Improved Corn Starch, 48, 49

Economics
of alcohol use, 115–117
of gaming casinos, 5–6, 276
Edison, Thomas, 79, 80–81, 88, 92
Education
in federal boarding schools, 98–99
sports and, 98, 99–101, 109
End of the Trail (sculpture), 214
*Enquiry into the Natural History of
Medicine Among the Indians of North
America and a Comparative View of
Their Diseases and Remedies, with
those of Civilized Nations, An* (Rush),
114
Enterprise Bone, Shell, and Corn Mills,
55–56, 57
Environmental issues
industrialism vs., 197
media framing of, 181–191
Eroticism. *See* Sexuality
Eskimo (film), 233
Ethnic pride movements, 197
Ethnographic realism, 91
Ethnography
cinematic, 79–92
tourism and, 161–162, 178
Evans, Lawton B., 131
Everglades, 152–153
Expedition of Citizenship, 86, 87
Exterminationism, 133

Falsey, John, 230
Familienroman der Neurotiker, Der
(Freud), 197
Family romance, 197–198, 205
Far Side, The (Larson), 265
Fearless warrior image, 211, 212–214,
221
Feminism, 246
Fiedler, Leslie A., 195, 196, 198, 204
Films
colonial revisionism in, 264
ethnographic, 79–92
going-Indian ideal in, 195–207
sexual appeal of American Indian male
in, 212, 213, 217–218, 219, 221, 224,
225

stereotyped Indians in, 1–3, 7, 10, 86–92
See also names of specific films
First Lessons in Georgia History (Evans),
131
First Seminole War, 151
Fiske, John, 230
Flag presentation ceremonies, 86
Flambeau Mine controversy
background of, 182–183
journalistic study on, 183–184
news framing in, 181–182, 184–191
Florida
Everglades of, 152–153
history of Seminoles in, 150–152
Seminole tourism in, 153–160
Football
Indian participation in, 105–109
See also Sports
Ford, John, 30
"Forepaugh's Equestrian Spectacular
Tragedy," 58
Forrest, Edwin, 7, 13, 15, 17–24, 25(n22),
26(n40)
Forts, U.S.
Buford, 30, 31, 32
Custer, 169, 170
Marion, 98
Mims, 133, 143
Moultrie, 135
Randall, 32–33, 35, 37, 41
Yates, 32
Franca, Ozz, 215
Francis, Daniel, 8, 19, 248, 258
Franklin, Benjamin, 117
Fraser, James, 214
French culture, 114
Freud, Sigmund, 197, 205

Gaiashkibos, 182, 184, 186, 187
Gambling casinos, 5–6, 158–159, 276
Garden of Eden myth, 197, 198
Garfield, James, 31
Garrick, David, 18
Gay Head peoples, 27(n53)
Geller, Peter, 8, 65
George, Chief Dan, 202
Geronimo, 29, 221, 266

Geronimo (film), 221, 246
"Geronimoo" cartoon character, 11,
    265–267, 275, 279(n4)
Ghost Dance religion, 124
Glenn, James L., 155
Godsell, P. H., 66, 70, 71, 76(n18)
Goff, Orlando Scott, 32
Goffman, Erving, 56
Going-Indian myth, 195–207, 208(n20),
    255
Gold Rush of 1829, 134
Good Housekeeping, 271
Goodyear, Frank, 8, 29
Grant, Rodney, 213
Green, Rayna, 72, 249, 284(n3)
Green Corn Dance, 161–162
Greene, Graham, 200, 218
Griffiths, Alison, 8, 79
Guerilla readings, 230
Gunsmoke (TV series), 231, 236

Haidas Indians, 238, 239
Half-breeds, 216–217, 283
Hall, James, 121, 136
Hall, Stuart, 257
Hampton Institute, 98
Handsome Lake, 118, 119–121, 122
Hanley, R. E., 106, 107
Harper's, 4
Harris, Richard, 202
Harrison, Gabriel, 19, 20, 25–26(nn 23, 40)
Haskell Homecoming, 98, 101–109
Haskell Institute, 98, 101, 103, 105, 106,
    108
Hawk (TV series), 232, 233
Hawkeye and the Last of the Mohicans (TV
    series), 231
HBC. *See* Hudson's Bay Company
Hemingway, Ernest, 198
Hero archetype
    American Indian male as, 211–226
    contemporary changes in, 226, 227(n32)
Hertzberg, H. W., 124
Hiawatha (film), 95(n50)
Hiawatha (poem by Longfellow), 84, 212
Hickock, Wild Bill, 30
High Chaparral, The (TV series), 245

Hillerman, Tony, 218, 219
Hinsley, Curtis, 83
History of Alabama (Pickett), 135, 140
Hoffman, Dustin, 202
Hooper, Johnson Jones, 137, 138
Hopi Indians, 271–272
Hopi Snake Dance, 263
Horse, Michael, 279(n6)
Horseshoe Bend National Military Park
    Museum, 143–144
Hudson, Henry, 115
Hudson's Bay Company (HBC), 65–75
Hudson's Bay Company, The (Schooling),
    75(n1)
Hughte, Phil, 272
Humor
    of Indians, 249
    from southwestern U.S., 137, 140
Hunt, George, 89

Ignoble savage stereotype, 3, 9, 137, 245,
    249
Imaginary Indian, 248, 249, 253
Imperialism
    in advertising imagery, 59–61
    collective memories and, 178
    defined, 112
    suppression of native customs by, 74,
        77(n33)
    See also Colonialism
Indian Act, Canada, 74
*Indian Communication: Sign Language of
    the North American Indian* (film), 84
Indian in the Cupboard, The (film), 11
Indian Leader, 105, 106
Indian Queen Perfume, 52, 53
Indian Reception, Red River Pageant,
    68–70
Indian Removal Act (1830), 132
Indians. *See* American Indians
Indian Tribes of North America, The
    (McKenney and Hall), 121, 136
Indian War Council and Sioux Ghost Dance
    (film), 81
Indigenous theory, 125
Ingrams, F. C., 67
Intermarriage, 133, 283

In the Land of the Head-Hunters (film), 86, 88–90, 94(n25)
In the Land of the War Canoes (film), 94(n25)
Inuit Eskimos, 238, 240
Inupiat Eskimos, 232, 239
Iron Tail, Chief, 84–85
Iroquois Indians, 119
Irving, Washington, 13, 15
Isleta Pueblo, 267, 272

Jackson, Andrew, 16, 132, 133, 136, 139, 143, 151
Jackson, Royal, 167
Jacobs, W. R., 116
James, George Wharton, 81–82, 92
Jameson, Frederic, 259
JanMohamed, Abdul, 112, 126(n6)
Jay, Robert, 48
Jesuits, 116
Jesup, Thomas S., 151
Jesup North Pacific Expeditions, 89
Jim Crow laws, 141
Johnson, William, 116
Jojola, Theodore S., 1, 11, 263
Jones, Sally, 7–8, 13
Jorgensen, J. G., 188
Joseph, Chief, 29
Josephy, Alvin M., Jr., 167
Journalism
    ethnocentricity in, 107–108
    framing issues through, 181–182, 184–191
    racial stereotyping in, 100, 106–107
    sports, 100, 106–107
"J.R." cartoon character, 11, 267–278

Kansas City Journal, 104
Kansas City Times, 107
Kennecott Copper Company, 182
Kesey, Ken, 198
Kewley, Mary Jo, 190
Keystone Agricultural Implements, 62, 63
Kickapoo Indian Remedy, 51, 59
Kindersley, Robert Molesworth, 65, 66, 69–70
Kinetoscope films, 80–81

King, Richard, 9
King Philip's War, 14
Kingsolver, Barbara, 221
Kinnewakan, Chief, 66, 69–70, 73
Kiowa Indians, 123
Klondike (TV series), 233
Kodiak (TV series), 233
Krouse, Susan Applegate, 84
Kwakiutl Indians, 86, 88, 89

Lac Courte Oreille band, 181, 182, 183
LaDuke, W., 188
Ladysmith News, 183, 189
Lakota Indians, 245
Lambert, Henry, 7
Lame Deer, 29
Lame White Man, 173
L'Amour, Louis, 225
Land allocations
    for Alaska Natives, 233
    Dawes Act and, 98, 109(n1)
    Indian defense of, 181–191
Lando, Joe, 247
Language
    naming process and, 202–204
    sign language, 84
Lansbury, Angela, 246
Larson, Gary, 265
Last of the Breed (L'Amour), 225
Last of the Mohicans, The (novel/film), 135, 217, 219, 224, 240, 246
Last Stand Hill, 169, 171–173
Law of the Plainsman (TV series), 231
Lawrence, D. H., 196
Laws
    Jim Crow, 141
    prohibiting Indian drinking, 117
Laziness stereotype, 37
Lears, Jackson, 46, 51, 52
Le Fleische, Francis, 83
Legends of the Fall (film), 225
Legitimation frames, 182, 188–189
Levi-Strauss, Claude, 196
Levoi, Ray, 225
Lewis, R. W. B., 197
Lindsay, Vachel, 90
Lipsitz, George, 110(n11), 258

Little Bighorn, 30, 31
Little Bighorn Battlefield National
    Monument, 9, 167–178
Little Big Man (film), 201
Little House on the Prairie (TV series), 253,
    257
Lomawaima, K. Tsianina, 108
Lone Ranger, The (TV series), 231, 268,
    279(n6)
Lonesome Dove (TV miniseries), 205
Long, John, 116
Longfellow, Henry Wadsworth, 84, 212
Longstreet, Augustus Baldwin, 137
Louisiana Purchase, 151

MacDonnel, Diane, 126(n6)
Magpie, George, 171
Maine Woods, The (Thoreau), 199
Making the Movies (Dench), 91
Malmsheimer, Lonna, 110(n18)
Man Called Horse, A (film), 202
Manifest destiny argument, 59, 197
Map of the Human Heart (film), 217, 225
Mardi Gras, 141
Mardi Gras Indians, 142
Marriage
    interracial, 133, 283
    sexuality in, 224, 227(n26)
Martin, Joel, 9, 129
Mashpee Indians, 22, 27(n53)
Massacres
    and going-Indian ideal, 200–202
    at Sand Creek, 251
    television's portrayal of, 251
    at Wounded Knee, 178
    See also Battles
Massasoit, 13–14
Mass media. *See* Media
McCoy, Michael, 168
McGirt, Zachariah, 130
McKay, W. C., 69, 70
McKenney, Thomas L., 3–4, 121, 136
Mead, John L., 30, 32–33, 42(n13)
Means, Russell, 1
Mechling, Jay, 9, 149
Media
    ethnocentricity in, 107–108

framing of issues by, 181–182, 184–191
noble savage stereotype portrayed in,
    104–107, 201, 202, 222, 245, 248
    See also Films; Newspapers; Television
"Medicine woman" role, 255, 257
Medina, Louisa, 22
Meek, Alexander Beaufort, 135, 138, 139
Melting-pot theory, 197
Men
    character appeal of, 218–222
    hero archetype and, 226, 227(n32)
    physical appeal of, 214–218
    sexual idealization of Indian, 211–226
    situational appeal of, 222, 224–226
Mercando, Larry, 189
Merskin, Debra L., 11, 281, 282
Mescalero Apaches, 123
Metacom, 13–15
Metamora; or the Last of the Wampanoags
    (Stone), 8, 13, 16–24
Miccosukee Culture Center and Indian
    Village, 159
Miccosukee Indians, 149–150, 151, 155,
    159–160
Middle-ground ideology, 132
Mikasuki. *See* Miccosukee Indians
Miles, Elaine, 234
Miles, Nelson A., 29
Mining controversy, Wisconsin, 181–191
Minstrel shows, 45–46
Missionaries, 102, 133
Mixed-race individuals, 216–217, 283
Model, The (painting), 215–216, 218–219,
    220
Mohawk Indians, 119
Moki Snake Dance by Wolpi Indians (film),
    81
Momaday, Scott, 222
Moore, F. E., 95(n50)
Morgan, J. Pierpont, 88, 89
Morrison, Toni, 47
Morrow, Rob, 236
Morrow, Stanley J., 42(n12)
Mossman, E. D., 101
Movies. *See* Films
Moving Picture World, 89, 91
Murdoch, James, 17

Musa Isle Grove, 154–155, 159, 160, 162, 163
Musgrove, Mary, 130–132
Muskogee Daily Phoenix, 104–105
Muskogee Indians, 138, 151
Mythmaking
  in advertising, 51–53
  in early ethnographic films, 86–92
  going-Indian ideal and, 195–207
  on television shows, 231–233, 242, 248, 253, 255, 257–259
  of "White Man's Indian," 2–6
  See also Stereotypes

Nakia (TV series), 232, 233
Names, Indian
  going-Indian myth and, 202–204, 208(n20)
  for places in southern states, 135, 138
  women and, 208(n20)
Nanook of the North (film), 233
NatChat, 1, 12(n4)
National Geographic, 161–162
National Parks, 171
National Park Service, 167–171
National Portrait Gallery, 23, 24
Native American Church, 118, 123–124
Native Americans. *See* American Indians
Native Shaker Church, 124
Navajo Indians, 219, 271
Neill, Wilfred T., 156, 162
Nelson, Henry, 156
Neville Brothers, 142
New Age Indian, 264, 270
News coverage
  defining legitimacy through, 181–182
  of Flambeau Mine controversy, 183–189
Newspapers
  ethnocentric descriptions in, 107–108
  framing issues in, 181–182, 184–191
  noble savage representations in, 104–107
  sports coverage in, 100, 107
New-York Dispatch, 18
New-York Mirror, 19
New York Times, 31, 32, 35, 91
Nick of the Woods (Medina), 22
Noah, Mordecai M., 15

Noble princess image, 259(n1)
Noble savage stereotype
  in advertising, 61
  cultural reinforcement of, 3, 4, 7, 16, 30, 80
  in ethnographic filmmaking, 82, 91
  media portrayal of, 104–107, 201, 202, 222, 245, 248, 249
  photographic narratives and, 31, 37
  Seminole Indians and, 153
  sexuality of Indian male and, 211
  Wild Man image vs., 113, 248
Nordstrom, Alison Devine, 165(n29)
North American Indian (Curtis), 88
Northern Exposure (TV series), 10, 229–230, 233, 234–242, 243(n15), 246, 284(n3)
North of Sixty (TV series), 217
Northrup, Jim, 11
Notman, William, 43(n22)
Nudity appeal, 217–218, 221
Nye, Bill, 4, 5

Office of Indian Affairs, 156
Ojibwa Indians, 4, 7, 11, 73, 116, 181–191, 254, 257, 259
Okalee Indian Village, 158
Oklahoma
  homesteading land in, 282
  relocation of Seminole Indians to, 151
One Bull, 35
Opper, Frederick, 6, 118
Oral tradition, 282
Oriard, Michael, 100, 106, 107
Osceola, 135–136, 142, 151

Panther, Joe, 158
Parker, Quanay, 124
Patriotism, 189
Pawnee Indians, 202
Peace pipe, 68–69
Peairs, H. B., 102, 107
Penn, Arthur, 201
Penn, William, 55–56
Perdue, Theda, 136
Peter Pan (film), 3
Peyote religion, 123–124

Philia, 224

Philip of Pokanoket, "King," 14–15, 19

"Phil Thomas" cartoon character, 11,
    267–274

Photographic Western (Bailey, Dix &
    Mead), 29–41, 42(n4)

Physical sexiness, 214–218

Pickett, Albert J., 135, 138, 140

Piegan Indians, 199

Pitt, Brad, 225

Place-names, Indian, 135, 138

Plains Indians, 29–31, 46, 169, 173–177,
    231, 268, 269

Playing Indian, 263

Plessy v. Ferguson, 141

Poarch Creek Indians, 144

Pocahontas (film), 1–3, 7, 263, 264, 275

Pocahontas myth, 2–3, 10, 197

Political economy
    of alcohol, 115–117
    of gaming casinos, 5–6, 276

Porter, William T., 137

Postcards, Seminole, 153–154, 155, 156,
    157

Postcolonial, defined, 125

Pratt, Richard Henry, 98–99

Pre-Removal period (1783–1830), 130–134

Printed ephemera, 46

Progress frames, 182, 186–187

Prophet's Town, 122, 123

Pueblo Indians, 267, 269, 270, 271,
    272–273, 274

Puri Indians, 198

*Purpose and Achievements of the Rodman
    Wanamaker Expedition of Citizenship
    to the North American Indian, The*
    (Dixon), 86

Quakers, 119

Quasi-ethnographic films, 79–80, 81

Racial ideologies
    advertising imagery and, 45–63
    cultural containment and, 45–46
    in early ethnographic films, 86–92
    school sports heroes and, 100, 106–107

on television, 242, 245, 255
    See also Stereotypes

Raleigh, Sir Walter, 208(n20)

Ramharter, Robert, 187

Reagan, Ronald, 241

Reconstruction period, 140

Red Eagle: A Poem of the South, The
    (Meek), 135

Red Jacket, 19

Red River Pageant, 66–75

Redsticks, 133, 143

Remington, Frederic, 29, 31, 199

Remington and Russell (Dippie), 199

Removal, Indian, 132, 140, 143

Renaming process, 202–204

Renegade image, 258

Reno-Benteen Battlefield, 169, 170

Resistant readings, 256–257

Revere, Paul, 14

Revisionism, colonial, 264

Reynolds, Burt, 232

Rituals
    Christian missionary suppression of,
        102
    ethnographic filming of, 81–82
    journalistic description of, 107–108
    Seminole tourism and, 161–162
    See also Customs

Romance novels, 216–217, 219–220, 221,
    222, 224, 225

Romance of the Far Fur Country, The
    (film), 65

Roop, John A., 154

Roosevelt, Theodore, 152

Ross Allen's Reptile Institute, 156, 160

Roughing It (Twain), 37

Rousseau, Jean-Jacques, 15, 16

Rowlandson, Mary, 200

Rush, Benjamin, 114

Russell, Charles M., 31, 199, 208(n26)

Sachem, 13

Said, Edward, 112, 117

Sand Creek massacre, 251

Sanjek, Roger, 83

Sante Fe railway, 263–264

Savagery
    in advertising images, 59–61
    association of African Americans with,
        141
    ignoble savage stereotype and, 3, 9, 137,
        245, 249
    Indian warfare associated with, 133, 143
    sexuality and, 211
    Wild Man image and, 112–113
    See also Noble savage stereotype
Schooling, William, 68, 70, 75(n1)
Schools
    federal boarding, 97–99
    sports participation by Indians in, 97,
        99–101, 105–106
Scientific frames, 182, 187–188
Scott, Duncan Campbell, 73, 74
Searchers, The (film), 207, 254
Second Seminole War, 151
Segregation
    Jim Crow laws requiring, 141
    at Little Bighorn Battlefield National
        Monument, 173–177
Seminole Indians
    cultural authenticity of, 9, 149–150,
        160–163
    history of, 150–152
    landscape of, 152–153
    tourism and, 153–163
    wars with, 135, 139
Seminole Tribe of Florida, 151
Seneca Indians, 119
Sexuality
    in advertising imagery, 59, 64
    character attractiveness and, 218–222
    in marriage, 224, 227(n26)
    native Indian dances and, 107
    physical attractiveness and, 214–218
    in popular image of Indian male,
        211–226
    situational attractiveness and, 222,
        224–226
    suppression of, 73, 108
    victimization and, 224–225
Seymour, Jane, 246, 247
Shaman, 270

Shawnee Indians, 122
Shawnee Prophet, 118, 121–123
Sheridan, Philip H., 32, 222
*She Would Be a Soldier; or The Plains of
    Chippewa* (Noah), 15
Shiveley, JoEllen, 254, 257
Sierra Club, 181, 182, 183, 186
Silent films
    Indian representations in, 79–92
    See also Films
Silver Springs Seminoles, 156–157, 162
Simms, William Gilmore, 135, 137, 138
"Simon Becomes Captain" (Hooper), 137
Sioux Indians, 31–32, 41, 46, 172, 176, 177,
    202, 203–204
Sitting Bull, 8, 29, 30–35, 38–41, 43(n21),
    176
Six Nations, 120
Skinner, Alanson, 91, 95(n50), 152
Slaves
    Indian ownership of, 139
    See also African Americans
Sleeping Indian (painting), 222, 223
Slotkin, Richard, 202
Smith, John, 2
Smithsonian Institution, 81, 88
Snake dances, 81–82
Snake handling, 161
Social unity principle, 120
Son of Morning Star (TV movie), 201,
    240
Southern history of Indians
    antebellum period, 134–140
    Civil War and post-War era, 140–142
    personal account of, 281–283
    pre-Removal period, 130–134
    present era, 142–145
    Seminole commercialism and, 153–163
Sports
    in Indian boarding schools, 98, 99–101,
        108–109
    noble savage image and, 105–107
    stereotyped Indian mascots in, 263
Springsteen, Bruce, 1
Squanto (film), 217, 246
Squaw, defined, 284(n3)

Stallone, Sylvester, 226
Standing Rock Agency, 32, 35, 41, 101
Stands-with-a-Fist, 201–202, 204
St. Clair, James D., 27(n53)
Steele, Jeffrey, 8, 45
Stereographs, 30, 33, 36–38, 42(n4)
Stereotypes
  advertising images using, 45–63
  cartoon, 264–278
  in contemporary films, 1–3, 7, 10
  on *Dr. Quinn, Medicine Woman*,
    248–257
  drunken Indian, 9, 113, 114–115, 116,
    121, 125
  in early ethnographic films, 86–92
  fearless warrior, 211, 212–214, 221
  ignoble savage, 3, 9, 137, 245, 249
  Northern Exposure's treatment of, 230,
    237, 239–241
  on physical characteristics of Indians,
    283–284
  role playing of, 70–73
  of school sports heroes, 100, 105–107
  stoic Indian, 19, 249, 253, 256
  of "White Man's Indian," 2–6
  See also Noble savage stereotype
Stevenson, Augusta, 208(n20)
Stewart, Jimmy, 197, 201
Stoic Indian stereotype, 249, 253, 256
Stone, Elizabeth, 198
Stone, John Augustus, 13, 17, 21, 23
Storge, 224
Story of Florida's Seminole Indians, The
  (Neill), 157
St. Paul Pioneer Press, 31
St. Regis Mohawk Reservation, 226
Strong, Pauline Turner, 3
Subservient-to-savage squaw image,
  259(n1)
Superior Evening Telegram, 185
Swinnerton, Jimmy, 271

Tamiami Trail, 151, 154, 159
Taylor, Annette M., 10, 229
Taylor's Sure Cure, 59
Team mascots, 263

Technological frames, 182, 187–188
Tecumseh, 123, 133
Television
  cartoon stereotypes on, 264–278
  mythmaking on, 231–233, 242, 248, 253,
    255, 257–259
  presentation of American Indians on,
    229–242, 245–259
  treatment of Alaska Natives on, 233,
    236–242
  Westerns on, 231–232, 236, 245, 259
  See also names of specific television
    shows
Temperance movements, 118–124
Tenskwatawa, 118, 121–123
Terry, Alfred, 31
Theatrical recreations, 13–24
Third Seminole War, 151
Thomson, James, 67
Thoreau, Henry David, 195, 198–199
Thorpe, Jim, 97, 100
Thunderheart (film), 218, 219, 225, 246
Tillman, Ben, 139
Tilton, Robert, 2, 249
Tippecanoe Spring Preparation, 48, 50
Tippecanoe tonic, 58
Tlingit Indians, 232, 238, 239–240
Topeka Daily State Journal, 106
Tourism
  at Little Bighorn Battlefield National
    Monument, 167–178
  of Seminole Indians, 153–163
Trade cards, 46–63
Trail of Broken Treaties, 171
Trail of Tears march, 134
Trails Plowed Under (Russell), 199
Treat, Henry H., 101–102
Treaty of Fort Stanwix (1784), 119
Treaty of Paris (1783), 119
Tribalism, 264
Tropical Hobbyland, 155, 156
Tsimshian Indians, 238
Tumbleweeds cartoon series, 271
Turner, Frederick Jackson, 152
Turner, Martha, 42(n13)
Turner, Nat, 134

Turner, William W., 83
Tuscaloosa, Chief, 142
Twain, Mark, 37
Twin Peaks (TV series), 242(n2)
Two Moons, Chief, 84, 85
Tyson, Charles, 97

Umatilla tribe, 87
Unconquered Seminole Indians, The, 161
Unto These Hills pageant, 143

van Lent, Peter, 10, 211
Victim image, 224–225
Virginia Dare: Mystery Girl (Stevenson), 208(n20)
Vision quest, 250
Voisine, Roch, 212

Wagon Train (TV series), 231
Walcott, Charles D., 88
Walden (Thoreau), 198
Walker, Mort, 272
Walker, Texas Ranger (TV series), 242(n2)
Waltons, The (TV series), 253
Wampanoags, 13–14, 22, 24
Wanamaker, Rodman, 84, 86, 87
War of the Northwest Territory, 119
Washington, George, 140, 142
Washington *Intelligencer*, 22
Wausau Daily Herald, 190
Wayne, John, 254
Weatherford, William, 136, 139, 143
Welles, Orson, 229
West, Patsy, 163
Westerman, Floyd Red Crow, 242(n2)
Western Iroquois Confederacy, 119
Westernization process, 140–141
Westerns
   going-Indian myth and, 197, 207
   on television, 231–232, 245, 259
Where Eagles Soar (painting), 220
White, Corby, 225
White, J. H., 81
White Dawn, The (film), 233
White Fang (film), 233

White Man's Indian, The (Berkhofer), 226
Whitman, Walt, 26(n40), 203
Whittridge, Worthington, 36
Wild Man image, 112–113, 248, 249
Wild West C.O.W.-Boys of Moo Mesa, The, 264–278
Wild West shows, 41, 43(n21), 45–46, 58, 74, 81, 94(n20)
Williamson, Joel, 141
Willis, Bruce, 226
Willson, Minnie Moore, 153
Wilson, Jim, 205
Wilson, John, 124
Wilson, Louis E., 71
Wind-in-His-Hair, 212–213, 224, 225
Winnipeg Bulletin, 71–72
Winnipeg Tribune, 73
Wintke, 204
Wisconsin Greens, 183
Wisconsin State Journal, 184, 185
Wissler, Clark, 80, 83, 88, 92
Women
   bloomers worn by, 108
   fur trade involvement by, 73, 77(n29)
   Indian names and, 208(n20)
   mixed-race, 283–284
   responses to *Dr. Quinn, Medicine Woman*, 254–255
   sexual attraction to Indian males by, 212–213, 217–218
   stereotyped images of Indian, 259(n1)
Wood Cree Indians, 70–71
World's Fair (1904), 83
World's Work, 83
Worthington, Rogers, 185
Wounded Knee Massacre, 178

Yataalii, 219
Yemassee: A Romance of Carolina, The (Simms), 135
Yuit Eskimos, 232

Zuni Pueblo Indians, 272